The multinational corporation
A radical approach

Papers by Stephen Herbert Hymer

The multinational corporation
A radical approach

Papers by Stephen Herbert Hymer

Edited by Robert B. Cohen, Nadine Felton, Morley Nkosi, and Jaap van Liere, with the assistance of Noel Dennis

Cambridge University Press

Cambridge
London   New York   New Rochelle
Melbourne   Sydney

Published by the Press Syndicate of the University of Cambridge
The Pitt Building, Trumpington Street, Cambridge CB2 1RP
32 East 57th Street, New York, NY 10022, USA
296 Beaconsfield Parade, Middle Park, Melbourne 3206, Australia

First published 1979

Printed in the United States of America
Typeset by Science Press, Ephrata, Pennsylvania
Printed and bound by Vail-Ballou Press, Inc., Binghamton, New York

Library of Congress Cataloging in Publication Data

Hymer, Stephen.

The multinational corporation.

Bibliography: p.

Includes index.

1. International business enterprises – Addresses, essays, lectures.
2. Marxian economics – Addresses, essays, lectures.
I. Cohen, Robert B.   II. Title.
HD2755.5.H95   338.8′8   79-52327
ISBN 0 521 22695 3

The Stephen Hymer Papers Collective dedicates
this book to Steve's family:
Bernice and the late Leo Hymer, his brother Bennett,
and his sons David and Jonathan

Contents

Editors' preface

At the time of his death on February 2, 1974, Stephen Herbert Hymer was recognized internationally as a leading analyst of the multinational corporation and as one of its most noted North American critics. Although many people within and outside of academia acknowledged the originality of his scholarship, much of his work, especially his later papers reflecting his contribution to Marxian analysis, had not been published in readily available journals, nor had his work been collected in a single volume. Shortly after his tragic death, several friends and colleagues decided to carry on the work he had begun and share with the public his path-breaking scholarship. They planned two projects: to publish a volume of Hymer's manuscripts and to archive his notes and finish those papers he was unable to complete before his death.

In March 1974, several people met in New Haven, Connecticut, and formed the Stephen Hymer Papers Collective. The collective appointed David Gordon and Heidi Hartmann literary executors of Hymer's estate and formed two subgroups: One would complete articles in progress and the other would collect and edit articles for publication. After this meeting, the second subgroup continued to work on what has resulted in this collection of Hymer's essays. The members of this editorial collective are: Robert B. Cohen, Noel Dennis, Nadine Felton, Morley Nkosi, and Jaap van Liere.

Initially, based on the suggestions we received from many people, the editorial collective planned to publish a longer volume that traced the development of Hymer's work and thought from that of a liberal economist to a Marxian analyst. This book was to include his work on Ghana, economic development, the multinational corporation, and the internationalization of labor and capital. However, while preparing the book, we received comments and criticisms that caused us to organize the collection in its current form. Although this volume is not as long as the one we had originally planned, it enables us to present more cohesively Hymer's critique of the multinational

ix

corporation and its effects on the internationalization of capital and the international division of labor.

The book is organized in several divisions. In the general introduction, we discuss the work of the mainstream and Marxian thinkers on multinational corporations and international economy, dealing in particular with those issues that Hymer addressed in his own examination of the corporation. We relate Hymer's work to the analysis of these writers and trace Steve's development from a representative of the antitrust school to one who became its critic to finally his emergence as a Marxian theorist of some stature. Hymer's essays are organized in three parts, which reflect both the evolution of his analysis and the areas of his study. [Some editorial changes have been made in the essays published in this edition. As originally published, a number of papers contain certain sections that are repetitious. In those essays where substantial overlapping occurs, we have omitted sections in such a way as not to lose the thrust of the argument. "The Multinational Corporation and the International Division of Labor" (Chapter 6) and "The United States Multinational Corporations and Japanese Competition in the Pacific" (Chapter 10) have been substantially edited. In each case, where a portion of an essay was eliminated, we include an editorial footnote that refers the reader to the original paper where he or she may find the entire discussion. In several essays, we have omitted or reduced the length of quotes that were repeated in other essays in this collection.] Each part includes an introduction written by a colleague and friend of Steve's who is familiar with his work in that area. The authors of the part introductions analyze the major issues raised in the essays and include some discussion of Steve's intellectual and personal development at the time he was writing those papers. Following Part III is a biography of Steve's life tracing the relationship between his intellectual, political, and personal development. Following the biography, the reader will find a complete bibliography of Hymer's published and unpublished papers and a memorial poem written for Steve by Ama Ata Aidoo, a close friend of his from Ghana.

This book of essays is the result of collective effort on the part of many people during the past five years. We hope it stands as a partial memorial to Stephen Hymer's scholarship and inspiring intellect, but we also hope it represents a tribute to Steve's belief in the importance of people working and sharing ideas collectively. Many people have acted in this spirit and given of their time willingly and unselfishly. We would like to thank the members of the Stephen Hymer Papers Collective, in particular Heidi Hartmann and David Gordon, for their help and encouragement throughout these five years. Heidi and David read over the manuscript in its various stages of development, gave us information and editorial help with the general introduction and biography and, most importantly, acted as supportive friends. Vahid Nowshirvani also provided invaluable assistance to us, especially in the early stages of the project. The other members of the collective, Amy Bridges, Bob Sherry, and Ross Thomson, have been most helpful in reading over and giving us information for the biography.

We want to thank Kari Levitt, Jim O'Connor, and Bob Rowthorn for writing introductions to the three parts of the book. As friends and colleagues of Steve, they shared with us their personal and professional experiences with him, thus making the part introductions more meaningful than a traditional introduction would have been. We would also like to thank Samir Amin, who wrote a similar introduction to the part on Ghana for the first draft of the book, even though it has not been included.

Many people assisted us with different parts of the book. We would like to thank Harry Magdoff, Stephen Resnick, the late Harry Braverman, Batya Weinbaum, Carlos F. Díaz-Alejandro, Paul Semonin, Gustav Ranis, Tom Weisskopf, Reginald Green, and Polly Hill for suggestions on how the book should be organized. In particular, we wish to thank Charles Kindleberger, Robert Heilbroner, Paul Sweezy, and Ronald Findlay both for their suggestions and their support for the book's publication.

Several of Steve's friends provided us with information for the biography and made criticisms of the drafts: Carole Reynolds; Lillian Salzman; Peter Bell; Sean Gervasi; Herbert Gintis; Geoffrey Kay; Alan Kellock; K. Osafo-Gyimah; Stephen Resnick; Frank Roosevelt; Paul Semonin; Richard Wolff; Ama Ata Aidoo, whose memorial poem to Steve is published in this edition; and Leah Margulies, who also helped with the bibliography. We also wish to thank Folker Fröbel, Jürgen Heinrichs, and Otto Kreye at the Max-Planck-Institut zur Erforschung der Lebensbedingungen der wissenschaftlich-technischen Welt at Starnberg, West Germany, for their helpful comments. Special thanks to Mel Watkins, who not only commented on and criticized the biography but also helped with other divisions of the book. We would also like to thank Hugh Patrick of the Yale University Economic Growth Center for his help with the biography and the bibliography.

Charles-Albert Michalet and Arthur Domike, of the United Nations Centre on Transnational Corporations, read the general introduction and made important criticisms and suggestions; Anwar Shaikh, Thomas Vietorisz, and Harry Magdoff were also especially helpful with the general introduction.

We wish to thank David Stohlberg for his help in preparing earlier drafts of the book's outline.

Although this collection is dedicated to Steve's family, we want to make special mention of the help they gave us while we were preparing the manuscript. Gilda Guttman, Steve's former wife, most generously provided us with biographical information, and Steve's brother Bennett and parents, Bernice and the late Leo Hymer, made many helpful suggestions.

We appreciate the advice and support we received from our publishers,

Cambridge University Press, and the work of Alfred Imhoff, who copyedited the manuscript.

The following people put much of their time and effort into typing, editing, and preparing the manuscript, and we wish to extend our special thanks to them: to Charles Frederick for helping to edit the biography and general introduction, to Victoria Brent and Joanne Koehler for typing drafts of the part introductions and general introduction, and to Constance Blake for preparing the index.

To all people who are not mentioned by name and yet helped us, we give our heartfelt thanks.

R. B. C.

N. D.

N. F.

M. N.

J. v L.

General introduction

Robert B. Cohen, Nadine Felton, Morley Nkosi,
and Jaap van Liere

The multinational corporation has become the dominant organizational form of modern capitalism. It now commands tremendous influence and power over the economic, social, political, and cultural lives of many nations and people. This development has given rise to many conflicts, contradictions, and very often destabilizing forces within both the national and international economies. The late Stephen Herbert Hymer addressed these and other aspects of the multinational corporation. He analyzed the root causes of some of its most disturbing characteristics and suggested how these could be eliminated and a world established in which exploitation and domination would be replaced by sharing and equality.

I. Questions posed by Stephen Hymer

Hymer's doctoral dissertation[1] is generally acknowledged to be a path-breaking work, critical for the reformulation of the theory of direct foreign investment. Indeed, as C. Fred Bergsten, Thomas Horst, and Theodore H. Moran have written, "much of the research done in the past fifteen years can be seen as a refinement or an extension of it."[2] However, little attention has been paid to his later writings. These papers may eventually be recognized as even more innovative than his thesis and particularly enlightening for understanding the crucial role played by multinational corporations.

This book consists of eleven papers that the editors selected as representative of Hymer's best work and illustrative of the context in which he and his work developed. (This introduction will not cover the social and political context in which Hymer lived and worked. This is discussed in the biography at the end of the book.) The first few papers show his involvement with international trade theory, industrial organization, and the study of direct foreign investment. But they soon move to analyzing the organization of production, the relations of production, and the social consequences of the capitalist system from a Marxian perspective. The papers he wrote during the

1

last years of his life were based on his deeper understanding of Marxian theory and dealt with the hierarchical organization of capitalist firms that functioned to control and dominate economic and social life under capitalism.

Our intention in this introduction is to situate Hymer's work in relation to the major mainstream and Marxian writers who have examined the multinational firm. To do this, we have tried to extract what we consider to be the central issues raised by Hymer and to examine what the selected major mainstream and Marxian writers have had to say about them. In the first part of this introduction, we consider mainstream analyses; the specific issues discussed are: (1) the capitalistic model of development and growth as developed and applied by North American theorists; (2) the efficiency and control of the multinational firm in terms of resource allocation, technology transfer, product distribution, and, most importantly, critical decision making regarding investments and the location of production facilities; (3) the conflict between the multinational corporation and the state, in which the sovereign powers of the state are being eroded and threatened by the multinational corporation; and (4) the future of the world economy that is shaped and determined by the multinational corporation.

The second part of the introduction addresses questions about the multinationals and the internationalization of capital raised by those with a Marxian perspective. Here, we deal with: (1) capitalist accumulation, both in its "primitive" (or primary) and modern senses, and the internationalization of capital; (2) the rise of the world market; (3) the international division of labor; and (4) the role of the state and its relation to the multinational corporation.

II. Mainstream analyses of the multinational corporation: the inherited framework

When Hymer first began studying direct foreign investment, three main approaches to the phenomenon seemed to dominate the literature.

The first approach, argued by Bertil Ohlin, was that international capital movements in and out of countries occur in response to the different interest rates prevailing in those countries.[3] Ohlin reasoned that interest rates would vary according to the differences in factor endowment ratios of labor and capital, and that as capital moves from low-interest to high-interest countries, equilibrium is achieved. With perfect international capital markets, there would be one world interest rate. But, because risks of default and confiscation vary, each country requires different risk premiums.[4] Ohlin qualified his theory by taking into account certain institutional and technical barriers to equilibrium. Nevertheless, his theory explains international capital movements, not direct foreign investment.

The second explanation, generally attributed to R. Z. Aliber, argued that there are risk premiums in international equity markets designed to cover uncertainty about the exchange risk on shares bought in weak-currency countries. These premiums do not apply to foreign-owned (therefore hard-currency country) subsidiaries that operate in soft-currency countries.[5] David Forsyth added to this theory by claiming that a higher capitalization rate will be applied to the profit stream of "foreign-owned subsidiaries (whose equities are denominated in home country currencies) than is applied to the income of host-country firms, whose liabilities are denominated in host-country currencies."[6] This tendency reflects the strong tendency of international equity markets to favor equities issued in the country where the corporation is headquartered against equities issued in the host country. But, again, this theory does not shed enough light on the causes of direct foreign investment.

Charles Kindleberger's early explanation held that direct foreign investment resulted from both the expansion of a firm's market and its use of internally generated funds.[7] This argument holds that when firms attempt to maximize their sales' growth rates, they have to set up plants wherever large markets exist. The internally financed growth argument says that these funds are cheaper than externally raised funds and should be used for expansion abroad.

Hymer argued that these three approaches were inadequate to explain international capital movements, especially direct investment abroad. In his dissertation, he demonstrated that the corporations' desire to *control* foreign operations was the central motive for direct investment. Hymer viewed control by the foreign investor not merely as a desire to determine the prudent use of assets but as a strategic move to eliminate competition between the investing enterprise and enterprises in other countries.[8] Alternatively stated, control is necessary in order to appropriate fully the returns on certain skills and abilities that the investing enterprise possesses. He was the first to suggest this reason for international capital movements. He also noted that international firms do not operate under conditions of perfect competition.[9] On the contrary, some firms have advantages over others, such as economies of scale, absolute costs, patent rights, and the ability to command large capital and technological resources. Certain firms' enterprises are interdependent and may be located in different countries. Thus, profits in one country may be up while in another they may be down.[10]

The initial perspectives that were criticized by Hymer did not dominate the literature for long. Multinational corporations became increasingly important during the 1960s. Mainstream economists quickly appreciated the importance of multinational firms' impact on direct investment and incorporated into their analysis many of the ideas developed by Hymer in his dissertation. However, the basic premises of mainstream theories remained the same and continued to underlie current explanations of the multinational corporation and the development of the modern world economy.

In the following section, we discuss these theoretical presumptions and their implications for an understanding of the world system.

A. *The capitalist model of development and growth*

Most mainstream writers accept the assumption that the global expansion of capitalism is desirable and perhaps inevitable. Occasional doubts are expressed about the possible conflict with socialism and the unsettling effect of Third World political and economic alliances such as, respectively, the Group of Seventy-seven and the Organization of Petroleum Exporting Countries (OPEC). Nonetheless, the generally accepted model for developing the "less-developed countries," as they are referred to in the literature, is capitalistic. This type of development is characterized by the infusion of foreign capital, technology, and managerial skills from developed countries. The consequent growth due to this injection tends to occur mostly in sectors of the economy that are perceived by foreign capital as being profitable or able to generate foreign exchange. It is this type of growth that is often associated and equated with development in less-developed countries.

It is also assumed that less-developed countries generally want rapid industrialization. In order to achieve this goal, capital and technology transfers are commonly regarded as two ways in which the Western countries can assist. Capital transfers consist mostly of direct and portfolio investments as well as loans, all seeking safety, high rates of return, and as much control as possible. Technology transfers contain the process know-how (the technology embodied in the production processes themselves), the ability to choose the appropriate technologies, the capability for engineering design and plant construction, and the technical know-how required to operate the production facilities, as well as the expertise necessary for conducting feasibility and market studies.[11] Both capital and technology are strictly *controlled* by multinational corporations from Western countries through direct investment and licensing agreements. Technological advantages are the source of quasi-monopoly power and increase profits to multinational corporations operating in situations with imperfect markets, particularly in the Third World.[12]

American economists tend to associate capitalism with the American model of capitalist development and growth. They assume that the American path to development offers the most promising results for the development of the rest of the world. Even traditional economists from Europe and the Third World are uncomfortable with this assumption. They find that it contains numerous contradictions, especially when the roles of American political, economic, cultural, and military power are considered. But despite the questions and discomfort caused by the American model, most if not all traditional economists hardly ever question the assumption that capitalism as a *system* is the most efficient way to allocate the world's resources for the benefit of all.

Perhaps the most sanguine view of the multinational corporation is offered by Charles Kindleberger in his book *American Business Abroad*.[13] He draws a parallel between the emergence of national firms, which increased the efficiency of markets for goods and factors within nations, and the rise of multinational firms, with their capacity to increase the efficiency of *international markets* for goods and factors. Kindleberger argues that multinationals can help equalize incomes among developed nations by supplementing trade and factor movements. As a consequence, they also offer the possibility of equalizing incomes between rich and poor countries.[14] The international firm engages local directors, hires local executives, employs local labor, and may utilize other local resources. In the course of maximizing its total earnings worldwide, it may sometimes be detrimental to the interest of its home economy,[15] because its object is to increase the efficiency (profits) of the world economy as a whole.

Kindleberger is aware of broader changes caused by multinational corporations, but he examines them in purely economic terms.[16] He also views government attempts to limit foreign investment as interfering with the proper workings of the market, where investments are made on the basis of liquidity preference or on the basis of differences in comparative rates of profit. Political issues are not really a concern.

B. The efficiency and control of the multinational corporations

Orthodox economists view the multinational corporation as the most efficient instrument of the capitalist system for both the optimal allocation of factors of production and the efficient distribution of products internationally. The neoclassical postulate underlying this view is that competition in the marketplace will result in a state of equilibrium, a condition that happens also to be an optimum one. The extent to which competition within the national market is enhanced by multinational corporations is regarded as a positive attribute. But once such corporations, because of their large size, begin to restrict entry into the marketplace and produce oligopolistic market structures, regulation is advocated.

In the view of many mainstream economists, even though the national marketplace is distorted by multinational corporations and the international economy is fraught with numerous trade barriers, multinational corporations are still the most efficient vehicle for allocating and using the world's productive resources. Richard E. Caves, a leading representative of this school of thought, goes on to suggest that competitive forces in the global economy "complement one another in limiting the distortions that can occur in national markets" and that whatever the industry's structural features, some international force can be pointed to as "the most likely potential constraint on departures from a reasonable competitive outcome."[17]

If the multinational corporation is seen as the most efficient instrument of investment to allocate the world's resources, how is it controlled? The thesis put forth by Adolf Berle and Gardiner C. Means,[18] regarding the divergence of stockholders' and managements' interests as the firm grew in size, states that managements' interests tend to dominate even though they are constrained by the need to assure stockholders dividend payments as well as an acceptable rate of growth of the firm. From this, and subsequent similar theses on the behavior of the firm, it is clear that critical investment decisions (including decisions concerning direct foreign investments) are to a very large extent determined by management or its designated committees.

In her study of the petroleum industry, Edith Penrose examines the suitability of the international firm as a vehicle for the flow of direct investment and finds that it is "defective, not so much because of the nature of the institution itself . . . nor even because of the monopolistic power it possesses, but because these characteristics, given the international environment in which the firms operate, may seriously distort the international distribution of the benefits obtainable from foreign investment."[19] Specifically, the chief dangers from multinationals arise from the fact that they are forced to discriminate among countries in their pursuit of profits. She finds that one solution to this dilemma would be to incorporate such firms under international law, freeing them from the control of the home government and setting up an international tax that would eliminate the significance of different tax rates imposed by various nations.[20] This stance is congruent with her view that one of the strongest arguments in favor of private enterprise is that such firms are not "instruments for the implementation of the economic or political policies of any particular government."[21]

In her more recent statements, Penrose has noted that the poorer the nation that is the host to foreign investment, the greater the likelihood that there may be adverse impacts of large amounts of such investment. She has warned that the acceptable costs of investment must be considered on an international level, and has proposed that monetary risks ought to be established for multinationals in case they violate acceptable international standards.[22]

C. The multinational corporation and the nation-state

Mainstream economists prefer to define and see the state as external to their method of analysis. They would like to believe that the state, or political sphere, and the corporate, or economic, sphere, are independent of each other and only distantly related. To them, the determining force is the economic; political, cultural, and other factors are external forces that tend to distort and disrupt the economy. The conflict between the multinational corporation and the nation-state raises the question of compatibility between the two, and if this is not possible the question becomes which is and/or will become the dominant power, the multinational corporation or the nation-state?

For most mainstream writers, the fundamental dilemma of the modern state is how to retain national control over the effective implementation of domestic economic and political policies while guaranteeing the openness of boundaries for multinational corporations to operate efficiently as well as to expand. In most cases, these writers assume that governments or some proposed international agency will regulate the excesses of multinational corporations, thus increasing their efficiency and ensuring their future growth and development.

Two mainstream writers who have included a discussion of the nation-state in their analysis of the multinational corporation are John Dunning and Raymond Vernon. Dunning has been more critical of the role of multinationals then either Kindleberger or Penrose.

In examining the problems associated with U.S. investment in the United Kingdom, Dunning emphasizes that foreign investors, besides bringing new capital and technology to Britain, may also attract and absorb scarce domestic capital and skills, and may purposefully try to acquire British companies that have valuable technical and managerial expertise.[23] On the technological side, Dunning finds that although the British firms probably do not have the resources to compete with the giant international firms in the future, there is no reason why the country should have to surrender its economic independence. Dunning suggests that the alternatives to internal direct investment to attain technological skills need to be assessed by the government and that policies to review foreign investments ought to be established.[24] Yet, at the same time, he finds that there is no evidence that the "UK is misallocating its resources by investing too much overseas. Indeed . . . British companies may well be seen to be investing too little overseas."[25] On the other hand, however, because foreign investments are a vital element in establishing the international competitive strength of firms, Dunning argues that the government should do little to restrict such operations, because they may have substantial detrimental impacts on the home economy.[26] In essence, although he is aware of the fundamental conflicts, Dunning still argues that the growth of the multinational corporation and its continued domination of the international economy offer the best prospects for the future.

Raymond Vernon finds that the multinational enterprise, by transmitting knowledge, technology, and resources efficiently across national boundaries, contributes to greater global welfare. Although troubled by some of the changes that have resulted from the growth of multinationals – particularly that many flows of goods, services, and money no longer result from arm's-length transactions between national economies but from transactions between sister affiliates of multinationals – he has been most interested in the decline of national sovereignty as a consequence of the rise of international firms. Vernon has always recognized the tensions that have existed between the multinationals and the nation-state, but he was optimistic that the global perspective of some of the multinationals, especially those from the United States, might enable them to transcend their narrow nationalism.[27] He, like Penrose, has suggested that a supranational authority might do much to lessen any conflicts that might arise. However, the international oil crisis has led him to reevaluate his past views.[28]

Two main events in the oil crisis impressed Vernon. The first was the inability of home governments, particularly those from Western Europe or the United States, to affect the actions of multinationals. As Vernon notes, the U.S. government was particularly slow to respond to the oil crisis brought on by the quadrupling of oil prices. The top levels of the administration, engrossed in the problems of Watergate, remained unaware of the full implications of the crisis until nearly six months after it broke. Other governments, like the French, used the crisis to begin foreign policy initiatives that would assert their independence from the United States.[29] The Japanese Ministry for International Trade and Industry used the crisis to shore up its declining ability to control the Japanese economy.[30]

Secondly, whereas Vernon had previously seen host countries as being relatively weak in comparison to the multinationals,[31] the oil crisis underscored the increased bargaining power of the OPEC nations. They had been able to improve their ability to collect and interpret the information that affected their negotiating position.[32]

On the other hand, Vernon also points to the continuing, or possibly enhanced, political power of the multinational corporations. He notes that they play a large role in the economies of most industrialized nations and carry considerable weight in their governments. In future years, the struggle over support for national sovereignty will take place both within the industrialized nations and in international organizations.[33] While recognizing that little action to resolve the conflicts has occurred, Vernon argues that codes of conduct leave the underlying problems unresolved. The basic problem is to find an international approach to disentangle conflicting national jurisdictions so actions by individual nations will not harm others, and to secure agreement among nations over what types of public actions are needed.[34]

D. The multinational corporation and the future of the world economy

For Vernon and a number of other mainstream commentators, the oil crisis marked a major shift in the distribution of power.[35] In the view of these writers, the rise of a new group of resource-rich nations not only presented industrialized nations with a new political and economic environment, but brought to the fore new macroeconomic problems that were unprecedented in the postwar period. Chief among these was the accumulation and transfer of massive financial resources by OPEC nations.

Thus, in the eyes of many mainstream writers, multinational corporations must now operate in a very different setting than at any point during the 1950s or 1960s. They will not fade away, but will be faced with increasing pressures from both home and host nations. The new world economy will, for many firms, make long-range planning much more difficult than in the past and may create extremely disruptive breakdowns in the international financial system. For most mainstream writers, it is unclear how multinational corporations are going to adapt to the evolving economy of the seventies and beyond. A resolution seems to depend upon how any future confrontations between new power groups in the world economy are resolved.

Yet there are still those mainstream writers who, like George Ball, believe that the U.S. multinationals must dominate world development. For Ball, a former Under Secretary of State in the Johnson administration, the survival, expansion, and growth of capitalism is vital and necessary. In his view, capitalism depends on U.S. economic and political leadership and on the central role played by U.S. multinationals.[36] Ball, a major proponent of a supranational state, argues that U.S. foreign policy used in concert with and in support of U.S. economic interests, especially international businesses, can indeed ensure the survival and expansion of capitalism.[37] He believes that the dialogue between the Northern and Southern hemispheres such as discussions sponsored by the Conference on International Economic Cooperation, would be incomplete if it did not take into account the important role of U.S. multinational corporations, "those institutions by which we conduct our economic affairs with developing countries."[38]

For Ball, conflicts between a multinational corporation and host country arise basically because of the different goals and objectives the two tend to pursue. Contractual agreements entered into by both parties are at best compromise attempts designed to accommodate each party's objectives.[39] In order to reduce conflict he recommends regulation, not by the "parochial interests of a single state," but by a supranational body responsible for chartering companies to operate in countries that are signatories of a negotiated multinational treaty consisting of established laws concerning international companies.[40]

Although such an arrangement might prohibit the most flagrant infringements on host-country rights, it could also serve as a means to legitimize the overwhelming power of multinationals, particularly those with extensive control over international markets. Thus, supranational codes of conduct, if adopted, may only make it easier for Ball's vision of the world to come true. Ball provides us with a way to settle future conflicts,[41] which will most likely be to the detriment of Third World nations.

E. International labor and the multinational corporation

The analysis of how the labor force has been affected by the rise of multinationals did not begin in earnest until the flight of factories from "more-developed nations" grew substantially. After the "runaway" plant phenomenon appeared in the popular press, writers began to explore two major questions: (1) What effects have multinationals had on the labor force in both the home and host countries? and (2) can labor, through transnational collective bargaining, have an impact on the growing power of the multinationals? Much of the discussions concerning these questions were extensions of earlier ideas about multinationals.

Several different approaches mark the most recent work. Mainstream commentators, like Raymond Vernon, felt that unions had to come to terms with multinationals. Duane Kujawa devised ways to measure the effectiveness of international collective bargaining by international labor in an internationalized industry such as the automobile industry. Judd Polk tried to reconcile the differences between multinationals and international labor. Among those whose work was more critical of the multinational corporations were Charles Levinson, who felt that international collective bargaining was gaining strength and that industrial democracy was helping this process, and Richard Cox, who was aware of the new divisions in international labor that have been exacerbated by the growing internationalization of capital.

Raymond Vernon believes that although capital and management are mobile, the state and labor are not.[42] Thus, labor is generally under the jurisdiction of a single state and its "appeal for the use of public power on its behalf" can be directed only to the government of that state.[43] As Vernon sees it, labor can respond to the growth of the multinational enterprise in two ways. Either it adopts an approach, characterized by measures such as the Burke-Hartke Bill, which Vernon says "invoke the shades of the machine-busting Luddites and saboteurs of the early 1800s"[44] and presumes that the world can be told to stop. Or it comes to terms with the "powerful underlying forces" of the multinational enterprise that have reduced national and regional differences in manufacturing and consumption patterns, and that enable multinational organizations to plan and control large parts of the world.[45]

International labor, in Vernon's opinion, has been weak because labor unions tend to be nationally oriented and espouse different ideologies.[46] National unions are passive toward government policies that reward businesses for using more capital than labor.[47] In fact, in the more industrialized countries, businesses have been particularly successful in obtaining support for technological innovations in order to respond to high labor costs. According to Vernon, these developments have helped to destroy the union's base. Therefore, the only alternative open to labor in its response to multinational enterprises is to "recognize the strength of the forces that are reducing the space between nations and find a course of action that increases the opportunities and rewards for labor in a world that continues to shrink."[48]

Duane Kujawa has examined whether or not labor in the highly internationalized automotive industry has been able to achieve better contracts than labor in more nationally oriented firms. He measured benefits received by the negotiating parties, including "direct wages, job classifications, wage supplements, vacations, holidays, personal insurance, pensions, and severance (layoff) benefits,"[49] and specific labor–management relationships, which included "work rules, grievance procedures, employee (or employer) representation units, and limitation on the use of strikes and lockouts."[50]

Kujawa analyzed industrial relations in the United Kingdom, West Germany, and France and investigated how constraints upon benefits and specific labor–management relationships influence transnational bargaining. In studying the Chrysler Corporation, the Ford Motor Company, and General Motors,[51] he found that collective bargaining in a single country seems to be more successful in controlling multinational enterprises than transnational collective bargaining.[52] In fact, Kujawa concludes that labor in multinational firms has achieved benefits that are only slightly better than those obtained by workers in more nationally based firms. The expansion of codetermination (workers' participaton in boardrooms) in Europe has strengthened the power and influence of national labor unions.[53]

Judd Polk has evaluated those criteria that may be useful in resolving the conflict between labor and U.S. multinational corporations over the impact of direct foreign investment on U.S. jobs.[54] There was a time, he says, when U.S. labor supported international free trade and enjoyed the resulting benefits that flowed from the classical notions of comparative advantage and national specialization. Now U.S. labor asserts that American workers are losing jobs and that their standard of living is being threatened because U.S. investments have gone to low-wage areas and a growing volume of imports is entering the country.[55] Organized labor still supports international free trade, but wants the government to impose quotas on a list of imports from U.S. firms in low-wage areas.

In order to resolve this conflict, Polk favors cooperation between U.S. multinational corporations and U.S. labor. The first cooperative task would be a national assessment of the "facts and implications of differential labor standards" to find the best ways of improving substandard conditions.[56] Secondly, in response to changes in national and international competition both corporations and labor should encourage U.S. research and development. This would maintain and probably increase the U.S. lead in high technology. It would also stimulate efforts to retrain workers for employment in more technologically sophisticated jobs and would force industry and government to plan the use of labor more effectively.[57]

International production is growing rapidly but without a clear goal. Polk's proposed minimum goal is the achievement of a $2,250 worldwide per capita income.[58] He believes that U.S. management and labor are able to cooperate in achieving a smooth adjustment for labor to the new problems of the world economy.[59] He also suspects that ever-increasing production will force answers to technical as well as social questions. Polk finds that one of the pressing social questions "almost certainly will involve a restatement of a labor theory of value."[60]

Charles Levinson, a Canadian who is general secretary of the International Chemical, Energy, and General Workers Unions (ICEF), has been particularly concerned with the erosion of unionized workers' wages and the consequent decline in their standard of living as well as the need to strengthen the structures and processes of international collective bargaining or "multinational unionism." He has suggested a way for labor to maintain its benefits in light of the continuing inflationary process that he finds is inherent in the operations of multinational firms because of their ability to pass along higher costs to their subsidiaries and consumers. Based on his experience with collective bargaining at the national and international levels, Levinson has concluded that wages cannot keep up with prices and that even escalation clauses in contracts are ineffective. He has proposed the use of "asset formation," the setting aside of a percentage of the accumulated assets of industry to create savings and equity for workers, which would provide a "new dimension of wealth and ownership"[61] for the working class.

According to Levinson, labor can and should respond to automation, new technology, and the rise of multinationals by helping to create conditions that encourage the growth of retained earnings, easier money policies through lower discount rates, and the maintenance of higher wages in key capital-intensive industries (which are strongly unionized) with relatively low unit labor costs.[62] These conditions would help increase company cash flows, ease interest rates, increase capacity utilization rates, and stimulate the output of consumer goods.[63] Asset formation would help labor create a greater equality of income and ownership of wealth and would counter the threat to democratic processes posed by the concentration of ownership of capital assets.[64]

Richard Cox, former director of the International Institute for Labor Studies in Geneva, has taken a more critical view of multinationals and labor. In his view, the emergence of a world economy has resulted in a hierarchical structuring of the world's labor force. Those workers directly employed by multinationals represent a labor aristocracy, a relatively privileged minority of the world's workers. Transnational bargaining has taken this segment— what Cox calls the primary labor markets – as its constituency and excluded other workers. The quandary faced by this relatively privileged group is whether or not to ally itself with the state for its own benefit, supporting corporate statism and political authoritarianism,[65] or to stand up for the rights of all workers, including those who are not privileged.

Cox finds that international production has resulted in the emergence of a pyramidal, global class structure. The apex consists of a transnational managerial class; the middle is occupied by "established labor" or members of the primary labor market; and the bottom comprises the social marginals, members of the secondary labor market.[66] Labor's response to international production has been to attempt transnational collective bargaining. These efforts have had limited success because: (1) Multinational corporations are big and powerful and operate within several national jurisdictions, whereas unions are weak because of ideological differences; (2) the distance between rank and file members and union leadership is large; and (3) the sophisticated and manipulative management techniques used by multinational corporations undermine union organization.[67]

Cox finds that a transnational collective bargaining strategy is most likely to work where unions are strongly organized at the plant level, where a relatively flexible national leadership exists, and where the union regards itself as an instrument for protecting its members' interests within an acceptable economic system.[68] Yet transnational bargaining really focuses only on the aristocracy of labor. This group will try to maintain the transnational bargaining strategy but in so doing may be confronted by the nationalism of the less-favored majority of workers.[69] Labor has two fundamental choices. Trade union leaders either acquiesce in the movement toward corporate statism and coercive authoritarianism – a process of symbiosis – or resist these tendencies by exercising the option of protecting all the workers – showing solidarity.[70]

III. Critics of the mainstream analyses of the multinational corporation

There is a growing number of critics of the mainstream perspective on and traditional approach to the study of the multinational corporation. These critics differ greatly in their ideological and philosophical orientations and thus in their methods of analyses and critiques of multinational corporations. In addition to Levinson and Cox, other critics, such as Sanjaya Lall and Paul Streeten, believe that multinational corporations can be made more sensitive and responsive to human needs in the context of clearly stated development priorities. Others, like Richard Barnet and Ronald Müller, see a more fundamental transformation occurring in the world economy because of the power and influence of multinational corporations, and they challenge their claim to being "engines of development."

A well-known document representing the non-Marxist critics' perspective is Streeten and Lall's study[71] on the impact of direct foreign investment on six developing countries. This research showed that 90 percent of the 159 sample firms in those countries had a negative effect on the host country's balance of payments and nearly 40 percent of the firms had a negative effect on social incomes.[72] The method of analysis used by the two authors was based on conventional economics and deliberately ignored socio-political factors. Yet the results of this study have grave implications for the development of underdeveloped countries and for negotiations between the governments of these countries and investing firms.[73]

It is clear that the terms permitting foreign companies to operate in host countries differ from country to country, depending upon the oligopolistic character of the companies involved and the level of economic development of the host country.[74] But host countries in general have very little, and in some cases no, experience or expertise in dealing with multinational corporations or direct foreign investment. Streeten and Lall propose specific guidelines (which incorporate some basic development requirements) that developing countries should take in carefully evaluating and selecting foreign investment.[75] They presume that foreign investment, if properly chosen, effectively controlled, and synchronized into development plans, will indeed help stimulate the development process.[76] This remains to be seen, especially when the excluded socio-political factors are taken into consideration.

Richard Barnet and Ronald Müller developed another critical analysis of multinational corporations, which includes socio-political as well as economic factors.[77] They focused on the pervasive impact such firms have on both underdeveloped and developed countries. Barnet and Müller argued that underdevelopment is still the greatest management problem multinationals have. What "were once the richest and most culturally alive areas of the globe" are now underdeveloped areas (and decaying industrial cities) that sustain three social classes consisting of a few very rich persons, a relatively small but growing middle-class whose tastes and preferences are similar to those of their counterparts in the U.S., and the overwhelming majority of poor people.[78] They pointed to the critical role finance capital played and continues to play in the history and actual process of underdevelopment. Finance capital controls the economic surpluses that were garnered in the past[79] by capitalists in the developed nations. These surpluses were not used for local development but were taken to the metropoles for consumption and further investment. According to Barnet and Müller, these surpluses continue to leave underdeveloped countries in the form of profits, dividends, royalties, technical fees, and interest on debt while these countries remain poor.[80] A number of poor countries have now become new major centers of production using high technology and cheap labor.[81] Their products are distributed and sold mainly in the rich nations that control much of the world's capital. Such outflows of capital from the U.S., for instance, have resulted in the decline of manufacturing and assembly jobs, changes in the character of the U.S. labor force, unemployment in certain industries, and redistribution of wealth and income.[82]

But the "big question" posed by Barnet and Müller is whether the multinational corporation, given its power and scope of operations, can "modify its behavior in ways that will significantly aid the bottom 60 percent of the world's population" in both poor and rich nations.[83] Their criterion for determining whether or not a social force is progressive is "whether it is likely to benefit the bottom 60 percent of the population."[84] Judging by present and projected strategies adopted by multinational corporations, the bottom 60 percent are condemned to increasing poverty because the multinational corporations have failed to assist development. Barnet and Müller propose that multinational corporations be regulated[85] and forced to disclose their dealings by opening their books to the public and to regulatory agencies,[86] both national and international.[87] And, in their view, "the precondition for effective international governments and regulation . . . is the restoration of certain powers to national governments and local communities to manage their own territory.[88]

For Barnet and Müller, multinational corporations are more adaptable than governments because their goals are simpler, their bureaucracies are generally more authoritarian, their planning cycles are shorter, and conflicting interests are fewer.[89] These advantages, plus mobility and control of information, have created a structural lag in policy formulation. Governments have continued to treat multinational corporations as national institutions when, in fact, they are global social institutions.[90] The heart of the problem is the excessive power wielded by multinational corporations and the limitations of self-imposed restraints upon that power.[91] The solution lies in regulation and disclosure.

IV. Marxian analyses of the internationalization of capital

Stephen Hymer's dissertation on the multinational corporation was not Marxian in its analysis. Neither was his early postdissertation work, which was characterized by a liberal, antitrust orientation. It was not until he wrote the "trilogy" of papers that appear in the first part of this book – "The Efficiency (Contradictions) of Multinational Corporations," "The Multinational Corporation and the Law of Uneven Development," and "The Internationalization of Capital" – that he began to analyze the multinational corporation as a global development in capitalist class relations rather than as a further growth of the firm, or as a result of the extension of market relations. In this later work, the role of labor became central to comprehending the evolution and structure of the international economy. The conflicts and contradictions raised by multinational corporations are not limited to market relations, nor to the nature of the firm itself, but rather are found in the need to control labor power.

In this section of the introduction, we discuss both the contributions of Marxian analysts to the debates on the internationalization of capital as well as their differences with and similarities to Stephen Hymer's work.

A. The inherited framework – Lenin's analysis of the international economy

Up to the 1960s, the Marxian analysis of international trade and the world economy was largely shaped by V. I. Lenin's concept of imperialism and the monopoly stage of capitalism as discussed in his essay "Imperialism, the Highest Stage of Capitalism."[92]

Lenin defined imperialism as "the monopoly stage of capitalism," in which the dominance of monopolies and finance capital is established:

Finance capital is the bank capital of a few very big monopolist banks, merged with the capital of the monopolist associations of industrialists; and . . . the division of the world is the transition from a colonial policy which has extended without hindrance to territories unserved by any capitalist power, to a colonial policy of monopolist possession of the territory of the world, which has been completely divided up.[93]

He believed that there were five basic features that were the briefest definition of the economic concepts of imperialism:

(1) the concentration of production and capital has developed to such a high stage that it has created monopolies which play a decisive role in economic life; (2) the merging of bank capital with industrial capital, and the creation, on the basis of this "finance capital," of a financial oligarchy; (3) the export of capital as distinguished from the export of commodities acquires exceptional importance; (4) the formation of international monopolist capital associations which share the world among themselves; and (5) the territorial division of the whole world among the biggest capitalist powers is completed. Imperialism is capitalism at that stage of development at which the dominance of monopolies and finance capital is established; in which the export of capital has acquired pronounced importance; in which the division of the world among the international trusts has begun, in which the division of all territories of the globe among the biggest capitalist powers has been completed.[94]

Lenin felt that imperialism enabled a handful of "exceptionally rich and powerful states" to "plunder the whole of the world"[95] by extracting enormous surplus value from the other nations; thus, it was marked by "parasitism and decay," which affected both rich and poor nations.[96] However, he did not believe the tendency toward parasitism and decay precluded the rapid growth of capitalism.[97] He argued that, at the monopoly stage, large firms could achieve better technological development. In general, he argued that development becomes more and more uneven, a phenomenon particularly visible in the richest capitalist nations.[98] Lenin's original formulation involved, therefore, a dual focus – both on surplus-value appropriation through circulation and surplus-value extraction from production.

Recent Marxian writings on the international economy have been marked by a lively debate around the framework inherited from Lenin and a reaction to the political developments and changes in the world system during the 1960s. (The editors recognize that there exists in the Marxian literature a distinction between the terms "surplus" and "surplus value." We have tried, wherever possible, to remain true to the terminology used by the particular authors under discussion.) This debate has reflected two new developments: First, world conditions have changed and Marxists have been forced by objective circumstances to reconsider earlier formulations. Second, the political situation in which radical work is done has become more open to new discussions about traditional ideas. But the present debates still reflect Lenin's dual foci, although most do not fully integrate those foci. There remain differences in emphasis – with some writers highlighting surplus extraction from poorer nations and some emphasizing the creation of new conditions for the production and accumulation of surplus value on a world scale.

B. Issues in modern Marxian interpretations

1. The accumulation and internationalization of capital

Paul Baran, Harry Magdoff, and Paul Sweezy, and to some degree Samir Amin, have all emphasized surplus appropriation. The early analysis of Baran and Sweezy[99] saw foreign investment as a device for transferring wealth from poorer to richer countries. This enabled the richer nations to expand their control over the economies of the poorer ones. Magdoff and Sweezy[100] extended this analysis by arguing that the large firm behaved very differently in the monopolistic phase. It had to regulate the increase in production carefully and found it necessary to expand both industrially and geographically because of the need to maintain monopoly prices. Control over its market share was emphasized as a means of preventing other investors from eroding monopolistic prices and reducing corporate profits. The advantages of the large, multinational firm, as enumerated by Magdoff and Sweezy,[101] were: (1) its plentiful supplies of capital and easy access to relatively inexpensive credit; (2) its large pool of managerial talent; (3) its sizable sales apparatus; and (4) its major research and development facilities. Magdoff also noted that although competition among capitalists has always been obstructed by various people-made and natural barriers, which introduced inequalities into the ranks of capitalists, some capitalists were particularly able to "transfer surplus value out of the pockets of other capitalists into their own."[102] This meant that capital was not just a relation of exploitation between one class and another, but was a complex of relations between classes and groups within classes – although the conflict between classes remains fundamental.

The multinational corporation was the vehicle through which many of these changes in the capitalist system were carried out. Baran and Sweezy[103] found that the new corporate giants were large and consistent importers of capital into the United States. Their complex structures and diversity of interests were highly different from their predecessors, and that the large-scale of exports from the foreign subsidiaries of U.S.-based companies to the United States itself was a major cause of the lagging growth of the U.S. economy and contributed to the rising unemployment. National firms are unable to compete with foreign subsidiaries of U.S. multinationals because they lack the capital, managerial, and organizational resources of the multi-national corporations. These subsidiaries can provide more profits than can be easily reinvested because they come to occupy a leading position in the new field and begin to participate in the monopolistic pricing practices of the large foreign corporations in any new industry they enter. Thus, foreign branches of corporations, which begin life as outlets for surplus capital, become sources of additional surplus capital and spur the corporation to find still other areas in which to expand, leading to further geographical and industrial diversity.

Amin[104] situates the process of accumulation in a more general historical framework, focusing on the inherent contradiction between the growing social nature of productive forces and the persistently narrow nature of productive relations. This contradiction is overcome by the continual expansion of the capitalist system and the renewal of its accumulation model, revolutionizing production relations to adjust them to the requirements of the progress of productive forces. "Every phase of expansion is characterized by a particular accumulation model, a type of propelling industry, a specific context defining the methods of competition and the status of the firm, etc. ... (and) corresponds to a certain stage of geographical expansion of the capitalist system, to a particular organization of international specialization in this context and, more specifically, to a distribution of the functions of its centre and its periphery, and finally to a certain balance (or imbalance) between the various central nation-states."[105] For Amin, however, the rise of the multina-tional corporation and the growing intervention of the state in the economy is not new, but rather "ways and means of prolonging the declining stage of the system."[106]

Although Amin does argue that a major contribution is made by the periphery in countering the falling rate of profit in the center because surplus value can be increased there more easily than at the center,[107] much of the analysis of accumulation in Amin's model is based on the shift of a surplus from the peripheral nations to the nations of the center. This shift is accomplished through the operation of the market and is based in the sphere of circulation.[108] Whereas increased exploitation characterizes the production relations in the periphery, Amin does not explore the role of the exploitation of labor, but rather focuses on the need for capitalism to constantly expand its markets.

Stephen Hymer's Marxian analysis, although influenced by the first approach discussed here, turned rapidly from a concern with the multinational firm to an analysis of the role of labor in the world economy. He argued[109] that capitalism expands by accumulating surplus value through the addition of a new proletariat at the point of production. In this context, some theories of imperialism seem inadequate because they focus on expansion of the market and not of production. As a result, Hymer concluded that the emphasis of such theories upon rivalries between capitalists is misplaced; more emphasis should be given, he thought, to the basic contradictions of capitalism that occur between capital and labor, and the fundamental basis of agreement among capitalists as against the working class.

Hymer's contribution to an understanding of accumulation is thus twofold. First, he demonstrated how "the development of business enterprise can . . . be viewed as a process for centralizing and perfecting the process of capital accumulation,"[110] by extending the analysis of the firm that had been done by a number of mainstream economists and economic historians, including R. H. Coase, Alfred Chandler, and Fritz Redlich. This work, which is most fully developed in his essays "The Multinational Corporation and the Law of Uneven Development" and "The Multinational Corporation and the International Division of Labor," was a radical extension of his thesis work and was particularly interesting because it raised numerous questions about the nature of hierarchy and control in the world economy.

Second, Hymer in his earlier essays, such as "The Internationalization of Capital," pointed to the divergence of an interlocked system of world capitalism, which differed from the Leninist view of interimperialist rivalries. This analysis reflected his belief, at the time, that multinational firms served as a substitute for the market. Capitalists would tend to unify their interests when those interests were threatened by growing competition in the world market as well as by noncapitalist groups and the working class.

This analysis later changed as Hymer was able to see that what had really happened with the rise of the multinational corporation was not an end to interimperialist rivalries (as in nation-states). Rather, a new and a more complex economic and political situation had developed in which the multinational corporation, as the institutional development of the international capitalist class, provided cohesiveness but did not signal the end of the contradictory and opposing forces both at the national (nation-state) level as well as at the regional level. Hymer's later work, especially in "The Multinational Corporation and the International Division of Labor" and "International Politics and International Economics: A Radical Approach," shows that his analysis saw the historical development of the multinational corporation not just as a further expansion of the same capitalist classes and institutions that had existed in the nineteenth century, but rather as their transformation into a new world economic order, dominated by the multinational corporation and not yet controlled by it.

Although Hymer did not draw upon a more formal Marxian model to discuss accumulation in the world market, others, such as Christian Palloix, have shown how the models presented by Marx in Volumes 2 and 3 of *Capital* can be used to analyze the internationalization process.[111] Much of this formalization of the radical analysis of world capitalism was similar to the ideas developed by Hymer in his Marxian writings. Indeed, Palloix's work is significant because it analyzes in detail the different ways in which particular European nations have chosen to foster the growth of selected industries in response to the new world situation. The necessity for the transformation of the nation-state's role in the modern era is a theme that is interwoven into many of the papers collected here.

2. The rise of the world market

The rise of the world market must be seen in terms of an historical development. The increasingly important role of the multinational corporation should be seen in the context of this developing world market. It is this relationship between historical development and the multinational corporation that has not been focused on by Marxists. They have tended to see the multinational largely as an extension of the firm and not as an indicator of qualitative change in the world economy. Amin and Hymer have been two exceptions, although each approached the world market from a somewhat different perspective.

Amin emphasizes that accumulation takes place on a world scale, rather than solely between advanced capitalist nations and "less-advanced" nations. By this he means that capitalist accumulation occurs both in the center and the periphery; he does not see accumulation as the result simply of siphoning off surplus, as in the era of merchant capitalism. He sees his theory of accumulation as being a theory of the relations between the center, the most advanced capitalist nations, and the periphery, which is being integrated into the world system through a transition to "peripheral capitalism."[112] Amin thus concentrates upon an analysis of how the periphery is integrated into the system, the development of unequal international specialization that is beneficial to the center, and a critique of the neoclassical theories of international trade. These theories fail to comprehend that the main need for foreign markets is not based on the lack of a market for products at home but rather upon the inevitable unlimited growth of production under capitalism that was pointed out by Lenin. In his examination of Rosa Luxemburg's contribution to the analysis of capital accumulation, Amin argues that Luxemburg fails to comprehend that the main need for foreign markets is not based on the lack of a market for products at home, but rather upon the inevitable unlimited growth of production under capitalism that was pointed out by Lenin. "[T]he standing contradiction [of the capitalist mode of production] between the capacity to produce and capacity to consume . . . is constantly being overcome both by deepening the internal . . . market and by extending the market externally."[113] Amin, however, still sees foreign expansion as a means to combat the tendency of the rate of profit to fall, a phenomenon that is reinforced by the growth of monopolies. Thus, the domination of the center causes the periphery to continually adjust to the center's requirements for accumulation.[114]

Hymer not only underscores both the centralization of capital, which has taken place on a world scale, and the effects of centralization – the industrialization of the Third World, the changing pattern of regional interdependence, and the increasing linkage of new forces, like the Japanese, to the world market; he also, like Amin, highlights the structural changes of the classical, competitive world market.[115] Hymer's work on this latter aspect was heavily influenced by his empirical study of the large corporations operating in Europe, which he did with Robert Rowthorn. In "Multinational Corporations and International Oligopoly: The Non-American Challenge," Hymer and Rowthorn illustrate how a new form of protectionism has emerged in Western Europe, where governments assist corporations in their penetration of foreign markets. Thus, the expansion of a few dominant firms becomes in the national interest and the growth of a specific part of the private sector becomes a national goal. This, however, strengthens a few corporations, but divorces their interest from the national interest. In his later papers, Hymer becomes more intrigued with the question of how classes operate on an international level, clearly alluding to the fact that a new superstructure is being evolved for international capitalist economic development.[116] Since Japan and Western Europe have been integrated into a new international alliance, Hymer notes, the capitalist system can survive despite the weakening of the United States.

3. The international division of labor

Two main radical views of the international division of labor derive from the work on imperialism of Rudolf Hilferding and Lenin.[117] The first sees a dualistic structure of the world economy, a separate center and periphery, as we have cited in Amin's work; the second sees a trend toward nationalization, which is dominant over the trend toward internationalization. Nikolai

Bukharin was one of the first to make the latter argument. He was sensitive to the conflicts that might emerge from the process of internationalization and to the centralization of capital on a world scale that was occurring after the First World War. He realized that the "international division of labor turns the private 'national' economies into parts of a gigantic all-embracing labor process, which extends over almost the whole of humanity."[118]

Although several more recent radical analyses have provided us with more than adequate documentation of the exploitation of the periphery of the Third World by the multinational corporations, few envision the world economy as an integrated whole. One of the important achievements of Stephen Hymer's work is that he progressed from an analysis of the firm to an interpretation of the dynamics of the world economy as a whole. Hymer emphasized four main dimensions of the international division of labor: the expansion of the firm itself; the creation of a world hierarchy of classes; the conflict between the international capitalist class and the working class; and the internationalization of production. Hymer saw multinational firms as "elaborate corporate superstructures to unite labor in production, but divide it in power,"[119] that had been erected by capital to maintain the separation between work and control. On a series of other levels, capital can maintain control via the multinational corporation through the division of labor in a number of dimensions that Hymer discusses in "The Multinational Corporation and the International Division of Labor": horizontal, vertical, spatial, and temporal. Not only did the multinational firm set up a hierarchy in the international economy that paralleled the division of labor within the firm, but it also utilized such a structure to divide and rule.[120]

Hymer's later shift from emphasizing the firm to examining the fundamental relationships under capitalism led him to argue that, on a national level, capitalists had forged a common front, "a veritable freemason society vis-à-vis the whole working-class," as Marx had remarked.[121] While such an association was formed, the intense rivalry among capitalists would continue unabated. In "The United States Multinational Corporations and Japanese Competition in the Pacific," Hymer extends his analysis of consolidation of interests to the international scene, indicating that the creation of an international hierarchy of classes was in progress. This conclusion has had significant implication for any interpretation of the conflict between capitalists and the working class in the modern age. Hymer, in his last article, where he discusses international politics and international economics, indicates that the emergence of the world market has brought capitalism to a critical point, particularly in the labor market. The old strategies of labor no longer work and the new response of an international labor movement, which would take a political form in the struggle over state power and the continuance of capitalism, would inevitably erode the power of capital.[122]

Hymer was also aware of the growing internationalization of production, which has been described more fully in the work of György Ádám and Christian Palloix.[123] "The internationalization of production via the multinational corporate system," Hymer notes, "was a reaction on the part of capital" to the fact that the "growth of world trade brings labor of different countries into closer contact and competition." Thus the competitive process, "which both brings labor together and separates it, has now taken on an international dimension."[124] Because things could be produced more cheaply abroad and there was growing competition from foreign firms, U.S. corporations and other developed nations invested abroad or entered into agreements that enabled them to maintain their growth and preserve their market position. Thus, as Hymer emphasizes, the tendencies to concentration and centralization were shifted to an international plane. In extending the investigation of the internationalization of production, Ádám was particularly concerned with examining why "lines of production that previously made cost sense in a national setting, lose their justification in a global setting, being followed by the international shifting of production."[125] Palloix has shown how the internationalization of production is linked to expanding the surplus value garnered by firms in the most-developed nations. He also examined the shift of European industries to the periphery of Europe. This work provides us with an initial description of a process that needs to be investigated in much more detail.

4. The role of the nation-state and interimperialist rivalries

The major question raised about the role of nation-states during the process of internationalization of capital is whether their power will be eroded or enhanced. Although this question is explored in several writings of neoclassical economists, particularly in Raymond Vernon's book *Sovereignty at Bay,* it has become a major point of contention among radicals. Indeed, if we must begin to question whether or not capital has a nationality, we may have to reexamine some of the basic assumptions in theories of imperialism.

Baran and Sweezy's early critical analysis of the international corporation[126] drew the inference that such firms were no more concerned with the interests of advanced nations than they were with those of the developing countries, because their decisions and actions were based solely on promoting their own interests. Magdoff's view[127] differed somewhat from this early interpretation. Although he found that multinational firms were "multinational" because they operated in a number of nations with the aim of maximizing profits for the company as a whole, in all other decisive respects they are national. Ownership and control are still located in one nation, and the link between capital and the state is fundamental to the existence of capital. What is new, Magdoff claims, is the fact that multinationals demand such sweeping freedom for their own operations. He concludes that nations will be unable to grant such freedoms and thus contradictions will occur between the states and the international firms.[128]

Bill Warren argues along lines similar to Magdoff.[129] He finds that examining the historical function of the state leads one to note that, if anything, the power of the nation-state has increased, and the interdependence between firms and the nation-state, which is enhanced by the growing internationalization of capital, leads states to intervene much more extensively in their domestic economies. Warren cites the British experience to support his contention that as firms get larger and fewer firms remain in each industry it is "easier for the state to control them by administrative fiat, monetary and taxation policy and so on."[130] Warren argues (in contrast to Robin Murray, whose views we will examine below) that although the postwar expansion of firms has created new problems for each nation-state's economic policy, these problems have not been generated by greater independence of the large firms in relation to the state. Rather, they are evidence of an increasing interdependence, in areas such as balance of payment problems, exchange rate difficulties, inflation, and international competitiveness.[131]

Robin Murray's contribution to this debate takes a rather different approach. He finds that although capital does require the performance of what he calls "primary public functions" – the guaranteeing of property rights, economic orchestration, input provision, intervention for social consensus, management of the external relations of the capitalist system, and the establishment of the conditions for free, competitive exchange – when it extends beyond a strictly national setting, these functions do not necessarily need to be performed by capital's home government.[132] The interests of capital in the types of public functions that need to be performed and the bodies that will perform them, according to Murray, differ depending upon a number of factors, including the degree of productive centralization, the strength of foreign competition, and the stage of overseas company development.[133] Murray points to a number of examples whereby corporations can operate within a system of using different sets of nation-states to support either their intranational or international interactions and concludes that multinationals and states are not fundamentally and irrevocably opposed to each other. However, weaker states in the period of internationalization will come to suit neither the interests of their own capital nor that of foreign investors, and the contradiction between the state and capital needs to be examined more closely to understand imperialism in the modern age.

Hymer's view, although close to that of Murray, has evolved through a number of stages. In an early paper, "The Efficiency (Contradictions) of Multinational Corporations," he suggests that the multinational firm is setting up a New Imperial System by centralizing decision making in a few centers and creating a division of labor between nations that corresponds to the division of labor between various levels of the corporate hierarchy.[134] In his later co-authored paper with Robert Rowthorn, he is more concerned with the consequences of nation-states' support for direct foreign investment by their national firms. This leads to a weakening of the link between country performance and company performance and erodes the power of the state to regulate multinationals. However, because the corporation cannot itself deal with the problems of the business cycle, social security, and unbalanced regional growth, Hymer and Rowthorn suggest that multinational firms will require multinational nation-states. Although this may not occur very quickly, it certainly seems to be the main trend, despite numerous obstacles.[135] This view is elaborated further in Hymer's later papers, which emphasize the emergence of a new system to maintain international capitalism, forged on the basis of a hierarchy of capitalists not limited by patriotic ties. Hymer finds that the most important change has not been the emergence of multinationals, but rather the rise of an international capital market, which has led to the creation of an international capitalist class with a material base for its international consciousness. Wars are no longer in the capitalist interest, and a series of linkages will be developed between the strongest capitals in order to revive the superstructure of the world capitalist system, which has been somewhat undermined by the conflicts and contradictions that have emerged in recent years.[136]

V. Future directions

In the last year of his life, Hymer was beginning to synthesize a number of highly provocative areas of thought. This process led him to consider formulating a very different agenda for the analysis of the international corporation and the world capitalist system. Hymer stood at the threshold of what appeared to be an exciting period of work, one which most of his colleagues expected would be highly productive and would contribute significantly to our understanding of the fundamental social and economic relations of capitalism. Although the "agenda" he had begun to formulate was never carried out, it is possible to point in the directions his work was heading.

Hymer believed that the end of the twentieth century would be marked by increasing international movements of capital coupled with a growing class of international capitalists. The internationalization of capital would be characterized by greater concentration and control in fewer and larger international firms. The technology chosen and used by these firms would be more sophisticated and basically capital intensive because of corporate goals of higher productivity, increased rates of return, and control. Hymer saw these trends as reducing the power of the nation-state to control international capital movements; as changing the capitalist class's relationship to its nation of origin; and as creating greater unemployment and increasing the industrial reserve army in both Western and Third World countries. In the latter, in particular, he envisaged accelerated destruction of precapitalist forms and modes of production, the increasing proletarianization of the populations, and the formation and rapid growth of the industrial reserve army, as well as sharper uneven development. According to Hymer, these events would cause the problems for labor and capital to be qualitatively different in the last quarter of the twentieth century.

Hymer concentrated his analytical talents on examining how changes in the accumulation of capital and the proletarianization of labor would alter the form of class conflict. He was also convinced that the uses made of patriarchy and hierarchical divisions would significantly condition the form of the class struggle. In his analysis of the recent changes in capital accumulation, he perceived three emerging contradictions: those on an international scale between the capitalist powers, those between the capitalist and socialist countries, and those between capitalist and Third World nations. In the first place, the capitalist countries were experiencing growing competition and rivalry among themselves, a fact illustrated by the competition U.S.-based corporations were meeting from Western Europe- and Japan-based corporations. Secondly, the contradictions and conflicts between capitalist and socialist countries continue to grow, partly because of their fundamental ideological orientation, their social systems, their international political objectives, and their differing positions in the world hierarchy of communications. Thirdly, the capitalist nations' multinational corporations were being challenged by Third World countries that wished to break with capitalist control. This was the result of internal struggles of national liberation, whose participants wanted to sever their ties to the Western nations, and the demands of an emerging bourgeois class, which feared the pressure from the local impoverished populace and needed to establish its own industrial base to defuse rival political movements.

In the international struggle, states and multinational corporations were competing for spheres of influence. This competition was conditioned by the conflicts that resulted from changes in the international division of labor. The emerging world configuration had altered those earlier alliances labor made with capital or the understanding labor had of its conflict with the capitalist class. Of course there were differences between countries, but generally the development of the labor movement in the capitalist nations was to a great extent controlled by the policies adopted by the labor unions. The unions believed that the conflict between labor and capital would take place within nations and that the policies adopted by unions to protect more favored sections of the working class would still be effective in the era of international capital mobility. However, capital became increasingly able to relocate its production facilities abroad; not only labor-intensive industries, but also capital-intensive industries as well. This began to erode the power of unions and threatened the collective bargaining agreements of the 1950s and 1960s. The unions were now faced with an increasingly non-unionized work force, a growing army of the unemployed supplemented by migration within their nations. Internationally, the work force of capitalist countries faced "competition" for jobs from proletariats and the "surplus population" in Third World countries. To make matters worse, the working class was further divided as a result of sexism, racism, and hierarchical divisions within occupations and between labor markets. Hymer saw that the significance of this was to control the class conflict, much in the same way as he saw the hierarchical division of the world with centers of control located in the advanced capitalist countries and production taking place in the Third World countries.

At the end of his life, Hymer integrated his analysis with a Marxian perception of the contradictory nature of these developments. He was impressed with the political movements of the late 1960s and early 1970s – the struggles for national liberation in the Third World and in the United States, the development of the women's movement, and the "counter-cultural" and working-class movements against hierarchy – and thought and hoped these movements would challenge the hegemony of capital.

Hymer also knew that many of these developments would have policy implications for the major actors in the international arena. Some of his suggestions are raised in the last paper in this volume, "International Politics and International Economics: A Radical Approach." He also discussed this perspective in many of his last lectures and conversations. At this time, he was becoming more concerned about the role labor unions would adopt vis-à-vis these changes – would they develop international collective bargaining agreements or maintain a national and, by implication, increasingly defensive stance? Or would the unions take into account the problem of organizing the unorganized workers in their own countries, as well as those in the industrial reserve army? Surely many of the ideas he raised were undeveloped, and perhaps he was unclear about the enormity of the task, but he recognized the need for unions to change their understanding of collective bargaining and organizing tactics. He also was very aware of the contradictions between the nation-states and the multinational corporations, and subscribed neither to the view that multinationals dominated the states, nor to the theory that saw the nations as the dominant actors. As for the conflicts between the Western and socialist countries and their struggles with the Third World, he could only raise these issues and try to understand them. But he believed that these conflicts, like the contradictions between the states and the multinational corporations, were being acted out on a level far more intense and more worldwide then ever before in the history of capitalism.

Part I

The nature and contradictions of the multinational corporation

Introduction

Kari Polanyi Levitt

I first met Stephen Hymer in 1967 while he was in Canada in connection with his assignment on the federal government Task Force on the Structure of Canadian Industry set up under the chairmanship of Professor Mel Watkins of the University of Toronto, a friend of Hymer since M.I.T. Hymer and I were excited to discover many similarities of approach. At this time I was completing "Economic Dependence and Political Disintegration: the Case of Canada,"[1] the initial version of my book *Silent Surrender,*[2] and was also working with Lloyd Best on an analysis of dependency in the Caribbean.[3] Over the next two years, we exchanged papers and ideas – Hymer's work on Ghana[4] and that of Best and other West Indian economists.[5] In 1968, Hymer and Watkins were commissioned to undertake a study for the Canadian International Development Agency (CIDA) on measures to speed the flow of Canadian investment to the Commonwealth Caribbean. They were soon persuaded that there was an inconsistency in resisting foreign investment in Canada and encouraging Canadian investment in the West Indies – Hymer made amends in a paper presented to a conference in Jamaica on the topic of "External Aid in the Caribbean Region: Effects and Influences in 1970."[6] The work of Caribbean economists interested Stephen sufficiently so that he arranged to spend several months of his 1968–9 sabbatical leave at the Trinidad campus of the University of the West Indies early in 1969.

During the years 1967 to 1970, there was a flurry of encounters as a number of individuals, long separated by the initial absence of communication links between peripheral locations, and all grappling with the related themes of mechanisms of dependent economies and the effects of multinational corporations on hinterland or peripheral countries, learned of each other's existence and work. It was Osvaldo Sunkel[7] who, under the auspices of the Max-Planck-Institut in Germany and the World Law Fund, drew up the invitation list for a small and informal colloquium in Hamburg in May 1970. Invited were people who had been working along similar lines but whose work was largely unknown by one another. The theme of the conference was deliberately vague – the economic order in the year 2000 – and the participants were people who, by and large, took their point of departure in their own work from the perspective of the periphery. Among those present who were from Canada: Hymer, Watkins, and Levitt; from the Caribbean: Best; from Latin America: Sunkel, Celso Furtado, and Keith Griffin; from Europe: Arghiri Emmanuel, Giovanni Arrighi, and some staff members of the Max-Planck-Institut. At the conference, Hymer presented an early version of his paper "The Multinational Corporation and the Law of Uneven Development," which is included in this part. Hymer's encounter with the Max-Planck-Institut developed into a continuing relationship.

After May 1970 I saw Hymer only infrequently, generally during the Christmas holiday season when it was his habit to visit Montreal to see his family and that of his wife, Gilda. Our ultimate farewell was at Paperman's Funeral Home on Côte de Neiges in Montreal on a bleak winter day. The following day Canada's leading newspaper, the Toronto *Globe and Mail,* carried an obituary report under the headline: "Watkins Economist Dies at 38." In typical fashion, Hymer had the last word even from the grave on the matter of the provincialism of his native country, whose citizenship he never relinquished and whose students of economics will, thanks to the New York compilers of this anthology to be published in England, become acquainted with this most unusual Canadian.

I. The efficiency (contradictions) of multinational corporations

The principal thesis of the three essays reprinted below holds that the enterprise (multinational corporation) is the microcosm; the international economic order is the macrocosm; and the relationship between them is explained in terms of two laws of economic development: the Law of Increasing Firm Size and the Law of Uneven Development. In "The Internationalization of Capital," Hymer attempts to cast the argument into more explicitly Marxian language and suggests that a "new world system" of transnational corporate capital is in the making.

This first article is best understood as a spin-off from Hymer's involvement with the Canadian policy debate on the effects of the rapid increase in control by U.S.-based corporations over Canada's economic sovereignty. In the context of that debate, nearly everyone conceded that the multinationals were more efficient, in strictly economic terms, than the indigenous national firms they were busily buying out. Foreign multinationals, so the argument went, should be welcomed, indeed encouraged. Encroachment on political sovereignty – the question of whose law should govern their conduct, that of their corporate citizenship or that of the country in which they operate – was a matter for legislation, separate and distinct from their contribution to the economy. To this day, the predominant opinion the world over is that the multinationals are efficient in terms of economic criteria. The question that Hymer attempts to answer in this article is one to which I also addressed myself during this same period and in the context of the same Canadian debate: Efficient for what and efficient for whom? Hymer's answer is that they are efficient at oligopolistic decision making and at securing their own expansion and survival.

Hymer observes that although most parent firms are large enough to have exhausted economies of scale without foreign investment, and although some of their foreign subsidiaries are unquestionably too small for efficient operation, firms continue to expand. There has been a steady increase in the size of firms since the middle of the nineteenth century so persistent as to be formulated as a general law of capitalist accumulation. In subjecting D. H. Robertson's "islands of conscious power in an ocean of unconscious co-operation" [8] to further examination, Hymer utilizes the writings of Professor A. D. Chandler [9] to explain the advantages of larger multinational firms over smaller national ones. Following Chandler, he traces the evolution of the firm from its early (Marshallian) days, when a single capitalist-entrepreneur decided just about everything concerning his single-industry factory; to the merger movement at the end of the nineteenth century and the formation of vertically integrated production and marketing corporations; to the multidivisional corporations of the 1920s with greatly enlarged head-office "brains"; and finally to the full-blown multinational corporations with highly complex and sophisticated central coordinating structures.

Ever more effective coordination through the head office is necessary precisely because there is an ever more elaborate internal division of labor, within the large firm not regulated by impersonal market signals, but subject to overall administrative corporate planning.

The modern transitional enterprise is a much more powerful and sophisticated business organization than the national corporation. It appears to be capable of integrating world production and exchange to an ever greater extent. Commodity trade and portfolio capital movements of the nineteenth century are being displaced by the international transfer of organizational capacity (foreign direct investment), which integrates world production within the private horizons of global corporate entities. In other words, the multinational corporation is the international manifestation of the process of concentration, and of oligopolistic and monopolistic competition.

One of the central images of Hymer's writing is that of a pyramid of power, whereby the microcosm of the multinational corporation shapes the world to its image, creating a macrocosmic division of labor between countries that corresponds to the various levels of the corporate hierarchy. It will tend to centralize high-level decision making in a few key cities – New York, London, Paris, Frankfurt, and Tokyo. The rest of the world will be confined to lower levels of activity and income; its settlements will be the provincial capitals, towns, and villages of the New Imperial System. Income, status, authority, and consumption patterns will radiate out from the centers in a declining fashion and the hinterland will be denied independence and equality. This, so Hymer argues, is the macrocosmic projection of the internal structure of the hierarchy within the corporation. Here day-to-day management is left to the nationals of subsidiaries who remain rooted in one spot. Above them is a layer of more senior corporate management personnel who move around freely from country to country, as bees among flowers, gathering and transmitting information. These people for the most part are citizens of the country of the parent corporation. At the apex or controlling center are individuals drawn from a relatively small homogeneous cultural and social group, quite distinct from the population of the metropole as a whole.

The multinational corporation is indeed a far cry from the Marshallian firm whose owner ruled his factory from an office on the second floor not far above the noise and clatter of his mechanical machinery. In the world of today, executive managers rule from the top floors of skyscrapers, linked by instant electronic communication to scores of corporate operations all over the world, likewise linked to the scene of the action wherever it might happen to be. On a clear day, as Hymer so graphically put it, they can almost see the world.

Gone is the simple world from which the propositions of welfare economics are drawn, the world of impersonal market decisions in which the famous invisible hand brings harmony between private profit maximization and the general public interest.

In a brief concluding paragraph, Hymer summarizes as follows: The multinational corporation reveals the power of size and the danger of leaving it uncontrolled. The trend is in the direction of international integration along the communication lines of large corporations, each engaged in planning with long time horizons: Noncorporate linkages between national economies are eroding; the system of transnational economic integration by means of multinationals eventually leads to national disarticulation and the subversion of public policy by the power of very big business. The alternative to integrating one industry or one firm over many countries is to integrate many industries over one country, and develop free, that is, noncorporate, links of trade and information between countries. Present trends, however, are not in that direction.

II. The multinational corporation and
the law of uneven development

This next article focuses on the manner whereby inequality is built into the growth mechanisms of the contemporary world capitalist system, reproducing hierarchies of dominance and dependence, wealth and poverty, at every level, including that of the cities of the Third World, so well described by Frantz Fanon and quoted by Hymer as an overture to his article. The argument takes its point of departure from the proposition that the factory and the market represent two different ways of coordinating the division of labor.

The roots of the modern corporation are traced back to the small workshops and "manufactories" organized by the emergent capitalist class during the Industrial Revolution. The capitalist, that is, "the person with sufficient funds to buy raw materials and advance wages," could gather a number of people under one roof and obtain his or her reward from the increased productivity resulting from the division of labor, that is, from social production. The direct coordination of tasks within the factory is consciously organized in a hierarchical and authoritarian manner. Complementing the *conscious* division of labor within the factory, between those who plan and those who work, is the *unconscious* decentralized and impersonal division of labor operating through the market process.

Hymer suggested that in the precapitalist system of production the division of labor was hierarchically structured at the macro level, that is, for society as a whole, but not at the micro level, that is, in the process of production. Individuals were largely independent in production, and individual craftspeople could produce work of high standard and high quality, but only in limited quantity because output per head was low. The capitalist system, he suggests, reversed this: The macro system became unconsciously structured as a self-regulating coordinator as restrictions on capital markets and labor mobility were removed, whereas at the micro level labor was gathered in ever larger factories under the authoritarian direction of the entrepreneur-capitalist. Robertson's "islands" grow ever larger, crowding the ocean much as cancerous cells destroy their host. Eventually the microcosmic corporation shapes the macrocosm to its own image as corporate capital becomes internationalized and the international economic and social system more hierarchical, authoritarian, and unequal.

The mechanisms whereby the corporations shape the international system in their own image comes into view when Hymer superimposes a spatial and ethnic dimension onto the three-level pyramid of decision making already described. This he calls the "correspondence principle"; it is apparently taken from location theory.

Level I activities are located close to the capital market, the media, and the levers of power of the metropolitan governments. Here top executives determine corporate goals and strategies – the ultimate decisions concerning people and money. This is the hub from which radiates information – new technology, new products, new fashions and tastes. In brief, the multinationals, backed by state power, have created a communications network of the imperial type, radiating out from the center.

Level II activities are basically those of the corporate civil service, a select corps of white-collar middle-level executives who move from country to country, from lower levels of the hierarchy to the apex of power, transmitting information and coordinating the work of the Level III managers. If Level I are the executive generals, Level II managers are commissioned officers of the global corporate system. They are largely drawn from a small culturally homogeneous group of Europeans or North Americans because they move more easily in higher managerial circles.

Level III management is localized and spread all over the globe in accordance with the pull of labor power, markets, and raw materials. Nationals remain rooted to one spot, their horizons limited to the level of the branch plants. Although playing an influential role in the political, social, and cultural life of the host country, these people, whatever their title, occupy at very best a medium position in the corporate structure. They are its noncommissioned officers. The governments with which they deal tend to take on the same middle-management outlook, because this is the only range of information to which they have access. Corporate and public civil servants at the host-country level are part of the same middle class, and their nationalism is basically one of seeking promotion within the corporate structure, not a break with it.

This hierarchical system, according to Hymer, requires the continued growth of the "modern" sector in Third World countries in order to secure class alliances necessary for minimal political stability. To this end it must solve four critical problems: (1) the foreign-exchange shortage; (2) labor skill and educational capacity; (3) the urban food problem; and finally (4) it must keep the excluded two-thirds of the population under control. The solutions suggested to these four problems are (1) cheap-labor-manufactured exports; (2) expanded aid programs and reformed government bureaucracies; (3) agribusiness and the green revolution; and (4) population control and counterinsurgency. Hymer concludes that it is doubtful whether the center has sufficient political stability to finance and organize such a program. Thus, the age of the multinational corporation may well be at its end, rather than its beginning.

III. The internationalization of capital

In the final article in this part, Hymer argues that competition between national capitalists is becoming less and less a source of rivalry between nations. By cross-penetration of investments in each other's markets, American, European, and Japanese corporations have been able to diversify and stabilize their corporate competitive situations. This process has many aspects, including the cross-purchase of corporate claims and the general diversification of portfolios through a rapidly growing and widening international superstructure of credit-drawing capital from all over the world.

Associated noncorporate private capital flows from one country to another are at least as large as direct investments, and probably are growing faster. Conflicts between firms on the basis of nationality are transformed into international oligopolistic market sharing and collusion. This incidentally explains why European and Canadian capitalists preferred the positive response to *le defi americain* – that is, becoming multinational themselves – rather than the negative one of blocking American penetration.

The overriding interest of the capitalist class is not the war of each against each, but the common need of all to maintain the capitalist society within a multinational corporate system whereby the 1 percent of the world's population that owns the vast majority of corporate stock can better preserve its interest as it absorbs and crowds out the others. In this connection, Hymer cites the famous quotation from Marx that "capitalists form a veritable freemason society vis-à-vis the whole working class, while there is little love lost between them in competition amongst themselves."

Hymer deduces that a "new world system" is in the making as international corporations are "unifying world capital and world labour into an interlocking system of cross-penetration that completely changes the system of national economies that has characterized world capitalism for three hundred years." This three-pronged process of an internationalized capital market, internationalized capitalist production, and international government is far from complete – especially with respect to the formation of supranational political institutions and unified codes of laws on the rights and limits of private property – but, says Hymer, "it has moved further and faster than is commonly realized." Its outlines can be discerned, and so can its cracks.

He tells us that the two powerful levers for the concentration of capital are *competition* and *credit,* and that these operate on a world scale. From competition derives the need for the constant reinvestment of profit, the constant extension of markets, and the constant search for new techniques. Availability of credit, or more generally the existence of an international capital market, is the prerequisite of expanded capitalist production on a world scale. Very true. Not for nothing did Marx call his capitalist Mr. Moneybags, nor Schumpeter assign a key role to credit in his cycle of the creation and destruction of rentier profit or quasi rents.[10]

In my view, Marx's basic proposition concerning the contradiction between extended *social* production (internal and international division of labor) and *private* concentrated power and appropriation has such general validity as to be incapable of proving or disproving the contention that a "new world system" is in the making in the decades of the 1970s and 1980s. Much the same holds for the Schumpeterian concept of "creative destruction" as a mechanism for the renewal and concentration of capital.

The real problem with Hymer's argument in this particular article is that it does not adequately treat the overall political economy of the process, that is, the international political prerequisites for the transnationalization of production. In the final analysis, to quote Hymer, "markets come out of the barrel of a gun, and to establish an integrated world economy on capitalist lines requires the international mobilization of political power." The question thus shifts to the nature of the relationship between the transnational corporation, the international capital market, and the sovereign nation-states that constitute the international political system. Hymer is right that the transnationalization of production, including the international allocation of labor on a world scale, requires some form of international government. A system of enforceable international codes of the rights and duties of international property has been the dream of George Ball, strategist of U.S. corporate business and a key member of the Trilateral Commission.[11] Legitimated by the liberal rhetoric of free movement of goods, capital, and labor and the efficiency of the global allocation of resources on a world scale, the strategy requires the emasculation of national sovereignty and the assertion of the primacy of economic forces over cultural and political collectivities. In the world in which we live, however, these economic forces are not the self-regulating market responses of millions of atomistic producers and consumers, but the conscious outcomes of the strategies of a few hundred global enterprises, that have access to the levers of political and administrative power in virtually every country of the so-called free world.

Although the governments and bureaucracies of nation-states have been infiltrated, one might even say subverted, by the innumerable "connections" of the corporate world, it remains a stubborn fact of the international political order that the only law that has legitimacy is national law. Moreover, the system of nation-states, unlike the system of capitalist economic transactions, has no international integrating mechanism, save for the pecking order of military might and the "checks" of the great powers' balance of terror. Paradoxically, the further internationalization of corporate capital as described by Hymer ultimately may yet depend on the continued hegemony of one undisputed superpower in the capitalist world – the model of a polycentric capitalist world being perhaps somewhat of an economistic myopia. Is not the penultimate source of political power in international affairs in fact military power, in all its various manifestations? The only political umbrella (providing essential security of property) under which the internationalization of the capitalist production of the 1970s and 1980s can proceed may ultimately prove to be the military might and political influence of the United States.

Both Germany and Japan remain demilitarized by virtue of the allied victory in the Second World War; the United Kingdom is bankrupt and explicitly satellitic vis-à-vis the United States; France is neither able nor will it be permitted to rival the United States in military power. If this argument has any validity, then Hymer's "new world system" is not as drastically different from the post–Second World War period as is claimed.

Perhaps the apparent novelty of corporate internationalization rests on the questionable assumption that big capital has ever had any sense of national allegiance. It was, I believe, Adam Smith who stated long ago that financial and mercantile capital knows no country, has no *patrie*. Perhaps relations between international capital and the metropolitan state have never been more than arrangements of convenience? In the ultimate analysis, it may turn out that Hymer was perhaps mistaken in dismissing the great mercantilist trading companies as antecedents of the multinational corporation. Far from begin "extinct dinosaurs" (Hymer's phrase), is there not an historical continuity from the mercantile enterprises engaged for the past 300 to 400 years in international commerce and exploitation to the transnational corporate-financial entities of the present day? Insofar as the capitalist metropolitan power system is progressively more (not less) hierarchical, the "polycentricity" of the international political system corresponds to Hymer's Level II. In this view, the Level I headquarters of the "international government" of the worldwide corporate system remain located in the United States – albeit perhaps in the New York offices of the Trilateral Commission. It follows that the most important "diplomatic" relationship of all the very large global corporations, wherever they are headquartered, is ultimately their relationship with the state machinery of the United States and its international ramifications. Underlying these relationships are structures of private economic power. Ultimately the system within which we are enmeshed cannot be understood without reference to the insights of Marx. The three articles in this part form a continuum of the expanding understanding by Stephen Hymer of the nature and structure of the world capitalist system in both microcosm and macrocosm.

The tragedy is that Hymer is no longer with us to explore the complicated relationship between the system of private economic and financial power on the one hand, and the international political system of states and governments on the other.

1 The efficiency (contradictions) of multinational corporations

Multinational corporations are a substitute for the market as a method of organizing international exchange. They are ". . . islands of conscious power in an ocean of unconscious cooperation," to use D. H. Robertson's phrase.[1] This essay examines some of the contradictions of this latest stage in the development of private business enterprise.

At the outset, we should note that the multinational corporation raises more questions than economic theory can answer. Multinational corporations are typically large firms operating in imperfect markets and the question of their efficiency is a question of the efficiency of oligopolistic decision making, an area where much of welfare economics breaks down, especially the proposition that competition allocates resources efficiently and that there is a harmony between private profit maximization and the general interest. Moreover, multinational corporations bring into high definition such social and political problems as want creation, alienation, domination, and the relationship or interface between corporations and national states (including the question of imperialism), which cannot be analyzed in purely "economic" terms.

I. Division of labor and the extent of the firm

Our starting point is the fact that there are two kinds of division of labor: the division of labor between firms coordinated by the markets; and the division of labor within firms, coordinated by entrepreneurs. International trade theory has been mainly concerned with the first of these and has long stressed the desirability of widening international markets to increase the division of labor and exchange. Far less attention has been paid to the parallel proposi-

This essay originally appeared in the *American Economic Review*, Vol. LX, No. 2, May 1970, pp. 441–8. Copyright ©1970 by the American Economic Association. Reprinted by permission of the American Economic Association.

tion that the division of labor within a firm is limited by the extent of the firm and the economic and social questions this raises.

Unfortunately, the empirical evidence is not very helpful in deciding the degree to which large international firms should be encouraged in order· to reap the benefits of internal specialization and exchange. Few studies have been made on the relationship of foreign investment to a firm's overall efficiency and as far as quantitative evidence is concerned, we must view this question as a completely open one. With regard to the effect of size, the evidence is more plentiful but not conclusive. A number of studies on differences in performance of large and small firms have in general concluded that firms experience economies of scale up to a certain minimum size, after which there is little relationship between size and performance. Applying these results to the multinational corporation suggests that most parent firms are large enough to have exhausted economies of scale without foreign investment, although many of their subsidiaries may be too small to stand on their own feet.

These tests, however, have several inadequacies and may seriously underestimate the advantages of size. The major difficulty is that large firms are seldom engaged in exactly the same activities as medium-sized or smaller firms and their performance is not really comparable. The fact that very large firms do not seem to be significantly more profitable than their smaller rivals or to grow significantly faster does not preclude the possibility that they are specializing in activities where size is of great advantage and which would not be undertaken if the large firms did not exist. The structure of output within a country could well be a function of the size distribution of its firms without there being observable differences between large and small firms with regard to the more commonly studied characteristics.

The qualitative evidence on the structure of business enterprise and its evolution through time suggests that both size and internationality have important positive effects on a firm's strength and ability. Since the beginning of the industrial revolution there has been a steady increase in the size of manufacturing firms, so persistent that it might almost be formulated as a general law of capital accumulation. These increases in size were accompanied by important changes in organizational structure involving both increased subdivision or differentiation of tasks and increased integration through the creation of new organs of control. Business administration became a highly specialized activity with its own elaborate division of labor; and the corporation developed a brain to consciously coordinate the various specialties and to plan for the survival of the organism as a whole.

Chandler[2] distinguishes three major stages in the development of corporate capital. First, the Marshallian firm, organized at the factory level, confined to a single function and a single industry, and tightly controlled by one or a few men who, as it were, see everything, and decide everything. The second stage emerged in the United States at the end of the nineteenth century when rapid growth and the merger movement led to large national corporations, and a new structure of administration was developed to deal with the new strategy of continent-wide, vertically integrated production and marketing. The family firm gave way to the modern corporation with a highly elaborate administrative structure to organize the many disparate units of a giant enterprise. The next stage, the multidivisional corporation, began in the 1920s and gathered great momentum after the Second World War. It too was a response to a new marketing strategy. To meet the conditions of continuous innovation, corporations were decentralized into several divisions, each specializing in one product line and organized as an almost autonomous unit similar in structure to the national corporation. At the same time, an enlarged corporate brain was created in the form of the general office to coordinate the various divisions and to plan overall growth and survival. This form is highly flexible and can operate in several industries and adjust quickly to rapidly changing demands and technology.

With each step in the development of business administration, capital obtained new power and new horizons. As Chandler and Redlich[3] point out, there are three levels of business administration. Level three, the lowest level, is concerned with managing the day-to-day operations of the enterprise; i.e., keeping it going within the established framework. Level two is responsible for coordinating the managers at level three. Level one's function is goal determination and planning; i.e., setting the framework for the lower levels. In the Marshallian firm all three levels are embodied in one entrepreneur. In the national corporation, the top two levels are separated from the bottom level. In the multidivisional corporation, differentiation is far more complete; level one is completely split off from level two and is concentrated in the general office whose specific function is strategy, not tactics.

In other words, the process of capital accumulation has become more and more specialized through time. As the corporation evolved, it developed an elaborate system of internal division of labor, able to absorb and apply both the physical sciences and the social sciences to business activity on a scale which could not be imagined in earlier years. At the same time, it developed a higher brain to command its very large concentration of wealth. This gave it the power to invest on a much larger scale and with a much wider time-horizon than the smaller, less developed firms that preceded it. The modern multidivisional corporation is thus a far cry from the Marshallian firm in both its vision and its strength. The Marshallian capitalist ruled his factory from an office on the second floor. At the turn of the century, the president of a large national corporation was lodged in a higher building, say on the seventh floor, with wider perspectives and greater power. In the giant corporation of today, managers rule from the tops of skyscrapers; on a clear day, they can almost see the world.

Each step in the evolution of business enterprise had important implications for the structure of the international economy, just as each excursion into the international economy provided new challenges to the corporation and speeded its evolutionary development. In a world of Marshallian firms, commodity trade and portfolio capital were the main engines of international exchange. Movement of enterprise between countries was sharply limited because firms were small and lacked the appropriate administrative structure. The diffusion of Marshall's vital fourth factor, organization, from advanced to less advanced countries was therefore exceedingly slow. Movements of portfolio capital were substantial, at times, because the small Marshallian firms were associated with a highly developed banking and financial system. But the ability of less advanced countries to absorb capital (and technology) was limited to the rate at which they could build up their own organizations, a slow and difficult process given the negative policies of most governments in Africa, Asia, and Latin America, especially those in colonial dependencies. The range of goods which could be produced was thus restricted and the possibility for international trade to equalize factor prices was severely limited.[4]

The national corporation opened new possibilities of transferring organizational abilities internationally. The new administrative structure and financial power enabled firms to undertake direct foreign investments and organize large-scale production in mining and manufacturing in foreign countries. However, this migration of business enterprise occurred only on a limited scale and was usually restricted to a narrow activity; i.e., to acquiring raw materials used by the parent company or to exploiting some technological advance or differentiated product developed by the parent company. Moreover, to the extent that investment strengthened the firm's market control, its effect was considerably less beneficial and perhaps even negative.

The modern multidivisional or conglomerate enterprise is a much more powerful organizational form than the national corporation and appears capable of integrating world production and exchange to a much larger extent. Larger size and a more advanced administrative structure give it a much wider horizon leading in many cases to a global outlook and a transformation to the stage of multinational enterprise. It seems that after a certain point, a corporation comes to think in terms of its world market position rather than merely its United States or European market position and to plan in terms of worldwide factor availabilities and demand patterns. Since the process is just beginning, it is difficult to evaluate how strong this tendency will be. However, it is clear that at present large corporations are consciously moving towards an international perspective much faster than other institutions and especially much faster than governments, and are in the vanguard of planners of the new international economy created by the aeronautical and electronic revolutions. Since multinational corporations also have great financial and technical resources, they will certainly have many successes and will be able to speed up the spread of technology and to organize activities until now impossible. They are a large step forward but this is not, however, the same thing as saying that they serve the general interest as well as their own, that they are the best way to exploit the possibilities of modern science, or that they do not create certain highly intractable problems which greatly impede their efficiency. We turn to these considerations.

II. Bigness and fewness

Multinational corporations enlarge the domain of centrally planned world production and decrease the domain of decentralized market-directed specialization and exchange. Bigness is thus paid for, in part, by fewness, and a decline in competition since the size of the market is limited by the size of the firm. The precise effect of the present wave of direct investment on seller concentration in world markets is not well established. On the one hand, improved communications are breaking down barriers to trade and widening the market facing most buyers. On the other hand, direct foreign investment tends to reduce the number of alternatives facing sellers and to stay the forces of international competition. A great deal of statistical work needs to be done to evaluate the net effect of these two tendencies and establish the exact trend in the level of seller concentration, taking into account the growing international nature of the market. All that can be said at present is that the world level of concentration is much higher than it would be if foreign investment and domestic mergers were restricted. Since most countries are encouraging mergers at home and foreign investment abroad, for better or worse, the opportunity to increase competition by maintaining numbers is not being taken up.

Direct foreign investment thus has a dual nature. It is an instrument which allows business firms to transfer capital, technology, and organizational skill from one country to another. It is also an instrument for restraining competition between firms of different nations. Analyzing any particular case is an exceedingly complex matter, as the antitrust literature shows.[5] For present purposes, the important point is to note that the general presumption of international trade economists in favor of free trade and free factor movements, on the grounds of allocative efficiency, does not apply to direct foreign investment because of the anticompetitive effect inherently associated with it. Just as in antitrust theory there are recognized reasons, within the framework of neoclassical economics, for preventing a firm from merging with another firm or from increasing its share of the market by growth, there are also international antitrust reasons for preventing a firm of one country from taking over a firm in another country or from acquiring or increasing its share of foreign production. Since this point can be easily misunderstood, it is important to stress that this is not a second-best argument but a genuine argument on antimonopoly grounds for interfering in international markets. A restriction on direct investment or a policy to break up a multinational corporation may be in some cases the only way of establishing a higher degree of competition in that industry. National antitrust measures cannot substitute for international antitrust when, for example, one of the major potential competitors to a domestic firm is its sister or parent affiliate within the same multinational group. In short, when we leave the conditions of perfect competition we lose the assumption of the invisible hand.

This argument, it should be noted, provides an important rationale for the infant entrepreneur argument supporting protection. Temporary protection of a weak firm from a stronger firm can improve the competitive structure of the industry in future periods by maintaining numbers. In the present context, the cost of this protection would have to be borne by the country that offers it while the benefits would accrue to the world as a whole. Thus, in reverse of the usual arguments, myopic behavior will lead to too little protection rather than too much. This presents a particularly acute problem in the case of underdeveloped countries. These countries typically do not sell commodities or buy capital or technology in competitive markets where there is an established price at which they can trade whatever quantity they want. Instead, they frequently face only a few potential buyers of their raw materials or their manufactured goods and a few potential sellers of a particular technology. The price they receive or pay therefore depends on their skill and strength in bargaining and not on market conditions alone. The less developed the country, the greater its disadvantage in the bargaining process because it has fewer organizations that are in any way a match for the giant companies with which it is dealing. Given the oligopolistic front maintained by the firms from developed countries, the underdeveloped countries need to devote an important share of their scarce resources to building up national enterprises which they can control and use in bargaining with foreign oligopolists. Ironically, their stronger bargaining position, by increasing competitiveness, may improve general welfare in the rich countries as well – although it will harm those in the monopoly position.

III. The international "trickle down"

Many economists, in dealing with oligopoly, prefer to stress, as Schumpeter did, that the competition that counts lies in creative destruction through the introduction of new technology and new products. In that case, an oligopolistic market structure, even though it interferes with static optimum allocation, may be a necessary or at least a contributing factor to dynamic optimum allocation in a private enterprise system, because it allows innovators to capture some of the benefits of their discoveries and thus provides the incentive for research and development. The record of the United States shows that one certainly cannot fault oligopoly on the grounds that it does not produce a very rapid rate of technological change and product innovation. (Indeed it is easier to argue that the rate of change is too high.) One can expect international oligopoly via multinational corporations to provide the same kind of dynamic environment for the world economy as a whole.

The question of efficiency therefore hinges on the direction of change rather than the rate of change. An analysis of this problem involves an excursion into unexplored terrain since we do not now have an adequate theory on how corporations choose between the available paths of innovation. We certainly cannot assume that market forces compel firms to choose the optimum path. It is true that an innovation must, to some extent, meet the market test for a corporation to survive. However, what is at stake here is not whether the consumer has some choice but rather whether an oligopolistically competitive market structure provides him with the full range of choices possible.[6] Oligopolists tend to copy each other, and their predictions as to what the consumer wants are often self-fulfilling, since in fact this is all that the consumer is offered. If we had only large numbers of independent decision centers could we assume that all avenues had been explored?

Since we cannot possibly treat this complex topic in any detail in the present paper, let us simply examine one theory of innovation closely associated with the multinational corporation and the international demonstration effect. The marketing literature suggests new products typically follow a cycle known as trickle-down or two-stage marketing. An innovation is first adopted by a small group of individuals who act as opinion leaders and is then copied by others via the demonstration effect. In this process, the rich get more votes than everyone else, first of all because they have more money, second of all because they have discretionary income and can afford to be experimental, and, third, because they have high status and are more likely to be copied. The principle of consumer sovereignty cannot easily be applied to this process since, at most, only the special group in the first stage of the marketing process has something approaching a free choice. The rest have only the choice between conforming or being isolated.

In the international economy, trickle-down marketing takes the form of the international demonstration effect. Products are first introduced in the United States or Europe and then spread to other countries. Multinational corporations speed up this process by making it easier to transfer new products and marketing methods to less-advanced countries. One of the key motives for direct investment, cited by corporations, is to gain control over marketing facilities in order to facilitate the spread of their products. If firms were denied control over communication and marketing facilities in the foreign countries and we had a regime of national firms (private or socialized) rather than multinational firms, the pattern of output would almost certainly be quite different than the one that is now observed. There would be more centers of innovation, and probably more variety of choices offered to the consumers, as each country developed products suited to its particular characteristics. Products from one country would spread to other countries either through trade or imitation but the movement would be coordinated by market competition rather than the planning decisions of top management in a few corporations whose interest it is to foreclose competition, to restrict the choices offered, and to insure the survival of their own organizations. It is difficult to speak with professional certainty in this badly neglected field, but it does not appear to be socially efficient to allow corporations to monopolize information on new possibilities created by science.

IV. The international hierarchy of decision making

Marshall, like Marx, thought that the "chief fact in the form of modern civilization, the kernel of the modern economic problem . . ."[7] was the division of labor within the factory between those who plan and organize economic activity and those who work for them. In the modern corporation the hierarchical structure of command and authority has been greatly elaborated from the simple division between owners and workers in the Marshallian firm, but the tensions and conflicts of autocracy remain. They take on particular importance in the multinational corporation where problems of nationalism and problems of authoritarianism intertwine.

Multinational corporations are torn in two directions. On the one hand, they must adapt to local circumstances in each country. This calls for decentralized decision making. On the other hand, they must coordinate their activities in various parts of the world and stimulate the flow of ideas from one part of their empire to another. This calls for centralized controls. They must therefore develop an organizational structure to balance the need to coordinate and integrate operations with the need to adapt to a patchwork quilt of languages, laws, and customs. One solution is division of labor based on nationality. Day-to-day management in each country is left to nationals of that country who are intimately familiar with local conditions and practices and best suited to deal with local problems and local government. These nationals remain rooted in one spot, but above them is a layer of people who move around from country to country, as bees among flowers, transmitting information from one subsidiary to another and from the lower levels to the general office at the apex of the corporate structure. In the nature of things, these people, for the most part, will be citizens of the country of the parent corporation, just as we now find that the top executives of most of the major corporations in the United States are drawn from a relatively small homogeneous cultural group quite distinct from the population of the United States as a whole.

This creates two types of problems. In the first place, there is the internal problem of creating incentives for foreigners whose access to the top corporate positions will be necessarily limited. The second problem is far more important and is in the nature of an external diseconomy. The subsidiaries of multinational corporations are frequently amongst the largest corporations in their country of operations and their top executives play an influential role in the political, social, and cultural life of the country. Yet these people, whatever their title, occupy at best a medium position in the corporate structure and are restricted in authority and horizons to a lower level of decision making. The country whose economy is dominated by the foreign investment can easily develop a branch plant outlook, not only with reference to economic matters, but throughout the range of governmental and educational decision making.

Thus there are important social and political costs to international specialization in entrepreneurship based on multinational corporations. The multinational corporation tends to create a world in its own image by creating a division of labor between countries that corresponds to the division of labor between various levels of the corporate hierarchy. It will tend to centralize high-level decision-making occupations in a few key cities in the advanced countries (surrounded by regional subcapitals) and confine the rest of the world to lower levels of activity and income; i.e., to the status of provincial capitals, towns, and villages in a New Imperial System. Income, status, authority, and consumption patterns will radiate out from the centers in a declining fashion and the hinterland will be denied independence and equality.[8]

This pattern contrasts quite sharply with the free trade system, which offered both income equality and national independence. According to the factor price equalization theorem, trade allows a country to choose its own style and still share fully in the riches of the world. Whether large or small and even if its resource endowment is highly skewed, it can achieve factor price equalization with the rest of the world by varying the composition of output without surrendering its control over its capital stock and without the need for its members to leave the country to find employment elsewhere. Now the stakes seem to have gone up. In order to reap the gains from international exchange, a country has to become integrated into a corporate international structure of centralized planning and control in which it plays a very dependent role.

Countries may not be willing to play this game nor to completely break with it and the possibility arises, in part suggested by the Canadian experience, of getting the worst of both worlds. Canada has allowed an almost unrestricted inflow of capital and as a result has surrendered a great deal of national independence. At the same time, she has adopted a number of policies, including high tariffs, which prevent international corporations from fully rationalizing production on a continent-wide basis. The record shows that foreign subsidiaries in Canada tend to perform at levels equal to their Canadian counterparts rather than at the higher levels of efficiency of their parent corporations. This suggests that many of the benefits of foreign investment have been emasculated while many of the costs remain.

V. Big corporations: small countries

The efficiency with which multinational corporations can allocate resources internationally depends in large part on government policy decisions. If government decision making were independent of the structure of the private sector, we could view it as an exogenous factor and safely ignore it in an essay devoted to the multinational corporation. However, an increase in the importance of multinational corporations relative to national corporations will clearly have an important impact on both the ability and willingness of governments to carry out certain types of economic policies. An analysis of the efficiency of multinational corporations must take this into account and analyze, for example, its effect on government capital formation in the crucial sectors of infrastructures and human capital. This aspect is particularly important with regard to the problem of underdevelopment – clearly the greatest instance of inefficiency in today's international economy.[9]

Analyses of the role of foreign investment in underdeveloped countries often focus on the great disparity between the bargaining power of the corporation and the bargaining power of the government. The corporations are large and modern and have international horizons. The governments are typically administratively weak and have very limited information outside their narrow confines. In any particular negotiation between one country and one company, power in the form of flexibility, knowledge, and liquidity is usually greater on the private side than on the public side of the table.

The problem of unequal bargaining power can be illustrated with a simple model (developed in collaboration with Stephen Resnick).[10] This model focuses on the feedback relationship between the government and the foreign corporation. The government provides certain support services to the corporation: protection, infrastructure, help in the creation of a labor force, land laws, etc. The corporation in return pays the government taxes and royalties. This is a trading relationship in which two main variables are involved: (1) the tax rate (t); and (2) the fraction of government expenditure devoted to support services (g). The outcome is determined by a process of bargaining which, for simplicity, can be viewed in a purely duopolistic form – one government and one country – though it, in fact, usually arises in a more complicated structure where there are several corporations and several power groups involved. The government, we assume, is interested in maximizing its surplus (total revenue from foreign firms less the cost of support services). The corporation is interested in maximizing profits after taxes. At one extreme the government may be very strong and choose (g) and (t) such as to make profit zero (we assume normal profits are included in cost) and to make the government surplus as large as possible. This seldom, if ever, occurs in underdeveloped countries where the bargaining tends to go in the opposite direction. The corporation sets (t) as low as possible, subject to the constraint that the government has enough money to: (*a*) provide necessary infrastructures; (*b*) remain in power and maintain law and order for the corporation. Since the government has little surplus it does not have the money to provide capital or services for other industries. This is in keeping with the foreign investor's interest, since the growth of other industries would compete away factors of production and would create interest groups who might challenge the corporation's hegemony. Provided that the political forces are kept under control in this system, the country can remain in its state of underdevelopment for a long period.

Such extreme cases are no longer possible because of the increased political strength of the local middle class in most underdeveloped countries and because of the changed nature of foreign investment. Modern multinational corporations are interested in manufacturing in underdeveloped countries and not just in raw materials and therefore want a growing market for advanced products and an educated, urbanized labor force. They are no longer tied to traditional backward governments, but have a stake in an active government sector which promotes growth and provides education and infrastructure. The "new foreign investment" is, then, a far cry from the "Banana Republic" kind, but important dangers remain. Statistics on income distribution show that the top one-third of the population typically gets about 60 percent of the total income. It is this top group which provides the direct and indirect labor force for large-scale manufacturing as well as the market. An alliance between this group and foreign investors represents a formidable bargaining force vis-à-vis the remaining two-thirds of the population. A government expenditure policy based on such an alliance would concentrate on the modern high-income sector, leaving the rest of the population as a source of unlimited supply of cheap labor for services and for menial work. Growth in these circumstances would retain its uneven quality and all the inefficiency that implies, albeit in a more advanced and progressive form than characterized the enclave economies of the previous round of foreign investment.

VI. Multinational corporations and supranationality

Multinational corporations create serious problems in the developed world as well. The most important of these, from the limited perspective of this essay, is that they reduce the ability of the government to control the economy. Multinational corporations, because of their size and international connections, have a certain flexibility for escaping regulations imposed in one country. The nature and effectiveness of traditional policy instruments – monetary policy, fiscal policy, antitrust policy, taxation policy, wage and income policy – change when important segments of the economy are foreign-owned. This has long been recognized in countries such as Canada, but it is now becoming obvious that even the United States has reached the point where the international commitments of its corporations reduce the room for flexibility in national economic policy formation. If foreign investment continues to grow at anything like the rate of the last ten or fifteen years, this problem will become an extremely serious one for all North Atlantic countries.[11]

This contradiction between multinational corporations and nation-states has important bearing on the efficiency of the multinational corporation. The main problem, stated most simply, is as follows: if national power is eroded, who is to perform the government's functions? For example, if nation-states, because of the openness of their economy, cannot control the level of aggregate economic activity through traditional monetary and fiscal policy instruments, multinational agencies will need to be developed to maintain full employment and price stability. Yet such organizations do not exist at present, nor can they be quickly built. Either one must argue that the Keynesian problem has somehow been solved by the creation of the multinational corporation (along with a host of other problems) or else one must agree that it is not feasible to have international business integration via direct foreign investment proceeding at a much faster rate than political integration. Yet, this seems to be precisely what is happening. Most of the large American firms have already staked out their claims in the European market and many of the leading European firms are now rapidly entering foreign markets, including those of the United States. A predominance of multinational corporations in the North Atlantic economy seems therefore to be a *fait accompli*. Government cooperation is not growing at anywhere as rapid a rate. If serious problems arise, governments are likely to reassert their power and attempt greater regulation and control over the business enterprises within their jurisdictions. Economists will rightly point out that these restrictions create inefficiencies in the allocation of the economic resources. It is important, however, to realize the role played by a too liberal policy towards private capital, movements and mergers that created the multinational industrial structure.

VII. Conclusion: some subjective evaluations

This essay has presented a list of advantages and disadvantages of multinational corporations. Assuming there are no important omissions and that each point taken by itself is valid, the question arises as to what weights should be attached to the various arguments. One simple summation, offered here without proof, is as follows: The large corporation illustrates how real and important are the advantages of large-scale planning, but it does not tell us how best to achieve wider domains of conscious coordination. Broadly speaking, there are two main directions in which one can proceed. Multinational corporations integrate one industry over many countries. The alternative is to integrate many industries over one country and to develop noncorporate linkages between countries for the free flow of goods and, more important, the free flow of information. The advantage of the second direction is that it keeps the economy within the boundary of the polity and the society. It thus causes less tension and creates the possibility of bringing economic power under control by removing the wastes of oligopolistic anarchy. This would allow more scope for solving the two major economic problems of today, affluence and poverty, than the first alternative. The trend, however, is clearly in the direction of the first alternative. The coming age of multinational corporations should represent a great step forward in the efficiency with which the world uses its economic resources, but it will create grave social and political problems and will be very uneven in exploiting and distributing the benefits of modern science and technology. In a word, the multinational corporation reveals the power of size and the danger of leaving it uncontrolled.

2 The multinational corporation and the law of uneven development

"The settler's town is a strongly-built town, all made of stone and steel. It is a brightly-lit town; the streets are covered with asphalt, and the garbage-cans swallow all the leavings, unseen, unknown and hardly thought about. The settler's feet are never visible, except perhaps in the sea; but there you're never close enough to see them. His feet are protected by strong shoes although the streets of his town are clean and even, with no holes or stones. The settler's town is a well-fed town, an easy-going town, its belly is always full of good things. The settler's town is a town of white people, of foreigners.

The town belonging to the colonized people, or at least the native town, the Negro village, the medina, the reservation, is a place of ill fame peopled by men of evil repute. They are born there, it matters little where or how; they die there, it matters not where nor how. It is a world without spaciousness; men live there on top of each other, and their huts are built one on top of the other. The native town is a hungry town, starved of bread, of meat, of shoes, of coal, of light. The native town is a crouching village, a town on its knees, a town wallowing in the mire. It is a town of niggers and dirty Arabs. The look that the native turns on the settler's town is a look of lust, a look of envy . . ."
–Fanon, *The Wretched of the Earth.*

We have been asked to look into the future towards the year 2000. This essay attempts to do so in terms of two laws of economic development: the Law of Increasing Firm Size and the Law of Uneven Development.[1]

Since the beginning of the Industrial Revolution, there has been a tendency for the representative firm to increase in size from the *workshop* to the *factory* to the *national corporation* to the *multi-divisional corporation* and now to the *multinational corporation*. This growth has been qualitative as well as quantitative. With each step, business enterprise acquired a more

This essay originally appeared in *Economics and World Order*, J. W. Bhagwati, ed. (New York: Macmillan, 1971), pp. 113–40. Copyright, © 1971, by Macmillan Publishing Co., Inc. Reprinted by permission of Macmillan Publishing Co., Inc.

complex administrative structure to coordinate its activities and a larger brain to plan for its survival and growth. The first part of this essay traces the evolution of the corporation stressing the development of a hierarchical system of authority and control.

The remainder of the essay is concerned with extrapolating the trends in business enterprise (the microcosm) and relating them to the evolution of the international economy (the macrocosm). Until recently, most multinational corporations have come from the United States, where private business enterprise has reached its largest size and most highly developed forms. Now European corporations, as a by-product of increased size, and as a reaction to the American invasion of Europe, are also shifting attention from national to global production and beginning to "see the world as their oyster."[2] *If* present trends continue, multinationalization is likely to increase greatly in the next decade as giants from both sides of the Atlantic (though still mainly from the U.S.) strive to penetrate each other's markets and to establish bases in underdeveloped countries, where there are few indigenous concentrations of capital sufficiently large to operate on a world scale. This rivalry may be intense at first but will probably abate through time and turn into collusion as firms approach some kind of oligopolistic equilibrium. A new structure of international industrial organization and a new international division of labor will have been born.[3]

What will be the effect of this latest stage in the evolution of business enterprise on the Law of Uneven Development, *i.e.,* the tendency of the system to produce poverty as well as wealth, underdevelopment as well as development? The second part of this essay suggests that a regime of North Atlantic Multinational Corporations would tend to produce a hierarchical division of labor between geographical regions corresponding to the vertical division of labor within the firm. It would tend to centralize high-level decision-making occupations in a few key cities in the advanced countries, surrounded by a number of regional sub-capitals, and confine the rest of the world to lower levels of activity and income, *i.e.,* to the status of towns and villages in a New Imperial System. Income, status, authority, and consumption patterns would radiate out from these centers along a declining curve, and the existing pattern of inequality and dependency would be perpetuated. The pattern would be complex, just as the structure of the corporation is complex, but the basic relationship between different countries would be one of superior and subordinate, head office and branch plant.

How far will this tendency of corporations to create a world in their own image proceed? The situation is a dynamic one, moving dialectically. Right now, we seem to be in the midst of a major revolution in international relationships as modern science establishes the technological basis for a major advance in the conquest of the material world and the beginnings of truly cosmopolitan production.[4] Multinational corporations are in the vanguard of this revolution, because of their great financial and administrative strength and their close contact with the new technology. Governments (outside the military) are far behind, because of their narrower horizons and perspectives, as are labor organizations and most non-business institutions and associations. (As John Powers, President of Charles Pfizer Corporation, has put it, "Practice is ahead of theory and policy."[5]) Therefore, in the first round, multinational corporations are likely to have a certain degree of success in organizing markets, decision making, and the spread of information in their own interest. However, their very success will create tensions and conflicts which will lead to further development. Section III of this essay discusses some of the contradictions that are likely to emerge as the multinational corporate system overextends itself. These contradictions provide certain openings for action. Whether or not they can or will be used in the next round to move towards superior forms of international organization requires an analysis of a wide range of political factors outside the scope of this essay.

I. The evolution of the multinational corporation

The Marshallian firm and the market economy

Giant organizations are nothing new in international trade. They were a characteristic form of the mercantilist period when large joint-stock companies, *e.g.,* The Hudson's Bay Co., The Royal African Co., The East India Co., to name the major English merchant firms, organized long-distance trade with America, Africa and Asia. But neither these firms, nor the large mining and plantation enterprises in the production sector, were the forerunners of the multinational corporation. They were like dinosaurs, large in bulk, but small in brain, feeding on the lush vegetation of the new worlds (the planters and miners in America were literally *Tyrannosaurus rex*).

The activities of these international merchants, planters and miners laid the groundwork for the Industrial Revolution by concentrating capital in the metropolitan center, but the driving force came from the small-scale capitalist enterprises in manufacturing, operating at first in the interstices of the feudalist economic structure, but gradually emerging into the open and finally gaining predominance. It is in the small workshops, organized by the newly emerging capitalist class, that the forerunners of the modern corporation are to be found.

The strength of this new form of business enterprise lay in its power and ability to reap the benefits of cooperation and division of labor. Without the capitalist, economic activity was individualistic, small-scale, scattered, and unproductive. But a man with capital, *i.e.,* with sufficient funds to buy raw materials and advance wages, could gather a number of people into a single shop and obtain as his reward the increased productivity that resulted from social production. The reinvestment of these profits led to a steady increase in the size of capitals, making further division of labor possible and creating an opportunity for using machinery in production. A phenomenal increase in productivity and production resulted from this process, and entirely new dimensions of human existence were opened. The growth of capital revolutionized the entire world and, figuratively speaking, even battered down the Great Wall of China.

The hallmarks of the new system were *the market* and *the factory,* representing the two different methods of coordinating the division of labor. In the factory entrepreneurs consciously plan and organize cooperation, and the relationships are hierarchical and authoritarian; in the market coordination is achieved through a decentralized, unconscious, competitive process.[6]

To understand the significance of this distinction, the new system should be compared to the structure it replaced. In the pre-capitalist system of production, the division of labor was hierarchically structured at the *macro* level, *i.e.* for society as a whole, but unconsciously structured at the *micro* level *i.e.,* the actual process of production. Society as a whole was partitioned into various castes, classes, and guilds, on a rigid and authoritarian basis so that political and social stability could be maintained and adequate numbers assured for each industry and occupation. Within each sphere of production, however, individuals by and large were independent and their activities only loosely coordinated, if at all. In essence, a guild was composed of a large number of similar individuals, each performing the same task in roughly the same way with little cooperation or division of labor. This type of organization could produce high standards of quality and workmanship but was limited quantitatively to low levels of output per head.

The capitalist system of production turned this structure on its head. The macro system became unconsciously structured, while the micro system became hierarchically structured. The market emerged as a self-regulating coordinator of business units as restrictions on capital markets and labor mobility were removed. (Of course the State remained above the market as a conscious coordinator to maintain the system and ensure the growth of capital.) At the micro level, that is the level of production, labor was gathered under the authority of the entrepreneur capitalist.

Marshall, like Marx, stressed that the internal division of labor within the factory, between those who planned and those who worked (between "undertakers" and laborers), was the "chief fact in the form of modern civilization, the 'kernel' of the modern economic problem."[7] Marx, however, stressed the authoritarian and unequal nature of this relationship based on the coercive power of property and its anti-social characteristics. He focused on the irony that concentration of wealth in the hands of a few and its ruthless use were necessary historically to demonstrate the value of cooperation and the social nature of production.[8]

Marshall, in trying to answer Marx, argued for the voluntary cooperative nature of the relationship between capital and labor. In his view, the *market* reconciled individual freedom and collective production. He argued that those on top achieved their position because of their superior organizational ability, and that their relation to the workers below them was essentially harmonious and not exploitative. "Undertakers" were not captains of industry because they had capital; they could obtain capital because they had the ability to be captains of industry. They retained their authority by merit, not by coercion; for according to Marshall, natural selection, operating through the market, constantly destroyed inferior organizers and gave everyone who had the ability – including workers – a chance to rise to managerial positions. Capitalists earned more than workers because they contributed more, while the system as a whole provided all its members, especially the workers, with improved standards of living and an ever-expanding field of choice of consumption.[9]

The corporate economy

The evolution of business enterprise from the small workshop (Adam Smith's pin factory) to the Marshallian family firm represented only the first step in the development of business organization. As total capital accumulated, the size of the individual concentrations composing it increased continuously, and the vertical division of labor grew accordingly.

It is best to study the evolution of the corporate form in the United States environment, where it has reached its highest stage.[10] In the 1870s, the United States industrial structure consisted largely of Marshallian type, single-function firms, scattered over the country. Business firms were typically tightly controlled by a single entrepreneur or small family group who, as it were, saw everything, knew everything and decided everything. By the early twentieth century, the rapid growth of the economy and the great merger movement had consolidated many functions over many regions. To meet this new strategy of continent-wide, vertically integrated production and market-ing, a new administrative structure evolved. The family firm, tightly controlled by a few men in close touch with all its aspects, gave way to the administrative pyramid of the corporation. Capital acquired new powers and new horizons. The domain or conscious coordination widened and that of market-directed division of labor contracted.

According to Chandler the railroad, which played so important a role in creating the national market, also offered a model for new forms of business organization. The need to administer geographically dispersed operations led railway companies to create an administrative structure which distinguished field offices from head offices. The field offices managed local operations; the head office supervised the field offices. According to Chandler and Redlich, this distinction is important because "it implies that the executive responsible for a firm's affairs had, for the first time, to supervise the work of other executives."[11]

This first step towards increased vertical division of labor within the managment function was quickly copied by the recently-formed national corporations which faced the same problems of coordinating widely scattered plants. Business developed an organ system of administration, and the modern corporation was born. The functions of business administration were sub-divided into *departments* (organs) – finance, personnel, purchasing, engineering, and sales – to deal with capital, labor, purchasing, manufacturing, etc. This horizontal division of labor opened up new possibilities for rationalizing production and for incorporating the advances of physical and social sciences into economic activity on a systematic basis. At the same time a "brain and nervous system," *i.e.,* a vertical system of control, had to be devised to connect and coordinate departments. This was a major advance in decision-making capabilities. It meant that a special group, the Head Office, was created whose particular function was to coordinate, appraise, and plan for the survival and growth of the organism as a whole. The organization became conscious of itself as organization and gained a certain measure of control over its own evolution and development.

The corporation soon underwent further evolution. To understand this next step we must briefly discuss the development of the United States market. At the risk of great oversimplification, we might say that by the first decade of the twentieth century, the problem of production had essentially been solved. By the end of the nineteenth century, scientists and engineers had developed most of the inventions needed for mass producing at a low cost nearly all the main items of basic consumption. In the language of systems analysis, the problem became one of putting together the available components in an organized fashion. The national corporation provided *one* organizational solution, and by the 1920s it had demonstrated its great power to increase material production.

The question was which direction growth would take. One possibility was to expand mass production systems very widely and to make basic consumer goods available on a broad basis throughout the world. The other possibility was to concentrate on continuous innovation for a small number of people and on the introduction of new consumption goods even before the old ones had been fully spread. The latter course was in fact chosen, and we now have the paradox that 500 million people can receive a live TV broadcast from the moon while there is still a shortage of telephones in many advanced countries, to say nothing of the fact that so many people suffer from inadequate food and lack of simple medical help.

This path was associated with a choice of capital-deepening instead of capital-widening in the productive sector of the economy. As capital accumulated, business had to choose the degree to which it would expand labor proportionately to the growth of capital or, conversely, the degree to which they would substitute capital for labor. At one extreme business could have kept the capital–labor ratio constant and accumulated labor at the same rate they accumulated capital. This horizontal accumulation would soon have exhausted the labor force of any particular country and then either capital would have had to migrate to foreign countries or labor would have had to move into the industrial centers. Under this system, earnings per employed worker would have remained steady and the composition of output would have tended to remain constant as similar basic goods were produced on a wider and wider basis.

However, this path was not chosen, and instead capital per worker was raised, the rate of expansion of the industrial labor force was slowed down, and a dualism was created between a small, high wage, high productivity sector in advanced countries, and a large, low wage, low productivity sector in the less advanced.[12]

The uneven growth of per capita income implied unbalanced growth and the need on the part of business to adapt to a constantly changing composition of output. Firms in the producers' goods sectors had continuously to innovate labor-saving machinery because the capital output ratio was increasing steadily. In the consumption goods sector, firms had continuously to introduce new products since, according to Engel's Law, people do not generally consume proportionately more of the same things as they get richer, but rather reallocate their consumption away from old goods and towards new goods. This non-proportional growth of demand implied that goods would tend to go through a life-cycle, growing rapidly when they were first introduced and more slowly later. If a particular firm were tied to only one product, its growth rate would follow this same life-cycle pattern and would eventually slow down and perhaps even come to a halt. If the corporation was to grow steadily at a rapid rate, it had continuously to introduce new products.

Thus, product development and marketing replaced production as a dominant problem of business enterprise. To meet the challenge of a constantly changing market, business enterprise evolved the multidivisional structure. The new form was originated by General Motors and Du Pont shortly after World War I, followed by a few others during the 1920s and 1930s, and was widely adopted by most of the giant U.S. corporations in the great boom following World War II. As with the previous stages, evolution involved a process of both differentiation and integration. Corporations were decentralized into several *divisions,* each concerned with one product line and organized with its own head office. At a higher level, a *general office* was created to coordinate the division and to plan for the enterprise as a whole.

The new corporate form has great flexibility. Because of its decentralized structure, a multidivisional corporation can enter a new market by adding a new division, while leaving the old divisions undisturbed. (And to a lesser extent it can leave the market by dropping a division without disturbing the rest of its structure.) It can also create competing product-lines in the same industry, thus increasing its market share while maintaining the illusion of competition. Most important of all, because it has a cortex specializing in strategy, it can plan on a much wider scale than before and allocate capital with more precision.

The modern corporation is a far cry from the small workshop or even from the Marshallian firm. The Marshallian capitalist ruled his factory from an office on the second floor. At the turn of the century, the president of a large national corporation was lodged in a higher building, perhaps on the seventh floor, with greater perspective and power. In today's giant corporation, managers rule from the tops of skyscrapers.

U.S. corporations began to move to foreign countries almost as soon as they had completed their continent-wide integration. For one thing, their new administrative structure and great financial strength gave them the power to go abroad. In becoming national firms, U.S. corporations learned how to become international. Also, their large size and oligopolistic position gave them an incentive. Direct investment became a new weapon in their arsenal of oligopolistic rivalry. Instead of joining a cartel (prohibited under U.S. law), they invested in foreign customers, suppliers, and competitors. For example, some firms found they were oligopolistic buyers of raw materials produced in foreign countries and feared a monopolization of the sources of supply. By investing directly in foreign producing enterprises, they could gain the security implicit in control over their raw material requirements. Other firms invested abroad to control marketing outlets and thus maximize quasi-rents on their technological discoveries and differentiated products. Some went abroad simply to forestall competition.[13]

The first wave of U.S. direct foreign capital investment occurred around the turn of the century followed by a second wave during the 1920s. The outward migration slowed down during depression but resumed after World War II and soon accelerated rapidly. Between 1950 and 1969, direct foreign investment by U.S. firms expanded at a rate of about 10 percent per annum. At this rate it would double in less than ten years, and even at a much slower rate of growth, foreign operations will reach enormous proportions over the next 30 years.[14]

Several important factors account for this rush of foreign investment in the 1950s and the 1960s. First, the large size of the U.S. corporations and their new multidivisional structure gave them wider horizons and a global outlook. Secondly, technological developments in communications created a new awareness of the global challenge and threatened established institutions by opening up new sources of competition. For reasons noted above, business enterprises were among the first to recognize the potentialities and dangers of the new environment and to take active steps to cope with it.

A third factor in the outward migration of U.S. capital was the rapid growth of Europe and Japan. This, combined with the slow growth of the United States economy in the 1950s, altered world market shares as firms confined to the U.S. market found themselves falling behind in the competitive race and losing ground to European and Japanese firms, which were growing rapidly because of the expansion of their markets. Thus, in the late 1950s, United States corporations faced a serious "non-American" challenge. Their answer was an outward thrust to establish sales production and bases in foreign territories. This strategy was possible in Europe, since government there provided an open door for United States investment, but was blocked in Japan, where the government adopted a highly restrictive policy. To a large extent, United States business was thus able to redress the imbalances caused by the Common Market, but Japan remained a source of tension to oligopoly equilibrium.

What about the future? The present trend indicates further multinationalization of all giant firms, European as well as American. In the first place, European firms, partly as a reaction to the United States penetration of their markets, and partly as a natural result of their own growth, have begun to invest abroad on an expanded scale and will probably continue to do so in the future, and even enter into the United States market. This process is already well underway and may be expected to accelerate as time goes on. The reaction of United States business will most likely be to meet foreign investment at home with more foreign investment abroad. They, too, will scramble for market positions in underdeveloped countries and attempt to get an even larger share of the European market, as a reaction to European investment in the United States. Since they are large and powerful, they will on balance succeed in maintaining their relative standing in the world as a whole – as their losses in some markets are offset by gains in others.

A period of rivalry will prevail until a new equilibrium between giant U.S. firms and giant European and Japanese firms is reached, based on a strategy of multinational operations and cross-penetration.[15] We turn now to the implications of this pattern of industrial organization for international trade and the law of uneven development.

II. Uneven development

Suppose giant multinational corporations (say 300 from the U.S. and 200 from Europe and Japan) succeed in establishing themselves as the dominant form of international enterprise and come to control a significant share of industry (especially modern industry) in each country. The world economy will resemble more and more the United States economy, where each of the large corporations tends to spread over the entire continent and to penetrate almost every nook and cranny. What would be the effect of a world industrial organization of this type on international specialization, exchange, and income distribution? The purpose of this section is to analyze the spatial dimension of the corporate hierarchy.

A useful starting point is Chandler and Redlich's[16] scheme for analyzing the evolution of corporate structure. They distinguish "three levels of business administration, three horizons, three levels of task, and three levels of decision making ... and three levels of policies." Level III, the lowest level, is concerned with managing the day-to-day operations of the enterprise, that is with keeping it going within the established framework. Level II, which first made its appearance with the separation of head office from field office, is responsible for coordinating the managers at Level III. The functions of Level I – top management – are goal-determination and planning. This level sets the framework in which the lower levels operate. In the Marshallian firm, all three levels are embodied in the single entrepreneur or undertaker. In the national corporation a partial differentiation is made in which the top two levels are separated from the bottom one. In the multidivisional corporation, the differentiation is far more complete. Level I is completely split off from Level II and concentrated in a general office whose specific function is to plan strategy rather than tactics.

The development of business enterprise can therefore be viewed as a process of centralizing and perfecting the process of capital accumulation. The Marshallian entrepreneur was a jack-of-all-trades. In the modern multidivisional corporation, a powerful general office consciously plans and organizes the growth of corporate capital. It is here that the key men who actually allocate the corporation's available resources (rather than act within the means allocated to them, as is true for the managers at lower levels) are located. Their power comes from their ultimate control over *men* and *money* and although one should not overestimate the ability to control a far-flung empire, neither should one underestimate it.

The senior men could take action because they controlled the selection of executive personnel and because, through budgeting, they allocated the funds to the operating divisions. In the way they allocated their resources – capital and personnel – and in the promotion, transferral and retirement of operating executives, they determined the framework in which the operating units worked and thus put into effect their concept of the long term goals and objectives of the enterprise ... Ultimate authority in business enterprise, as we see it, rests with those who hold the purse strings, and in modern large-scale enterprises, those persons hold the purse strings who perform the functions of goal setting and planning.[17]

What is the relationship between the structure of the microcosm and the structure of the macrocosm? The application of location theory to the Chandler-Redlich scheme suggests a *correspondence principle* relating centralization of control within the corporation to centralization of control within the international economy.

Location theory suggests that Level III activities would spread themselves over the globe according to the pull of manpower, markets, and raw materials. The multinational corporation, because of its power to command capital and technology and its ability to rationalize their use on a global scale, will probably spread production more evenly over the world's surface than is now the case. Thus, in the first instance, it may well be a force for diffusing industrialization to the less developed countries and creating new centers of production. (We postpone for a moment a discussion of the fact that location depends upon transportation, which in turn depends upon the government, which in turn is influenced by the structure of business enterprise.)

Level II activities, because of their need for white-collar workers, communications systems, and information, tend to concentrate in large cities. Since their demands are similar, corporations from different industries tend to place their coordinating offices in the same city, and Level II activities are consequently far more geographically concentrated than Level III activities.

Level I activities, the general offices, tend to be even more concentrated than Level II activities, for they must be located close to the capital market, the media, and the government. Nearly every major corporation in the United States, for example, must have its general office (or a large proportion of its high-level personnel) in or near the city of New York because of the need for face-to-face contact at higher levels of decision making.

Applying this scheme to the world economy, one would expect to find the highest offices of the multinational corporations concentrated in the world's major cities – New York, London, Paris, Bonn, Tokyo. These, along with Moscow and perhaps Peking, will be the major centers of high-level strategic planning. Lesser cities throughout the world will deal with the day-to-day operations of specific local problems. These in turn will be arranged in a hierarchical fashion: The larger and more important ones will contain regional corporate headquarters, while the smaller ones will be confined to lower level activities. Since business is usually the core of the city, geographical specialization will come to reflect the hierarchy of corporate decision making, and the occupational distribution of labor in a city or region will depend upon its function in the international economic system. The "best" and most highly paid administrators, doctors, lawyers, scientists, educators, government officials, actors, servants, and hairdressers, will tend to concentreate in or near the major centers.

The structure of income and compensation will tend to parallel the structure of status and authority. The citizens of capital cities will have the best jobs – allocating men and money at the highest level and planning growth and development – and will receive the highest rates of remuneration. (Executives' salaries tend to be a function of the wage bill of people under them. The larger the empire of the multinational corporation, the greater the earnings of top executives, to a large extent independent of their performance.[18] Thus, growth in the hinterland subsidiaries implies growth in the income of capital cities, but not *vice versa*.)

The citizens of capital cities will also be the first to innovate new products in the cycle which is known in the marketing literature as trickle-down or two-stage marketing. A new product is usually first introduced to a select group of people who have "discretionary" income and are willing to experiment in their consumption patterns.[19] Once it is accepted by this group, it spreads, or trickles down to other groups via the demonstration effect. In this process, the rich and the powerful get more votes than everyone else; first, because they have more money to spend, second, because they have more ability to experiment, and third, because they have high status and are likely to be copied. This special group may have something approaching a choice in consumption patterns; the rest have only the choice between conforming or being isolated.

The trickle-down system also has the advantage – from the center's point of view – of reinforcing patterns of authority and control. According to Fallers,[20] it helps keep workers on the treadmill by creating an illusion of upward mobility even though relative status remains unchanged. In each period subordinates achieve (in part) the consumption standards of their superiors in a previous period and are thus torn in two directions: If they look backward and compare their standards of living through time, things seem to be getting better; if they look upward they see that their relative position has not changed. They receive a consolation prize, as it were, which may serve to keep them going by softening the reality that in a competitive system, few succeed and many fail. It is little wonder then, that those at the top stress growth rather than equality as the welfare criterion for human relations.

In the international economy trickle-down marketing takes the form of an international demonstration effect spreading outward from the metropolis to the hinterland.[21] Multinational corporations help speed up this process, often the key motive for direct investment, through their control of marketing channels and communications media.

The development of a new product is a fixed cost; once the expenditure needed for invention or innovation has been made, it is forever a bygone. The actual cost of production is thus typically well below selling price and the limit on output is not rising costs but falling demand due to saturated markets. The marginal profit on new foreign markets is thus high, and corporations have a strong interest in maintaining a system which spreads their products widely. Thus, the interest of multinational corporations in underdeveloped countries is larger than the size of the market would suggest.

It must be stressed that the dependency relationship between major and minor cities should not be attributed to technology. The new technology, because it increases interaction, implies greater interdependence but not necessarily a hierarchical structure. Communications linkages could be arranged in the form of a grid in which each point was directly connected to many other points, permitting lateral as well as vertical communication. This system would be polycentric since messages from one point to another would go directly rather than through the center; each point would become a center on its own; and the distinction between center and periphery would disappear.

Such a grid is made *more* feasible by aeronautical and electronic revolutions which greatly reduce costs of communications. It is not technology which creates inequality; rather, it is *organization* that imposes a ritual judicial asymmetry on the use of intrinsically symmetrical means of communications and arbitrarily creates unequal capacities to initiate and terminate exchange, to store and retrieve information, and to determine the extent of the exchange and terms of the discussion. Just as colonial powers in the past linked each point in the hinterland to the metropolis and inhibited lateral communications, preventing the growth of independent centers of decision making and creativity, multinational corporations (backed by state powers) centralize control by imposing a hierarchical system.

This suggests the possibility of an alternative system of organization in the form of national planning. Multinational corporations are private institutions which organize one or a few industries across many countries. Their polar opposite (the antimultinational corporation, perhaps) is a public institution which organizes many industries across one region. This would permit the centralization of capital, *i.e.*, the coordination of many enterprises by one decision-making center, but would substitute regionalization for internationalization. The span of control would be confined to the boundaries of a single polity and society and not spread over many countries. The advantage of the multinational corporation is its global perspective. The advantage of national planning is its ability to remove the wastes of oligopolistic anarchy, *i.e.*, meaningless product differentiation and an imbalance between different industries within a geographical area. It concentrates *all* levels of decision-making in one locale and thus provides each region with a full complement of skills and occupations. This opens up new horizons for local development by making possible the social and political control of economic decision-making. Multinational corporations, in contrast, weaken political control because they span many countries and can escape national regulation.

A few examples might help to illustrate how multinational corporations reduce options for development. Consider an underdeveloped country wishing to invest in education in order to increase its stock of human capital and raise standards of living. In a market system it would be able to find gainful employment for its citizens within its *national boundaries* by specializing in education-intensive activities and selling its surplus production to foreigners.

In the multinational corporate system, however, the demand for high-level education in low-ranking areas is limited, and a country does not become a world center simply by having a better educational system. An outward shift in the supply of educated people in a country, therefore, will not create its own demand but will create an excess supply and lead to emigration. Even then, the employment opportunities for citizens of low-ranking countries are restricted by discriminatory practices in the center. It is well-known that ethnic homogeneity increases as one goes up the corporate hierarchy; the lower levels contain a wide variety of nationalities, the higher levels become successively purer and purer. In part this stems from the skill differences of different nationalities, but more important is the fact that the higher up one goes in the decision-making process, the more important mutual understanding and ease of communications become; a common background becomes all-important.

A similar type of specialization by nationality can be expected within the multinational corporation hierarchy. Multinational corporations are torn in two directions. On the one hand, they must adapt to local circumstances in each country. This calls for decentralized decision making. On the other hand, they must coordinate their activities in various parts of the world and stimulate the flow of ideas from one part of their empire to another. This calls for centralized control. They must, therefore, develop an organizational structure to balance the need for coordination with the need for adaptation to a patch-work quilt of languages, laws, and customs. One solution to this problem is a division of labor based on nationality. Day-to-day management in each country is left to the nationals of that country who, because they are intimately familiar with local conditions and practices, are able to deal with local problems and local government. These nationals remain rooted in one spot, while above them is a layer of people who move around from country to country, as bees among flowers, transmitting information from one subsidiary to another and from the lower levels to the general office at the apex of the corporate structure. In the nature of things, these people (reticulators) for the most part will be citizens of the country of the parent corporation (and will be drawn from a small, culturally homogeneous group within the advanced world), since they will need to have the confidence of their superiors and be able to move easily in the higher management circles. Latin Americans, Asians, and Africans will at best be able to aspire to a management position in the intermediate coordinating centers at the continental level. Very few will be able to get much higher than this, for the closer one gets to the top, the more important is "a common cultural heritage."

Another way in which the multinational corporations inhibit economic development in the hinterland is through their effect on tax capacity. An important government instrument for promoting growth is expenditure on infrastructure and support services. By providing transportation and communications, education and health, a government can create a productive labor force and increase the growth potential of its economy. The extent to which it can afford to finance these intermediate outlays depends upon its tax revenue.

However, a government's ability to tax multinational corporations is limited by the ability of these corporations to manipulate transfer prices and to move their productive facilities to another country. This means that they will only be attracted to countries where superior infrastructure offsets higher taxes. The government of an underdeveloped country will find it difficult to extract a surplus (revenue from the multinational corporations, less cost of services provided to them) from multinational corporations to use for long-run development programs and for stimulating growth in other industries. In contrast, governments of the advanced countries, where the home office and financial center of the multinational corporation are located, can tax the profits of the corporation as a whole, as well as the high incomes of its management. Government in the metropolis can, therefore, capture some of the surplus generated by the multinational corporations and use it to further improve their infrastructure and growth.

In other words, the relationship between multinational corporations and underdeveloped countries will be somewhat like the relationship between the national corporations in the United States and state and municipal governments. These lower-level governments tend always to be short of funds compared to the federal government which can tax a corporation as a whole. Their competition to attract corporate investment eats up their surplus, and they find it difficult to finance extensive investments in human and physical capital even where such investment would be productive. This has a crucial effect on the pattern of government expenditure. For example, suppose taxes were first paid to state government and then passed on to the federal government. What chance is there that these lower level legislatures would approve the phenomenal expenditures on space research that now go on? A similar discrepancy can be expected in the international economy with overspending and waste by metropolitan governments and a shortage of public funds in the less advanced countries.

The tendency of the multinational corporations to erode the power of the nation-state works in a variety of ways, in addition to its effects on taxation powers. In general, most governmental policy instruments (monetary policy, fiscal policy, wage policy, etc.) diminish in effectiveness the more open the economy and the greater the extent of foreign investments. This tendency applies to political instruments as well as economic, for the multinational corporation is a medium by which laws, politics, foreign policy, and culture of one country intrude into another. This acts to reduce the sovereignty of all nation states, but again the relationship is asymmetrical, for the flow tends to be from the parent to the subsidiary, not *vice versa*. The United States can apply its antitrust laws to foreign subsidiaries or stop them from "trading with the enemy" even though such trade is not against the laws of the country in which the branch plant is located. However, it would be illegal for an underdeveloped country which disagreed with American foreign policy to hold a U.S. firm hostage for acts of the parent. This is because legal rights are defined in terms of property-ownership, and the various subsidiaries of a multinational corporation are not "partners in a multinational endeavor" but the property of the general office.

In conclusion, it seems that a regime of multinational corporations would offer underdeveloped countries neither national independence nor equality. It would tend instead to inhibit the attainment of these goals. It would turn the underdeveloped countries into branch-plant countries, not only with reference to their economic functions but throughout the whole gamut of social, political, and cultural roles. The subsidiaries of multinational corporations are typically amongst the largest corporations in the country of operations, and their top executives play an influential role in the political, social, and cultural life of the host country. Yet these people, whatever their title, occupy at best a medium position in the corporate structure and are restricted in authority and horizons to a lower level of decision making. The governments with whom they deal tend to take on the same middle management outlook, since this is the only range of information and ideas to which they are exposed.[22] In this sense, one can hardly expect such a country to bring forth the creative imagination needed to apply science and technology to the problems of degrading poverty.

III. The political economy of the multinational corporation

The viability of the multinational corporate system depends upon the degree to which people will tolerate the unevenness it creates. It is well to remember that the "New Imperialism" which began after 1870 in a spirit of Capitalism Triumphant, soon became seriously troubled and after 1914 was characterized by war, depression, breakdown of the international economic system, and war again, rather than Free Trade, Pax Britannica, and Material Improvement.

A major, if not the major, reason was Great Britain's inability to cope with the by-products of its own rapid accumulation of capital; *i.e.,* a class conscious labor force at home; a middle class in the hinterland; and rival centers of capital on the Continent and in America. Britain's policy tended to be atavistic and defensive rather than progressive, more concerned with warding off new threats than creating new areas of expansion. Ironically, Edwardian England revived the paraphernalia of the landed aristocracy it had just destroyed. Instead of embarking on a "big push" to develop the vast hinterland of the Empire, colonial administrators often adopted policies to slow down rates of growth and arrest the development of either a native capitalist class or a native proletariat which could overthrow them.

As time went on, the center had to devote an increasing share of government activity to military and other unproductive expenditures; they had to rely on alliances with an inefficient class of landlords, officials, and soldiers in the hinterland to maintain stability at the cost of development. A great part of the surplus extracted from the population was thus wasted locally.

The new Mercantilism (as the Multinational Corporate System of special alliances and privileges, aid and tariff concessions is sometimes called) faces similar problems of internal and external division. The center is troubled: Excluded groups revolt and even some of the affluent are dissatisfied with their roles. (The much talked about "generation gap" may indicate the failure of the system to reproduce itself.) Nationalistic rivalry between major capitalist countries (especially the challenge of Japan and Germany) remains an important divisive factor, while the economic challenge from the socialist bloc may prove to be of the utmost significance in the next thirty years. Russia has its own form of large-scale economic organizations, also in command of modern technology, and its own conception of how the world should develop. So does China to an increasing degree.[23] Finally, there is the threat presented by the middle classes and the excluded groups of the underdeveloped countries.

The national middle classes in the underdeveloped countries came to power when the center weakened but could not, through their policy of import substitution manufacturing, establish a viable basis for sustained growth. They now face a foreign exchange crisis and an unemployment (or population) crisis – the first indicating their inability to function in the international economy, and the second indicating their alienation from the people they are supposed to lead. In the immediate future, these national middle classes will gain a new lease on life as they take advantage of the spaces created by the rivalry between American and non-American oligopolists striving to establish global market positions. The native capitalists will again become the champions of national independence as they bargain with multinational corporations. But the conflict at this level is more apparent then real, for in the end the fervent nationalism of the middle class asks only for promotion within the corporate structure and not for a break with that structure. In the last analysis their power derives from the metropolis and they cannot easily afford to challenge the international system. They do not command the loyalty of their own population and cannot really compete with the large, powerful, aggregate capitals from the center. They are prisoners of the taste patterns and consumption standards set at the center, and depend on outsiders for technical advice, capital, and when necessary, for military support of their position.

The main threat comes from the excluded groups. It is not unusual in underdeveloped countries for the top 5 percent to obtain between 30 and 40 percent of the total national income, and for the top one-third to obtain anywhere from 60 to 70 percent.[24] At most, one-third of the population can be said to benefit in some sense from the dualistic growth that characterizes development in the hinterland. The remaining two-thirds, who together get only one-third of the income, are outsiders, not because they do not contribute to the economy, but because they do not share in the benefits. They provide a source of cheap labor which helps keep exports to the developed world at a low price and which has financed the urban-biased growth of recent years. Because their wages are low, they spend a moderate amount of time in menial services and are sometimes referred to as underemployed as if to imply they were not needed. In fact, it is difficult to see how the system in most underdeveloped countries could survive without cheap labor, since removing it (*e.g.,* diverting it to public works projects as is done in socialist countries) would raise consumption costs to capitalists and professional elites. Economic development under the Multinational Corporation does not offer much promise for this large segment of society and their antagonism continuously threatens the system.

The survival of the multinational corporate system depends on how fast it can grow and how much trickles down. Plans now being formulated in government offices, corporate headquarters and international organizations, sometimes suggest that a growth rate of about 6 percent per year in national income (3 percent per capita) is needed. (Such a target is, of course, far below what would be possible if a serious effort were made to solve basic problems of health, education, and clothing.) To what extent is it possible?

The multinational corporation must solve four critical problems for the underdeveloped countries, if it is to foster the continued growth and survival of a "modern" sector. First, it must break the foreign-exchange constraint and provide the underdeveloped countries with imported goods for capital formation and modernization. Second, it must finance an expanded program of government expenditure to train labor and provide support services for urbanization and industrialization. Third, it must solve the urban food problem created by growth. Finally, it must keep the excluded two-thirds of the population under control.

The solution now being suggested for the first is to restructure the world economy allowing the periphery to export certain manufactured goods to the center. Part of this program involves regional common markets to rationalize the existing structure of industry. These plans typically do not involve the rationalization and restructuring of the entire economy of the underdeveloped countries but mainly serve the small manufacturing sector which caters to higher income groups and which, therefore, faces a very limited market in any particular country. The solution suggested for the second problem is an expanded aid program and a reformed government bureaucracy (perhaps along the lines of the Alliance for Progress). The solution for the third is agri-business and the green revolution, a program with only limited benefits to the rural poor. Finally, the solution offered for the fourth problem is population control, either through family planning or counterinsurgency.

It is doubtful whether the center has sufficient political stability to finance and organize the program outlined above. It is not clear, for example, that the West has the technology to rationalize manufacturing abroad or modernize agriculture, or the willingness to open up marketing channels for the under-developed world. Nor is it evident that the center has the political power to embark on a large aid program or to readjust its own structure of production and allow for the importation of manufactured goods from the periphery. It is difficult to imagine labor accepting such a re-allocation (a new repeal of the Corn Laws as it were[25]), and it is equally hard to see how the advanced countries could create a system of planning to make these extra hardships unnecessary.

The present crisis may well be more profound that most of us imagine, and the West may find it impossible to restructure the international economy on a workable basis. One could easily argue that the age of the Multinational Corporation is at its end rather than at its beginning. For all we know, books on the global partnership may be the epitaph of the American attempt to take over the old international economy, and not the herald of a new era of international cooperation.

Conclusion

The multinational corporation, because of its great power to plan economic activity, represents an important step forward over previous methods of organizing international exchange. It demonstrates the social nature of production on a global scale. As it eliminates the anarchy of international markets and brings about a more extensive and productive international division of labor, it releases great sources of latent energy.

However, as it crosses international boundaries, it pulls and tears at the social and political fabric and erodes the cohesiveness of national states.[26] Whether one likes this or not, it is probably a tendency that cannot be stopped.

Through its propensity to nestle everywhere, settle everywhere, and establish connections everywhere, the multinational corporation destroys the possibility of national seclusion and self-sufficiency and creates a universal interdependence. But the multinational corporation is still a private institution with a partial outlook and represents only an imperfect solution to the problem of international cooperation. It creates hierarchy rather than equality, and it spreads its benefits unequally.

In proportion to its success, it creates tensions and difficulties. It will lead other institutions, particularly labor organizations and government, to take an international outlook and thus unwittingly create an environment less favorable to its own survival. It will demonstrate the possibilities of material progress at a faster rate than it can realize them, and will create a worldwide demand for change that it cannot satisfy.

The next round may be marked by great crises due to the conflict between national planning by governments and international planning by corporations. For example, if each country loses its power over fiscal and monetary policy due to the growth of multinational corporations (as some observers believe Canada has), how will aggregate demand be stabilized? Will it be possible to construct super-states? Or does multinationalism do away with Keynesian problems? Similarly, will it be possible to fulfill a host of other government functions at the supranational level in the near future? During the past twenty-five years many political problems were put aside as the West recovered from the depression and the war. By the late sixties the bloom of this long upswing had begun to fade. In the seventies, power conflicts are likely to come to the fore.

Whether underdeveloped countries will use the opportunities arising from this crisis to build viable local decision-making institutions is difficult to predict. The national middle class failed when it had the opportunity and instead merely reproduced internally the economic dualism of the international economy as it squeezed agriculture to finance urban industry. What is needed is a complete change of direction. The starting point must be the needs of the bottom two-thirds, and not the demands of the top third. The primary goal of such a strategy would be to provide minimum standards of health, education, food, and clothing to the entire population, removing the more obvious forms of human suffering. This requires a system which can mobilize the entire population and which can search the local environment for information, resources, and needs. It must be able to absorb modern technology, but it cannot be mesmerized by the form it takes in the advanced countries; it must go to the roots. This is not the path the upper one-third chooses when it has control.

The wealth of a nation, wrote Adam Smith two hundred years ago, is determined by "first, the skill, dexterity and judgement with which labor is generally applied; and, secondly by the proportion between the number of those who are employed in useful labor, and that of those who are not so employed."[27] Capitalist enterprise has come a long way from his day, but it has never been able to bring more than a small fraction of the world's population into useful or highly productive employment. The latest stage reveals once more the power of social cooperation and division of labor which so fascinated Adam Smith in his description of pin manufacturing. It also shows the shortcomings of concentrating this power in private hands.

Epilogue

Many readers of this essay in draft form have asked: Is there an alternative? Can anything be done? The problem simply stated is to go beyond the multinational corporation. Scholarship can perhaps make the task easier by showing how the forms of international social production devised by capital as it expanded to global proportions can be used to build a better society benefiting all men. I have tried to open up one avenue for explanation by suggesting a system of regional planning as a positive negation of the multinational corporation. Much more work is needed to construct alternative methods of organizing the international economy. Fortunately businessmen in attacking the problem of applying technology on a world level have developed many of the tools and conditions needed for a socialist solution, if we can but stand them on their head. But one must keep in mind that the problem is not one of ideas alone.

A major question is how far those in power will allow the necessary metamorphosis to happen, and how far they will try to resist it by violent means. I do not believe the present structure of uneven development can long be maintained in the light of the increased potential for world development demonstrated by corporate capital itself. But power at the center is great, and the choice of weapons belongs in the first instance to those who have them.

Theodor Mommsen summed up his history of the Roman Republic with patient sadness.

It was indeed an old world, and even the richly gifted patriotism of Caesar could not make it young again. The dawn does not return till after the night has run its course.[28]

I myself do not view the present with such pessimism. History moves more quickly now, the forces for positive change are much stronger, and the center seems to be losing its will and self-confidence. It is becoming increasingly evident to all that in contrast to corporate capitalism we must be somewhat less "efficient" within the microcosm of the enterprise and far more "efficient" in the macrocosm of world society. The dystopia of the multinational corporate system shows us both what is to be avoided and what is possible.

3   The internationalization of capital

The multinational corporation, or the multinational corporate system, has three related sides: international capital movements; international capitalist production; and international government.

By international capital movements I refer first to the direct investment of corporations in their overseas branches and subsidiaries, which at present amounts to about $80 billion for American multinationals and about $50 billion for non-American multinationals. Second, I refer to the associated flows of short-term, long-term, and equity capital stimulated by the multinational corporation, which in turn stimulate the growth of international finance, that is, deposits in foreign banks, investments in the Eurocurrency and Eurobond market, investments in corporate stock of multinational firms by non-nationals, and so forth. The direct foreign investment by corporations has served as a base for a vast superstructure of credit drawing capital from all over the world; the associated noncorporate private capital flows from one country to another are at least as large as direct investments by corporations, and probably are growing faster.

International capitalist production refers to the incorporation of labor from many countries into an integrated worldwide corporate productive structure. American firms, for example, directly employ from 5 to 7 million people in foreign countries, and a growing but unknown number indirectly through subcontracting, licensing, and so forth. By comparison, the total employment of the 500 largest American firms is 13 or 14 million (this figure includes some, but not all, foreign employees), which means that many large corporations have 30, 40, or 50 percent and more of their labor force outside the United States.

This essay originally appeared in *The Journal of Economic Issues,* Vol. 6, No. 1, March 172, pp. 91–111. Copyright, © 1972 by the Association for Evolutionary Economics. Reprinted by permission of the Association for Evolutionary Economics.

International government refers to the erosion of the traditional powers of nation-states and the emergence of international economic policy instruments in line with the tendency of the multinational corporation to internationalize capital and labor. When a corporation invests abroad, it not only sends capital and management out, but also establishes a system for drawing foreign capital and labor into an integrated world network. When many firms from many countries do this together on an expanded scale, as has been true over the last decade and will be increasingly true in the next, they are forming a new world system. They are unifying world capital and world labor into an interlocking system of cross-penetration that completely changes the system of national economies that has characterized world capitalism for the past three hundred years. This process reduces the independence of nation-states and requires the formation of supranational institutions to handle the increased interdependence. To create a world market where state frontiers disappear, a world system is needed in which the separate interests, laws, governments, and systems of taxation and regulation are lumped together into a unified code of laws on the rights and limits of international private property.

This three-pronged process is far from complete and is anything but smooth, but it has moved further and faster than is commonly realized. The outlines of a new international system already can be discerned, and it must be quickly added, so can its cracks. American firms have been in the vanguard, but European corporations are close on their heels; Japanese corporations, who have just started, are moving very quickly. International capital markets and international banking also are growing by leaps and bounds, and the combined movement of these forces is rapidly reducing the autonomy of governments. The pressure for international governmental agencies is very great and a start has been made on many fronts, but the process has been zigzagging and is far from off the ground.

The argument

In this essay I wish to concentrate on the political economy of the process, that is, the political consolidations accompanying the multinationalization of business. In the last analysis, markets come out of the barrel of a gun, and to establish an integrated world economy on capitalist lines requires the international mobilization of political power.

The central image of my analysis is the pyramid of power, and the focus of study is the merging of the separate pyramids of nation-states into an international pyramid. "When two primitive feudal states amalgamate," wrote Franz Oppenheimer in his classic treatise on the state, "their social layers stratify in a variety of ways, which to a certain extent are comparable to the combinations that result from mixing together two packs of cards."[1]

The process of integration now going on in the international economy may be thought of in a similar way – as the interpenetration of national corporation and capital into a new multinational system of ownership and control. The shuffle is neither random nor even, nor are the decks of the same size. Aces, kings, and queens are trying to remain on top, but instead of lording over their separate piles, they are cross-penetrating into a more complex structure.

I have chosen the image of cross-penetration instead of American imperialism pure and simple because I believe that the American hegemony which characterized the past twenty-five years has ended with the recovery of Europe, Japan, and Russia. American capital may well be able to retain a position of dominance, but it is under severe challenge and will have to share power with other capitalists far more than it has done in the past.

I wish in my analysis to stress how competition in the product and capital markets helps forge a unified interest among capitalists, while the corporate hierarchy and competition in the labor market divide and weaken popular power. The dynamic of the multinational corporation is thus a contradictory one. True, it expands the social nature of production to a world level; but only on the basis of minority power, and a conflict emerges between the general social power into which capital develops, and the private power of individual capitalists over these social conditions. As capital unites many workers in production and collectivizes many capitals in ownership, it becomes an alienated independent power which stands opposed to society and checks the full development of human productivity and its universal application. *Pace* Adam Smith, who thought the magic of competition could turn private interests into the general interest (but who later began, as Robert Heilbroner has shown, to sense the severe limitations of this method based on madness[2]), the capitalist organization is fraught with contradictions whose cost becomes more onerous as productivity is developed and the system broadens to worldwide scope.

Under capitalism, the mutual and universal interdependence of individuals who remain indifferent to one another constitutes the social network that binds them together. In the *market,* capitalism unites producers, who fundamentally acknowledge no other authority but that of competition, and who are not able to develop a social outlook commensurate with the social production they create. In the *factory* or *corporation,* an authoritarian hierarchy is used to coordinate labor, to keep the worker ignorant of the cooperative process of which he is part, and to alienate him from his work, his instruments and machines, and his product. Because of the undemocratic nature of the work process, the possibilities for human development created by science cannot be realized, while the fact that workers are not cooperating voluntarily, but are coerced by an alien force, means that capital must continuously squander energy wrestling with their insubordination. An attempt is made through the *state* to coordinate capitalism on a plane above that of the market so that the waste of externalities can be reduced, and the conflicts between capitals and between capital and labor can be ameliorated. But the state has to operate with its hands tied. It has to solve problems without damaging the system of private property that produces these problems. The good intentions of public policy always founder on this rock, and society must continue to bear the costs of constant rivalry, the inability to meet social needs, and the frustration of human development.

A Marxian bias is evident in my presentation. Unfortunately, Marx's promised volumes on wage labor, foreign trade, and the state and the world economy were never written (or have not been found), and the elements of his analysis are scattered throughout his many writings. However, a succinct statement of his basic argument, which the reader may find useful, is found in Volume 3 of *Capital*. There he identifies "three cardinal facts of capitalist production," as follows:

1) Concentration of means of production in few hands, whereby they cease to appear as the property of the immediate labourers and turn into social capacities. Even if initially they are the private property of capitalists. These are the trustees of bourgeois society, but they pocket all the proceeds of this trusteeship.
2) Organization of labour into social labour; through competition, division of labour, and the uniting of labour with the natural sciences.
In these two senses, the capitalist mode of production abolishes private property and private labour, even though in contradictory forms.
3) Creation of the world market.
The stupendous productivity developing under the capitalist mode of production relative to population . . . contradicts the basis, which constantly narrows in relation to the expanding wealth, and for which all this immense productiveness works. They also contradict the conditions under which this swelling capital augments its value. Hence the crisis.[3]

Internationalization of corporations

"When labour cooperates systematically," Marx wrote, "it strips off the fetters of its individuality and develops the capability of its species."[4] But in order for labor to cooperate, it must be brought together and linked through exchange. Under capitalism, the cooperation of laborers is entirely brought about by the capital that employs them. The history of social labor is the history of social capital since the number of laborers who can work together depends upon the degree to which capital is concentrated and centralized.

The two powerful levers for concentrating capital into larger and larger aggregates and then integrating these aggregates into a unified whole are *competition* and *credit*. Competition drives firms to continuously reinvest their profits and extend their markets as a means of self-preservation. The credit system unites individual capitals and stimulates further increases in their size. It acts as an immense social mechanism above that of the individual firm for the centralization of capital and the preservation of its collective interest. The market forces are now operating on a world scale and leading to the internationalization of corporations and capital.

The dynamics of corporate expansion

Business enterprises usually are built around some special discovery or advantage. Before their innovation becomes general, they can undersell their competitors and still sell at a price well above cost of production. But their position is constantly threatened by new entrants who may discover a new technology, a new product, a new form of organization, or a new supply of labor. The dialectic of the product cycle gives capitalism its forward motion. An innovation is introduced; if it suceeds, the product enjoys a high rate of growth as it displaces other products and more and more consumers come to use it. As the market becomes saturated, growth tapers off while profitability is squeezed. Simultaneously, other firms try to enter the market because the very success of the innovation provides tangible proof that the new product works and that a market exists. With the secret out, production costs begin to dominate. The competition of other firms using cheaper labor or accepting a lower rate of profit eats into the original innovator's profit.

There are two ways of coping with the competitive threat. First, a continuous effort can be made to develop new products; when the rate of growth slows, the firm can switch tracks and continue at a high rate of profit. Second, the product cycle can be prolonged by gaining control of marketing outlets, searching for and moving to places of cheaper labor, and secrecy. These two methods, of course, are intertwined, for the wider a firm's market, the more it can spread the costs of innovation, and the more it can afford to spend on research and development.

Both these methods require further investment. At a given point of time, a corporation may be earning a high rate of profit because it is onto a good thing, but competition and technological change threaten to wipe out its advantage. It must plough back its profits in order to improve production and expand its scale "merely as a means of self-preservation and under threat of ruin." Thus under capitalism change becomes normal and businessmen can never afford to look upon and treat the existing form of a process as final. The incessant revolutions in production and the depreciation of the existing capital this implies spur them on to new methods and new places.

International competition in the fifties and sixties

This dialectic played an important role in the postwar expansion of American firms in foreign countries. The American giants who were or became multinational possessed numerous advantages in organization technology, access to capital, and product differentiation. They could supply some of the foreign market through exports, gaining a certain protection for their secrets from the long distance between production and consumption. The recovery of Europe and Japan soon challenged them, and they began to see many foreign firms using their technology and methods, or improving upon them. They could see their own expansion being thwarted by the formation of new capitals in other countries, and they discovered their advantages would be short-lived if they did not undertake foreign investment to preserve them.

These firms had three motives for expansion: (1) They saw a rapid growth in the *markets* for goods in which they specialized; (2) they saw *cheaper labor* (productivity divided by wage) which made it profitable to produce abroad; and (3) they saw *foreign competitors* growing faster than themselves and gaining an increased share of the world market.

To the individual firm these might appear as separate phenomena, but they are closely connected to each other through the labor market. Europe and Japan emerged from the devastation of the war with consumption patterns and expectations well below the American standard. However, their potential productivity was not nearly as far below that of America's, given the work habits and levels of skills of the labor force. A large surplus was available if the labor force could be organized and consumption kept from rising too fast.

With American help the threat of a socialist alternative was avoided, and the state built an infrastructure, reformed education, adopted new foreign trade policies, and developed an administrative structure for channeling capital and planning investment. The way was cleared for a rapid expansion of private industry. National capitalists were able to draw upon the technology which had accumulated during the war, earn high rates of return, and grow rapidly. This growth, switching people from agriculture to industry and from old industries to new, expanded the market for new products.

American firms were thus presented with an opportunity and a challenge. Growth of foreign markets and labor supply made it attractive to invest abroad; growth of European and Japanese firms made it necessary. American firms did not invest substantially in continental Europe and Japan in the late forties and early fifties when they had the most political influence. Only after the development of the Common Market did they make their greatest effort, just as it was serious competition from Japanese firms that spurred the great drive to get into Japan. It is more competitive pressure than foresight which guides capitalists to expand.

International competition in the seventies and eighties

The world economy now presents new opportunities and challenges. The unlimited supply of labor in Europe is drying up as they exhaust their own populations and the possibilities for importing cheap labor. Twenty years of prosperity have changed labor's expectations about consumption standards and work intensity. The greening of Europe is about to begin. A similar tendency toward labor shortage, that is, a decline in the margin between labor's production and consumption, is emerging in Japan. In the United States resistance to work seems about to reach acute proportions from capital's point of view. Firms from all these countries are looking more and more toward labor in outlying fields.

In Eastern Europe, low consumption standards and a great expansion of infrastructure, health services, and education have resulted in a potentially very high rate of surplus value now bogged down in undemocratic socialism. The managers of these economies are trying, through economic reforms, to channel this surplus into the accumulation of capital and wealth. They could provide a great challenge to Free World capitals. (The threat would be greater, but different, if these countries chose socialist development.) The scramble for East–West trade and technical agreements is an attempt to change this challenge into an opportunity. China, less advanced and less amenable, also presents an important commercial and industrial challenge. (This article was written with a perfect replica of a Parker pen – as far as I could tell – manufactured in China; it sells in Iran for 50 cents, and in Singapore for 40 cents.) The scramble for China's surplus labor is just beginning.

The Third World also will be an important battleground in the coming years. "Capitalist production," wrote Marx, "first makes the production of commodities general, and then, by degrees, transforms all commodity production into capitalist commodity production."[5] The great commercial revolution in the late nineteenth and early twentieth centuries transformed the Third World into export economies, based for the most part on plantation, peasant, or contract labor systems rather than free markets for capital and labor. The resulting evolution led in the forties and fifties to national independence movements and a great increase in urbanization, infrastructure, and education. Large absolute numbers of people (often still a small percentage of the population) became concentrated in the cities, ready, able, and willing to sell their labor power. Standards of consumption have remained low due to the large supply of this free labor, while potential productivity has increased substantially due to the government's expansion of education, urban and industrial infrastructure, and other services.

Potential surplus labor is large, while the local capitalist class is weak, due to the restraints placed on it during the colonial period. Many multinationals have begun to tap this cheap labor supply, originally to displace imports, but now to expand exports to other underdeveloped countries and to the developed world. This phase of international investment is just beginning, but is likely to grow rapidly when one considers the plentiful supply of labor. The big danger to the multinationals is the possibility of socialism or state capitalism which will prevent the transformation of commodity production into capitalist commodity production, that is, prevent the transfer of the power of Asiatic and Egyptian kings, Etruscan theocrats, and so forth, over collective labor to the multinational capitalist.

The large firms of the world are all competing for these various sources of future growth, but in an oligopolistic rather than in a cutthroat way. They recognize their mutual interdependence and strive to share in the pie without destroying it. As they do so, they come to be less and less dependent on their home country's economy for their profits, and more and more dependent on the world economy.Conflicts between firms on the basis of nationality are thereby transformed into international oligopolistic market sharing and collusion.

Internationalization of capital

The second great lever of capital concentration and centralization is the credit system. The formation of a world capital market has only begun, but if its development continues at the present rate, it soon will be a factor of great significance in the world economy.

The multinational corporation and the international capital market should be seen as parallel, symbiotic developments. The multinational corporation's need for short-term loans and investment arising from the continuous inflow and outflow of money from all nations, never quite in balance, has encouraged international banking and has helped integrate short-term money markets; its long-term financial requirements and excellent credit rating have broadened the demand for international bond and equity capital. This provides an impetus for free international capital mobility.

The Eurobond market, for example, attracts capital from all over the surface of the globe (a significant portion comes from underdeveloped countries, particularly the oil wealth of the Middle East and the war wealth of Southeast Asia), concentrates it in an organized mass, and redirects it via multinational corporations and other intermediaries back to the country from which it came. It then bears the stamp of international capital and its privileges.

The development of the international capital market, in turn, gives multinational corporations increased access to the savings of many nations, enables larger undertakings to be formed, and fosters mergers and consolidations. Most important, it helps forge an identity of interests between competing national capitals, a vital ingredient for the survival of the multinational corporate system. We saw in the last section how international competition in the product market raised the horizons of corporations from the national to the international plane. Similarly, the international flow of private capital, through the multinational corporation or alongside it, gives individual wealth-holders a stake in the international capitalist system as a whole, in proportion as their income comes less and less from their home country, and more and more from the world economy at large.

The overseas expansion of American firms, for example, has substantially diversified the investment portfolio of American shareholders internationally. In addition, Americans have purchased stock in non-American corporations, or invested in land or other assets abroad, and thus further transferred their interests from the United States to the world as a whole. Given the prospects for industrial growth outside the United States and the social and political problems within the United States, this diversification is likely to continue as a sort of capital flight. At the same time, capitalists from other countries have been buying corporate stock in the United States, lending money to multinationals in regional or local capital markets, and in this way shedding their national character and becoming part of international capital.[6]

National corporations and national finance capital

An analogy might be made here to the development of the national corporation and national capitalism in the United States at the turn of the century. Prior to that time, the typical industrial enterprise was the closed family firm with only a few outside shareholders. With the merger movement and the development of a national capital market for industrial equity stock, the modern corporation began to emerge with many shareholders, none of whom owned a majority of stock.

Much has been written about how the dispersion of ownership and the lessening of direct control over management by owners has created an autonomous technostructure which operates independently of the specifically capitalist character of the production process. However, it seems to me to be more appropriate to look upon this process in exactly the opposite way. From the point of view of the large capitalists, that is, the 1 percent of the population that owns the vast majority of corporate stock, the modern corporation was an institutional device for maintaining their control and ensuring the continued accumulation of their wealth.

What happened, in effect, was that the wealthy exchanged shares among themselves, thus forging a common front. Far from relinquishing their interests, they generalized them. Instead of each family capital being locked into a specific firm, it became diversified over many firms and over other assets, such as government bonds and land. In this system, competition more or less assures the equalization of the rate of return; and each capital, if it is sufficiently diversified and prudently managed, will share in the general social surplus, according to its size. Rivalry remains as each capitalist strives to obtain an above-average rate of return, but a dominant general interest in the aggregate rate of profit emerges. At this higher level "capitalists form a veritable freemason society vis-à-vis the whole working class, while there is little love lost between them in competition among themselves.[7]

The corporate structure and the development of a managerial class enabled capital to delegate the work of supervising labor to others and to rely on the market and the government to maintain the rate of profit and the rate of accumulation. In this connection Marx quotes Aristotle: "Whenever the masters are not compelled to plague themselves with supervision, the manager assumes *this honour* while the masters attend to affairs of state or study philosophy."[8] Or one might use Plato's system and say that owners of capital have been elevated to the position of guardians, while the technostructure performs the function of auxiliaries. The interests of the Rockefellers are no longer tied solely to Standard Oil , but their propensity to accumulate has not diminished now that they study economics and attend to the affairs of state as guardians in banking and government.

Multinational corporations and international capital

From this point of view, the national corporation abolished "private" property through collectivization and gave it a general social character as essentially the common capital of a class. The overriding interest of this class is not the war of each against each, but the common need of all to maintain the capitalist society, that is, the rights of property to income and the assurance of an adequate supply of labor to generate that income. Similarly, the multinational corporate system tends to abolish national capital and create a world system in which output is produced cooperatively to a greater degree than ever before, but control remains uneven; capitalists, as trustees of society, continue to pocket a good share of the proceeds.

Without the multinational corporate system, the growth of American capital, and European and Japanese capital, would be thwarted by the growth of new capitals or new socialisms based on the increasing productivity of world labor. With the multinational corporate system, the interests of the 1 percent can be better preserved as they absorb and co-opt some of their potential creditors while crowding out others.

The great pull of this system toward international class consciousness on the part of capital can be illustrated by the ambivalence of the successful industrial capitalist in underdeveloped countries. In the short run he may find it better to remain independent of international capital and continue his successful challenge, but his long-run interest often lies eleswhere. No matter how successful the family firm, it is faced with the problem of managerial succession and limited possibilities of obtaining capital for expansion as long as its shares are tightly held. In addition, there is the ever-present threat of nationalization. If this capitalist allows himself to be taken over by a multinational corporation, he can solve most of these problems. In return for a profitable but inflexible investment in a national firm, he obtains shares of a multinational corporation, traded on the world market, and guaranteed by all the forces that lie behind the international law of private property. He is no longer locked into his industry or his country; the viability of his concern is ensured by its connections to the multinational firm, and he can probably stay on and manage it. Furthermore, his need for Swiss bank accounts and other ways of escaping his own government is diminished because now his capital receives the special privileges of foreign capital. Although every state is absolutely sovereign with regard to national property within its borders, foreign capital is protected by the rule of no confiscation without reparation.

These considerations apply to every capitalist in the world seeking protection and future growth. In my view they help explain why Canadian and European capitalists preferred the positive response to American expansion (that is, becoming multinational themselves), rather than the negative response of blocking American penetration. I think Japanese capital might go the same way. Who knows – perhaps the Russian elite also see outward expansion as necessary for maintaining their internal power and, hence, are opening their arms toward multinationals in the name of science and technology.

In sum, the wealthy of the world have a strong interest in internationalism in order to preserve their position. Freedom to intermingle and compete in the world capital market allows them to diversify their holdings and escape supervision of national governments, that is, control by the majority. It thus protects them from the vagaries of specific markets and specific governments and gives them diversified, general interests in the maintenance of the capitalist system as a whole. This continued flow of aggregate profit is then divided among them more or less in proportion to their wealth, as equalization of world rates of profit is brought about by competition.

International division of labor

As we have just seen, market forces lead corporations and capitalists toward internationalization and a greater recognition of their mutual harmony of interests. At the same time, they divide labor, to whom increased cooperation appears as increased competition. The expansion of the market does not, for the most part, help labor diversify and expand, as it does capital; rather, in many cases it takes away their security and stability.

In order for the multinational corporate system to survive and expand, it must maintain the rate of profit. At its most fundamental level this depends on the state of the labor market and the gap between the productivity of labor and the share labor is allowed to control. Capital can be threatened within the system by labor's unwillingness to work efficiently as a "reasonable wage," and ultimately it is threatened by political revolution which would destroy private property as the basis of income and investment.

To maintain the separation between work and control, capital has erected elaborate corporate superstructures to unite labor in production, but divide it in power. On the political plane, it has used the state bureaucracy to maintain, by force or by education, the general structural conditions which cause laborers to come to work each day and to accept the authority of the capitalist and his right to higher income, either as managerial compensation or as interest and dividends.

Corporate structure as divide and rule

"An industrial army of workmen under the command of a capitalist," wrote Marx, "requires like a real army, officers (managers), and sergeants (foremen, overseers) who, while the work is being done, command in the name of the capitalist."[9] Upon its various bases of national labor, the multinational corporation constructs local hierarchies to supervise and manage day-to-day operations, regional administrations to coordinate national branches, and, at the top, strategy apexes to give overall guidance and direction through the use of budgetary controls. At the bottom of this vertical hierarchy, labor is divided into many nationalities. As one proceeds up the pyramid, nationality becomes more homogeneous and increasingly north European.

The work of this hierarchy has a twofold character. In part, it fulfills functions of coordination and unification which are necessary wherever larger numbers cooperate; in part it fulfills functions that arise from the alienated nature of work in capitalist production. Under capitalism, the laborer does not think socially about his work, his machines, or his product. He regards his work as something he would rather not do, except that he needs the money. Because he does not participate voluntarily, each day is a constant struggle over labor time. The capitalist, or his representative, tries to get the laborer to do something he does not want to do. The laborer tries not to do it.

The twofold character of the technostructure is reflected in the twofold nature of division of labor, which partially is based on the greater productivity that results from specialization, and partially stems from the principle of divide and rule. The corporate hierarchy is essentially a structure to control the flow of information. It has strong vertical linkages so that information passes up and orders pass down easily, and it has strong lateral communication at the top in order to obtain concerted action. At the bottom, lateral communication is broken so that the majority cannot consolidate against the minority. This is done through a series of pyramids in which the president supervises n men, who in turn each supervise n men at the next lower level, and so on until everyone is integrated in a large pyramid that fans out from the center. Each supervisor controls the budget and promotion of the people below him.

In principle a person at any one level can only communicate with someone at the same level who is not in his group by going through his supervisor at the higher level. The higher up one goes, the more flexibility, opportunity, and discretion are permitted. At the bottom, people are rated on a daily or hourly basis, have little opportunity for advancement, and work within narrowly prescribed limits. At the management level, people have a career where promotion is the expected result of performance; the higher they rise, the more they move about, the greater the discretion (responsibility) given to them. People are rewarded doubly since the better the job, the higher the pay. People in the middle and at the top have positions rather than jobs, salaries rather than wages.

The vertical stratification of the corporation rests on a division of mental and manual labor. The higher-level intellectual functions concentrate at the top and vanish on the bottom. In the natural body, head and hand wait upon each other. In the corporation, they part company and become deadly foes. Although the multinational corporation spreads production over the world, it concentrates coordination and planning in key cities, and preserves power and income for the privileged.

The power of the bottom is thus weakened by the spatial division of labor. Each national or regional labor force performs a specialized function which is only meaningful to the integrated whole, yet it has no understanding of the whole. Its integration with other groups is not of its own doing, but is the act of capital (the head) that brings them together; it remains an isolated group whose connections to other groups are matters foreign and external to it. Even its national leaders – its government officials and local corporate executives – are only middlemen in a world system, and are themselves blocked from the information needed to obtain an overall picture. The national technostructures occupy an ambivalent position. On the one hand, they are in conflict with the top of the pyramid over their desire for better jobs or their nationalist identification with their country; on the other hand, they are subordinate and dependent because they lack the key ingredients of capitalist power – information and money.

The government may have apparent political sovereignty, but it too has limited real power and is forever looking to international corporations for technology and capital. It remains a weak state, subordinated to the dictates of the budget, the sternest taskmaster of all in a capitalist society. In this way, the corporate economy attempts to solve its dilemma: It requires an expanding state to solve its problems, but must prevent the state from coming under the actual control of the majority, who have formal control in a democratic state. As long as the state is barred from the process of production, it does not develop the capacity to generate capital and technology, which it always must seek from corporate headquarters, where it has been collected for redistribution. Yet the very process by which it obtains foreign aid ensures that the state will once again be dependent in the next round. The international division of labor keeps the head separate from the hand, and each hand separate from every other. It thus weakens the potential resistance to capital control.

The weakening of the state is a two-edged sword; it incapacitates the government from fulfilling social needs which require active participation, support, and understanding from the population as a whole. The demonstrative effect of capitalist growth creates rising expectations which it is unable to fulfill. In older established areas, resistance and unity grow, forcing capital to tap new untainted sources as a spatial industrial reserve army. Hence the contradictory nature of industrialization of the Third World.

The spread of technology potentially should make everyone better off, but it appears to labor in advanced countries as a conflict for jobs. This is because their jobs and income are in fact threatened by international competition since under capitalism the burden of adjustment is placed on them. The cycle of depressed areas and depopulation which happened when textiles left the northern United States, for example, now might well be occurring on a world scale. As capital leaves one group of workers for another, in a process resembling slash and burn agriculture, the advanced group is forced to lie fallow in unemployment for use later when their resistance has been weakened.

The wastefulness of capital

This process is extremely wasteful of labor, as the continuation of poverty in the United States shows. The labor of large numbers of people who cannot adapt to the discipline of the capitalist work process, or who are incapacitated by its shifting cultivation, is squandered; while the employed section is spurred on to accept discipline because of the fear of falling out. At the same time, the growth of consumption produced by capitalism has a shoddy inhuman aspect. In a society based on unequal distribution of power and private ignorance, the innovator does not appeal to human needs, but to excess and immoderation.

If the multinational corporations continue to expand and interpenetrate, we will have a world economy in which the leading sectors are dominated by a few giant world corporations, competing through advertising and innovation. The larger market, and the stress on nonprice competition, most likely will lead to a faster rate of innovation on a world scale. In turn, the uncertainties created by this rapid change will mean more resources devoted to research and innovation. This positive feedback can lead to furious competition, especially if the government accentuates it by subsidizing research, forcing growth, and centralizing international communications, making it possible to reach the whole world with one blow.

International competition is thus likely to at least continue to foster, and probably raise, the animal spirits of multinational corporations, and bring about a revolutionary reconstruction of world society by continuously destroying old needs and wants and creating new ones. The life styles of the present advanced centers will be transferred to the hinterlands, and new needs and wants will be created for the affluent. In turn, these will spread to the rest in a continuous cycle of innovation and trickling down, appropriately called "creative destruction" by Schumpeter.

"Hunger is hunger," wrote Marx, "but the hunger that is satisfied with cooked meat eaten with fork and knife is a different kind of hunger from the one that devours raw meat with the aid of hands and teeth."[10] The incredible technological progress of capitalism reduces the realm of natural necessity and replaces it with needs that are historically produced. There can be no doubt that the multinational corporation is a forward-moving organization, producing needs, destroying them, and producing new needs within a generation. The question that concerns us is the direction of change. Paradoxically, the new manifestation of human powers and the new enrichment of the human being created by technological change often have the opposite meaning within the corporate system. Wants are pushed forward in a one-sided direction, and the growth of needs and the means to satisfy them result in a lack of needs and of means. No matter how wealthy we grow, we continue to live from hand to mouth.

In the great cities of the United States, where the highest per capita income obtains, the need for decent housing and for fresh air ceases to be a need, while the automobile becomes a necessity. "Man returns to the cave dwelling again but it is now poisoned by the pestilential breath of civilization... Light, air, and the simplest animal cleanliness cease to be human needs. Filth, this corruption and putrefaction which runs in the sewers of civilization (this is to be taken literally) becomes the element in which man lives."[11] In New York, the home of the multinational corporation, this is almost literally true. Symbolically the Bowery abuts Wall Street and Fifth Avenue runs into Harlem. The same contradiction between poverty and wealth can be seen in the underdeveloped capitalist world where small islands of modern consumption are ringed by slums of poverty. "The savage in a cave does not feel himself a stranger ... but the cellar dwelling of a poor man is a hostile dwelling."[12]

If, instead of this perverse pattern of growth, underdeveloped countries aimed at producing a bundle of basic consumption goods on a mass scale, they could increase employment and reduce the worst aspects of poverty. They could use technology that has been known for decades, and less capital per unit of output would be required because of the long production runs and standardized output. They would have little need for multinational corporations whose special advantages for the most part lie in differentiated products and new goods.

The state

During the *Pax Americana* large corporations from all countries came more and more "to see the world as their oyster," to use the prophetic phrase of former Assistant Under Secretary of State Anthony Salomon.[13] It is not yet theirs. Just because capitalism *ideally* transcends the boundaries of the nation-state, it in no way means that it has really surmounted them. The nation-state was an integral part of the system under which capitalism grew; at this point it is seen as a barrier that limits the further growth of capital and must be overcome. However, the nation-state is a structure of power, and in order to supersede it, international capital must mobilize new power bases in its support.

Multinational corporations (and their owners) are only one sector of society. They are a few hundred giants with great power, but with a heavy past and great limitations on their ability to deliver the goods. They first must battle with the smaller businesses, state bureaucracies, and colonial remnants, whose more nationalistic outlook is antagonistic to the progress of world capitalism; second, with the minority that works directly or indirectly for them, and must accept their goals and rules; and, finally, with the majority of the world's population that lies outside their sphere and is largely excluded from the benefits of "modernization."

The historical role of the state

In its early days, capital allied itself with the central power of the sovereign against the feudal classes. This system, working in complex ways, helped to drive the population off the land to become a free wage labor force in the towns and cities. People became unencumbered by property in the twofold sense: They were free of feudal claims on their time and had no property of their own, and therefore had no alternative to working for others.

The international economy played two vital roles. (1) It commercialized the domestic economy, that is, converted the feudal self-sufficient economy into an economy producing commodities for the market, thus concentrating land holdings and freeing labor. (2) It fostered the accumulation of capital in a few hands. National rivalry – the competitive zeal of European nations to possess themselves of the products of Asia and the treasures of America, and the colonial system – was a basic propelling force, giving the nascent capitalist class a wider market and the chance to make a fortune. In this mercantilist age, gold became the ultimate aim. It was an age when foreign trade was a basic means of accumulating capital, that is liquidity, and to obtain gold was to obtain the power to become a capitalist in a market system where a plentiful supply of labor for hire was emerging.

If in the first world economy (sixteenth and seventeenth centuries), foreign commerce created industry under the symbiosis of capital and crown, in the second world economy (late nineteenth and early twentieth centuries), industry created commerce. The industrial revolution and the export of manufactured goods created a system of international specialization based on different levels of capitalist development. Cheap commodities were the heavy artillery to batter down even the Great Wall of China, figuratively speaking. However, some countries, now called developed, were able to resist British penetration by erecting national tariff barricades against the destructive force of British heavy industry. Again state power was necessary to institute capitalism by (a) creating a supply of labor for industry, and (b) protecting, subsidizing, and otherwise fostering the concentration of capital in a class willing to use it for manufacturing, investment, and associated activities.

With the spread of industry and the growth of multi-centered capitalism, the role of the state, or rather its methods, changed again. First, it continued to protect national capital from foreigners (hence imperialism, trade wars, subsidies, and so forth), thus creating an environment which led to two wars and a depression instead of the peace and prosperity liberal ideology promised. Second, it assumed more and more the task of coordinating capitalism at a level above that of the market in order to reduce the instability and wastes of unplanned competition through such means as banking and railroading regulation, antitrust legislation, regulation of hours of work, and counter-cyclical policy and planning. Third, it had to socialize labor into continued acceptance of capitalism through education, trade unions, unemployment compensation, social security, and so forth, which improved the welfare of labor while retaining the capitalist base.

Current political problems

The current needs of capitalism are, first, a reduction of the conflicts between national capitalists, which initially helped but later plagued capitalist development. Second, and at the same time, the labor market must be maintained by pacifying the advanced workers in the developed countries and by tapping the latent reserve army in the underdeveloped countries. The three major sources of difficulty for international capitalism are contradictions between the centers, competition between the centers and the hinterland, and contradictions within the centers.

Contradictions between the centers.   Although the bitter memories of the Great Depression and war remain, national rivalry – the use by national capital of the protective state to foster its growth – is far from gone. There remains not only the problem of settling differences between the Free World powers of the United States, Europe, and Japan, but also the challenge of Russia and China. In addition, the capitalists of the underdeveloped countries, although weak in general, are strong in particular places (for example, the overseas Chinese, the Philippines, the large Indian capitalists), and somehow must be integrated into a supranational system.

It is not merely a question of avoiding war between the rivals, but also the much more intractable problem of creating an international government apparatus to prevent depression and inflation, to work out a balance between big and small, and to prevent, when the going gets rough, the tendency of capitalists to rely on their individual strength and cunning in place of collusion and cooperation.

Competition between the centers and the hinterland.   Despite capitalism's advances, poverty remains a significant problem in the advanced world and an overwhelming problem in the underdeveloped nations. Even the most optimistic forecasters do not see great progress in this area over the next thirty or forty years, which, for political prognostication, is a rather long time. The excluded masses, united before in the national independence movements, are now united in much stronger forms of resistance. The United States is presently bogged down in one such struggle, and several more are on the horizon. It is true that the multinational corporate system is to some extent prospering because of the war, but its continued existence depends upon keeping such resistance in check.

Contradictions within the centers.   In order for an integrated worldwide system based on the relations of private property to exist, a vast imperial apparatus is necessary to administer the empire to fight when necessary. During the past twenty years the United States provided this apparatus. It now seems less able to carry on this function due to many internal struggles. Among these are : the revolt of the Blacks; the failure of some of the most promising youth to take up the call for which they were trained; a host of movements, such as the cultural revolution and women's liberation, which reject the whole social fabric of the society and the power system on which it is based; the low morale in the army; and other problems now manifested in drugs and an unwillingness to work hard, but soon perhaps to take political form.

Our present fiscal crisis at the municipal, state, and international level, despite growth of the GNP, the switch in the allegiance of intellectuals, and a loss of self-confidence in the ruling class were the three major signs of a disintegrating *ancien regime* identified by Crane Brinton in his study of the anatomy of revolution.[14] No wonder a sense of foreboding is dawning that capitalism is no solid crystal, but an organism capable of changing. Some are hopeful, most are frightened, a few have everything to lose.

In sum, it is my view that although the first round (the fifties and sixties) went to the multinational corporation, the coming rounds (the seventies and eighties) will take a quite different course, as the arena shifts from economic integration to political battle. With the fall of the United States from its position of predominance, Europe and Japan may try to substitute some system for American hegemony, but their record of foreign rule is a bad one. Furthermore, their faith in growth as a solution to all problems has been challenged, and they all face many of the same internal problems as the United States. These, at bottom, seem to stem from the fact that twenty-five years of prosperity erode the compliance to capitalism built up by wars and depression, and that economic growth under capitalism is not satisfying and does not fulfill human needs. As Keynes once put it in discussing capitalism, "it is not beautiful, it is not just, it is not virtuous – and it doesn't deliver the goods."[15] The multinational corporation is its swan song.

Part II

Accumulation, trade, and exploitation

Introduction

James O'Connor

Steve Hymer began his teaching and writing career as an orthodox (albeit liberal) bourgeois economist. At the end of his life he was the most creative and theoretically bold Marxist economist working in the English language. The three essays in this part (and the other parts) and above all his last conversations with friends and co-workers established beyond dispute that in the right hands Marxism remains the indispensable science of society. These studies are Marxist in the double sense that they can be read as critiques of bourgeois economics and simultaneously as scientific accounts of the real historical processes of capital accumulation. Careful readers will find critiques of the orthodox theories of international trade and foreign investment, economic development, the behavior of the capitalist enterprise, and last but not least the neoclassical theory of the "allocation of scarce economic resources." The same readers will also find scientific accounts of primitive capitalist accumulation, capitalist development on a world scale (including the process of uneven and combined development), and the hegemony of the multinational corporation (the form in which international capital is organized today). Every reader will discover in these three studies many important themes and contradictions inherent in the present-day capitalist accumulation process. Some of these themes are worked out in detail, for example, Steve's discussion of the relationship between the multinational corporation and the international division of labor. Other themes that are worked out in less detail highlight the relationship between market forces and political power in world capitalist history, for example, the essays on primitive accumulation and international trade and uneven development. The analysis of the connection between the so-called free market and political force and oppression is increasingly relevent today; for example, the impossibility of separating Milton Friedman's laissez-faire economics applied to Chile and the barbarism of the Chilean junta.

The first essay, "Robinson Crusoe and the Secret of Primitive Accumulation," is a brilliant and devastating critique of bourgeois neoclassical econom-

97

ics and perhaps the most important benchmark in Steve's development as a Marxist theoretician. Economists in the bourgeois tradition believe that capitalism and the "free market" are positive forces in the development of the human species. They argue that laissez-faire or free trade based on private ownership of the means of production not only is the best way, but the only rational way of economizing on "scarce resources" (e.g., land, labor). Steve believed in his last years that capitalism was an irrational system that distorted, crippled, wasted, and destroyed human beings in countless ways. In the Marxist tradition, he argued that capitalism transformed the direct producers into detail laborers with overdeveloped capacities for unskilled specialized work and undeveloped and crippled all-around physical, intellectual, sensual, and even spiritual capacities. He also believed that the theory of neoclassical economics (e.g., the theories of consumer choice and market demand and the theory of the firm) was in fact the theory of the capitalist (i.e., exploiting) class. He argued that the obsession with economizing on the use of time and human energy originated in the capitalist's need to control the living labor of the direct producers, and that economizing in this sense was irrelevant in a rational community that organized its own way of life and produced material objectives to meet human needs decided upon collectively and democratically. In such a community the whole meaning of efficiency and economizing is totally different from that in capitalism, where the capitalist class exploits the labor power of the working class, and hence has every incentive to utilize this exploited labor power "economically." Steve and I discussed these formulations subsequent to the original appearance of this essay, which cuts through the dreary theorems of bourgeois economic thought with a profundity yet simplicity such as is rarely achieved in works of social theory.

"Robinson Crusoe" is also outstanding for its revealing critique of the frequently oversimplified Crusoe analogy employed by bourgeois economic theorists, who empty Defoe's real message about the reality of capital accumulation. In Steve's essay, the real Robinson Crusoe emerges as a greedy, vicious, and frightened exploiter and murderer, not the intelligent, resourceful, and diligent human being motivated simply by making money as glorified in orthodox economics textbooks. Robinson Crusoe in reality lives in the period of primitive capitalist accumulation characterized by the slave trade, unequal exchange, racism, colonization, new emerging ruling classes, human alienation and oppression, the indispensability of exploited labor for the accumulation of capital, and last but not least the power of the gun. Nowhere in modern economic writing is the thesis that market economic power grows out of the barrel of a gun, that is, that economics and politics are the dirty sides of one another, argued so forcefully. Steve expounds the real process of early capitalist development with extraordinary clarity and sensitivity, not the least regarding the condition of Friday and his grandchildren, whose contribution to capitalist development as slave laborers typically is ignored by bourgeois economic science.

The next essay in this part, "International Trade and Uneven Development," co-authored with Stephen A. Resnick, was written earlier than "Robinson Crusoe." The latter work is clearly Marxist in method because of the central role Steve gives to the social relations of production and their effects on the productive forces. This essay illustrates the process whereby Steve was becoming a Marxist in outlook and method, and hence is flawed in significant ways to be discussed below. In this work, he and Resnick explain why and how the growth of international trade has resulted in a dual world economic structure – development in the metropoles or centers and underdevelopment on the peripheries. By contrast, orthodox trade theory asserts that international trade results in the equalization of "factor prices" and general worldwide development. Their analysis also exposes the weakness of orthodox government policy recommendations because such recommendations for development are based on economic criteria alone, that is, criteria that lend themselves to quantification. Economic orthodoxy normally excludes from analysis social and political factors involved in concrete situations. The authors of "International Trade and Uneven Development" focus on the economic, social, and political factors inherent in the growth of international trade dating from the late fifteenth century to the present. This method reflects a Marxist orientation to the degree that it emphasizes the real historical development of international trade and examines its contributions to and effects on the whole capitalist development process in which trade is only one element. This uneven development process is found to have had negative effects on the majority of the producing classes in Africa, Asia, Latin America, and to a much lesser degree in the metropolitan regions themselves (i.e., underdevelopment is located within the metropoles as well as on the peripheries). The authors then warned against the development of economic and political power among the national bourgeoisie in the Third World, "who become the middlemen in the international economic system" and assisting in the increasing penetration of capitalist institutions and consumption patterns in the underdeveloped world, thus ensuring the continuing dependence of the periphery on the center.

The authors sketch a schematic history of world capitalist development and underdevelopment based on a method that combines analysis of market forces and allocation of land and labor power on the one hand and political power on the other. This method is not fully adequate because it neglects the dialectical process of changing productive forces and production relations. Specifically, the authors fail to distinguish between "merchant capitalism" and industrial capitalism, hence the all-important distinction between monopoly in trade and monopoly of means of production is lost. Changes in income distribution are explained in terms of shifts in market patterns and political relations rather than in terms of changes in production relations, specifically, the transformation of independent commodity production to wage labor in the center and of slavery to various forms of semiproletarian status on the periphery. The absence of analysis of changing production relations also leads the authors to neglect the important problem of the reproduction costs of labor power in the center and their relationship with raw material production and colonialism on the periphery. In sum, the article places undue emphasis on the role of market forces and political relationships and government policies but pays little attention to systemic accumulation laws and tendencies (e.g., concentration and centralization of capital, reserve army of labor as the lever of accumulation).

The third essay, "The Multinational Corporation and the International Division of Labor," is Steve's most ambitious exposition and analysis of the internationalization of production and capital, as well as of the multinational enterprise as the primary vehicle of capital accumulation on a world scale today. The critical dimensions of the present-day accumulation process that Steve brings out include conflicts between the multinational companies and nation-states (and interest groups within both); competition among the multinationals for raw materials and markets; the internal dimensions of the multinationals and the differentiation of their component parts; the vertically organized hierarchical control structures within the multinational company; the multinationals as a motive force in the world economy in the forms of foreign investment and the product cycle; and their worldwide spatial dimensions and the effects on the world hierarchy of urban centers.

Steve analyzes the relationship between the growth of international corporate capital in the form of horizontal and vertical integration and multiproduct production on the one hand and the internal specialization and development of the corporate administrative apparatus on the other. Corporate growth means the transformation of market mechanisms into administrative mechanisms; in place of a multitude of specialized market activities we have a multitude of specialized administrative activities. Steve next works out the spatial configurations of the modern worldwide accumulation process. He writes that the multinational corporation "may well be a force for diffusing industrialization to the less-developed countries and creating new centers of production." Here we find the elements of the theory of dependent development or a world economy in which production and related activities are decentralized but where middle-level coordinating activities and high-level planning are concentrated geographically and racially. Steve shows how the spatial division of labor is "a vertical one between different levels of activities. . . A regime of multinational corporations would tend to produce a hierarchical division of labor between geographic regions corresponding to the vertical division of labor within the firm." This essay is a lucid outline of the many-sided process of capital accumulation in the world today as well as a clear summary history of the capitalist enterprise, U.S. foreign investment, and the relative position of European and Japanese capital today. His conclusion is that a new equilibrium has been established between U.S. and European multinational firms and that capital from both regions is engaged in a major investment drive in the underdeveloped countries to establish and consolidate market positions. In sum, this essay, like the corpus of Steve's work, is unsurpassed in its portrayal of the role, methods of operation, and power of the multinational corporation in the world economy today.

4   Robinson Crusoe and the secret of primitive accumulation

Every living being is a sort of imperialist, seeking to transform as much as possible of the environment into itself and its seed.

Bertrand Russell

Note on primitive accumulation
The word *primitive* is here used in the sense of "belonging to the first age, period, or stage," i.e., of being "original rather than derivative," and not in the sense of "simple, rude, or rough." Marx's original term was "ursprüngliche akkumulation," and as Paul Sweezy suggests, it would have been better translated as "original" or "primary" accumulation. But it is too late to change current usage, and the word *primitive* should be interpreted in a technical sense, as in mathematics, where a *primitive* line or figure is a line or figure "from which some construction or reckoning begins." In economics primitive accumulation refers to the period from which capitalist accumulation springs. It was not simple, though it was rude and rough.

The solitary and isolated figure of Robinson Crusoe is often taken as a starting point by economists, especially in their analysis of international trade. He is pictured as a rugged individual – diligent, intelligent, and above all frugal – who masters nature through reason. But the actual story of Robinson Crusoe, as told by Defoe, is also one of conquest, slavery, robbery, murder, and force. That this side of the story should be ignored is not at all surprising, "for in the tender annals of political economy the idyllic reigns from time immemorial." The contrast between the economist's Robinson Crusoe and the genuine one mirrors the contrast between the mythical description of international trade found in economics text books and the actual facts of what happens in the international economy.

The paradigm of non-Marxist international trade theroy is the model of a hunter and fisherman who trade to their mutual benefit under conditions of

This essay originally appeared in *Monthly Review*, September 1971, pp. 11–36. Copyright © 1971 by Monthly Review Inc. Reprinted by permission of Monthly Review Press.

equality, reciprocity, and freedom. But international trade (or, for that matter, interregional trade) is often based on a division between superior and subordinate rather than a division between equals; and it is anything but peaceful. It is trade between the center and the hinterland, the colonizers and the colonized, the masters and the servants. Like the relation of capital to labor, it is based on a division between higher and lower functions: One party does the thinking, planning, organizing; and the other does the work. Because it is unequal in structure and reward it has to be established and maintained by force, whether it be the structural violence of poverty, the symbolic violence of socialization, or the physical violence of war and pacification.

In this essay I would like to go over the details of Crusoe's story – how, starting as a slave trader, he uses the surplus of others to acquire a fortune – in order to illustrate Marx's analysis of the capitalist economy, especially the period of primitive accumulation which was its starting point.

For capitalist accumulation to work, two different kinds of people must meet in the market (and later in the production process); on the one hand, owners of money eager to increase their capital by buying other people's labor power; on the other hand, free laborers unencumbered by pre-capitalist obligations or personal property. Once capitalism is on its legs, it maintains this separation and reproduces it on a continuously expanding scale. But a prior stage is needed to clear the way for the capitalist system and get it started – a period of primitive accumulation.

In the last part of Volume I of *Capital,* Marx sketched the historical process by which means of production were concentrated in the hands of the capitalist, leaving the worker no alternative but to work for him. He showed how a wage labor force was created through the expropriation of the agricultural population and he traced the genesis of the industrial capitalist to, among other things, the looting of Africa, Asia, and America "in the rosy dawn of the era of capitalist production."[1] In the story of Robinson Crusoe, Defoe describes how a seventeenth-century Englishman amassed capital and organized a labor force to work for him in Brazil and in the Caribbean. Of course what Crusoe established was not a market economy such as emerged in England but a plantation and settler economy such as was used by capitalism in the non-European world. It might therefore be called the story of primitive underdevelopment.

Defoe (1659–1731) was particularly well placed to observe and understand the essence of the rising bourgeoisie and the secrets of its origins. The son of a London butcher, he was engaged in the business of a hosiery factory and was a commission merchant until he went bankrupt. During his life he wrote many essays and pamphlets on economics, discussing among other things, banks, road management, friendly and insurance societies, idiot asylums, bankruptcy, academies, military colleges, women's education, social welfare programs, and national workshops. He was one of the first writers to rely on the growing market of the middle class to earn his living.[2]

I. Merchants' capital

Robinson Crusoe's story can be told in terms of a series of cycles, some running simultaneously, through which he accumulates capital. In the early days these take the form M–C–M, i.e., he starts off with money, exchanges it for commodities, and ends up with more money. In the later phases when he is outside the money economy, they take the form C–L–C, as he uses his stock of commodities to gain control over other people's labor and to produce more commodities, ending up with a small empire.

Robinson Crusoe was born in 1632. The son of a merchant, he could have chosen to follow the middle station of life and raise his fortune "by application and industry, with a life of ease and pleasure." Instead he chose to go to sea – partly for adventure, partly because of greed.

In his first voyage he starts off with £40 in "toys and trifles," goes to the Guinea Coast (as mess-mate and companion of the captain whom he befriended in London), and comes back with five pounds nine ounces of gold worth £300. This is the first circuit of his capital. He leaves £200 of this sum in England with the captain's widow (the captain died soon after their return) and, using the remaining £100 as fresh capital, sets off on a second voyage as a Guinea trader in order to make more capital. Instead he meets with disaster. The ship is captured by Moors and he becomes a slave in North Africa. He escapes slavery in a boat taken from his master, accompanied by a fellow slave Xury, a black man, to whom he promises, "Xury, if you will be faithful to me, I'll make you a great man." Together they sail a thousand miles along the coast of Africa, until they are met and rescued by a Portuguese captain.

Fortunately for Robinson, there is honor among capitalists. The captain, who is on his way to Brazil, feels it would be unfair to take everything from Robinson and bring him to Brazil penniless. "I have saved your life on no other terms than I would be glad to be saved myself. . . When I carry you to Brazil, so great a way from your own country, if I should take from you what you have, you will be starved there, and then I only take away that life I have given."

Robinson of course does not tell the captain that he still has £200 in England. Instead, he sells the captain his boat (i.e., the boat he took when he escaped) and everything in it, *including Xury*. An African is an African, and only under certain conditions does he become a slave. Robinson has some pangs of guilt about selling "the poor boy's liberty who had assisted me so faithfully in procuring my own." However the captain offers to set Xury free in ten years if he turns Christian. "Upon this, and Xury saying he was willing to go to him, I let the captain have him" (for sixty pieces of eight).

Commodities are things and cannot go to market by themselves. They have to be taken. If they are unwilling, they can be forced.

Robinson arrives in Brazil where he purchases "as much land that was uncured as my money would reach, and formed a plan for my plantation and settlement, and such a one as might be suitable to stock which I proposed to myself to receive from England." He soon finds "more than before, I had done wrong in parting with my boy Xury," for he needed help and found there was "no work to be done, but by the labor of my hands."

He sends a letter to the widow in England through his Portuguese captain friend instructing that half of his £200 be sent to him in the form of merchandise. The captain takes the letter to Lisbon where he gives it to some London merchants who relay it to London. The widow gives the money to a London merchant who, "vesting this hundred pounds in English goods, such as the captain had writ for, sent them directly to him at Lisbon, and he brought them all safe to me to Brazil; among which, without my direction (for I was too young in my business to think of them), he had taken care to have all sorts of tools, ironwork, and utensils necessary for my plantation, and which were of great use to me."

The cargo arrives, bringing great fortune to Robinson. The Portuguese captain had used the £5 the widow had given him for a present to purchase and bring to Robinson, "a servant under bond for six years service, and would not accept of any consideration, except a little tobacco which I would have him accept, being of my own produce." Moreover, he is able to sell the English goods in Brazil "to a very great advantage" and the first thing he does is to buy a Negro slave and a second indenture servant.

This series of transactions presupposes an elaborate social network of capitalist intercommunications. The mythical Robinson is pictured as a self-sufficient individual, but much of the actual story, even after he is shipwrecked, shows him as a dependent man belonging to a larger whole and always relying on help and cooperation from others. The social nature of production turns out to be the real message of his story as we shall see again and again. There is no real paradox in this. To capitalism belong both the production of the most highly developed social relations in history and the production of the solitary individual.

Robinson now integrates himself into the community as a successful planter and accumulates steadily. But he cannot be content and soon leaves "the happy view I had of being a rich and thriving man in my new plantation, only to pursue a rash and immoderate desire of rising faster than the nature of the thing admitted."

The plantations in Brazil were short of labor, for "few Negroes were brought, and those excessive dear" since the slave trade at that time was not far developed and was controlled by royal monopolies of the kings of Spain and Portugal. Robinson had told some friends about his two voyages to the

Guinea Coast and the ease of purchasing there "for trifles not only gold dust but Negroes in great numbers." (N.B. that the trifles listed are beads, toys, knives, scissors, hatchets, bits of glass, and the like – all but the first two are by no means trifles, as Robinson would soon find out.) These friends approached him in secrecy with a plan for outfitting a ship to get slaves from the Guinea Coast who would then be smuggled into Brazil privately and distributed among their own plantations. They asked Robinson to go as "supercargo in the ship to manage the trading part and offered [him] an equal share of the Negroes without providing any part of the stock."

Robinson accepts, and it is on this voyage that his famous shipwreck occurs. Years later, in the depths of isolation, he had cause to regret this decision which he views in terms of his original sin of "not being satisfied with the station wherein God and nature hath placed [him] . . ."

What business had I to leave a settled fortune, a well-stocked plantation, improving and increasing, to turn supercargo to Guinea, to fetch Negroes, when patience and time would have so increased our stock at home that we could have bought them from those whose business it was to fetch them? And though it had cost us something more, yet the difference of that price was by no means worth saving at so great a hazard.

In fact he comes out ahead for by the end of the story Robinson has succeeded in accumulating much faster than if he had remained content, for he adds a new fortune from his island economy to the growth of his plantation. True, he must suffer a long period of isolation, but in many ways his solitary sojourn represents the alienation suffered by all under capitalism – those who work and receive little as well as those like Robinson who accumulate and always must Go on, Go on.

II. Island economy: the pre-trade situation

The key factors in Robinson Crusoe's survival and prosperity on his island in the sun are not his ingenuity and resourcefulness but the pleasant climate and the large store of embodied labor he starts out with. In thirteen trips to his wrecked ship he was able to furnish himself with many things, taking a vast array of materials and tools he never made but were still his to enjoy. These he uses to gain command over nature and over other men. Of chief importance in his initial stock of means of production is a plentiful supply of guns and ammunition, which give him decisive advantage in setting the terms of trade when his island economy is finally opened up to trade.

Robinson himself is fully aware of the importance of his heritage (see Table 1). "What should I have done without a gun, without ammunition, without any tools to make anything or work with, without clothes, bedding, a tent, or any manner of coverings?" he asks. And "by making the most rational judgment of things every man may be in time master of every

Table 1. *Items taken by Robinson Crusoe from the shipwreck*

Defense: ammunition, arms, powder, 2 barrels musket bullets, 5–7 muskets, large bag full of small shot
Food: biscuits, rum, bread, rice, cheese, goat flesh, corn liquor, flour, cordials, sweetmeats, poultry feed, wheat, and rice seed
Clothing: men's clothes, handkerchiefs, colored neckties, 2 pairs of shoes
Furniture and miscellaneous: hammock, bedding, pens, ink, paper, 3 or 4 compasses, some mathematical instruments, dials, perspectives, charts, books on navigation, 3 Bibles
Tools: carpenter's chest, 203 bags full of nails & spikes, a great screwjack, 1 or 2 dozen hatchets, grindstone, 2 saws, axe, hammer, 2 or 3 iron crows, 2 or 3 razors, 1 large scissors, fire shovel and tongs, 2 brass kettles, copper pots, gridiron
Raw materials: rigging, sails for canvas, small ropes, ropes and wire, ironwork, timber, boards, planks, 2–3 hundredweight of iron, 1 hundredweight of sheet lead
Animals: dog, 2 cats
Things he misses badly: ink, spade, shovel, needles, pins, thread, smoking pipe

---

mechanic art. I had never handled a tool in my life, and yet in time, by labor, application, and contrivance, I wanted nothing but I could have made it, *especially if I had had the tools*" (emphasis added). A European is a European and it is only under certain conditions that he becomes a master. It was not their personal attributes that gave Robinson and other European adventurers their strength vis-à-vis non-Europeans but the equipment they brought with them, the power of knowledge made into objects. This material base was the result of a complicated social division of labor of which they were the beneficiaries not the creators.

His island is a rich one, again thanks in part to the activities of other people. He surveys it with little understanding since most of the plants were unfamiliar to him. He makes no independent discovery but finds certain familiar items – goats, turtles, fruits, lemons, oranges, tobacco, grapes – many of which I imagine could not have gotten there except if transplanted by previous visitors from other islands. His own discovery of agriculture is accidental. Among the things he rescued from the ship was a little bag which had once been filled with corn. Robinson seeing nothing in the bag but husks and dust, and needing it for some other purpose, shook the husks out on the ground. A month or so later, not even remembering he had thrown them there, he was "perfectly astonished" to find barley growing.

Conditioned by capitalist tradition, Crusoe tries to keep account of his activities and "while my ink lasted, I kept things very exact; but after that was gone, I could not, for I could not make any ink by any means I could devise." He draws up a cost–benefit analysis of his position, stating in it "very impartially like debtor and creditor, the comforts I enjoyed, against the miseries I suffered." He finds his day divided into three. It took him only about three hours going out with his gun, to get his food. Another portion of his day was spent in ordering, curing, preserving, and cooking. A third portion was spent on capital formation, planting barley and rice, curing raisins, building furniture and a canoe, and so forth.

This passion for accounting might seem to confirm the economist's picture of Robinson as the rational man par excellence, allocating his time efficiently among various activities in order to maximize utility. But then comes this astonishing observation, "But my time or labor was little worth, and so it was as well employed one way as another!" Contrary to the usual models of economic theory, Robinson Crusoe, producing only for use and not for exchange, finds that there is no scarcity and that labor has no value. The driving force of capitalism, the passion for accumulation, vanished when he was alone. "All I could make use of was all that was valuable. . . The most covetous, griping miser in the world would have been cured of the vice of covetousness, if he had been in my case."

Robinson's own explanation of this phenomenon is mainly in terms of demand. Because he is alone, his wants are limited and satiated before he exhausts his available labor time:

> I was removed from all the wickedness of the world here. I had neither the lust of the flesh, the lust of the eye or the pride of life. I had nothing to covet; for I had all that I was now capable of enjoying. I was lord of the whole manor; or if I pleased, I might call myself king, or emperor over the whole country which I had possession of. There were no rivals. I had no competitor. . .

This is true as far as it goes, but it is one-sided. Robinson's greed went away because there were no people to organize and master. Marx's proposition was that surplus labor was the sole measure and source of capitalist wealth. Without someone else's labor to control, the capitalist's value system vanished; no boundless thirst for surplus labor arose from the nature of production itself; the goals of efficiency, maximization, and accumulation faded into a wider system of values.

Later, when Robinson's island becomes populated, the passion to organize and accumulate returns. It is only when he has no labor but his own to control that labor is not scarce and he ceases to measure things in terms of labor time. As Robinson's reference to the miser shows, it is not merely a question of the demand of consumption goods. The miser accumulates not for consumption but for accumulation, just as the purposeful man in the capitalist era, as Keynes noted, "does not love his cat, but his cat's kittens; nor, in truth, the kittens, but only the kittens' kittens, and so on forward forever to the end of cat-dom. For him jam is not jam unless it is a case of jam tomorrow and never jam today."[3] Money and capital are social relations representing social power over others. Regardless of what goes on in the minds of misers and capitalists when they look at their stock, it is power over people that they are accounting and accumulating, as they would soon find out if they, like Robinson, were left alone.

Robinson is partially aware of this when he meditates on the uselessness of gold on his island:

> I smiled to myself at the sight of this money. "O drug!" said I aloud, "what are thou good for? Thou art not worth to me, no not the taking off of the ground, one of those knives is worth all this heap; I have no manner of use for thee; e'en remain where thou art, and go to the bottom as a creature whose life is not worth saving." However, upon second thoughts, I took it away. . . .

He thus negates the Mercantilist system which made a fetish out of gold, but does not fully pierce the veil of money to uncover the underlying basis of surplus labor – does not in his theories, that is; in his daily practice he is fully aware of the real basis of the economy. This shows up when he discusses the concept of Greed. In Robinson's eyes, his original sin is the crime of wanting to rise above his station instead of following the calling chosen for him by his father. Isolation and estrangement are his punishment, and he feels that his story should teach content to those "who cannot enjoy comfortably what God has given them." He feels guilty for violating the feudal institutions of status, patriarchy, and God. He does not consider that when he accumulates, he violates those whom he exploits – Xury, the Africans he sold into slavery, his indentured servants, and soon Friday and others. From the ideological point of view, Robinson is a transitional man looking backward and upward instead of forward and downward. This is why he learns nothing (morally speaking) from his loneliness. The miser is not in fact cured, the vice of covetousness easily returns.

Since the relationship of trade, accumulation, and exploitation is so crucial to understanding economics, we might dwell on it a little longer. The argument can be traced back to Aristotle, who felt that a self-sufficient community would not be driven by scarcity and accumulation, since natural wants were limited and could easily be satisfied with plenty of time left over for leisure. Such a community would practice the art of householding which has use value as its end. But Aristotle, an eyewitness to the growth of the market at its very first appearance, noted that there was another art of wealth getting – commercial trade – which had no limit, since its end was the accumulation of exchange value for its own sake. Aristotle was more interested in the effects of the rise of commerce than in its base and did not make the connection between exchange value and surplus labor. But it was there for all to see. The emergence of the market in ancient Athens was a by-product of its imperial expansion, the looting of territories liberated from the Persians, the collection of tribute and taxes from other Greek states for protection, and the forced diversion of the area's trade to Athens' port.[4]

Keynes, though analytically imprecise, glimpsed the same point in his article on "National Self-Sufficiency" where he instinctively saw that some withdrawal from international trade was necessary to make the life made possible by science pleasant and worthwhile. He wanted to minimize rather than maximize economic entanglements among nations so that we can be "our own masters" and "make our favorite experiments toward the ideal social republic of the future." He was all for a free exchange of ideas, knowledge, science, hospitality, and travel, "but let goods be home-spun whenever it is reasonably and commercially possible, and, above all let finance be primarily national." He knew that it was not invidious consumption that was the problem, but the desire to extend oneself by penetrating foreign markets with exports and investment which in the end comes down to an attempt to transform as much as possible of the world into oneself and one's seed, i.e., imperialism.[5]

To return to Robinson Crusoe. It is important to note that his isolation was accompanied not so much by loneliness as by fear. The first thing he did when arrived on his beautiful Caribbean paradise was to build himself a fortress. It was only when he was completely "fenced and fortified" from all the world that he "slept secure in the night." His precautions during the first eleven years when he is completely alone are astonishing. Yet during these years he is in no danger from wild animals or any living thing. His chief problem comes from birds who steal his seeds. He deals with them with dispatch, shooting a few and then "I took them up and served them as we serve notorious thieves in England, viz., hanged them in chains for a terror to others." And, as we shall see in the next section, when signs of other human beings come to him, he does not run out with joy, ready to risk everything to hear a human voice after so many years in solitary confinement. Instead his fears and anxieties rise to a frenzied pitch, and he fences and fortifies himself more and more, withdrawing further and further into isolation.

Perhaps this is what one should expect from a man isolated for so long a period. But at times it seems to me that Defoe, in describing Robinson Crusoe, was not only talking about a man who by accident becomes isolated, but is presenting an allegory about the life of all men in capitalist society – solitary, poor, uncertain, afraid. The isolation is more intense in Robinson's mind than in his actual situation. For what comes out clearly, in encounter after encounter, is that whenever Robinson has to face another person he reacts with fear and suspicion. His isolation, in short, is no more nor less than the alienation of possessive individualism, repeated a million times in capitalist society, and in our days symbolized by the private civil-defense shelter protected from neighbors by a machine gun.

III. Opening up of trade: forming an imperial strategy

The opening of his economy to the outside world does not come to Robinson Crusoe in the form of abstract prices generated in anonymous markets but in the form of real people with whom he must come to terms. After fifteen years on the island, he comes upon the print of a naked man's foot on the shore. His first reaction is fear. He was "terrified to the last degree, looking behind me at every two or three steps, mistaking every bush and tree, and fancying every stump at a distance to be a man." He goes to his retreat. "Never frightened hare fled to cover, or fox to earth, with more terror of mind, than I." From then on he lived "in the constant snare of the fear of man . . . a life of anxiety, fear and care."

He thinks of destroying his cattle enclosure, cornfield, and dwelling, "that they might not find such a grain there . . . and still be prompted to look further, in order to find out the persons inhabiting." He builds a second wall of fortifications, armed with seven muskets planted like a cannon and fitted "into frames that held them like a carriage, so that I could fire all the seven guns in two minutes' time. This wall I was many a weary month a-finishing and yet never thought myself safe till it was done." He pierces all the ground outside his wall with stakes or sticks so that in five or six years' time he had "a wood before my dwelling growing so monstrous thick and strong that it was indeed perfectly impassable; and no men of what kind soever would ever imagine that there was anything beyond it."

Three years after he sees the footprint, he comes across bones and other remains of cannibalism. (We leave aside the historical question of whether or not cannibalism was practiced by the Caribbeans. It is enough that Robinson thought so. European readiness to believe other people were cannibals, regardless of fact, plays the same role in determining trade patterns as the inter-European solidarity exhibited, for example, between the Portuguese captain and Robinson.) He withdrew further and "kept close within my circle for almost two years."

Gradually fear wears off, and he begins to come out more. But he proceeds cautiously. He does not fire his gun, for fear it would be heard, and he is always armed with a gun, two pistols, and a cutlass. At times he even thinks of attack, and builds a place from which he can "destroy some of these monsters in their cruel bloody entertainment and, if possible, save the victim they should bring hither to destroy." But then he thinks, "These people had done me no injury . . . and therefore it could not be just for me to fall upon them." He chastises the Spaniards for their barbarities in America "where they destroyed millions of these people . . . a mere butchery, a bloody and unnatural piece of cruelty, unjustifiable either to God or man; as for which the very name of a Spaniard is reckoned to be frightful and terrible to all people of humanity or of Christian compassion." He decides it is "not my business to meddle with them unless they first attacked me."

During the next few years he keeps himself "more retired than ever," seldom going from his cell. Fear "put an end to all invention and to all the contrivances I had laid for my future accommodations." He was afraid to drive a nail, or chop a stick of wood, or fire a gun, or light a fire for fear it would be heard or seen. He wants "nothing so much as a safe retreat," and finds it in a hidden grotto. "I fancied myself now like one of the ancient giants which were said to live in caves and holes in the rocks, where none could come at them." Yet even in this deep isolation, it is only people that he feared. With some parrots, cats, kids, and tame seafowl as pets, "I began to be very well contented with the life I led, if it might but have been secured from the dread of the savages."

In his twenty-third year he finally sights some of the Caribbeans who periodically visit the island. He first retreats to his fortifications; but, no longer "able to bear sitting in ignorance," he sets himself up in a safe place from which to observe "nine naked savages sitting around a small fire." Thoughts of "contriving how to circumvent and fall upon them the very next time" come once more to his mind and soon he is dreaming "often of killing savages." His loneliness intensifies when one night he hears a shot fired from a distressed ship and next day finds a shipwreck. He longs for contact with Europeans. "O that there had been one or two, nay, or but one soul saved out of this ship, to have escaped to me, that I might have one companion, one fellow creature to have spoken to me and to have conversed with!"

His thoughts move from defense to offense. His moral misgivings about Spanish colonization recede into the background, and he begins to form an imperial strategy. The plan comes to him in a dream in which a captured savage escapes, runs to him, and becomes his servant. Awaking, "I made this conclusion, that my only way to go about an attempt for an escape was, if possible, to get a savage into my possession; and if possible it should be one of the prisoners." He has some fears about whether he can do this and some moral qualms about whether he should; but though "the thoughts of shedding human blood for my deliverance were terrible to me," he at length resolved "to get one of those savages into my hands, cost what it would."

About a year and a half later a group of about twenty or thirty Caribbeans come ashore. Luck is with him. One prisoner escapes, followed by only two men. "It came now very warmly upon my thoughts and indeed irresistibly, that now was my time to get me a servant, and perhaps a companion or assistant."

Robinson knocks down one of the pursuers and shoots a second. The rescued prisoner, cautious and afraid, approaches. "He came nearer and nearer, kneeling down every ten or twelve steps . . . At length he came close to me, and then he kneeled down again, kissed the ground, and laid his head upon the ground, and taking me by the foot, set my foot upon his head; this, it seems, was in token of swearing to be my slave forever." Robinson has his servant. An economy is born.

IV. Colonization

Friday, tired from his ordeal, sleeps. Robinson evaluates his prize. The relationship they are about to enter into is an unequal and violent one. ("Violence," writes R. D. Laing, "attempts to constrain the other's freedom, to force him to act in the way we desire, but with ultimate lack of concern, with indifference to the other's own existence or destiny."[6]) It requires an ideological superstructure to sustain it and make it tolerable. Friday is an independent person with his own mind and will. But Robinson's rule depends upon the extent to which his head controls Friday's hand. To help himself in his daily struggle with Friday, Robinson begins to think of Friday not as a person but as a sort of pet, a mindless body that is obedient and beautiful. ("The use made of slaves and of tame animals is not very different; for both with their bodies minister to the needs of life." Aristotle, *The Politics*.[7]) The following is a verbatim quote of his description of Friday, except for the substitution of "she" for "he," "her" for "him." This is not done to suggest homosexuality but to emphasize how rulers conceive of the ruled only as bodies to minister to their needs. (To quote Aristotle again, "the male is by nature superior, and the female inferior; and the one rules, and the other is ruled."[8])

She was a comely, handsome woman, perfectly well made, with straight strong limbs, not too large, tall and well-shaped, and, as I reckon, about twenty-six years of age. She had a very good countenance, not a fierce and surly aspect, but seemed to have something very manly in her face and yet she had all the sweetness and softness of a European in her countenance too, especially when she smiled. Her hair was long and black, not curled like wool; her forehead very high and large; and a great vivacity and sparkling sharpness in her eyes. The color of her skin was not quite black, but very tawny; and yet not of an ugly yellow, nauseous tawny, as the Brazilians and Virginians, and other natives of America are; but of a bright kind of a dun olive color that had in it something very agreeable, though not very easy to describe. Her face was round and plump; her nose small, not flat like the Negroes', a very good mouth, thin lips, and her fine teeth well set, and white as ivory.

Robinson has a gun, but he cannot rule for force alone if he wants Friday to be productive. He must socialize his servant to accept his subordinate position. Robinson is at a great advantage for he has saved the man's life, but a careful program is still necessary, going through several stages of development, before the servant internalizes the authoritarian relationship and is able to act "independently" in a "dependent" fashion. The parallels between Robinson's education of Friday and the actual procedures of colonization used in the last two hundred years are striking.

Step 1. The first thing Robinson does is set the stage for discourse by giving himself and Friday names that are humiliating to Friday and symbolic of his indebtedness. "First I made him know his name should be Friday, which was the day I saved his life; I called him so for the memory of the time; I likewise taught him to say Master, and then let him know that was to be my name."

Step 2. Robinson further establishes relative status by covering Friday's nakedness with a pair of linen drawers (taken from the shipwreck) and a jerkin of goat's skin and a cap of hareskin he had made himself. He "was mighty well pleased to see himself almost as well clothed as his master."

Step 3. Robinson gives Friday a place to sleep between the two fortifications, i.e., a middle position, partly protected but outside the master's preserves. He sets up a burglar alarm so that "Friday could in no way come at me in the inside of my innermost wall without making so much noise in getting over that it must needs waken me," and takes other precautions such as taking all weapons into his side every night. Yet as Robinson says, these precautions were not really needed, "for never man had a more faithful, loving, sincere servant than Friday was to me; without passions, sullenness, or designs, perfectly obliged and engaged; his very affections were tied to me like those of a child to a father; and I dare say he would have sacrificed his life for the saving of mine upon any occasion whatsoever." The allocation of space helps remind Friday of his position and keeps him subordinate.

Step 4. Friday is then given the skills necessary for his station and his duties, i.e., the ability to understand orders and satisfy Robinson's needs. "I . . . made it my business to teach him everything that was proper to make him useful, handy, and helpful; but especially to make him speak and understand me when I spoke."

Step 5. Next comes a crucial moment in which Robinson, through a cruel show of force, terrifies poor Friday into complete submission. Robinson takes Friday out and shoots a kid with his gun. (He is no longer afraid of being heard.)

> The poor creature, who had at a distance indeed seen me kill the savage, his enemy, but did not know or could imagine how it was done, was sensibly surprised. . . He did not see the kid I had shot at or perceive I had killed it, but ripped up his waistcoat to feel if he was not wounded, and as I found presently, thought I was resolved to kill him, for he came and kneeled down to me, and, embracing my knees, said a great many things I did not understand; but I could easily see the meaning was to pray me not to kill him.

In this ritual death and rebirth, Friday learns the full extent of Robinson's power over him. Robinson then kills various animals, and teaches Friday "to run and fetch them" like a dog. But he takes care that Friday never sees him load the gun, so that he remains ignorant of the fact that you have to put in ammunition.

Step 6. The first stage of initiation is completed; Robinson can move on to establishing the social division of labor on a more subtle base. He teaches Friday to cook and bake, and "in a little time Friday was able to do all the work for me, as well as I could do it for myself." Then Robinson marks out a piece of land "in which Friday not only worked very willingly and very hard, but did it cheerfully." Robinson explains that it was for corn to make more bread since there were now two of them. Friday, by himself, discovers the laws of property and capitalist distribution of income in fully mystified form. "He appeared very sensible of that part, and let me know that he thought I had much more labor upon me on his account than I had for myself, and that he would work the harder for me, if I would tell him what to do."

Step 7: Graduation. Robinson now instructs Friday in the knowledge of the true God. This takes three years, during which Friday raises such difficult questions that Robinson for a time withdraws, realizing that one cannot win by logical argument alone, and only divine revelation can convince people of Christianity. Finally, success. "The savage was now a good Christian." The two become more intimate, Robinson tells Friday his story, and at long last "let him into the mystery, for such it was to him, of gunpowder and bullet and taught him how to shoot." Robinson gives Friday a knife and a hatchet and shows him the boat he was planning to use to escape.

Step 8: Eternal policeman. Even after granting independence, Robinson cannot trust Friday. The master can never rest secure. One day, while watching the mainland from the top of a hill on the island, Robinson observes

an extraordinary sense of pleasure appeared on Friday's face ... and a strange eagerness, as if he had a mind to be in his own country again; and this observation of mine put a great many thoughts into me, which made me at first not so easy about my new man Friday as I was before; and I made no doubt but that if Friday could get back to his own nation again, he would not only forget all his religion, but all his obligation to me; and would be forward enough to give his countrymen an account of me, and come back, perhaps with a hundred or two of them, and make a feast upon me, at which he might be as merry as he used to be with those enemies, when they were taken in war.

Robinson continuously pumps Friday to see if he could uncover any cracks; then he feels guilty over his suspicion. Imperialism knows no peace.

V. Partnership and expanded reproduction

For roughly ten years, between the time he first saw the print of a foot in the sand until he met Friday, Robinson Crusoe led a life of fear, anxiety, and care during which time his productive activities were reduced to a minimum and he scarcely dared to venture outside the narrow confines of his strongholds. When Friday comes, he becomes expansive again, teaching, building, accumulating. Though no mention is made of accounting, one can deduce that labor again became valuable, for Robinson is once more purposeful, and interested in allocation and efficiency, as he orders, causes, gives Friday to do one thing or another, instructs him, shows him, gives him directions, makes things familiar to him, makes him understand, teaches him, lets him see, calls him, heartens him, beckons him to run and fetch, sets him to work, makes him build something, etc., etc. Through his social relation with Friday, he becomes an economic man. Friday becomes labor and he becomes capital – innovating, organizing, and building an empire.

About three years after Friday arrives, Robinson's twenty-seventh year on the island, an opportunity for enlargement comes. Twenty-one savages and three prisoners come ashore. Robinson divides the arms with Friday and they set out to attack. On the way, Robinson again has doubts as to whether it was right "to go and dip my hands in blood, to attack people who had neither done or intended me any wrong." "Friday," he observes, "might justify it, because he was a declared enemy, and in a state of war with those very particular people; and it was lawful for him to attack them," but, as he could not say the same for himself, he resolves unilaterally for both of them not to act unless "something offered that was more a call to me than yet I knew of."

The call comes when he discovers one of the victims is a white man and he becomes "enraged to the highest degree." As it turns out, the prisoner is a Spaniard; given what Robinson had previously said about Spanish colonial policy, one might have thought he would have some doubts about what was lawful. But he does not, and along with Friday, attacks – killing seventeen and routing four. (Friday does most of the killing, in part because he "took his aim so much better" than Robinson, in part because Robinson was directing and Friday doing.) The Spaniard is rescued and they find another victim in a boat who turns out to be Friday's father, his life luckily saved because his fellow captive was white.

Now they were four. Robinson has an empire which he rules firmly and justly with a certain degree of permissiveness and tolerance.

My island was now peopled, and I thought myself very rich in subjects; and it was a merry reflection, which I frequently made, how like a king I looked. First of all, the whole country was my own property, so that I had an undoubted right of dominion. Secondly, my people were perfectly subjected. I was absolute lord and lawgiver; they all owed their lives to me, and were ready to lay down their lives, if there had been occasion of it for me. It was remarkable, too, we had but three subjects, and they were of three different religions. My man Friday was a Protestant, his father was a pagan and a cannibal, and the Spaniard was a Papist. However I allowed liberty of conscience through my dominions.

The period of primitive accumulation is over. Robinson now has property. It is not based on his previous labor, but on his fortunate possession of arms. Though his capital comes into the world dripping blood from every pore, his ownership is undisputed. Friday was not a lazy rascal spending his subsistence and more in riotous living, yet in the end he still has nothing but himself, while the wealth of Robinson Crusoe increases constantly although he has long ceased to work.

With time, more people arrive on his island. Robinson shrewdly uses his monopoly of the means of production to make them submit to his rule. As the empire grows, its problems become more complex. But Robinson is ever resourceful in using terror, religion, frontier law, and the principle of delegated authority to consolidate his position and produce a self-reproducing order.

Robinson learns that there are fourteen more Spaniards and Portuguese staying with the Caribbeans, "who lived there at peace indeed with the savages." They had arms but no powder and no hope of escape, for they had "neither vessel, or tools to build one, or provisions of any." Robinson of course has the missing ingredients for their rescue, but how can he be sure he will be paid back? "I feared mostly their treachery and ill usage of me, if I put my life in their hands, for that gratitude was no inherent virtue in the nature of man; nor did men always square their dealings by the obligations they had received so much as they did by the advantages they expected."

Robinson cannot depend on the law to guard his property. Instead he uses religion. Europeans do not require so elaborate a socialization procedure as Friday because they have come by education, tradition, and habit to look upon private property as a self-evident law of nature. The Spaniard and Friday's father are to go to where the other Europeans are staying. They would then sign a contract, "that they should be absolutely under my leading, as their commander and captain; and that they should swear upon the Holy Sacraments and the Gospel to be true to me and to go to such Christian country as that I should agree to, and no other; and to be directed wholly and absolutely by my orders." Robinson converts their debt to him into an obligation towards God. Thus men are ruled by the products of their mind.

The trip is postponed for a year, while Robinson's capital stock is expanded so that there will be enough food for the new recruits. The work process is now more complicated because of the increase in numbers. A vertical structure separating operations, coordination, and strategy is established on the basis of nationality – a sort of multinational corporation in miniature. "I marked out several trees which I thought fit for our work, and I set Friday and his father to cutting them down; and then I caused the Spaniard, to whom I had imparted my thought on that affair, to oversee and direct their work."

When the harvest is in, the Spaniard and Friday's father are sent out to negotiate. While they are away, an English ship arrives at the island. Robinson is filled with indescribable joy at seeing a ship "manned by [his] own countrymen, and consequently friends." Yet at the same time, "some secret doubts hung about [him]," for perhaps they were thieves and murderers. This we have seen is a typical reaction of Robinson Crusoe to other people; it is a prudent attribute in a society of possessive individuals where all are the enemy of each. *Caveat Emptor.*

Some of the crew come ashore with three prisoners. When the prisoners are left unguarded, Robinson approaches them: "I am a man, an Englishman, and disposed to assist you, you see; I have one servant only; we have arms and ammunition, tell us freely, can we serve you?" The three prisoners turn out to be the captain of the ship, his mate, and one passenger. The others are mutineers, of whom the captain says. "There were two desperate villains among them that it was scarce safe to show any mercy to"; but if they were secured, he believed "all the rest would return to their duty."

The charges being laid, a quick decision and verdict is reached. Robinson sides with authority. The captain offers a generous contract to Robinson:

"Both he and the ship, if recovered, should be wholly directed and commanded by me in everything; and if the ship was not recovered, he would live and die with me in what part of the world soever I would send him; and the other two men the same." Robinson asks for much less: recognition of his undisputed authority while they are on the island, free passage to England for himself and Friday if the ship is recovered.

The men who brought the captain ashore are attacked, The two villains are summarily executed in the first round, the rest are made prisoners or allowed to join the captain and Robinson. More men are sent to shore from the ship, and are soon captured. One is made prisoner, the others are told Robinson is governor of the island and that he would engage for their pardon if they helped capture the ship. The ship is seized with only one life lost, that of the new captain. Robinson, still posing as governor, interviews the five prisoners and hearing the "full account of their villainous behavior to the captain, and how they had run away with the ship and were preparing to commit further robberies," offers them the choice of being left on the island or being taken to England in chains to be hanged. They choose the island and Robinson is so much the richer. Law makes criminals and criminals make settlers. In a repeat of his lesson to the birds, Robinson orders the captain "to cause the new captain who was killed to be hanged at the yardarm, that these men might see him."

On the 19th of December, 1686, twenty-eight years and two months after his arrival, Robinson goes on aboard the ship, taking with him his great goatskin cap, his umbrella, one of his parrots, and the money he had taken off the ship. He also takes Friday but does not wait for the return of Friday's father and the Spaniards. Instead he leaves a letter for them with the prisoners being left behind, after making them "promise to treat them in common with themselves."

He returns to civilization and discovers capital's power for self-sustaining growth. His trustees

had given in the account of the produce of my part of the plantation to the procurator fiscal, who had appropriated it, in case I never came to claim it, one third to the king, and two thirds to the monastery of St. Augustine, to be expended for the benefit of the poor and for the conversion of Indians to the Catholic faith; but for that if I appeared, or anyone for me, to claim the inheritance, it should be restored: only that the improvements, or annual production being distributed to charitable uses, could not be restored.

He was thus a rich man, "master all on a sudden of about £5,000 sterling in money, and had an estate, as I might well call it, in Brazil, of about a thousand pounds a year, as sure as an estate of lands in England."

He also had his island, to which he returns in 1694. He learns how the Spaniards had trouble with the villians when they first returned but eventually subjected them, of their battles with the Caribbeans, "of the improvement they made upon the island itself and of how five of them made an attempt upon the mainland, and brought away eleven men and five women prisoners, by which, at my coming, I found about twenty young children on the island." Robinson brings them supplies, a carpenter, and a smith and later sent seven women "such as I found proper for service or for wives to such as would take them."

Before he leaves the island, he reorganizes it on a sound basis. Dividing it into parts, he reserves to himself the property of the whole, and gives others such parts respectively as they agreed upon. As to the Englishmen, he promised to send them some women from England, "and the fellows proved very honest and diligent after they were mastered and had their properties set apart for them." With property and the family firmly established, the ground is clear for steady growth.

VI. Moral

We may stop at this point and consider the very high rate of return earned by Robinson on his original capital of £40. He cannot be said to have worked very hard for his money, but he was certainly a great organizer and entrepreneur, showing extraordinary capacity to take advantage of situations and manage other people. He suffered the pains of solitude and the vices of greed, distrust, and ruthlessness, but he ends up with "wealth all around me" and Friday – "ever proving a most faithful servant upon all occasions."

The allegory of Robinson Crusoe gives us better economic history and better economic theory than many of the tales told by modern economics about the national and international division of labor. Economics tends to stay in the market place and worry about prices. It has more to say about how Robinson's sugar relates to his clothing than how he relates to Friday. To understand how capital produces and is produced, we must leave the noisy sphere of the market where everything takes place on the surface and enter into the hidden recesses of the factory and corporation, where there is usually no admittance except on business.

Defoe's capitalist is transported to a desert island outside the market system, and his relations to other people are direct and visible. Their secret of capital is revealed, namely, that it is based on other people's labor and is obtained through force and illusion. The birth certificate of Robinson's capital is not as bloody as that of many other fortunes, but its coercive nature is clear.

The international economy of Robinson's time, like that of today, is not composed of equal partners but is ordered along class lines. Robinson occupies one of the upper-middle levels of the pyramid. (The highest levels are in the capitals of Europe.) Captains, merchants, and planters are his peer group. With them he exchanges on the basis of fraternal collaboration. (Arab captains excepted.) They teach him, rescue him, do business for him, and keep him from falling beneath his class. He in turn generally regards them as honest and plain-dealing men, sides with them against their rebellious subordinates, and is easy with them in his bargaining. Towards whites of lower rank he is more demanding. If they disobey, he is severe; but if they are loyal, he is willing to share some booty and delegate some authority. Africans and Caribbeans are sold, killed, trained, or used as wives by his men, as the case may be. About the white indentured servants, artisans, etc., little is said by Defoe in this story.

The contradictions between Robinson and other members of the hierarchy give the story its dynamics. He is forever wrestling with the problem of subordinating lower levels and trying to rise above his own. The fact that he does not see it this way but prefers to make up stories about himself makes no difference. He denies the conflict between himself and Friday by accepting Friday's mask of willing obedience. And he conceives of his greed as a crime against God instead of against man. But his daily life shows that his social relations are antagonistic and that he knows it.

In the last analysis, however, the story is only partly dialectical. We hear only of how Robinson perceives the contradictions and how he resolves them. In this work of fiction he is always able to fuse two into one. In actual life one divides into two, and the system develops beyond the capitalist's fantasy of proper law and order. Economic science also needs the story of Friday's grandchildren.

5   International trade and uneven development

co-authored with Stephen A. Resnick

Our goal in this paper is to analyze the historic origins of underdevelopment using a framework that includes political as well as economic factors. Our purpose is to explain why the growth of the international economy over the course of the last few centuries has failed to equalize factor prices but instead has created a dualism between the developed and underdeveloped areas of the world.

Among other things, we want to show the frail base upon which rest so many of the orthodox economists' policy recommendations for development. Since international trade theory tells only a portion of the story of the gains and losses from trade, it is seriously misleading when used by itself in empirical analysis and policy prescription. As the following simple econometric model of supply response demonstrates, the cost of ignoring political factors is an inability to identify economic relations and, therefore, an inability to make policy recommendations.

Equation 1 describes the usual economic supply function. Equation 2 is a political equation relating government policy to world price.

$$x_t = a_1 + b_1 P_t (1 - t_t) + u_{1t} \tag{1}$$

$$t_t = a_2 + b_2 P_t + u_{2t} \tag{2}$$

where: x_t is exports in real terms, P_t is the world price, t_t is the net tax rate, i.e., taxes less subsidies including expenditures on infrastructure, and u_{it} is the error of the ith equation.

Solving these equations yields the reduced form,

$$x_t = a_1 + b_1(1 - a_2)P_t - b_1 b_2 P_t^2 - b_1 P_t u_{2t} + u_{1t}$$

$$= a_1 + B_1 P_t + B_2 P_t^2 + u_t \tag{3}$$

This essay originally appeared in *Trade, Balance of Payments and Growth,* J. W. Bhagwati, R. W. Jones, R. A. Mundell, and J. Vanek, eds. (Amsterdam: North-Holland, 1970), pp. 473–94. Copyright © 1970 by North-Holland Publishing Company. Reprinted by permission of North-Holland Publishing Company.

The first problem encountered in any attempt to evaluate the parameters of supply response in this model is the difficulty of obtaining data on t. One can sometimes measure tariffs and taxes accurately, but it is almost never possible to estimate other government instruments, e.g., the value of subsidies contained in the wide variety of services offered by the government to the private sector at reduced prices. Where t cannot be measured, one cannot estimate the structural equations of the model but must confine the analysis to the reduced form. This is not adequate for policy. To formulate policy (i.e., to decide how best to alter the decision rule implied by Equation 2), a government must know the value of b_1 and cannot rely merely on the reduced form estimates B_1 and B_2 so long as b_2 is not small.

Thus the question of whether "power" relationships should be included in economic models is an empirical one and not a matter of convenience or of specialization between economists and political scientists. Since economists usually ignore political factors, structural estimates are not available and policy is often severely hampered. Empirical work on input/output tables provides an important example of information based only on reduced form estimates. The coefficients of these tables, so frequently used by planners, are derived from the actual flows in a given year and do not reflect technological linkages alone, as they purport to, but also the tastes, interests, and limitations of the previous governments' decision rules. Thus there are good econometric reasons for a government interested in overcoming underdevelopment, i.e., changing policy and structure, to be wary of them.

This model also points to another important problem for policy making even where accurate estimates of t are available. Suppose that a previous government had been characterized by a decision rule which attempted to stabilize price to producers by varying t inversely to P (e.g., through a marketing board). This would reduce the observed variance of $P(1-t)$ and increase the difficulty of estimating the coefficients of Equation 1 thus making it difficult to use past experience as a basis for future policy. More generally, when a government attempts to change (i.e., develop) the structure of an economy, it often finds the data generated by the previous structure (i.e., the historical facts) to be unhelpful as a basis for policy. Revolution, by definition, implies values of a and b outside the historical sample, and only under very special conditions would the statistical estimates of those coefficients apply to nonmarginal changes. Ideology supplies the strength to ignore the facts. One of the important purposes of historical analysis is to show how power relations in the past constrained the full development of the productive potential of the economy.

This essay is divided into three parts corresponding to the three major stages of the international economy: *Mercantilism* (late 15th to 19th centuries), *Colonialism* (1870 to 1939), and *The Present*. For convenience we call these Mercantilism I, Mercantilism II, and Mercantilism III, respectively, since they represent successive stages of unequal trade and uneven development. The argument is conducted heuristically, but our hope is to proceed at a later point to theoretical and econometric models using sets of interdependent political and economic equations.

Mercantilism I: 15th century to 1870

The Mercantilist period created the first truly international economy. The oceans were transformed from a barrier separating Europe from Asia, America, and Africa, to a medium of exchange, and new dimensions for commercial intercourse were created. Ironically, the global integration that created *one world*, unified by mercantile and political relationships, also led to the fragmentation of its parts into a small set of developing countries and a large group of stunted and deformed economies which became the underdeveloped areas of the world. It is this historical process of uneven development that we will focus upon in the following analysis.

International trade theory[1] predicts that in a market system the fall in transport costs created by the age of exploration would lead to an increase in trade and improved welfare for the world as a whole as well as for each of its trading countries. Individuals and groups within a country may, of course, gain or lose depending on their ownership of the factors of production. In an egalitarian peasant economy, for example, all individuals will be better off, since they share equally in the resources of the country. In a more highly developed civilization such as existed in parts of Asia and South America, labor will lose and land will gain since imported manufactures will substitute for crafts and services while increased exports of primary products would raise the value of natural resources.

Our model yields different results, because it takes into account political as well as market relationships. Mercantilist trade changed the power structure within and between countries, and this radical break is of greater importance in explaining the patterns of trade and income distribution than is the market reaction to price focused upon in the orthodox model.

Figure 1 is a device to illustrate the employment structure of the traditional economy and the changes that occurred as a result of Mercantilism I trade. The diagram is based on an equation linking food production (and consumption) per capita $\bar{f}$ to: output per man hour in agriculture a, hours per man in agriculture h, and the proportion of persons engaged in agriculture n.

$$\bar{f} = ahn \tag{4}$$

For a given per capita food standard, Equation 4 traces out a rectangular hyperbola AA, describing possible distributions of the work force of a traditional society. It is assumed that a is unaffected by h and n.[2] At a point such as A_1 (which we shall argue represents one of the prevalent African

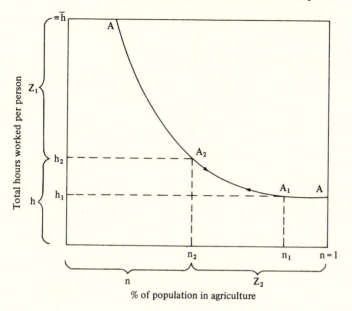

Figure 1.

modes of production) nearly the entire population is engaged in the agrarian sector (n approaches 1), but the hours worked per man in agriculture are low. At a point such as A_2 (Oriental despotism), a much larger fraction of the population is outside the agrarian sector, while those engaged in agriculture are more fully specialized and work substantially longer hours in farming in order to produce an agricultural surplus for the remainder of the population.

The distribution of time in nonagricultural activities can be illustrated in Figure 1 by dropping perpendiculars to each axis. The vertical distance between the total hours of labor per worker $\bar{h}$ and the actual hours worked in agriculture per worker h represents the time available in the agrarian sector for the production of household goods and services[3] [$Z_1 = (\bar{h} - h)n$ where Z_1 refers to hours per capita spent on rural household goods].

The horizontal distance between the total population ($n = 1$) and that fraction engaged in agriculture n represents the proportion engaged in what the physiocrats called the unproductive sector, i.e., the aristocrats, soldiers, servants, officers, clerks, traders, and artisans associated with the state sector. The size of this sector (per capita) is $Z_2 = \bar{h}(1 - n)$.

The African case was characterized by a small state sector, because its egalitarian political structure inhibited the appropriation of the surplus by a small group. Most families had full rights to land and paid little, if anything, in the way of rents or taxes either in kind or in labor services. The fraction Z_2

was, thus, very small (in many cases even the chief's family grew its own food), and while the portion of time spent on Z_1 was large, much of it was devoted to leisure and ceremony.[4]

An opposite pattern is found in the Asian case. Because of the great power of the state to extract a surplus, Z_2 is large and Z_1 is small. A large number of people are engaged in extracting the surplus from agricultural workers, managing the affairs of the bureaucracy, and providing consumption goods and services for the state. In order to meet their taxes, the agricultural population must reduce their consumption of Z_1 and devote their time to producing an agricultural surplus. In addition, the requirements of corvée further reduce the time available for household production.

In Figure 1, as we have drawn it, the standard of life for the majority of the population is clearly superior in the African case. Food consumption per capita is the same in both cases by assumption, while Z_1 is much greater in Africa than in Asia. This result depends crucially on the assumption that AA is a rectangular hyperbola. In reality, there are several reasons for believing that agricultural labor productivity associated with the Asian mode differs from that found in Africa. The advanced civilization associated with Oriental despotism was based on a hydraulic society which implied investment of resources in irrigation and other infrastructure to increase agricultural output. If a was sufficiently higher as a result of this investment, it would be possible then for h (hours per worker in agriculture) to be the same in both cases even though the Asian mode had a larger Z_2. This would have happened if the state in practice charged a tithe exactly equal to its social productivity so that the agricultural population did not suffer because of its existence. There is no historical reason to believe this was the case. Studies of Oriental despotism suggest that the state attempted to maximize the surplus and to reduce income in the agricultural sector to the minimum necessary for survival, and sometimes not even that.[5] Moreover, some of the government infrastructure was needed merely to compensate for diminishing returns resulting from the use of a higher labor/land ratio.[6]

The revolutionary impact of the new trading possibilities introduced by Mercantilism I led to the growth of the state in certain African economies and to a movement towards the Asian mode; while in certain Asian economies, it led to a decline in state power and a movement away from their original position. This movement is shown by the arrows in Figure 1. In both cases, there is a dramatic change in the composition of output and its distribution even though national income did not necessarily increase and in some cases fell.

In the African case, the new opportunities for foreign trade provided both an incentive and the means for the growth of a state sector. Economic factors were not the sole cause of state formation but were an important contributing factor. A military group that succeeded in monopolizing coercive power in a given area could establish peace and security for traders and levy taxes accordingly. The state, in a word, substituted tolls and tariffs for banditry. The larger the area brought under control, the greater the taxes that could be charged, and the more powerful a military and bureaucratic establishment that could be supported. The strength of the state could also be used to capture slaves, to organize slave production of exportables (in gold mining for example), or to meet food requirements. It was thus possible to expropriate a surplus through exploitation of labor as well as through taxation of trade.

The impact of Mercantilism I on income in Africa and its distribution was very complex. The local elites benefited, as did both the plantation owners in the new world and the merchants who organized the elaborate mercantile system based on the slave trade. To the extent that it participated in the upsurge of economic activity on a voluntary basis, a certain portion of the population at large also benefited by trading food or manufactures for imported goods. Nonetheless, gains were in no way commensurate with the enormous deadweight loss associated with the capture of slaves and their exploitation in plantations. As regards Africa, therefore, the production possibilities of society shifted inward as a result of those losses from trade. Among those who remained, there was a reallocation of labor into Z_2 owing to the growth of the state (it is assumed that Z_2 includes plantation production) and out of Z_1 as free men substituted imported goods for domestic manufactures. The distribution of employment resembled more closely that of the Asian society, but the distribution of income among the living was quite different. The standard of life of slaves was repressed below the preceding levels; but the standard of life of free men was increased, because their marketed surplus was compensated by imported goods rather than simply taken away through taxes.

In the Asian case, the coming of the West led to the undermining of the power structure in countries or regions characterized by the Asiatic mode of production. The steady penetration of Western traders from the 16th century onward eroded the political and economic relationships based on Oriental despotism. In terms of Figure 1, there was a decline in Z_2 and an increase in Z_1 as labor was freed from activities serving the state. Thus the Asian mode moved somewhat in the direction of the African as the influence of the state declined and that of the West increased. The impact of Mercantilism I trade thus at first led to an improvement in welfare as the decline of Z_2 and rise in Z_1 distributed income in favor of the long exploited peasant. The decline of Oriental depotism with its unproductive class of retainers and its demands for corvée labor meant that the wage–rental ratio for the society as a whole rose contrary to the predictions of the classical model.

In some areas a new Z_2 arose in connection with the expansion of commercial activity as new trading routes to the West replaced the historical trade among China, India, and Southeast Asia. The flourishing of this trade, during the 17th and especially the 18th centuries, led to the growth of Western controlled coastal regions and port areas and the demand for a food surplus to service traders, soldiers, and consuls. In these areas, Z_2 (the new sector specializing in commercial activity) rose while Z_1 declined, replaced by imported manufactures, as the hinterland specialized in food or export production.

Through time, the West pushed steadily inward and established a new system of political control. The tendency to improve welfare increasingly came under pressure as the West increased its ability to control the indigenous work force, to enforce tribute, and to levy taxes. As the West's ability to extract a surplus grew, the share of the gains from trade going to the vast majority of the population declined, and only a small class of foreign traders and rulers or, in some regions, local elites benefited substantially. The peasant, freed from Oriental despotism, found himself increasingly bound to a new master, and there was once again a tendency for Z_2 (including plantation labor) to rise and for Z_1 to fall.

The Western impact in Latin America (Mexico and Peru) was different in that the existing political structure was quickly taken over and the population exploited at a maximal rate. So ruthless was the appropriation of the surplus in gold and silver mining that a large percentage of the population soon died. The complex pattern of Western rule and colonization that existed in Asia was, therefore, not duplicated in Latin America. There was a total collapse of society and enormous losses from trade.

Our models of trade in Mercantilism I have emphasized shifts in the power structures rather than movements along the production possibilities curve and have yielded quite different predictions about changes in production, employment, and distribution of income than those of international trade theory. Our analysis can be summarized in the following simple balance equation of the gains and losses from trade (providing one is willing to accept, for the sake of argument, the measurability of changes in welfare):

$$\begin{array}{l} \text{Gains to elite} \\ \text{in Europe} \end{array} + \begin{array}{l} \text{Gains (or losses) to} \\ \text{majority in Europe} \end{array} =$$

$$\begin{array}{l} \text{Gains from} \\ \text{trade} \end{array} - \begin{array}{l} \text{Gains to elite} \\ \text{in underdeveloped} \\ \text{countries} \end{array} + \begin{array}{l} \text{Losses of} \\ \text{exploited} \end{array} - \begin{array}{l} \text{Deadweight} \\ \text{loss} \end{array}$$

The crucial feature of Mercantilism I is that the overall gains from trade were small and the deadweight loss was large. It is hard to imagine any reasonable set of calculations that would show that the value of the increase in world income during the 16th, 17th, and 18th centuries could offset the tremendous costs associated with the murder and enslavement of Africans and Americans. This is true even if one were to argue that there was a net gain in welfare for those Asian countries in which the population was freed from Oriental despotism.[7] Many of the gains accruing to the elites in the underdeveloped world and Europe (and possibly to workers in Europe) arose mainly from the shifts in power and increased exploitation rather than from increased productivity. This slash and burn capitalism was possible only because Mercantilism I was able to use the human capital accumulated over previous centuries and did not worry about maintaining its reproduction.

If Mercantilism I caused an inward shift in the production possibilities curve in parts of Africa and America, it also caused an outward shift in Europe. Again, changes in the distribution of income and power were the crucial factors. It is not necessary to postulate that Europe as a whole (or even England as a whole) gained from Mercantilism I to explain the phenomenal rise in savings, investment, and income in the 19th century. The important feature is that some groups benefited and that a new class was formed out of the gains from trade. In other words, in place of the usual neoclassical formulation for investment ($I = sY$) we would substitute the equation ($I' = s'Y_c$) where I' refers only to investment in industry, Y_c refers to the income of the capitalist class, and s' refers to the capitalist savings rate. An increase in industrial capital could then occur even if Y fell, as long as Y_c/Y rose sufficiently. Empirically, it is difficult to estimate what happened to Y, but it is clear that Mercantilism I led to the growth of capitalist income and power in Europe.

The steps in this process are interesting. At first, the merchant capitalist class had little power and was subjected to discrimination by the feudalistic state. However, the new possibilities of maritime commerce and exploitation led to an alliance between the state and merchants (in some cases pirates). It was highly profitable for the monarch to subsidize international trade and offer it protection because of the profits to be gained. Thus the state and the emerging capitalist class grew in step, though much of the increased national power was dissipated in international rivalry. Eventually the capitalist class became sufficiently strong to take power and to switch government expenditure away from the agrarian sector, remove agrarian preferences and protection, and to increase agrarian taxes. This further enhanced the industrial capitalist class and led to its further growth. During the 19th century, industrial capital emerged triumphant, dismantled the corn law structure and the rest of the Mercantilist framework, and created a new technology based on iron and steam, and a new set of government policies (so called laissez-faire) with which it conquered the world and laid the basis for the second international economy. A total restructuring and reorganization of the hinterland occurred in Mercantilism II as Europe formulated a single strategic conception for the development of the world economy and planned a new division of labor. Many of the mainstays of Mercantilism I were cast away, like the first stage of a rocket, and new enclaves of growth were created. Mercantilism II began as an unequal partnership based on the asymmetrical results of Mercantilism I, and during the course of its lifetime, it further widened the gap between Europeans and non-Europeans.

Mercantilism II: 1870 to World War II

The period from 1870 to the 1920s was characterized by a fall in international transportation costs and an increase in the variety of manufactured goods available for trading. Trade theory predicts these events would cause the hinterlands of Africa, Asia, and America to expand export production and to replace the production of home goods by imported manufactures. The outward shift in the production possibilities curve would imply an increase in national income but not necessarily a corresponding improvement in welfare of every subgroup. The initial impact of this trade could, for example, lower wage rates and the standards of living of large parts of the populations as production of labor-intensive homes goods declined and the production of land-intensive export goods increased. Through time, however, the level of income would be expected to rise for everyone. Increased income would lead to increased savings and investment, and an outward shift in the production possibilities curve. A rise in wages would occur as the capital/labor ratio increased.

Broadly speaking, this scenario fits a large number of countries. It explains the great expansion of trade, the emergence of surplus labor, the strengthening of the landowning class, and the growth of mercantile capitalists. Furthermore, it also predicts the eventual investment in industry after the 1930s, the growth of the industrial labor force, and the emergence, in the late 1960s, of manufacturing exports. Even the attraction of foreign investment finds support in the predictive power of the theory because of the increased infrastructure and human capital financed by the export economy.

This scenario, however, should not be used in trade classes to illustrate the benefits of greater integration into the world economy, because it omits "power" equations and incorrectly identifies the structure of the system. Because so many underdeveloped countries with such diverse backgrounds followed the pattern outlined here indicates common biases in government policy rather than the power of the trade model. Neoclassical theory would predict a much greater variety of growth patterns given the great diversity of initial conditions and is to some extent falsified by this common experience. We suggest that the expansion of exports reflected in large part the similar policies of colonial rule, while the growth of manufacturing reflected the growing strength of the indigenous capitalist class associated with the "national independence" movements after World War II.

Colonial strategy squeezed the traditional economy to create an elastic supply of labor and biased infrastructure toward exports in order to transfer the surplus to the center in the form of lower prices. The specific labor policies used conformed to no single pattern, rather a variety of devices emerged to deal with the variety of initial conditions. In some cases the government levied labor taxes or poll taxes to stimulate an exodus from the "traditional" economy into the "commercial" economy. In other cases, the government seized the land or created a landlord class thus reducing the opportunity cost of wage labor. The fostering of a proletariat for the export sector (including the food surplus to feed it) was also stimulated through land concentration, intensification of tenure arrangements, and the growth of indebtedness. National and international mobility was encouraged as the government helped in recruitment and enforcement of contracts thus making possible vast transferences of population within continents as well as from Asia to Africa and America. In this way, labor and exports were generated in each colony.

The gains from trade generated during Mercantilism II were shared unevenly. Initially, there was a decline (sometimes drastic) in the standard of living for many people as they were coerced into export production. Through time, this decline tended to be reversed as new opportunities were made available in the commercial economy. Increased specialization led to new divisions of labor and created new dependencies as resources were reallocated from the traditional economy to export production and the personalized society of the village was fragmented. The striking feature of Mercantilism II, however, is that the standard of living for the vast majority of the population of Africa, Asia, and America rose very slowly in sharp contrast to the progress at the center.

Although exact statistics are not available, evidence suggests that the real wage for unskilled labor has risen slowly over the last 50 to 100 years, and this wage can be taken as a proxy for the level of income of perhaps two-thirds of the population. Moreover, other evidence suggests that debt peonage and tenure arrangements increased in the agrarian sector as peasants found themselves increasingly bound to money lenders and absentee landowners. No doubt there was some improvement in consumption patterns as superior European manufactures increasingly replaced native rural industry. However, the displacement of rural industry and traditional activities also led to the fragmentation of the agrarian society, and in many countries, especially those in which export specialization proceeded most rapidly, there was a serious deterioration of the social life of the society.[8]

The gains from trade were partly captured by local elites (some of whom were foreigners from the mother country) who accumulated land, capital, education, or the rights to higher paying employment in the government bureaucracy or in the commercial economy. Often an alien complex of production was established where the peasant cultivated the soil or worked in the mines, a foreign mercantile class grew in strength (in Asia, Chinese, and in Africa, Indian), and the Europeans controlled the import–export trade as well as determined colonial expenditure and labor policies. The distribution of income reflected the political power of this economic structure. Much of the gains from export growth went to the government (in the form of increased revenues), to the urban centers (where services and industry grew based on export growth), and to local and foreign elites of one type or another.

In part, the gains were passed abroad in the form of lower prices. The division between the metropole and the local elite depended largely on the propensities to import. If surplus receivers had a much higher propensity to import than the population as a whole, the "cheap labor" policies followed would be export biased to the benefit of the mother country. On the other hand, if local elites spent a high proportion of their income on local services, they would divert labor from export production. This would still involve an international transfer of surplus, since a high proportion of this elite income went to foreign settlers and colonial officials from the mother country. The surplus would, however, tend to be consumed locally rather than in the center.

This possible antitrade bias was offset, at least in the initial phase of colonialism, by a number of other policies designed to specifically encourage exports. Many labor policies directed labor towards particular industries, e.g., mining, whose only function was production for exports. Similarly, infrastructure was heavily biased towards export production and neglected the production of home goods or placed it at a disadvantage. In other words, the steps taken to produce cheap labor were combined with steps taken to induce it to flow into exports.

The observed high elasticity of exports in this period thus reflects government policy as well as market response. A high export price resulting from an expansion of demand would induce an increase in private investment because of high profits. It would also provide the government with extra revenue (since trade taxes were the dominant source of funds) and thus lead to the improvement of infrastructure and other support services which would further stimulate international supply because of their export bias. Thus a strong tendency towards immiserizing growth was built into the system, for any rise in price would trigger an expansion of export biased investment until price fell sufficiently.

An alternative development strategy would have allocated a greater share of public investment to home good industries and produced a more balanced investment program. This would have a substitution and an income effect. The substitution effect of removing the export bias in infrastructure might bias production away from exports, but this might be offset by the income effect from growth if importables were highly income elastic. Moreover, the development of the hinterland would have increased the variety of possible exports and provided new opportunities for mutually beneficial trade.

A more forward looking policy would have directed a large flow of funds from the center to the periphery for investment purposes. The dominant feature of Mercantilism II was the global capital market centered in London. For the first time in history, investment decisions throughout the world were coordinated in one place and subjected to a single strategic conception. It thus became technically possible to spread capital evenly throughout the world. In other words, capital accumulation after 1870 could have proceeded via capital widening rather than capital deepening, i.e., the capital/labor ratio could have remained constant and a far larger number of people activated as industrial workers. This would soon have exhausted the metropolitan labor force and either capital would have had to move to the hinterland or labor move to the center. This, combined with efficient trade, would have produced factor price equalization on a global basis. In other words, had this strategy been followed, industrial capitalism would have reproduced for the entire world population the higher level of living it achieved for Europeans. (The term Europeans is used to include people of European descent in all continents.)

The whole pattern of production and trade would have been quite different in such a system. Manufacturing production would have spread throughout the world, earnings and output per worker *employed* would have been much lower, but the work and its fruits would have been shared more equally. The structure of manufacturing output would be altered towards the mass production of basic consumption needs rather than towards the high income goods that account for most of industrial output. Instead of this, capital accumulation proceeded via capital deepening in the industrial countries and led to a widening differential in production and income between the center and the hinterland. Thus, the returns to labor were not equalized despite the great expansion of trade after 1870 and large migrations of Europeans, Asians, and Africans.

Capital per worker was raised and the expansion of the industrial labor force slowed down. This created a radically different structure of demand from the egalitarian one just described and led to an economy based on continuous "creative destruction" to use Schumpeter's phrase. Because the capital/labor ratio increased steadily, the producer good sector had to continuously innovate labor saving machinery. Raising per capita income for a small, favored group meant a continuous change in the basket of goods consumed since, according to Engel's law, people tend not to consume more of the same as they get richer but reallocate their consumption patterns away from old goods towards new goods. Thus, toward the end of the nineteenth century, product innovation and marketing became the dominant problems of business enterprise rather than the mass production of goods. Instead of applying the achievements of science widely and solving the basic problems of subsistence for the majority of the world's population, attention was focused on creating "new products" and lightening the work load of the privileged under the guise of technological change.

Why was the second path chosen rather than the first? It could have been the result of the exogenous factor of technological change or differences in production functions, as many economic models imply, but we would argue that political factors were an important if not dominant determinant. In our view, the observed uneven development represented uneven power, and the resulting distribution of income and demand was a social phenomenon rather than a technical one.

The control device was government expenditure. Private capital was highly mobile during this period and flowed to wherever profit could be made. But the rate of profit or the demand for investment in any country depended upon the extent of public investment in infrastructure and human capital. The colonial system centralized power over government expenditure policy and insured a much higher rate of public capital formation in the center than in the hinterland. This biased distribution of public capital provided "external economies" in the center and directed private industrial capital away from the hinterland.

That this policy neither maximized world income nor distributed it equally is not surprising. The imperial system did not weigh people equally in its social welfare function. Political power was used to foster the growth of the capital of the mother country (i.e., the capitalists), subject to the constraints of class conflict. Using Kindleberger's group behavior approach,[9] we might analyze the policy of this period in terms of the alliances and coalitions formed between the following groups:

	Center	Hinterland
Capital	C_1	C_2
Land	T_1	T_2
Labor	L_1	L_2

Let us first examine trade between Europe and the areas of European settlement in America, Oceania, and Africa. According to the theory of the time, colonization, i.e., the migration of Europeans to other continents, was a method of expanding land and warding off the tendency for profits to fall because of diminishing returns in agriculture. The resulting pattern of international trade initially involved the exchange of manufactures for raw materials because of two important historical advantages associated with the mother country: (1) a large domestic market giving rise to internal and external economies, and (2) a strong capitalist class (or stock of entrepreneurship). Through time, the colony developed its own manufacturing sector (aided perhaps by tariffs or other government instruments) as the internal market expanded and as the indigenous capitalist class acquired the strength and resources to engage in industrial activity. Two-way trade in manufactures could then begin based on differences in comparative advantage and tastes.

As Kindleberger noted, the smooth working of this model would only take place under specific political conditions. Since trade would tend to reduce rents, it could only occur where the resistance of landlords was weak. In England, where the industrial classes had reached a position of dominance, this condition prevailed and free trade allowed the importation of wheat, which helped to complete the liquidation of landlords as the most powerful economic group in Britain.[10] But in Germany, the agricultural class was sufficiently strong to stop this development from taking place. Ironically, growth and development proceeded much more rapidly after 1870 in Germany than in the rest of Europe, perhaps because of the balance struck between agricultural and industrial classes. The fusion of rye and steel created a powerful alliance that could use the state's power to pursue a growth-oriented strategy.

In terms of the earlier framework, the major conflict was between T_1 and T_2. The politics of labor were relatively unimportant, because it was not yet well organized and, in any case, labor tended to benefit from the cheap wheat. It also could migrate to the hinterland when severely hurt at the center.[11] The conflict between C_1 and C_2 was also muted in the early stage because of the low degree of capitalist development in America.

After 1870, this power structure changed drastically. The landed classes became unimportant as a separate interest group (in the center), because they were destroyed or absorbed into industrial capital. The English capitalist class lost its hegemonic position as native bourgeoisies arose on the Continent, in America, and in Japan. Rivalry between C's became a dominant element in the foundation of Mercantilism II.

Equally important, labor became a powerful force as it became concentrated in industrial centers. The class consciousness was accentuated in England because of the shock of the great transformation out of agriculture and into the city as a consequence of wheat imports.

The result of these changes was that the imperial centers were in no position to embark on a "big push" in the hinterland. Their main concerns were to ward off rivalry from competing centers and to satisfy the growing demands of labor. Their policies tended to be defensive rather than offensive, mercantilist (i.e., protectionist) rather than free trade; ironically Edwardian England revived the paraphernalia of the landed aristocracy it had just destroyed.

Many of the policies of Mercantilism II thus slowed down the rate of growth and prevented the full development of the potential created by the scientific revolution. The fact is masked by growth statistics that show what happened instead of what could have happened. Unlike Mercantilism I, where the deadweight losses exceeded the gains, technological achievements of the nineteenth century were so great as to overwhelm the inefficiencies and retarding elements of Mercantilism II.

Instead of promoting the growth of enterprise in the hinterland, colonial policy arrested the development of native capitalists by failing to provide positive incentives and by the application of negative measures including, in some cases, outright destruction of burgeoning entrepreneurship. For similar reasons, they preferred low-wage/low-productivity labor in the hinterland over high-wage/high-productivity workers, because the latter would have been a potential political threat. The dual of this policy was to create a labor aristocracy in the center and to protect it through tariffs and immigration policy. Education programs and expenditures were unequal, being biased towards labor in the center. The two parts of the labor force must be seen as one if this period is to be analyzed properly.

Finally, the center had to devote an increased share of government activity to military and other nonproductive expenditures and had to rely frequently in the hinterland on an alliance with an inefficient class of landlords, officials, and soldiers, to maintain stability at the cost of development. A great part of the surplus extracted from the population was thus wasted locally.

The ideology of Mercantilism II, as reflected in economic theory, was capitalism triumphant. By the early twentieth century, nearly all of the components needed to solve mankind's material problems had been discovered. The only task left was the systems analysis problem of organizing and applying them. Mercantilism II began with great promise, but after a brief time span became seriously troubled and increasingly characterized by war, depression, the breakdown of the international economy, and war again, rather than by free trade, pax brittanica, and material improvement.

Mercantilism III

Political change, i.e., national independence, is clearly at the heart of the policy changes that ushered in Mercantilism III. The depression and World War II weakened the center allowing the national bourgeois class (C_2), born in the colonial export economy, to assert independence and to divert government expenditures to their own ends. Their control was, however, far from complete, and the restrictions and biases of the international economic system governed much of their actions. They did not, for example, face perfectly competitive markets in which they could trade freely with other countries. Instead, they frequently encountered large oligopolistic corporations with whom they had to bargain for needed investment goods and technology. Moreover, the governments in the advanced countries, though no longer possessing legal control, continued to exert pressure to keep the hinterland open to capital and manufactured goods from the center. Finally, the tariff structure used by the center effectively closed the rich industrial markets to manufacturing exports from the hinterland.

The set of policy options open to the newly independent countries were thus severely restricted (especially with respect to their control over the export staples and the accompanying network of financial intermediaries) while their targets and search procedures reflected and were limited by their disadvantaged past. The national bourgeois were, in effect, middlemen who did not understand the wider system above them and who could not mobilize the people below them. Given the limited vantage point of their past, they became imitators rather than innovators; they were children of the Europeans, an underdeveloped middle class. Forced industrialization became their strategy and the goal was to create a national capitalist class by using protection and import-substitution policies. The result was uneven development.

Although there seems to be a variety of experiences in the postwar period, as each country endeavored to formulate a national policy peculiar to its circumstances, a common theme is found in the tendency to reproduce on a national scale the pattern of the international economy evolved during Mercantilisms I and II. Capital formation is concentrated in urban centers resulting in rising capital/labor ratios, productivity, and per capita income for a small group of people. The neglect of the agrarian sector leads to rural stagnation and an unlimited supply of labor at low wages. An income and class gap emerges parallel to the international gap between European and non-European, previously described.

Basically, the import-substitution policies result in a rapid growth of manufacturing, centered in urban areas with little generation of employment. The economic reasons usually given are the labor-saving nature of foreign technology coupled with imperfections in the factor market that cause the imported price of capital to be too low and lead to a steady increase in the organized manufacturing sector's capital/labor ratio.

Although we cannot analyze this system in detail here, we do want to point out, in the spirit of this paper, that the reasons behind this scenario lie as much in the "power" equations as the market equations. The biases in economic structure come from the governments' attempt to favor one sector over another. The devices used to protect the national capitalist class have long been studied by trade economists, i.e., the instruments of tariffs, quotas, exchange controls, import licensing, and internal subsidies. Less fully analyzed but equally important are the biases in government infrastructure towards urban industrial needs, the establishment of a discriminatory educational system, and the use of the police power of the state to suppress the rural population and maintain the surplus of labor at the existing wage. It is these policies and the political relationships involved, and not merely the shape of production functions, that help to explain the output mix, factor proportions, and factor prices observed. The symbiosis, between the national bourgeois and the state, favored capital and a select group of urban labor at the expense of the population as a whole, and this resulted in a rapid growth of manufacturing, an increase in industrial wages rather than employment, and an excess demand for jobs. It also resulted in an output mix aimed at the few, emphasizing import substitution rather than import displacement.[12] In other words, the "independence" strategy accepted foreign tastes and foreign technology and tried to reproduce them on a miniature basis instead of adapting to local needs and local endowments.

There is reason to believe that this strategy is reaching a turning point as it encounters increased imbalance in the labor market and the foreign exchange market. A new solution is therefore needed to deal with the crisis in population, employment, and balance of payments that results from growing political pressure from the excluded population and the international economy. The basis for it seems to be an alliance between C_2 and C_1, the native capitalist class and the multinational corporation. This new group behavior, if it continues to develop, will lead to new economic configurations and a new international division of labor. We cannot analyze it in detail here but we might conclude the essay with a few conjectures about the next round of Mercantilism III.

We argued that Mercantilism I led to the formation of C_1, while Mercantilism II broke down, in large part, because of rivalries between subgroups of C_1, i.e., the various national capitals of the center. In the first round of Mercantilism III, C_2 succeeded in establishing itself as a minor partner, secure but in no way powerful enough to challenge or replace C_1. Meanwhile, a new relationship has appeared within C_1 in the form of a growing trend towards multinationalization of private enterprise. Mergers and foreign investment by American and European firms are leading to interpenetration of markets and the weakening of links between particular countries and particular firms.[13]

Thus the stage is set for a new international industrial structure dominated by 300 to 500 large North Atlantic oligopolistic corporations that operate on a global basis in cooperation with smaller national firms who serve as suppliers, distributors, licensees, and in some ways, as competitors. The trade pattern associated with this international hierarchy of decision-making will lead to an exchange of goods and services based on skill differentials. The center will specialize in complex manufacture and high-level technology, i.e., systems design, research, marketing, finance, while the hinterland will specialize in labor-intensive production. The multinational corporation, if it succeeds, will reproduce on a world level the centralization of control found in its internal administrative structure.

Three major political questions dominate any attempt to predict the future course of the international economy. First, will there be some sort of alliance of L's to match the alliance of C's? Second, will multinational corporations be able to construct multinational political institutions to replace the nation-states whose power they are eroding? Third, will it be possible to resolve rivalry between the capitalist and socialist blocs and within the capitalist bloc itself (e.g., the problem of Japan and Germay)? The progression from Mercantilism I to Mercantilism II to Mercantilism III has seen an increased complexity of political and economic linkages between countries. Modern communications and the multinational corporations are increasing interconnectedness to so great an extent that a qualitatively new system is emerging. The greater the interactions between countries, the greater the interdependence, i.e., the higher are international multipliers and the lower are national multipliers. If we were dealing purely with market relationships, this would not present analytical problems, since a great deal is known by economists about the self-regulating properties of general equilibrium systems involving many decision units. These stability properties do not hold on the political plane where tariff struggles and "beggar my neighbor" policies, etc., lead away from Pareto optimality. International trade theory, because it does not include these political factors, is misleading in analyzing the current world economy.

6   The multinational corporation and the international division of labor

I. The actors

What is the nature of the Beast? People call it many names: Direct Investment, International Business, the International Firm, the International Corporate Group, the Multinational Firm, the Multinational Enterprise, the Multinational Corporation, the World Company, the Multinational Family Group, the Worldwide Enterprise, La Grande Entreprise Plurinationale, La Grande Unité Interterritorial, La Grande Entreprise Multinationale, La Grande Unité Pluriterritoriale; or as a French Foreign Minister called them, "The U.S. corporate monsters."[1]

Whatever its name, there are two aspects upon which everyone agrees: The "beast" is large in size and it operates over a wide territorial space.

Why is this a problem? Essentially, the issue is one of power. Who decides what and where? What does it mean that an executive of a giant corporation in New York closes a plant in London, Toronto, or Bangkok?

In legal terms, the corporation is a person operating under rights granted by a sovereign state. In practice, it is a social and political (power) structure that organizes large numbers of people, as employees, customers, suppliers, consultants, brokers, counselors, etc. The large corporation does not operate under the state but alongside it and in some cases above it.

Corporations argue that their freedom is limited by the outdated attempts of nation-states to control international exchange. George Ball says:

... the structure of the multinational corporation is a modern concept, designed to meet the requirements of a modern age; the nation state is a very old-fashioned idea and badly adapted to serve the needs of our present complex world.[2]

This essay is published here for the first time by permission of the Estate of Stephen Hymer. An earlier and shorter version of the essay appeared in French in *Etudes Internationales* (Quebec: Centre de recherche en relations internationales institut Canadien des affaires internationales), Vol. II, No. 1. March 1971, pp. 58–80. Paul Semonin assisted in researching and preparing both versions of this paper.

Defenders of the nation-state say that its sovereignty is limited by the ability of corporations to escape its regulations.

The problem therefore appears to us in the first instance as a conflict between institutions. The actors are corporations and nation-states. The arena is the evolving world economy. A disjunction exists between the corporation, which is coming to see the whole world as its own, and the nation-state, which operates with much narrower horizons. As *Business Week* observed, "for a worldwide company, national boundaries are drawn in fading ink."[3]

The conflict between the corporation and the nation-state takes place at the level of appearances. As we look further into the matter we shall come to see the conflicts as struggles between various interest groups in society. The real actors are the people within the corporations and nation-states, struggling over: Who gets what, where; who in London, Toronto, and Bangkok makes the decisions; how income and other values are to be shared. The study of the multinational corporation is thus a study of tthe international hierarchy of decision making and the world pattern of consumption.

The conflicts involve a wide range of interest groups both within individual countries and between groups in different countries. For example:

1   conflicts between large multinational firms over the share of the international market;

2   conflicts within a country between large firms who can meet the challenge of the international economy through foreign investment and small firms who can only do it through exports;

3   competition among middle classes of different countries for managerial and scientific jobs (this includes the question of location of scientific facilities as well as the amount of national participation in management);

4   competition between the high-wage labor in advanced countries and the low-wage labor in less-advanced countries over jobs;

5   conflicts over the amounts of taxes corporations will pay on a worldwide basis and what each government's share will be;

6   conflicts between excluded groups and the elites as to the direction of development.

Pyramids of power

To grasp fully what is at stake one must pose the question in the widest possible context. The world is organized into nations whose political relations are ordered hierarchically in pyramids of power.[4] These pyramids may be described in terms of class structure, as the Marxists do, or in terms of elites, as liberal social scientists prefer. These pyramids represent a fusion of social, economic, and political power. At any level there may be individuals who have wealth without political power, or vice versa, and considerable effort has been devoted to analyzing conflicts between different factions on the same level. Yet, when one looks at their relationships vertically, rather than horizontally, the striking feature of our society is that the number of people who have wealth or status or political power (or any combination of these) is few while the number who have little of any is many.

The relationships between nations are also unequal. The most important division in the distribution of values (power, wealth, well-being, dignity, etc.) is between the Northern Hemisphere and the Southern Hemisphere. Until the end of the Second World War most of the latter countries were in a politically subordinate position relative to the Northern powers. In the national independence period these countries obtained sovereignty but not equality in the shaping and sharing of values. From an analytical viewpoint they are not on the same plane as the major powers but rather lower down in the hierarchy.

These structures of power are not static but are constantly in motion and subject to tensions that periodically break out into open clashes – world wars, colonial wars, and civil wars. Due to increased communications between pyramids and the trend toward global perspectives, the late sixties and early seventies seem to be a period of great fluidity and realignment – one might even say a revolutionary period – in which things are falling out of place and history is going faster.

Because of their size and close contact with new technology, large corporations are in the vanguard of this revolution. They are among the first to establish international perspectives. Over the past twenty years they have been organizing production and consumption internationally, forming alliances with groups in other countries, and restructuring their activities on global lines.

The question is what will emerge from this period of change, that is, will the pyramids tend to be flattened or heightened?[5] Most people hope the new international order will represent some form of democratic interdependence – a global village – and projections of the futurists frequently imply that this will be the case. However, there are trends that suggest otherwise. The existing elites are particularly threatened by the new world forces. They may unify in order to establish a world hierarchy that will reproduce the pyramid of power on a global scale – a dystopia such as the one put forward by Harold Lasswell in what he calls the "unspeakable revolution."[6] It is now only a matter of a few years to the time when major breakthroughs in the human ability to control genetics can be expected. These scientific discoveries open up the possibility for great steps forward in the evolution of human life. They also present us with the horror that they may be used to "police the world medically," as Lasswell put it.

Some people see international capital as a leveling force that will help to integrate the world and provide increased opportunity for participation in the modern economy. Others see it as a force tending to maintain the present inequalities and to consolidate them on a worldwide basis. The argument of this paper is that a new world economy based on multinational corporations would in fact tend to produce a hierarchical division of labor between geographical regions corresponding to the vertical division of labor within the corporations.

II. The arena of the world economy

Other than raw materials, businessmen see foreign investment in terms of maintaining their share of the world market. They claim that they invest abroad rather than rely on exports because they would otherwise lose their ability to compete. They must also invest in foreign countries in order to protect their share of the U.S. market when imports threaten.

Foreign investment thus depends on three things: the size of the demand in the foreign market, the availability of labor and other factors of production for manufacturing, and the existence of competitors who can enter the industry if the multinational firm does not. Rapid growth of a foreign country attracts foreign investment both because of the expanding market and because of the growth of rival capitalists – local capital, capital from other countries, or state capital.

The first wave of U.S. direct foreign capital investment occurred around the turn of the century, followed by a second wave during the 1920s. The outward migration slowed down during the depression, but resumed after the Second World War and soon accelerated rapidly. A third wave of outward migration of U.S. capital followed the rapid growth of Europe and Japan. This, combined with the slow growth of the U.S. economy in the 1950s, threatened the dominant position of American corporations. Firms confined to the U.S. market found themselves falling behind in the competitive race and losing ground to European and Japanese firms, which were growing rapidly because of the expansion of their markets. Thus in the late 1950s the U.S. corporations faced a serious "non-American" challenge. Their answer was an outward thrust to establish sales production and bases in foreign territories.

What about the future? The present trend indicates further multinationalization of all giant firms, European as well as American. A period of intense rivalry will perhaps prevail until the major giants, American and non-American, have penetrated each other's territories and divided up the remaining ones so as to establish a roughly similar distribution of world operations (on an average). The world economy will come more and more to resemble the U.S. economy, where each of the large corporations is spread over the entire economy and has penetrated almost every nook and cranny. This solution has certain stability properties. At present unequal growth of different parts of the world economy upsets the oligopolistic equilibrium because the leading firms have different geographical distributions of production and sales. Thus if the European economy grows faster than the U.S. economy, European firms tend to grow faster than American firms, unless American firms engage in heavy foreign investment. Similarly, if the United States grows faster than Europe, U.S. firms will grow faster than European firms because Europeans have a lesser stake in the American market. However, when firms are distributed evenly in all markets, they share equally in the good and bad fortunes of the various submarkets, and oligopolistic equilibrium is not upset by the unequal growth of different countries. The fortunes of an individual multinational firm are no longer as closely connected with national economies.

The underdeveloped countries are likely to play a key role in the oligopolistic rivalry of the future. In the first place, they have a large and growing market in the very products that the American, European, and Japanese firms specialize in. Statistics on per capita income disguise the market potential in these countries. It should be realized that income is distributed very unevenly and that the top 10 percent of the population gets anywhere from 30 to 40 percent of the total income of the country. Thus within each country there is a group of consumers with consumption patterns roughly similar to those that prevail in the developed countries. This group is growing relatively rapidly and forms a moderately sizable market. Every major firm in the world has to ensure that it acquires a stake in this market. This means establishing marketing facilities and a certain degree of local manufacturing in each of these high-income areas scattered throughout the underdeveloped world.

The question arises why these markets appear more important than their actual size. The answer lies to some extent in the barriers to entry associated with oligopolistic competition. The failure of a firm to establish its market share early (i.e., set up the marketing channels for its products) could mean losing its market share in the future once competitors – be they local or foreign – have already established themselves. These underdeveloped areas are markets of the future and the investments by large firms there are often preemptive actions to preserve their market position.

We must add to all these reasons the fact that advertisers will soon be able to reach an entire continent at one blow by a cycle of TV. We have fairly convincing evidence, therefore, that a major part of the expansion of the multinational corporation in the next round will be directed toward the 2 billion (American billion) people in the underdeveloped world, or rather toward the top 200 million people. The potential of this market, of course, will not be realized unless certain economic and political reforms are put into practice to ensure the steady growth of its advanced sectors. The underdeveloped countries must be able to earn foreign exchange to pay for foreign investments; they must solve their agricultural problems to permit organization; they must provide infrastructure and education neede. modern sectors; they must embark on programs of population control; .. must also be able to maintain political stability among the excluded groups.

In the past, business groups seldom concerned themselves with such problems on a worldwide basis. But now some of the multinational corporations are sufficiently large and possess sufficiently wide horizons to appreciate the various problems involved in creating growing markets throughout the world. The underdeveloped countries are not only a market for American products, but a source of low-cost production for products exported to the American market. (For a discussion of Japan and East–West trade, see Chapter 10.)

Two major tendencies are likely to develop in the future. The first is the creation of a new equilibrium between the giant U.S. firms and the giant European firms. Until now, the relationship has been asymmetrical insofar as European firms seldom had direct investments outside their own country, whereas U.S. corporations typically had operations on a worldwide basis. This created certain tensions that have led firms from both sides of the Atlantic to become increasingly multinational. Although the direction of change taken by these firms is perhaps clear, it will take some time before a new equilibrium is reached. Thus, for perhaps the next ten or fifteen years, there will be a certain amount of flexibility until a new balance is reached, which will then probably coalesce and remain stable for a much longer period of time. The second tendency, which is closely connected to the first, is for a major investment drive toward the underdeveloped countries in order to stake out positions and begin the process of market (consumer) development.

III. The horizontal dimension: size and differentiation

Since the beginning of the industrial revolution, there has been a steady increase in the size of manufacturing firms from the *workshop* to the *factory* to the *national corporation* to the *multidivisional corporation* and now to the *multinational corporation*. The tendency has been so persistent that it might almost be formulated as a general law of capital accumulation. These increases in size were accompanied by important changes in organizational structure involving both subdivision or differentiation of tasks and organization through the creation of new organs of control.

As the firm grew horizontally, it developed a more complex administrative structure to control its dispersed operations and a larger brain to plan for its survival and growth. Lewin has shown that as an individual develops his or her life space increases, as does the variety of his or her behavior and his or her time perspective. Lewin's concept of the development of the individual is useful for understanding the evolution of the corporation:

Development seems to increase the number of relatively independent subparts of the person and their degree of independence, thus decreasing the degree of the unity of the individual. On the other hand, development involves integration which increases the unity of the person. As both of these processes advance at the same time, obviously, integration cannot be a process which is actually the reversal of differentiation. It does not eliminate differentiation, and it is not dedifferentiation. But, integration presupposes differentiation. To avoid misunderstandings we prefer, therefore, to use the term "organization" instead of integration.[7]

The main point is that increasing differentation is not the opposite of integration but the complement to it. The biological analogy is found frequently in the literature concerning the growth of firm size, and it was cited by Marshall himself.

The development of the corporation led to a great increase in the numbers and importance of advisory and administrative personnel. Simon has carried the analogy with the differentiation of the human body to its logical conclusion with his distinction between the head and the hand:

It is clear that the actual physical task of carrying out an organization's objectives falls to the persons at the lowest level of the administrative hierarchy. The automobile, as a physical object, is built not by the engineer or the executive, but by the mechanic on the assembly line. The fire is extinguished, not by the fire chief or the captain, but by the team of firemen who play a hose on the blaze . . .

How then, do the administrative and supervisory staff of an organization affect that organization's work? The nonoperative staff of an administrative organization participate in the accomplishment of the objectives of that organization to the extent that they influence the decisions of the operatives – the persons at the lowest level of the administrative hierarchy. The major can influence the battle to the extent that his head is able to direct the machine gunner's hand.[8]

The evolution of the corporation

The major steps in the evolution of the corporation were the workshop, the factory, the national corporation, the multidivisional corporation, and the multinational corporation. In the *workshop* a small number of people worked together with very little specialization in production; they sold their product jointly through middlemen who also may have financed some of their materials. The *factory* was based on a large concentration of people and a high degree of specialization of labor (Adam Smith's pin factory); many new specialties and subdivisions accompanied the introduction of machinery and a sharp division of labor emerged between those who planned and those who worked, between capitalists and laborers.

National corporation.   The evolution of the national corporation (multi-plant, multilocation, multimarket) is best studied in the U.S. environment, where it has reached its highest stages. In the 1870s the U.S. industrial structure consisted largely of Marshallian type single-function firms, scattered over the country. By the early twentieth century, the rapid growth of the economy and the great merger movement had consolidated many small enterprises into large national corporations engaged in many functions over many regions.

Whereas previously they had sold to wholesalers and bought their raw materials in the market, they now integrated forward and backward to create a multicity marketing structure and in some cases a far-flung control over the supply of raw materials. The life space of the firm, thus, comprised many occupations, many markets, many production units, and many functions. The administrative structure also became differentiated functionally – between finance, personnel, purchasing, engineering, and sales – and there was a great increase of specialization within these functions. The functions were organized in departments within a head office separate from the operations and field offices.

Multidivisional corporation.   The great national corporations by and large were restricted to one industry and one product line. They were mainly based on satisfying old demands on a mass basis and restricted themselves to one main product line such as meat, sewing machines, soap, tobacco, etc. The changing nature of the market after 1920 involved the continuing introduction of new products (Du Pont in chemicals, for example) and differentiation within each product line (General Motors). The leading corporations were subdivided into divisions to handle different products or different brands and to facilitate the development of new products. This led to the creation of a middle level of administration within the firm that coordinated activities of a product division and left the top management to concentrate on strategic planning.

Multinational corporation.   Some firms became multinational very early, but until recently most engaged in international operations as a by-product of domestic activity. As the importance of international operations grew in size, they tended to be organized under separate international divisions.

Though some multinational activities were organized as subsidiaries rather than as international divisions (for tax and legal purposes), these units were not substantially different in terms of their operating responsibilities. The actual organizational patterns for international operations vary, but the trend toward a centralizing of strategic controls apparently applies to most companies whatever their pattern. "The really decisive point in the transition to world enterprise is top-management's recognition that, to function effectively, the ultimate control of strategic planning and policy decisions must shift from decentralized subsidiaries or division locations to corporate headquarters, where a worldwide perspective can be brought to bear on the interests of the total enterprise."[9]

IV. The vertical dimension: hierarchy of control

Chandler and Redlich provide a rich contextual approach to the analysis of the basic levels of activity in the modern multidivisional enterprise.[10] They distinguish "three levels of business administration, three horizons, three levels of task, and three levels of decision-making . . . and three levels of policies." Level III, the lowest level, is concerned with managing the day-to-day operations of the enterprise, that is, with keeping it going within the established framework. Level II, which first made its appearance with the separation of head office from field office, is responsible for coordinating the managers at Level III. The functions of Level I – top management – are goal determination and planning. This level sets the framework in which the lower levels operate. In the Marshallian firm, all three levels are embodied in the single entrepreneur or undertaker. In the national corporation, a partial differentiation is made in which the top two levels are separated from the bottom one. In the multidivisional corporation, the differentiation is far more complete. Level I is completely split off from Level II and concentrated in a general office whose specific function is to plan strategy, rather than tactics. It is here that the key people who actually allocate the corporation's available resources (rather than act within the means allocated to them, as is true for the managers at lower levels) are located. Their power comes from their ultimate control over *people* and *money*. Although one should not overestimate their ability to control a far-flung empire, neither should one underestimate it.

The corporate hierarchy

The hierarchical structure of the corporation stems from the fundamental fact, as Barnard wrote, that ". . . all large formal organizations are constituted of numbers of small organizations" and "the clue to the structural requirements of large complex organizations lies in the reason for the limitations of the size of simple organizations."[11] In Barnard's eyes, the size of the unit was determined "by the limitations of effective leadership." Any leader or order-giver can only effectively hold a limited number of people accountable to him or her and must, therefore, delegate to others this function beyond a limit.

To view this another way, the ability of the primary group to work together is limited by its members' ability to communicate with each other, because the number of possible interactions between members,

$$\frac{N(n-1)}{2} = \frac{n^2 - n}{2}$$

increases more rapidly than the numbers involved.[12]

The limitations on the span of control lead to a pyramidal relationship in large organizations. Mathematically, if every leader has n immediate subordinates (or alternatively, every n people appoint one leader), and S is the total number of employees and L the number of levels of authority in the hierarchy, the following holds:

$$S = 1 + n + n^2 + \ldots n^{L-1} = \frac{n^L - 1}{n - 1} \simeq \frac{n^L}{n - 1}$$

The factors that determine the span of control are varied and a large literature has grown up discussing the limitations of the concept and its relation to methods of communications that need not concern us here.

Stratification within the corporation

The distinction between intellectual and manual labor in the corporate hierarchy has the most profound consequences for quality of life because of the differences in type of work and earnings. Quoting from Marshall, who viewed this separation as the "'kernel' of the modern economic problem":

> For the business by which a person earns his livelihood generally fills his thoughts during by far the greater part of these hours in which his mind is at its best; during them his character is being formed by the way in which he uses his faculties in his work, by the thoughts and the feelings which it suggests, by his relations to his associates in work, his employers or his employees.
> And very often the influence exerted on a person's character by the amount of his income is hardly less, if it is less, than that exerted by the way in which it is earned.[13]

Marx put it more strongly by asking us to imagine what it would be like if the whole society were organized like a factory:

> Division of labour within the workshop implies the undisputed authority of the capitalist over men, that are but parts of a mechanism that belong to him. . . . The same bourgeois mind which praises division of labour in the workshop, life-long annexation of the labourer to a partial operation, and his complete subjection to capital, as being an organization of labour that increases its productiveness – that same bourgeois mind denounces with equal vigour every conscious attempt to socially control and regulate the process of production, as an inroad upon such sacred things as the rights of property, freedom and unrestricted play for the bent of the individual capitalist. It is very characteristic that the enthusiastic apologists of the factory system have nothing more damning to urge against a general organization of the labour of society, than that it would turn all society into one immense factory.[14]

The question that arises here is that of power. The people at the top usually stress the limits of their power – perhaps to mystify those below – but also because that is what strikes them most. It is true that they are limited in what they can command because their employees can disobey orders, work inefficiently, or leave the company and take another job. Similarly, their ability to keep open a high-cost plant in a given region is limited by their need to make a profit in order to survive. But though it is true that the higher levels of the corporation to some extent act as brokers and mediators between conflicting interests and not as indpendent sources of influence and that they are driven by Adam Smith's invisible hand of God to do things independent of their will, they nonetheless have far more discretion and influence than the people below them do (Galbraith stresses how chief executives are limited by the techno-structure but has little to say about the alienation and limitations placed on the 80 percent of the people below the technostructure[15]).

Moreover, it is not the discretion of individuals acting separately or in small groups that is important, but the strength of the elite as a whole. For example, the power of a corporate executive to make his employees obey him depends on the alternatives available to the worker. These in turn are limited by class, sexual, racial, and national barriers as well as educational systems that suit people only for certain jobs.

Similarly, whether or not it is profitable for an executive to open or close a plant in a given spot depends upon the physical infrastructure, education, taxes, political stability, and other environmental factors provided by the government. As we shall discuss below, the government's ability and willing-ness to provide education and infrastructure depends on the corporate system. (This interdependence of economic and political power implies that one should not compare a single multinational firm to a local firm in the same circumstance, but rather the system of multinational corporations with the system of national development.)

Whatever the subtleties or ambiguities in measuring power, there is little doubt that status and rewards are distributed unevenly. Salary and wages are clearly a function of the level of the hierarchy and the compensation of executives tends to be highly correlated with the number of people under them. Other studies show that skills, rewards, authority, time span of discretion, time perspective, access to information, and mental demands also vary with the level of organization.

V. The temporal dimension: motion

As the corporation evolved, it developed an elaborate system of internal division of labor, able to absorb and apply both the physical sciences and the social sciences to business activity on a scale that could not be imagined in earlier years. At the same time, it developed a higher brain to command its very large concentration of wealth. This gave it the power to invest on a much larger scale and to plan over the various stages of the product cycle with a much wider time horizon than the smaller, less-developed firms that preceded it. The modern multidivisional corporation is thus a far cry from the Marshallian firm in both its vision and its strength.

The corporation is a process as well as a structure. Each activity it encompasses represents not only a different level of activity but also a

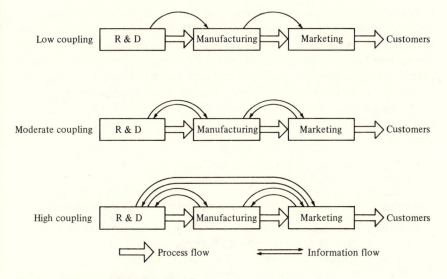

Figure 1.   Degrees of downstream coupling.

different point in time, that is, a different phase of the product cycle. The product cycle traces the operational flow of activities organized by the corporation through the phases of science, invention, innovation, production, marketing, distribution, and consumption.

The evolution of the corporation's ability to plan over the product cycle is shown in Figure 1.[16]

In the factory system the main concern of the industrial capitalist was production. The extension of the market necessary to absorb the increased production made possible by the industrial revolution fell to the merchants and the government. This division of labor, however, broke down with the advent of mass production. Mass production required the mass market. The new industrial manufacturers encountered great difficulties in selling their products through existing channels and, therefore, they integrated forward to take over the wholesale function in order to reach the customer more directly. This can be viewed as an attempt to integrate or to "couple" production and sales by *preselling* the customer so that he or she was prepared to buy the products coming off the assembly line. In nonintegrated systems, information about a product is passed on to the consumer at the point of sale. Through advertising and control of the contractual functions in the distribution channel, the corporation sends messages forward to potential buyers at the same time that it is sending messages downward through the corporate hierarchy instructing that the goods be produced. (For a complete discussion of the development of the market, see Chapter 2.)

Product development and marketing gradually replaced production as a dominant problem of business enterprise. The corporation placed increased emphasis on using scientists and engineers to invent, innovate, or adapt innovations to create new products. At the same time the marketing function rose in the corporate hierarchy and merged into the planning function. For corporations like Du Pont the process began in the 1920s. For other companies it took place after the Second World War. General Electric, for example, described the rise of marketing in product planning in its 1952 *Annual Report:*

> In 1952, your company's operating managers were presented an advanced concept of marketing, formulated by the Marketing Services Division. This, in simple terms, would introduce the marketing man at the beginning rather than at the end of the production cycle and would integrate marketing into each phase of the business.[17]

Robert J. Keith of the Pillsbury Company traced the evolution of his company's marketing function through four phases: the first, when they were production oriented (1869–1930); the second, which was sales oriented (1930s–50s); the third, when the company became marketing oriented in the 1950s; and the beginning of a fourth era, in the 1960s, of market control. The key development in this process took place during phase three:

> We needed, in fact, to build into our company a new management function which would direct and control all the other corporate functions from procurement to production to advertising to sales. This function was marketing. Our solution was to establish the present marketing department.[18]

The latest developments in marketing venture even further and begin to see the whole process of production, education, and consumption in an integrated framework. The movement in this direction is symbolized by the increased interest in technological forecasting and market segmentation. In both cases the corporation is attempting to go beyond its previous boundaries and to study the fundamentals of production and consumption. This stage is closely associated with the multinational dimension. Because the development of a global perspective has emphasized the cultural and sociological factors in consumption, the need has arisen to use science in new ways in order to penetrate markets in underdeveloped areas. With the instrument of the computer, the corporations are looking at countries as total systems.

This whole process of increasing integration of the product cycle is usually described in terms of technological imperatives. The corporation is seen as uniquely suited for incorporating the potentialities of science and taking advantage of economies of scale. To repeat George Ball's statement, "The structure of the multinational corporation is a modern concept, designed to meet the requirements of a modern age."[19]

Or as Max Ways put it in an article published in *Fortune* magazine in January 1968, "The corporation can stretch into any part of the world, deal attentively with any race or culture. It can combine to a unified purpose the most disparate skills, building internal order amidst the brisk clash of opinions."[20]

There is a certain degree of truth in these views. But it attributes far too much to the productivity of the corporation. Land and his associates may think that *they* invented the Polaroid camera, just as corporations claim responsibility for the new products they introduce. But a broader view realizes that for this act to have occurred a large number of people must have worked to produce various ideas and materials. The camera is in fact the product of many hands and many minds and the general development of society. If one traced through each of the components that enter directly or indirectly into the camera and each of the ideas, one would find that it, like every other product, is the result of a far-reaching network of labor, that is, that every product is the sum of the immediate labor and past dated labor of many people:

$$P = L_t + L_{t-1} + L_{t-2} + \ldots + L_{t-n}$$

Similarly, one must stress that for the camera to be produced, a market had to be available, which presupposes a communications system, a certain structure of income distribution, and the development of tastes.

Contrary to what George Ball says, it is the government sector, insofar as it represents the combined activities of people, that plays a crucial role in the modern age, because of its strategic importance in education, communication, science, and the overall development of the environment.

The accomplishments of the corporation in planning over the product cycle are largely concerned with its own survival and growth. To equate this with technology and scientific development in general is mystification. In many ways, corporations can frustrate the development potential because that would interfere with their own existence.

The corporate cycle is:

hire people $\longrightarrow$ produce goods and services $\longrightarrow$ sell $\longrightarrow$ repeat

This activity involves it in the constant accumulation of material production and knowledge and the ability to produce better goods.

The social reproductive cycle is:

$$\text{people} \longrightarrow \text{activity} \underset{\longrightarrow \text{goods}}{\overset{\longrightarrow \text{knowledge}}{\langle}} \longrightarrow \text{new people}$$

Looked at in this general way there is no reason to expect that the new people will want to repeat the old activities. They might, for example, choose to shorten the workday and devote themselves to activities outside the corporate sector; this would interfere with the corporation's productive cycle. For example, suppose we decided to have a zero GNP growth and, thus, a tendency in the sales and size of corporations to remain constant rather than grow steadily as in the past. This would disrupt their whole incentive and organization system, which is geared toward growth. It would strip importance from many of the higher-level activities and would eliminate the carrot of advancement provided by an expanding system.

The international operations of a corporation are an attempt to control that part of the product cycle that takes place in foreign countries. It does this under the guise of bringing capital, technology, and management skill, but its motive for direct investment is to defend its own quasimonopoly of knowledge and to assure its own stability and growth. This often has the effect of blocking independent sources of development. The vertical structure of the corporation is a method of coordination, but it is also one of control and the values are its own survival and a favorable environment, not the development of society as a whole.

VI. The spatial dimension

Suppose giant multinational corporations (say 300 from the United States and 200 from Europe and Japan) succeed in establishing themselves as the dominant form of international enterprise and come to control a significant share of industry (especially modern industry) in each country. The world economy will resemble more and more the U.S. economy (or perhaps more accurately the United States-Canadian complex), where each of the large corporations tends to spread over the entire continent and to penetrate almost every nook and cranny. What would be the effect of a world industrial organization of this type on international specialization, exchange, and income distribution? The purpose of this section is to analyze the geographical (or spatial) dimension of the corporate hierarchy.

What is the relationship between the structure of the microcosm and the structure of the macrocosm, that is, between the vertical dimension of the corporation and the spatial dimension? The application of location theory to the Chandler-Redlich scheme suggests a close correspondence between centralization of control within the corporation and centralization of control within the international economy.

Location theory suggests that Level III activities would spread themselves over the globe according to the pull of labor power, markets, and raw materials. Level II activities, because of the need for white-collar workers, communications systems, and information, tend to concentrate in large cities. Level I activities, the general offices, tend to be even more concentrated than Level II activities, for they must be located close to the capital market, the media, and the government. (For a complete discussion of the application of location theory to the Chandler-Redlich scheme, see Chapter 2.)

The importance of this can be understood in terms of communications and information flows, the key factor in control ("in an exhaustive theory of organization, communication would occupy a central place, because the structure, extensiveness, and scope of organization is almost entirely determined by communications technique"[21]).

Putting this in terms of the pyramid structure of corporate power, the important things for the maintenance of cohesion and control are:

1 having an efficient and effective system of vertical communication, so that information from the bottom flows rapidly and easily to the executive level as do orders from the top to the operatives below;

2 cementing lateral communication at the higher levels of the organization, so that the important decision makers do not work at cross purposes but have an opportunity to exchange information and reconcile differences;

3 the breaking of lateral communication at the lower levels, so as to prevent alliances and interchanges that lead to actions counter to those prescribed by higher management.

The exact point in the vertical hierarchy where lateral communication is broken instead of encouraged (i.e., the middle level) depends on the nature of the organization. In the military, for example, Karl Deutsch points out that the colonels are the strategic "middle level" because:

It is that level of communication and command that is "vertically" close enough to the large mass of consumers, citizens, or common soldiers to forestall any continuing and effective direct communication between them and the "highest echelons"; and it must be far enough above the level of the large numbers of the rank and file to permit effective "horizontal" communication and organization among a sufficiently large portion of the men or units on its own level. From this point of view, there are usually too few generals to receive direct information from, or give direct orders to, the large mass of private soldiers; and there are too many sergeants and lieutenants in most armies to permit their effective organization for political purposes.[22]

Cementing the lateral communications at the upper levels so that understanding and confidence are maximized requires face-to-face contact and an oral rather than written system of communication. In his classic analysis of the crucial role of New York, R. M. Haig has identified the importance of oral as opposed to written communication in its relationship to the architecture of the central city:

The exercise of this managerial function of coordination and control is at first glance singularly independent of transportation. It does not require the transfer of huge quantities of materials. It deals almost exclusively with information. What is all-important is transportation of intelligence. The mail, the cable, the telegraph, and telephone bring in its raw material and carry out its finished product. Internally easy contact of man with man is essential. The telephone is prodigally used, of course, but the personal conference remains, after all, the method by which most of the important work is done. Conferences with corporation officers, with bankers, with lawyers and accountants, with partners, with fellow directors, fill the day.[23]

As one businessman cited by Haig put it: "The skyscraper facilitates personal contacts in a way never possible before. From my office on the twenty-eighth floor of a building in the Times Square district, I can get to practically every person of importance in the architectural and business field in fifteen minutes' time."[24]

Another succinct statement of the same point:

"Physical propinquity may be a very real factor in determining the frequency of real communication," writes Simon, "and hence, the layout of offices is one of the important formal determinants of the communication system." This observation was verified all through our study. It was most obvious, of course, in the case of those firms which had works or offices in different localities, but it was also true with regard to the home plant or the head office. A different part of the building or even a different floor from that where the chief executive's office was situated meant in most cases a definite contact barrier.[25]

This analysis helps to explain why the function of finance, as well as banking services, is concentrated in a few (or one) capital markets. Capital is the key variable in the system and information and confidence in people as well as things are of the utmost importance. Of course, within the financial function there is a hierarchy where local banks lend small amounts to local firms or branches of large firms on secured collateral, but loans of large sums of money for a long period of time require decisions at a higher level in a centralized place. Similarly, a hierarchy is found in the marketing function. At the lowest level there are salespeople spread out over the entire market. These are coordinated at a regional level, integrating markets with a certain degree of homogeneity. But the overall strategic design involving the most advanced concepts of marketing is centralized in the location where there is most ready access to social scientists, publishers, media, designers, and competitors.

The research function has certain peculiar features. The lowest levels of research are done at the plant level almost as a by-product of the manufacturing process. Higher levels of research tend to be concentrated in research centers, but typically not in the general office or the central city. This is in part because scientists occupy a dual role as professionals and as members of the organization. They do not fit well into the regular chains of command and usually place a high premium on professional autonomy because, as professionals whose authority is based on knowledge, they expect and demand the authority to exercise their own judgment. In addition, it is very important, especially where basic science is concerned, that they be in contact with other scientists and act as "open cells" receiving and absorbing knowledge generated at the frontiers of science. On the other hand, it is very important that their results be channeled into the highest levels of management where they can be coupled with marketing functions in an overall strategy for product development. Thus, even though the research function may be located away from the high-density commercial centers, its communications are with these centers rather than with its local community, and it forms an enclave rather than an integrated part of the local economy.

Finally, the suppliers of various services to the corporations also vary according to the level. Each branch plant of a giant corporation is surrounded by local firms that supply it with certain components, materials, or services; that act as local competitors in the city or regional market; and that serve as distributors of the corporation's products (e.g., the automobile industry: parts suppliers located in Detroit and close to some assembly points; local car dealers, repair shops, service stations, used car dealers, etc.).

At the central places we find the top corporation lawyers, consultants, designers, artists, specialists, large wholesalers, brokers, etc.; in short, those whose stock in trade is specialized knowledge and broad horizons.

In summary, the spatial division of labor is not only a horizontal one between different industries but a vertical one between different levels of activity.

When one begins to seek the reasons for growth and decline in the center, he is immediately impressed by the inadequacy of the terminology ordinarily used in discussing the problem. Broad terms such as "industry," "manufacture," "commerce," and "trade," are not well adapted to the task in hand. If, for example, a silk mill, formerly located on Manhattan, moves to Pennsylvania but keeps its head office and salesroom in New York, it is not accurate to say that this "industry" has left New York. What has actually happened is that there has been a territorial subdivision of functions which were formerly united in the same place, certain activities being sent to Pennsylvania and certain others kept in the metropolis. Fabrication and certain other functions have gone, but selling and many of the other functions remain. Fourth Avenue is full of establishments bearing the names of manufacturing plants, but no fabrication is in evidence. Though it is the center of the silk industry, not a loom is to be found there. Nor is the situation changed fundamentally if the establishment, instead of retaining its New York office, delegates its selling to a jobber or agent operating in New York under its own name. The significant thing is the amount and the character of the activity which leaves and the amount and character of the activity which remains.[26]

A regime of multinational corporations would tend to produce a hierarchical division of labor between geographical regions corresponding to the vertical division of labor within the firm. It would tend to centralize high-level decision-making occupations in a few key cities in the advanced countries, surrounded by a number of regional subcapitals, and confine the rest of the world to lower levels of activity and income, that is, to the status of towns and villages in a New Imperial System. Income, status, authority, and consumption patterns would radiate out from these centers along a declining curve, and the existing pattern of inequality and dependency would be perpetuated.

The pattern would be complex, just as the structure of the corporation is complex, but the basic relationship between different countries would be one of superior and subordinate, head office and branch plant.

VII. Cities: dominance and subdominance

The city

As R. D. McKenzie points out,

> The city has ever been the symbol of civilization; which, even in its crudest form, represents a spatial pattern of a fixed center of dominance with tributary subordinate districts.[27]

The word "civilization" itself means city; in the ancient world empires were organized around cities. Their frontiers marked the boundary where the powers radiating from the center reached very low levels. Often the relation between the capital and its hinterland was parasitic, not symbiotic, being based on the extraction of tribute rather than the formation of an integrated economic structure. "Rome never became more than a city," as Marx said;[28] or in McKenzie's later remarks with regard to ancient empires: "Tribute rather than trade, however, defined the relation of the subordinate regions to the dominant centers."[29]

Medieval Europe began in the countryside and only gradually did the manufacturing activities separate from agricultural activities and become concentrated in towns. Because the political power lay with the feudal lords, the towns did not have a total dominance over the countryside, but rather were in struggle with it. Nonetheless, the guilds and other regulations of the town served to support a monopoly position in manufacturing and shifted the terms of trade against the countryside.

Trade between cities was beyond the control of any city. As Pirenne points out, a city could not regulate the prices of foreign merchants as it did local artisans and merchants because it could not know what their costs were.[30] The most it could do was insist that the foreign merchant sell through local merchants, thus attempting to appropriate part of the surplus for local citizens.

The consolidation of nation-states created a ring around the number of cities, protecting them from the competition of other countries but allowing free competition within its boundaries. This led to the emergence of a "primate city," that is, the concentration of population, higher-order functions (such as wholesaling, finance, etc.) and wealth and power in the capital city. In part, this could be explained by ecomonic or technical tendencies (e.g., Cristaller's central place theory).[31] But economic centralization is not sustainable without centralization of political power as well, because the government through various laws and ordinances and its construction of communication and transportation systems vitally affects the contours along which economic forces flow.

With the colonial era, the metropolitan cities extended their power beyond national boundaries and gained dominance over outpost cities, which coordinated the collection and transportation of the export staples and political administration of the countryside. McKenzie vividly describes the dual role of the parasitic colonial city:

> Whatever the nature of the modern frontier, it is usually more intimately connected with its distant centers of dominance than with its local *hinterland*. The Western world has established its outposts along the water rims of the backward continents and islands of the sea. Lines of transportation and communication connect the frontier with the foreign centers of control. Docks, go-downs, banks, office buildings are constructed as the essential mechanisms of control. The coast cities of China, Malaya, and India wear these European masks which give the visitor the impression that he is traveling along the shores of Europe or America. A short distance from the waterfront, however, he discovers the "native" city with its pristine organization and form, apparently unaffected, although not actually so, by the foreign invasion.[32]

One of the implications of this for the hinterland is the absence of a primate city. As Jefferson noted, primate city rule did not hold for countries recently unified, such as Italy, nor the dominions and colonies of the British Empire.[33] India, Australia, Canada, etc., for example, had several important centers rather than one, each associated with a particular region or export staple and linked to London rather than to each other (in the case of Canada, Toronto perhaps should be viewed more appropriately as being integrated into the American rather than the British system).

The United States does not have a primate city comparable to London or Paris partly because of its colonial past and partly because of its continental scale. Nonetheless, it does have a hierarchy in which New York and the eastern megalopolis occupy a prominent position.

We described above how the growth of the national corporation was associated with the urban expansion in the nineteenth and early twentieth centuries and the emergence of a national, or more correctly a multicity, market. Corporate centralization of control and dispersion of operations were a response to the challenge of operating over a continent-wide area. The mirror image of this process was the emergence of a structure of "national key cities." McKenzie's description is worth quoting in full (many other books bear out this process and its continuance):

> While the forces of competition tend to set cities and regions apart as separate economic and social entities, other forces at the same time are drawing them together in an ever finer web of functional interrelationship. The trend toward closer integration of settlement is represented in the expansion of communications – in the highways, airways, pipe lines, and particularly in the modern agencies for the dissemination of intelligence. The thickening of the web of routes, the increasing speed

of travel and transport, the development of the metropolitan press, of toll telephone service, the mails, and the radio, all are objective indices of the trend toward more intimate relations among the various units of settlement.

A national system of "key" cities, each dominating a more or less definable trade area, is arising in response to the growth of large-scale organization, based in turn upon recent developments in communication. The creation of the Federal Reserve Banking System in 1913, with its 12 regional cities, each with a tributary territory, mapped so as to cover the entire nation, gave official recognition to the key-center pattern of organization.

Once a city becomes established as a regional distributing center, its banking, transportation, and other facilities compel new concerns entering the region to select it as their point of operation. This cumulative process is one of the chief factors in explaining the recent rapid growth of many of the more isolated cities of the nation, particularly those in the South and Middle West where state rates of population increase have been relatively low. This tendency toward concentration of business function in certain types of cities is indicated roughly by statistics pertaining to the recent construction of office space. While increase in office space has been one of the conspicuous developments in the construction field in postwar years, it has been much more pronounced in the larger than in the smaller cities.[34]

The world hierarchy of cities

With the expansion of direct investment and the extension of the American frontier, New York has become a capital of the world. Plans for its future seem to reflect its new status and are predicated on a consolidation and strengthening of its position. Citibank of New York makes the following observations about that city's recently published *Master Plan* for federal aid and local planning:

The report wisely perceives the strengthening of New York's assets as a major ingredient in the package of solutions for the city's problems. It would foster the concentrations of national center activities, ranging from corporate head offices, mass media and Wall Street to Broadway theaters and Seventh Avenue fashions, within proper planning and design guidelines.

In this regard, it departs from the planning philosophy prevalent in a number of the world's capital cities. There, planners are opting for dispersal rather than further concentration of national center activities.[35]

However, New York will not be the only major capital in the world, and its position has been somewhat weakened recently by internal strife and the Vietnam War. Tokyo, London, Paris, and Frankfurt remain important centers of capital. In the future these, along with Moscow and perhaps Peking, will form an inner circle of high-level strategic planning centers. The lesser cities throughout the world will deal with day-to-day operations of specific local problems in a hierarchical fashion: Larger and more important ones will contain regional corporate headquarters and a middle-strength bourgeoisie, while the smaller ones will be confined to lower-level activities. Because business is usually the core of the city, geographical specialization in general tends to reflect the hierarchy of corporate decision making, and the occupational distribution of labor in a city or region depends upon its function in the international economic system. The "best," most highly paid administrators, doctors, lawyers, scientists, educators, government officials, actors, servants, and hairdressers tend to concentrate in or near the major centers.

The international hierarchy of labor

The structure of income and consumption will tend to parallel the structure of status and authority. The citizens of capital cities will have the best jobs – allocating people and money at the highest level and planning growth and development – and will receive the highest rates of remuneration. (Executives' salaries tend to be a function of the wage bill of people under them. The larger the empire of the multinational corporation, the greater the earnings of top executives, to a large extent independent of their performance. Thus growth in the hinterland subsidiaries implies growth in the income of capital cities but not vice versa.)

This is reflected in the internal structure of corporations. Multinational corporations are torn in two directions. On the one hand, they must adapt to local circumstances in each country. This calls for decentralized decision making. On the other hand, they must coordinate their activities in various parts of the world and stimulate the flow of ideas from one part of their empire to another. This calls for centralized control. They must therefore develop an organizational structure to balance the need for coordination with the need for adaptation to a patchwork quilt of languages, laws, and customs. One solution to this problem is a division of labor based on nationality. Day-to-day management in each country is left to the nationals of that country who, being intimately familiar with local conditions and practices, are able to deal with local problems and local government. These nationals remain rooted in one spot, while above them is a layer of people who move around from country to country transmitting information from one subsidiary to another and from the lower levels to the general office at the apex of the corporate structure. These people (reticulators) for the most part will be citizens of the country of the parent corporation (and will be drawn from a small, culturally homogeneous group within the advanced world), for they will need to have the confidence of their superiors and be able to move easily in higher management circles. Latin Americans, Asians, and Africans will at best be able to aspire to a management position in the intermediate coordinating centers at the continental level. Very few will be able to get much higher than this, for the closer one gets to the top, the more important is "a common cultural heritage."

Because the subsidiaries of multinational corporations are frequently among the largest corporations in their country of operations, their top executives play an influential role in the political, social, and cultural life of the country. Yet these people, whatever their title, occupy at best a medium position in the corporate structure, and are restricted in authority and horizons to a lower level of decision making. The country whose economy is dominated by foreign investment can easily develop a branch-plant outlook not only in economic matters but throughout the range of governmental and educational decision making.

International patterns of consumption

The people in the centers will also be leaders in consumption and the trickle-down, or two-stage, marketing cycle. A new product is usually first introduced to a select group of people who have discretionary income and are willing to experiment in their consumption patterns. Once it is accepted by this group it spreads, or trickles down, to other groups via the demonstration effect. In this process, the rich and the powerful get more votes than everyone else; first, because they have more money to spend; second, because they have more ability to experiment; and third, because they have high status and are likely to be copied. This special group may have something approaching a choice in consumption patterns; the rest have only the choice between conforming or being isolated.

The trickle-down system also has the advantage – from the center's point of view – of reinforcing patterns of authority and control. According to Fallers, it helps keep workers on the treadmill by creating an illusion of upward mobility even though relative status remains unchanged.[36] In each period, subordinates achieve (in part) the consumption standards of their superiors in a previous period and are thus torn in two directions: If they look backward and compare their standards of living through time, things seem to be getting better; if they look upward, they see that their relative position has not changed. They receive a consolation prize, as it were, which may serve to keep them going by softening the reality that, in a competitive system few succeed and many fail. It is little wonder, then, that those at the top stress growth rather than equality as the welfare criterion for human relations.

In the international economy, trickle-down marketing takes the form of an international demonstration effect spreading outward from the metropoles to the hinterland. Lee S. Bickmore, chairman of National Biscuit Company, sees a rapidly expanding market for convenience foods throughout the world as family income rises and the eating habits of consumers move on from bread to cookies and crackers. "Crackers and cookies are the only luxury products that sell nearly as cheaply as necessities,"[37] he points out. Bickmore reportedly sees the day coming when "Arabs and Africans, Latins and Scandinavians will be munching Ritz crackers as enthusiastically as they already drink Coke or brush their teeth with Colgate."[38]

Multinational corporations help speed up this process through their control of marketing channels and communications media. The development of a new product is a fixed cost; once the expenditure needed for invention or innovation has been made, it is forever a bygone. The actual cost of production is thus typically well below selling price, and the limit on output is not rising costs, but falling demand due to saturated markets. Corporations therefore have a strong interest in forestalling the entrance of independent centers of innovation and in maintaining a system of spreading their products widely. Thus, the interest of multinational corporations in underdeveloped countries is larger than the size of the market would suggest.

Communications

Spatial organization is closely associated with communication systems. R. D. McKenzie shows how the separation of communication from transportation made possible the separation of management from operations and the emergence of broad-based, integrated industrial systems:

> Prior to the middle of the nineteenth century, communications and transportation were practically synonymous terms. Intelligence was transmitted by the same agency as commodities and people; but the introduction of the telegraph, the telephone, and wireless forms of communication has completely changed this situation and produced revolutionary results in spatial organization. The first effect of this divergence is the rate of speed in the transmission of ideas and objects was to make for centralization of control and decentralization of operation. The function of management and direction is tending to become spatially removed from that of operations or application. Under the new order of communication, planning and direction of business or government can be more efficiently executed at the radial points of communication than the level of action itself.[39]

Many supporters of the multinational corporation argue that it is an imperative of modern communications. Sidney Rolfe, for example, maintains that "The conflict of our era is between ethno-centric nationalism and geocentric technology . . . and that history is not of the essence here, evolution is . . . and what the world faces is *le defi international* rather than *le defi americain.*"[40]

This view, thus, argues that the problem is one of horizontal integration rather than vertical subordination. This technological determinism should not be accepted. The new technology, because it increases interaction, implies greater *inter*dependence but not necessarily a hierarchical structure. Communications linkages could be arranged in the form of a grid in which each point was directly connected to many other points, permitting lateral communication as well as vertical communication. This system would be polycentric; messages from one point to another would go directly rather than through the center; each point would become a center on its own, and the distinction between center and periphery would disappear.

Such a grid is made *more* feasible by aeronautical and electronic revolutions that greatly reduce costs of communications. It is not technology that creates inequality; rather, it is *organization* that imposes a ritual judicial asymmetry on the use of intrinsically symmetrical means of communication; it arbitrarily creates unequal capacities to initiate and terminate exchange, to store and retrieve information, and to determine the extent of the exchange and the terms of the discussion. Just as colonial powers in the past linked each point in the hinterland to the metropolis and inhibited lateral communications, preventing the growth of independent centers of decision making and creativity, multinational corporations (backed by state powers) centralize control by imposing a hierarchical system.

Is in this light that the control and organization of international communications should be viewed. For example, one could imagine an alternative system of organization in the form of national planning. The multinational corporation is a private institution that organizes one or a few industries across many countries. Its polar opposite is a public institution that organizes many industries across one region. At the same time, modern communication could provide for a free flow of science and technology between nations and countries and counteract the danger of isolation. Regionalization would be substituted for internationalization. The span of control would be confined to the boundaries of a single polity and society and not spread over many countries. The advantage of the multinational corporation is its global perspective. The advantage of national planning is its ability to remove the waster of oligopolistic anarchy, that is, meaningless product differentiation and an imbalance between different industries within a geographical area. It concentrates *all* levels of decision making in one locale, and can thus provide each region with a full complement of skills and occupations. This opens up new possibilities for local development by making possible the social and political control of economic decision making. Multinational corporations, in contrast, weaken political contact because they span many countries and can escape national regulation.

Part III

The future of the world economy

Introduction

Robert Rowthorn

When I first met Stephen Hymer in London he had just completed a study on multinational corporations for the Canadian government's Task Force on the Structure of Canadian Industry and a paper on transatlantic reactions to direct investment. In these writings (one of which, "Direct Foreign Investment and the National Economic Interest," appears here as Chapter 7), Hymer approached the multinational corporation from a bourgeois nationalist standpoint, considering how the problems it creates can be handled within the existing framework of capitalist property rights. As always in such an approach, the government was assumed to express some kind of General Will and to act on behalf of the entire population. Any conflicts of interest between groups or classes were ignored and there was no discussion of the class character of various alternative policies toward the multinationals. Indeed, the entire analysis was conducted in terms of "countries" and corporations. On one level, this approach reflects the constraints imposed on anyone working for an official task force – an explicitly Marxist or class analysis would have been rejected out of hand by the Canadian government. On another level, however, it reflects Hymer's own intellectual position at the time. Politically and emotionally he had been influenced by the events and radical atmosphere of the midsixties, but as yet this radicalism had not seriously affected his method of analysis, which was that of a conventional business economist of the antitrust school.

The main thrust of these earlier writings was as follows. Multinational corporations are here to stay and ideally should be regulated by some kind of international agency, just as national corporations are at present regulated by national planning or antitrust agencies. Unfortunately, international cooperation on the required scale is not an immediate or even medium-term prospect, and in the meantime individual countries must do the best they can. Hymer and the task force argued that, for Canada, this meant taking unilateral action to limit the power of foreign capital and to ensure balanced economic development. Domestic capital should be strengthened and encouraged to purchase shares in the Canadian subsidiaries of foreign multinationals, and these subsidiaries should be regulated by a government agency. In the Canadian context these proposals were fairly radical, for they involved a major extension of state control over big business and a head-on clash with U.S. imperialism. Thus, starting from an avowedly capitalist standpoint, Hymer and the task force followed through the logic of nationalism to the point where the existing structure of capitalist power was brought into question, and for this reason their recommendations were never really accepted by the Canadian government.

Over the next few years, following the completion of his work with the task force, Hymer's view on the multinational corporation changed in a number of ways as he developed in depth ideas that were largely implicit in his earlier work. The task force study, for example, had contained very little on the organizational structure of the multinational corporation and its implications for national economic development, a subject discussed at length in a later paper, "The Multinational Corporation and the International Division of Labor" (Chapter 6 above). This paper, in my opinion, is his best and most complete analysis of the multinational corporation.

In another direction, concerned with international rivalry and the world pattern of capitalist expansion, Hymer and I were to collaborate in writing an article entitled "Multinational Corporations and International Oligopoly: The Non-American Challenge" (Chapter 8 below). The background of our article is as follows. For some time I had been thinking about British economic development and the problems a socialist government would face if it came to power. This had led me to study British imperialism and to consider the nature of world capitalist rivalry. At this point I met Stephen Hymer, who was visiting Britain for a few months. We soon realized how much our views had in common and, after a few days of hectic discussion, decided to collaborate in making a statistical analysis of the world's largest corporations. The results surprised us both. We found that, contrary to popular belief, American giants were not outpacing their European rivals, but were themselves being challenged. Moreover, big firms seemed to be at a disadvantage in comparison with medium-sized firms, whose growth rates were in general higher. The relatively slow growth of American firms was easy to explain – they had suffered from a locational disadvantage, being heavily dependent on sales in the U.S. market, which had been expanding relatively slowly. The faster growth of medium-sized firms, however, was something of a mystery to us, and we were never able to explain it. Indeed, I still cannot understand why big firms grew so slowly during the period in question. An obvious explanation is they they had overreached themselves and had begun to experience serious diseconomies of scale or growth. This seems implausible, but I cannot think of any better hypothesis.

In the light of our statistical analysis we went on to consider the dynamics of international investment, arguing that the multinational corporation can only be understood within the framework of oligopoly theory: Big firms exist in rivalry with other big firms, choosing their pattern of expansion with both offensive and defensive needs in mind, and they are as much influenced by the growth and location of markets as by technology and economies of scale. Moreover, multinational corporations bring few benefits that a medium-sized or large country cannot acquire in some other way. Japan, for example, has kept out the multinationals and yet has acquired a modern technology and reaped huge economies of scale by concentrating production in a few large corporations. And, if capitalist Japan could do this, so in our opinion could any medium or large socialist country. Indeed, a socialist country would be even better able to exploit economies of scale: The entire economy could be planned as an integrated whole and wasteful duplication could be eliminated by merging existing large firms into even bigger units. We concluded that existing nation-states were not yet out of date, and that socialism would enable individual countries to exploit modern technology without opening their frontiers to the multinationals and without sacrificing their independence to some supranational body.

On reflection, I think these conclusions need qualifying, for they only really apply to countries like Japan where multinationals do not yet occupy a dominant position in the economy. In most of Western Europe, however, particularly in Britain and the Netherlands, big firms are already highly international in operation and, it would be very costly to dismember them and set up a socialist economy of the kind we envisaged. Indeed, the countries of Western Europe are becoming rapidly more interdependent both through trade and the spread of multinationals, and the scope for independent national development is being correspondingly reduced. To deal adequately with the emerging European economy will require socialist planning on a continental scale. This is, however, a long-term solution, for it will take many years to establish the political conditions necessary for Europe-wide planning. In the meantime, individual Left-wing governments in, for example, France or Italy, may be forced to come to terms with the multinationals and establish a working relationship with them. There are many different forms such a relationship might take, ranging from contractual agreements about future investment and output plans through to state ownership of local subsidiaries. But these would only be stopgap measures and the long-term need would remain some form of international planning. The multinational corporation is making international socialism a necessity (and a possibility) in a way that trade never did.

The third article reprinted in this part is entitled "United States Investment Abroad" (Chapter 9). It contains little new material, but weaves together a number of diverse topics upon which Hymer had worked during the previous fifteen years, and updates some of the unpublished work contained in his doctoral dissertation of 1960. Much of the article is devoted to a detailed description of U.S. corporations' expansion abroad. Hymer shows how giant firms have been responsible for the bulk of overseas investment and how they have focused their expansion on certain specific industries such as automobiles, chemicals, and petroleum. In these industries the American subsidiary is usually "the dominant producer or one of a small number of producers." He argues that these characteristics imply an interaction between multinational corporations "and the government quite different from the traditional view, which pictures a large state acting on a plane above business. Large corporations, because of their cohesiveness, their access to information and modern technology, their worldwide network of communication, and their long-term perspectives, often act alongside the state or above it. In theory, the corporation is a person operating under the sovereignty of the state. In practice, the actual power of many national governments, relative to multinational corporations, is more like that of city governments than sovereign states." Hymer then considers how local firms react to foreign penetration of their domestic economy. Some take a nationalist position and call for the use of state power to protect their domestic markets. Others, however, take an "internationalist" position and oppose measures that discriminate against foreign capital or limit the freedom of action of multinationals. Among the latter group are many of the bigger local firms that are themselves multinational in operation or have aspirations in this direction, together with smaller satellite firms that supply the multinationals or distribute their products. Hymer argues that this alliance, of actual or would-be multinationals and their smaller hangers-on, is very powerful and is usually successful in its opposition to economic nationalism. This is a plausible argument and it helps explain why so few bourgeois regimes have resisted the spread of multinational corporations.

In "The United States Multinational Corporations and Japanese Competition in the Pacific" (Chapter 10), Hymer takes up a theme of the previous article that an international ruling class is emerging and that the epoch of multinationals has ended the old system of exclusive spheres of influence. He begins by calling our attention to the asymmetry of Japan's foreign economic position, that is, that Japan's direct foreign investment in relation to exports was only 10 percent in 1968 (compared with the United States' 168 percent). Hymer next shows that this low percentage conceals Japan's growing network of raw material production in the Pacific Rim and the fact that Japanese economic penetration has taken the form mainly of product sharing, guaranteed demand contracts, technical assistance, and so on, rather than branch plants and subsidiaries. But he foresees that the United States and Europe will force Japan to abandon its go-it-alone policy, which is expected to shift from "undercutting" to "interlocking." Looking at international capitalism from the standpoint of the underdeveloped world, Hymer warns that although the major imperialist powers compete in "offering suppliers credit" they "form a united front when collecting the debt." Further, he warns that technical assistance and similar agreements draw the underdeveloped countries "into a system of continued dependency as the big countries collude more and more." At this point Hymer's analysis of the capitalist product cycle becomes crucial. All major international firms have products in different stages of the product cycle and although these firms bring capital and technology to underdeveloped countries, they keep control over new technology and new products, hence deepening the web of dependency.

An interesting aspect of this paper is Hymer's rejection of the common view that imperialism makes capitalist development impossible in the Third World: "The question is not so much whether industry will grow rapidly but who will organize it – *national* capital, *state* capital, or *foreign* capital. What direction will it taken and who will benefit from it?" His criticism of economic dependency is not that it prevents industrial development, but that it implies a certain pattern of growth and income distribution, and reinforces capitalist power in the country concerned. This is, I am sure, correct.

In the last essay, "International Politics and International Economics: A Radical Approach" (Chapter 11), written in 1973, Hymer deals with the problem of class struggle for the first time in a systematic way. He argues that the uneven development of world capitalism has divided the working class along sectional lines, and created a labor aristocracy that accepts its subordinate position in return for real material benefits. He points out that during the 1950s and 1960s the major source of rebellion and protest was not the established proletariat, but rather "the new strata being incorporated into the wage labor force from their previous position in the latent surplus population" (e.g., the peasantry). But Hymer believes things are changing and that the labor movement in the advanced world will in the future be infused with "new dimensions of protest and militancy." He gives two reasons for this conclusion: Real wages will not grow in the future as they have in the past, and workers are disillusioned with the "consumer society." He argues that the response of labor "will take a political form, i.e. a struggle over state power around the central issue of capitalism and its continuance. Because states are territorial, the locus of the struggle will be largely national, or at least regional, even though the context is international. In the United States, it will probably tend to the formation of some sort of labor party. In Europe, it will probably lead to unification and a closer union between Social Democratic and Communist Parties. In the underdeveloped countries, it will lead to an increased role of labor in politics as the new proletariat emerges, and so on." If we ignore his rather fanciful reference to an American Labor Party, this seems a reasonable forecast. Hymer correctly points out, however, that the struggle is extremely complex and the outcome is not a foregone conclusion. There may even be a major shift to the Right as "a privileged part of the . . . working class in the advanced countries joins with capital in a new imperialistic alliance to get higher benefits in return for suppressing blacks, Third World people, foreign workers, the aged, etc." He thinks this is unlikely, but its very possibility is a warning against the dangers that may face us in future decades.

In sum, the articles in this section stand as a valuable contribution to our understanding of capitalism as a world system, and the potentialities inherent in the present epoch. The political position that both underlies and emerges from these articles is classic Marxist internationalism. Marx wrote about the European proletariat that the basic task of the workers' movement is the establishment of "regular cooperation between the employed and the unemployed." Hymer ends his last article with the call for "steady struggle to eliminate . . . [competition among workers] at higher and higher levels until it reaches a world historic perspective."

7　Direct foreign investment and the national economic interest

Does it really make a difference that so high a percentage of Canadian industry is owned by foreign firms? Most Canadian economists seem to answer that it does not.[1] "Foreign investment may create problems from a political point of view," they would argue, "but from an economic point of view, it is a great benefit to the country. A business firm's behavior is determined by supply and demand, not by its nationality. Whether a firm is American-owned or Canadian-owned, it invests by choosing the most profitable alternative use of its funds, and strives always to maximize profits. Nothing is lost by having Canadian industry controlled from abroad, while much is gained from the capital and technology which the foreigners bring to us. If we wish to place restrictions on foreign investment for political reasons, we shall have to pay for that action by lowering our economic welfare."

While there is much to be said for this line of reasoning, it is not fully convincing. Foreign firms do bring us capital and technology, but in some cases they may charge too high a price. By judicious regulation and restriction, we might be able to lower the price and obtain the happy combination of greater political independence and higher national income. Because I feel that the darker side of direct foreign investment has been neglected in the past by Canadian economists, I will concentrate on it. By exploring some problems associated with direct investment, I will argue a case for closer control than is customarily thought necessary.

The motive for direct investment: imperfect competition

Political concern about foreign investment centers primarily, and properly so, on the issue of foreign ownership and control. Not all foreign investment, or inflow of capital from abroad, is accompanied by foreign ownership; foreign

This essay originally appeared in *Nationalism in Canada,* Peter Russell, ed. (Toronto: McGraw-Hill Ryerson, 1966), pp. 191–202. Copyright © 1966 by McGraw-Hill Ryerson Ltd. Reprinted by permission of McGraw-Hill Ryerson Ltd.

purchases of bonds and of non-controlling equities are cases in point. Direct investment, on the other hand, refers to those cases where the foreigner, by exporting capital, does acquire control and retains the locus of decision-making.[2]

Now the proper place to begin any discussion of direct investment in Canada is to put the question: What motivates foreign firms to own branch plants and subsidiaries in Canada? It is not simply differences in the cost of capital; though these play a role, they are not crucial determinants. If the rate of return on capital is higher in Canada than in the United States, Americans admittedly will find it profitable to lend money to Canadians. But this does not explain why they choose to invest directly in subsidiaries which they wholly own and control. Other factors must be present to account for this choice of means.

Nor will it suffice to say that an American or British firm acquires a subsidiary in Canada because it needs a raw material found in abundance in Canada, for that fails to answer the question of why it chooses to acquire the raw material through direct investment rather than by some alternative means. It could, for example, buy the raw material from an independent Canadian firm instead of investing large sums of money in direct ownership and control. Similarly, a foreign firm wishing to use its superior technology or its brand name in Canada does not have to invest in a subsidiary in order to do so; it could rent, license, or otherwise sell its advantage to an independent Canadian firm. Why doesn't it?

It can be said with certainty that the foreign firm will choose the alternative that maximizes its own profits. The issue for Canadians however, is whether that particular alternative is also in the best interest of Canada. Is it to our advantage to have Canadian enterprise directly affiliated to foreign firms, or would we be better off if the Canadian firm was independent? Which form of business organization results in more Canadian production, lower prices for Canadian consumers, and higher prices for Canadian exports? We cannot be sure until we know what it is that the parent firm is trying to achieve through control of its Canadian subsidiary.

Let us consider a number of cases where the motive for direct investment stems from the fact that the relevant industry in the United States is made up of a small number of firms. This oligopolistic market structure, which exists in many industries, is a situation of imperfect competition which lies somewhere between the poles of monopoly of the single firm and pure competition of many firms. Confining our attention to oligopoly means neglecting the full spectrum of possibilities, but this is defensible, for empirical evidence in Canada and elsewhere shows that direct investment tends to be associated with industries where the market share is largely accounted for by a small number of firms.[3] It makes sense to look for causes and evaluate effects in terms of an industrial structure characterized by the small number of firms, or, in the parlance of the economist, high concentration.

Horizontal integration

Consider an industry where there are great economies of scale, or advantages from largeness, or where there are other barriers to entry facing potential competitors, with the consequence that there are only a few firms in each country. Since competition tends to lower price and reduce profits, these leading firms will have every incentive to agree amongst themselves to restrain competition. If international trade takes place, agreements with respect to price and market shares must extend across national boundaries to encompass foreign as well as domestic firms. International cartels based on price and market sharing agreements are one device which firms sometimes have used to achieve international collusion. Direct investment to achieve international integration of firms is another means. The integration is horizontal in the sense that it links different firms producing the same product. Direct investment can give a firm in one country control over price and output decisions of an enterprise in another country. To obtain perfect collusion, all of the enterprises in the world producing a given product would have to merge into one large international firm, controlling prices, production, and sales in each country, and maximizing global profits. In reality, collusion seldom goes this far, but stops at the point where there are a few large international firms which neither collude completely nor compete fully.

In such industries it is impossible to evaluate the goodness or badness of foreign investment without considering the effect of foreign ownership on the degree of competition. The operation of foreign ownership decreases the number of firms in the world and tends to encourage imperfectly competitive behavior. In general, imperfect competition reduces economic welfare because it decreases the efficiency with which resources (such as scarce labor and capital) are allocated. Prices facing consumers tend to be higher than they would otherwise be and consumers tend to be made worse off. Hence, direct investment which creates horizontal integration tends to have detrimental effects on world income. Within an individual nation, legal procedures exist to evaluate the performance of oligopolistic industries and to effect remedies when deemed appropriate; in principle, if not always in practice, this is the function of anti-combines legislation in Canada. There is a tendency, however, in Canada and elsewhere, to discuss market competition (or its absence) as if it were only of domestic origin, and to discuss foreign investment as if it created international problems unrelated to issues of competitive and oligopolistic behavior. Seldom are direct investment and anti-combines policy considered together. Direct investment is discussed as if it was a matter of capital and technology alone, while competition is investigated with little attention to direct investment.

In fact, anti-combines legislation designed to compel competitive behavior should be applied even more stringently in cases where foreign ownership is involved than in wholly domestic industries. For as well as misallocating resources and reducing efficiency, the existence of oligopoly increases the profits of firms, or redistributes income in favor of the oligopolists. In a completely Canadian industry, this redistribution effect takes from one set of Canadians and gives to another set of Canadians. Whether this is good or bad depends on who the givers and takers are, and what each does with his money. If, for example, the gainers tend to reinvest their profits and promote growth, oligopoly may not be such a bad thing after all. But where foreign ownership is involved, the outcome is necessarily different. The gains from oligopoly accrue to foreigners, and the redistribution effect reduces Canada's national income. Insofar as the foreigner gains by being paid for services rendered, there can be no complaint. Under oligopoly, however, some portion of the foreigners' gains may be paid for the disservice of restraining competition and reducing the efficiency of resource allocation.

It is unnecessary to look far to find out why the anti-combines implications of direct investment have been neglected. Firstly, it would mean investigating not only enterprises operating in Canada, but also parent and sister firms operating in other countries beyond Canada's jurisdiction. Secondly, any action taken by Canada would affect not only Canadian industry and welfare, but those of foreign countries as well. Regulation of international oligopoly, therefore, requires cooperation between Canada and other nations. At present, no mechanism for such cooperation exists, nor does its creation seem likely in the near future. There is a serious policy gap here, and room for Canadian initiative. The anti-combines or anti-trust legislation in Canada and in countries which invest in Canada is not adequate for a world in which international trade and international firms play ever more important roles.

Vertical integration

The complexities of dealing with direct investment can be further illustrated by considering the case of vertical integration, that is, the linking of firms that operate at different stages in the productive process (such as a steel mill and an iron ore mine). Consider an industry with two stages of production, with stage A in Canada producing the raw material and stage B in the United States engaging in further processing. For simplicity, suppose there is only one source of the raw material in Canada and only one firm, a monopolist by definition, producing from that source. Similarly, assume there is only one manufacturer, again a monopolist, doing the processing in the United States. How will the price of the raw material be determined in this case? The answer is important, for the higher the price of the raw material, the more profit accrues at stage *A* and the less at stage *B*. The firms cannot rely on competition to determine prices, for each party has no alternative but to deal with the other party. The raw material seller cannot find another outlet and the buyer cannot avail himself of any competing suppliers. The price will depend not on supply and demand in a competitive market, but on trials of strength. If, however, the two firms were owned jointly, the conflict of interest would be removed and the issue of setting a price on the raw material obviated. The vertically integrated firm would simply maximize the total profits of *A* and *B* taken together and would not worry about how to distribute them between the two stages.

Faced with a situation of this kind, what should be the government's attitude? The economics of this case are quite different from the preceding one of horizontal integration. Vertical integration, by permitting rationalization in the productive process, normally leads to lower prices and greater output, and is therefore desirable from the point of view of world efficiency. The demonstration of this proposition requires somewhat more technical analysis than is justifiable here, but an intuitive argument may suffice. In the vertical case just outlined, with no integration there were two stages of monopoly – one in the market where the raw material was sold, and one in the market where the product was sold after manufacturing. This sequential monopoly involves a doubling of the distortive influences conventionally attributed to monopoly. When the two stages are integrated under a single firm, one source of distortion, in the raw material market, is removed. Though this is far from an ideal solution, it is nonetheless an improvement, and there is thus a presumption that it is desirable.

Even though this vertical integration may lead to a more efficient allocation of the world's resources, Canada may not benefit. What matters in the latter regard is how the gains are distributed. Part of the gains take the form of lower prices of the final manufactured product to the consumer; here Canada gains only to the extent that these consumers are Canadians. The rest of the gains accrue as profits, and Canada's share will depend on tax policy. For accounting purposes, the (vertically integrated) company sets the price at which it sells the raw material from its stage *A* raw material wing to its stage *B* manufacturing wing, computes profits using this price, and endeavors to pay taxes accordingly. But this raw material price is an exceedingly arbitrary one. It does not reflect any economic transaction taking place at arm's length, but is rather a book entry linking a parent and its subsidiary. The company will try to set the price to minimize its total tax bill, but that price may or may not be one that maximizes Canada's share of taxes paid. This problem cannot be solved by resort to the handy device of a free market price, for if there was a free market, the stage *B* firm would have bought its raw material there and never have acquired direct control of the stage *A* supplier. Because this is not a competitive situation, there is no "just" (competitive) price. The profits that stem from closer coordination of firms in different countries accrue jointly to all of them and cannot be allocated to any single one by economic criteria. A political solution is necessary to distribute the gains resulting from the improved efficiency of vertical integration. It is possible that at present the benefits in many industries go out of Canada to a considerable extent, for Canadian raw materials are often owned abroad and used abroad. Certainly the Canadian tax authorities should very properly appraise all transactions of this type and strive to maximize the Canadian tax share.

Technology and entrepreneurship

Direct investment involves the flow not only of capital but also of technology and entrepreneurship. An analysis of market imperfection turns out to be a useful way to approach the complexities that inhere in analyzing these two critical factors in the process of economic growth.

Foreign ownership is frequently based on the foreigner's possession of superior technology. A firm which has a patent – or a unique (differentiated) product, or some other advantage – is a monopolist with respect to that advantage. Why does the firm not sell (or rent) the patent rather than make a direct investment? If there were many buyers, it would be tempted to do so, for it would then be in a strong position to extract maximum rent. But its bargaining position is much weaker if it faces only a few buyers. The small number of buyers tends to offset the company's monopoly power. To bypass this countervailing power, the company, rather than renting or selling its patent, may be induced to invest directly in its own foreign subsidiary. But while the company's position may thereby be improved, this does not mean that direct investment is therefore in Canada's interest. It might be possible for Canada to gain access to the superior technology at a lower cost in a way that yields the foreign firm an even lower return. This is a matter which has hardly been explored, and it is impossible to be specific. It is widely accepted, however, that restrictions should sometimes be placed on the use of patents; certainly special attention should be given to patents which prompt international investment.

The issue of technology can be looked at in terms of three targets. Firstly, we wish to ensure the rapid adoption in Canada of the best technology in the world. Secondly, we wish to avoid paying too high a price for this technology. Thirdly, we wish to encourage the formation of entrepreneurial talent in Canada. The analysis of oligopoly showed that too great an anxiety to achieve the first target could endanger the second. An argument can be made that restrictions on foreign ownership are needed as well in the interest of the third target.

The large volume of foreign investment in Canada seems to suggest a shortage of Canadian entrepreneurs. But which is cause and which is effect? We usually think of foreign investment as a consequence of a shortage of domestic entrepreneurs, but perhaps the former has helped create the latter. Suppose, in the extreme case, Canada forbade all foreign direct investment. This would certainly slow down the flow of technology and create a gap between techniques used in Canada and the best available elsewhere. What would happen then? Through time, the gap would grow and there would be an increasing incentive for Canadians to learn how to breach it. Might this not stimulate a growth of Canadian entrepreneurship? Once over their initial learning period, might not Canadian entrepreneurs be able to stand on their own feet? The shortage of entrepreneurs in Canada might disappear and with it the need for so much foreign investment. Just as there is an infant industry argument for a tariff, there may be an infant entrepreneurship argument for restricting foreign ownership.

It could be argued against this that foreign firms stimulate Canadian entrepreneurs by providing a demonstration effect and that banning direct investment would lead to less rather than more Canadian entrepreneurship. There is some case to be made along these lines, for the presence of firms from abroad certainly keeps already existing Canadian firms on their toes. But has the growth of new Canadian firms been stimulated or inhibited? One of the alarming features of the historical record in Canada is that there is no apparent tendency for the extent of foreign ownership and control to decline through time; the evidence is rather of a remarkable stability over time.[4] Both overall and within industries, foreign firms seem to maintain their market share and not give way to Canadian firms. This is true in many other countries as well. In general, direct investment seems to be self-sustaining, tending to hold its own or expand. The only important cases where foreign investment has given way to domestic investment occurred in the United States during the First and Second World Wars when special circumstances led to the Americanization of British and German subsidiaries. War, as it were, created artificial protection for American firms; perhaps protection is needed for Canadian firms.

Alternative sources of capital

No attention has been paid so far to capital. The reader may very well feel that we have thrown the baby out with the bathwater. If we try to improve the degree of competition in Canadian industries by restricting direct investment, will we not sacrifice the capital that foreign firms bring us, and will this not mean a net loss in economic welfare?

The first point to be made in this connection is that we are not discussing the *amount* of capital that Canada should borrow from abroad, but rather, the *form* that borrowing should take. If we restrict direct investment, we are still free to borrow as much as is desired in the market for bonds and non-controlling equities. Whether we could get enough of this portfolio investment to replace the lost direct investment would depend on how perfect the capital markets were. Suppose, to take an extreme case, Canada compelled all American firms to divest themselves of their Canadian subsidiares within a reasonable period of time. Clearly there would be a greatly increased demand for capital in Canada as American firms sought out Canadian buyers. But there would be created simultaneously an extra supply of an exactly equal amount of capital in the United States as the American sellers received the proceeds. In a perfectly functioning capital market, the result would be to lower interest rates in the United States and to raise interest rates in Canada, and to induce a flow of capital back into Canada. American investors would increase their holdings of Canadian bonds and of equity securities in Canadian firms. The end result in a perfect capital market would be about the same level of aggregate American investment in Canada, but in a different form; the investment would be held by American investors without control rather than by American corporations with control.

In the real world, however, capital markets are far from perfect. The loss on direct investment would probably not be completely offset by an increase in portfolio investment. There would, then, be a price to pay, but unless capital markets do not function at all, this price would be far less than the loss of the total amount of direct investment in Canada. Some of it would come back in a new form.

But there is also another argument on the side that no net loss need occur. Forcing American firms to sell their securities might lead to some pleasantly surprising results. One of the important characteristics of direct investment is the insistence of parent firms on nearly complete ownership of their subsidiaries. It has been argued throughout this paper that the motivation of the foreign direct investor is the maximization of global profits. To the extent that these profits rest on monopolistic (or oligopolistic) advantage, they are maximized when they are fully captured by the integrated decision-making unit, and this necessitates full control and wholly-owned subsidiaries. While some price would be high enough to induce the parent firm to sell shares in its Canadian operation to Canadians, a number of factors decrease the likelihood. The local capital market may be thin and prospective buyers may underestimate the profitability of the local operation. The parent firm may fear loss of control, or simply not wish to listen to a minority interest; it is, in any event, accustomed to operating an integrated concern at home and is geared to using the same methods abroad. The firm tends to see itself as a manufacturer, not an investor, and has no desire to be left with surplus funds through permitting local participation. Its view is that potential local shareholders should prefer to buy its shares, for they would then have access to global profits and avoid the risks associated with smaller or more specialized local operations.[5]

The foreign firm's preference for full control of its Canadian subsidiary has meant the exclusion of Canadians from participation in equity securities, except to the extent that they have been willing to buy the shares of the parent. The result may have been to deflect Canadian saving into other investments with lower rates of return. This, in turn, may have reduced total Canadian savings. By forcing foreign owners to sell shares in the Canadian operation in Canada one might raise rates of return to Canadians and elicit the extra savings necessary to finance capital investment in Canada.

The argument is an old one. In nearly every country where direct investment is important, there has been some move to compel the selling of local shares. The customary counter-argument is that this interferes with the efficient operation of the corporations. But what it might do is interfere with their efficient *monopolization* and that type of interference might be a very welcome one. It is interesting to note that though Canada has been a net recipient of foreign investment for a long time, it has not had an overall faster rate of economic growth than the United States. This suggests that either the Canadian propensity to save (for investment) is lower than the American, or that the productivity of capital is lower in Canada than in the United States. It is not beyond reason that the high degree of foreign investment is one cause of the lower Canadian saving propensity and/or the lower productivity of capital. There has been little empirical investigation of this issue in Canada and nothing can be said with certainty except that it deserves more study.

I have tried in this paper to counter the presumption that foreign investment is generally beneficial to the Canadian economic interest and its regulation generally detrimental. To argue against government interference in the working of free markets, economists appeal to Adam Smith's "invisible hand" as insuring that profit-maximizing firms promote the general welfare in attempting to promote their own. This argument, however, depends upon the existence of effective competition in the markets for goods and factors of production. There is empirical evidence to suggest that in many cases of foreign investment markets are highly imperfect. The presumption of the invisible hand is missing, and therefore it may be possible for the government to increase the level of income by interfering with the decisions of private corporations.

To the extent that market imperfections are important, the cost of political nationalism is lower than is usually thought. In fact, from the viewpoint of economic theory, restrictions on direct investment make far more sense than the high wall of tariffs that Canada has erected to stimulate Canadian industry. Most economic analyses suggest that these tariffs are quite detrimental to Canadian interests; Canadian per capita income is one-third lower than in the United States and a good part of this differential may be caused by the Canadian tariff.[6] In the case of foreign investment, however, some of the theoretical arguments suggest that the problem lies in the opposite direction of too little nationalism, rather than too much.

My primary purpose has been to analyze rather than to prescribe, but arguments for specific nationalist policies have flowed from the analysis. In particular, the Canadian authorities should consider the feasibility of the following remedies:

— use Canadian anti-combines legislation to ensure competitive behavior by foreign firms
— cooperate with other nations in the regulation of international oligopoly
— use tax policy to maximize the Canadian share of taxes paid by international firms with Canadian operations
— use patent legislation, and other means, to encourage the inflow of foreign technology into Canada without foreign ownership
— use restrictions on direct investment rather than the tariff to stimulate Canadian industry and entrepreneurship.

8 Multinational corporations and international oligopoly: the non-American challenge

co-authored with Robert Rowthorn

The large-scale migration of United States capital to foreign countries in recent years and the coming to prominence of the multinational corporation have stimulated a world-wide discussion about the nature and significance of this latest stage in the evolution of business organization. The purpose of this essay is to examine the problem of direct foreign business investment in its European context, using a simple oligopoly model combined with data on the 500 largest industrial corporations in the world (approximately 300 U.S. and 200 non-U.S.).[1] Our aim is to analyze what might be termed the dialectics of the multinational corporation, the thrusts and counterthrusts of U.S. and non-U.S. corporations as they compete for shares in the world market using direct foreign investment as one of their chief instruments. Our hope is to clarify the debate on the "American challenge," a debate that we think is in many ways a manifestation on the political level of the oligopolistic rivalry of large corporations on the business level. We also wish to draw out some of the implications of the current European policy to merge and rationalize in order to meet the "specter of the American Multinational Corporations."[2]

Servan-Schreiber's[3] analysis of the American challenge provides a useful starting point. His analysis rests on three basic propositions. First, modern technology requires large corporations. The large corporation, because of its ability to concentrate capital and administer it effectively, is an essential requisite of growth and modernity. The parallels on this point, between Servan-Schreiber's analysis and that of Galbraith in _The New Industrial State_,[4] are of course obvious. Second, a country (continent) without its own multinational corporations will become a colony. If Europe does not create corporate capitals to match the American giants it will be reduced to playing

This essay originally appeared in _The International Corporation_, C. P. Kindleberger, ed. (Cambridge, Mass.: M.I.T. Press, 1970), pp. 57–91. Copyright © 1970 by the M.I.T. Press. Reprinted by permission of the M.I.T. Press.

Table 1. *The size distribution of large industrial corporations*

Size class of sales (millions of dollars)	Cumulative number of firms							Cumulative sales (billions of dollars)						
	1957		1962		1967		U.S. as % of Total[a]	1957		1962		1967		U.S. as % of Total[a]
	U.S.	non-U.S.	U.S.	non-U.S.	U.S.	non-U.S.		U.S.	non-U.S.	U.S.	non-U.S.	U.S.	non-U.S.	
(1)	(2)	(3)	(4)	(5)	(6)	(7)	(8)	(9)	(10)	(11)	(12)	(13)	(14)	(15)
19,999 to 26,005	—	—	—	—	1	—	100	—	—	—	—	20.0	—	100
15,345 to 19,999	—	—	—	—	1	—	100	—	—	—	—	20.0	—	100
11,724 to 15,345	—	—	1	—	2	—	100	—	—	14.6	—	33.3	—	100
9,033 to 11,724	1	—	2	—	3	—	100	10.9	—	24.2	—	43.8	—	100
6,931 to 9,033	2	1	3	—	4	1	80	18.8	7.4	32.3	—	51.5	8.4	86
5,318 to 6,931	3	1	3	1	7	2	78	24.6	7.4	32.3	6.0	68.9	9.4	88
4,080 to 5,318	5	1	4	2	9	2	82	33.3	7.4	37.0	10.1	78.2	13.9	85
3,131 to 4,080	6	2	7	2	12	2	86	36.9	10.8	47.7	10.1	89.2	13.9	86
2,402 to 3,131	11	2	11	3	28	5	85	50.2	10.8	58.2	12.6	133.4	22.0	86
1,843 to 2,402	16	4	20	4	37	10	79	60.5	14.9	76.6	14.6	153.0	32.8	82
1,414 to 1,843	22	5	29	8	50	18	74	69.9	16.5	91.9	21.2	173.5	45.7	79
1,085 to 1,414	33	7	41	11	73	34	68	83.1	18.9	106.3	25.0	202.3	65.6	76
0,823.5 to 1,085	45	8	56	23	101	61	62	94.0	19.8	121.0	36.1	229.5	90.9	72
0,639.8 to 0,823.5	57	18	77	36	137	87	61	102.9	26.9	136.2	45.9	256.2	109.7	70
0,490.1 to 0,639.8	81	27	108	61	175	112	61	116.5	31.8	153.4	59.5	277.5	123.4	69
0,376.0 to 0,490.1	105	51	138	88	225	142	61	126.5	42.0	166.2	70.9	298.9	136.3	69
0,289.5 to 0,376.0	143	67	180	118	278	185	60	139.2	47.3	179.9	80.9	316.4	150.7	68
0,221.4 to 0,289.5	196	88	235	155				152.8	52.7	193.9	90.2			
0,169.9 to 0,221.4			284	183						203.3	95.5			

[a] 1967.

a secondary, colonial role, not just in the economic sphere, but in the political, social, and cultural spheres as well. Third, the appropriate remedy lies in positive rather than negative measures. Negative measures to restrict the inflow of U.S. corporation investment, as the Japanese have done, would in Servan-Schreiber's view avoid the American challenge rather than meet it. Instead he argues that positive measures are needed on a European-wide basis to create giant European corporations using advanced methods of business organization and working in close collaboration with universities and government to create an economic structure suited to modern technology.

This brief summary of Servan-Schreiber's analysis does not pretend to do justice to his views. Rather we have singled out certain key features, widely accepted in Europe and in the United States, which we feel require further investigation. The view that Europe's challenge is to emulate the United States model of industrial organization raises certain important questions for analysis, and the task of this essay will be to formulate some tentative answers to them:

1   What has been the relative performance of U.S. corporations and non-U.S. corporations in recent years and how much of an advantage has size been?
2   What is likely to be the impact of the European merger movement on the strength and performance of European corporations and on the pattern of trade and investment?
3   With regard to Servan-Schreiber's political analysis, how is the creation of European giant corporations likely to affect the "independence" of Europe?

An international comparison of the size and performance of U.S. and non-U.S. industrial corporations

Size.[5]   A major focus of the debate on the American challenge has been the large size of U.S. corporations. Table 1 shows the distribution of the 500 largest corporations by size of sales in 1967 and illustrates the "giantism" of the U.S. corporations. The United States accounts for about half of the industrial production of Organization for Economic Cooperation and Development countries but U.S. firms have a much larger share of the sales of corporations in larger-size categories.

The phenomenon of giantism can also be seen in Table 2, which shows that the sales of the top ten U.S. corporations are about 2½ times as large as the sales of the top ten non-U.S. corporations, but that the relative size ratio declines for smaller corporations and stabilizes at about 1.6 from the 40th largest corporations to the 200th. When size is measured by assets rather than sales, giantism, though still present, is less marked. The relative size ratio is

Table 2. *The relative size of U.S. and non-U.S. corporations*

Firms ranked[b]	1967 Sales (billions of dollars)		Relative size ratio in 1967[a]		
	U.S.	Non-U.S.	Sales	Assets	Employees
1–10	82.2	32.8	2.5	1.9	1.2
11–20	30.7	15.7	2.0	2.0	1.2
21–30	25.3	12.7	2.0	1.4	1.5
31–40	20.1	10.7	1.9	1.7	0.7
41–50	15.2	9.5	1.6	1.4	1.0
51–60	13.5	8.7	1.5	1.7	0.5
61–70	12.0	8.0	1.5	1.7	0.9
71–80	10.6	7.1	1.5	1.1	0.9
81–90	9.9	6.5	1.5	1.2	1.2
91–100	9.1	5.6	1.6	1.2	0.9
101–110	8.1	5.2	1.6	1.3	0.7
111–120	7.7	4.7	1.6	0.9	0.9
121–130	7.1	4.4	1.6	1.5	1.0
131–140	6.5	4.0	1.6	1.1	0.8
141–150	6.0	3.7	1.6	1.4	0.9
151–160	5.5	3.5	1.6	0.9	1.3
161–170	5.2	3.3	1.6	1.1	1.0
171–180	4.9	3.1	1.6	1.4	0.9
181–190	4.6	2.9	1.6	1.1	1.2
191–200	4.4	2.8	1.6	0.7	0.5
1–50	173.5	81.3	2.1	1.7	1.1
1–100	228.6	117.2	1.9	1.6	1.0
1–200	288.8	154.8	1.8	1.5	1.0

[a]The relative size ratio is the ratio of total sales, assets, or employees of U.S. corporations to non-U.S. corporations within a given ranking.
[b]1–10 means the 10 largest firms (by sales size), etc.

slightly under 2 for the 20 largest firms and about 1.5 thereafter. (The differences in the sales asset ratio may reflect differences in accounting practice.) When size is measured in terms of number of employees, U.S. firms have only a slight size advantage.

Table 3 compares the size of U.S. corporations to the size of leading non-U.S. corporations on a country-by-country basis. These binary comparisons exaggerate the giantism of U.S. corporations, and are of interest because countries and regions frequently compare their corporations directly with those of the United States and naturally feel overwhelmed. United States corporations, of course, are interested in the strength of their rivals collectively and not separately.

Table 4 shows that the relative size of U.S. and non-U.S. corporations differs substantially from industry to industry, and serves as a warning against overgeneralization. In the chemical industry, U.S. and non-U.S. corporations are just about evenly balanced; the large U.S. corporations are

Table 3. *Relative size ratio by country (1967 sales)*[a]

Rank of firm	U.K.	Sweden	Switzerland	Germany	France	Italy	Benelux	Canada	Japan
1	2.7	29.7	11.1	8.6	13.2	9.7	8.3	22.3	11.6
2	2.4	20.1	15.9	6.7	9.9	6.9	13.8	15.7	8.0
3	3.5	19.7	16.2	6.3	9.4	8.1	13.8	14.7	7.6
4	2.9	17.5	14.5	4.7	2.3	6.4	10.6	10.9	6.0
5	2.5	22.6	11.7	4.2	6.5	6.9	10.6	12.0	4.9
6	4.4		12.7	3.9	6.2	8.4	12.4	11.3	4.6
7	4.1		15.0	4.2	6.0	9.8	12.0	11.3	4.3
8	4.5		18.4	4.2	5.7	16.7	13.9	12.9	4.4
9	3.9			3.7	4.8		12.3	11.3	4.1
10	3.8			4.0	4.7		13.4	12.0	4.3
11	3.8			3.8	4.7			12.1	4.3
12	3.4			3.4	4.2				4.4
13	3.4			3.3	4.7				4.5
14	3.6			3.8	5.4				4.6
15	3.6			3.7	5.9				4.5
16	3.6			3.7	6.6				4.7
17	3.8			5.0	7.7				5.7
18	4.0			5.2	8.4				6.2
19	4.0			6.6	8.7				6.3
20	4.1			7.1	8.8				6.2
21	4.1			7.0	9.8				6.1
22	4.0			7.0	9.4				5.9
23	4.6			7.4	9.4				5.9
24	5.2			7.8					6.1
25	4.6			8.6					6.2

[a]See notes to Table 2.

smaller than their non-U.S. counterparts while medium-sized U.S. firms are a bit larger.[6] In the automobile industry, U.S. corporations have an overwhelming size advantage over the leading non-U.S. corporations because production is much more concentrated in the United States than in Europe (taken as a whole). In addition, large-scale foreign investments by the U.S. giants have enabled them to capture a significant proportion of the European market, and this accounts in part for the small size of their non-U.S. competitors. Other industries show variations on these two patterns.

United States corporations are thus formidable competitors. Their ability to mobilize very large amounts of capital for specific purposes gives them a great financial advantage, especially in modern industries. However, this advantage is somewhat overstated in the size comparisons, since many non-U.S. corporations, though operationally separate from each other, are linked through banks and financial institutions and form a corporate group not unlike the large U.S. corporations. United States corporations also appear to have a qualitative advantage in their administrative structures which gives

Table 4. *Relative size ratio by industry (1967 sales)[a]*

Firms ranked	1 Auto	2 Electrical machinery	3 Oil	4 Chemicals	5 Food	6 Iron and steel	7 Non-ferrous metal	8 Machinery and engineering
1	8.6	3.2	1.6	0.5	1.6	2.4	1.2	1.5
2	5.5	2.7	1.9	0.9	2.5	1.8	1.1	1.5
3	4.1	2.1	3.8	1.2	2.6	1.0	0.9	1.5
4	0.6	2.3	3.2	0.9	2.1	0.9	1.1	1.5
5	0.6	2.3	3.4	1.1	2.2	0.9	1.6	1.4
6	0.6	2.4	3.8	1.1	1.8	1.0	1.0	1.3
7	0.6	2.3	3.8	1.2	1.6	0.9	1.1	1.2
8	0.8	2.2	3.3	1.1	1.8	0.8	1.4	0.9
9	0.8	1.9	3.9	1.2	1.9	0.4	1.3	0.9
10	0.6	1.8	4.2	1.3	1.8	0.4	1.1	0.9
11	0.5	1.6	4.3	1.4	1.8	0.5		1.1
12	0.5	1.6	4.1	1.4	2.2	0.6		1.3
13	0.5	1.6	4.2	1.3	2.1			1.5
14	0.6	1.9		1.3	2.1			1.5
15	0.7	1.9		1.2	2.3			1.5
16	0.7	1.8		1.2	2.1			1.6
17	0.8	1.5		1.4	2.2			1.6
18		1.5		1.3	1.9			
19		1.5		1.2	2.0			
20		1.5		1.2	2.1			
21		1.5		1.1				
22		1.5		1.1				
23		1.5		1.2				
24		1.5		1.2				
25		1.4		1.2				
26		1.5		1.2				
27		1.5		1.2				
28		1.5		1.3				
29		1.5		1.3				
30		1.4		1.3				
31				1.3				
32				1.3				
33				1.2				
34				1.2				
35				1.1				
36				1.1				

[a]See notes to Table 2.

them a certain flexibility and mobility that non-U.S. corporations do not have. In order to meet the challenge of their peculiar market, U.S. corporations had to develop an administrative structure capable of managing units spread out over an entire continent in an environment of rapidly and continuously changing markets. Their answer – the national corporation (circa 1900), the multidivisional corporation (circa 1920), and now the multinational corporation[7] – involved enlargement of the corporate "brain,"

Table 5. *Changes in the relative size of U.S. and non-U.S. firms 1957 to 1962, 1962 to 1967*

	(Relative size ratio)[a]								
	Sales			Assets			Employees		
Firms ranked	1957	1962	1967	1957	1962	1967	1957	1962	1967
1–10	2.2	2.3	2.5	2.2	1.9	1.7	1.3	1.0	1.2
11–20	2.9	2.1	1.9	3.7	1.9	2.0	1.4	0.9	1.2
21–30	2.4	2.1	2.0	2.3	1.7	1.4	1.3	0.8	1.5
31–40	2.4	1.8	1.9	1.6	1.5	1.7	1.0	0.8	0.7
41–50	2.0	1.9	1.6	2.0	1.5	1.4	1.3	0.8	1.0
51–60	1.9	1.7	1.5	2.5	1.8	1.7	1.3	0.8	0.5
61–70	1.9	1.6	1.5	2.1	1.3	1.7	0.7	0.7	0.9
71–80	2.0	1.5	1.5	2.0	1.4	1.1	0.6	0.7	0.9
81–90	1.9	1.5	1.5	2.5	1.1	1.2	0.8	0.8	1.2
91–100	2.0	1.6	1.6	1.6	1.7	1.2	1.2	0.9	0.9
101–110		1.5	1.6		1.3	1.3		1.0	0.7
111–120		1.5	1.6		1.4	0.9		0.6	0.9
121–130		1.6	1.6		1.0	1.5		0.7	1.0
131–140		1.5	1.6		0.9	1.1		1.0	0.8
141–150		1.5	1.6		0.9	1.4		0.5	0.9
151–160		1.5	1.6		1.0	0.9		0.8	1.3
161–170		1.6	1.6		1.1	1.1		0.6	1.0
171–180		1.7	1.6		1.2	1.4		0.6	0.9
181–190		1.7	1.6		1.5	1.1		1.1	1.2
191–200		1.7	1.6		1.0	0.7		0.8	2.5

[a]See notes for Table 2.

and the development of business administration as a specialized profession with its own elaborate division of labor and its own system of education.

The U.S. corporation thus represents a very highly developed form of capital (where capital is defined in the businessmen's sense of a concentration of wealth combined with the ability to use it for productive activities) and it is no wonder that European business enterprises wish to emulate it in size and organization. But as we shall see, it is not sufficient to point to the large size of the U.S. corporation, the apparently smooth functioning of its mechanism, and its ability to defend itself in international competition to establish its superiority as a mechanism for organizing economic activity to meet today's problems.

Performance   Size comparisons by themselves are of little importance. What interests us is performance. The available evidence on the growth of industrial corporations in the ten years following the formation of the Common Market (1957 to 1967) shows that U.S. corporations have not been outstripping their rivals in recent years. Rather, they fell behind from 1957 to 1962 and only managed to keep pace between 1962 and 1967. Table 5 shows a shift in the

Table 6. *Changes in the relative size of U.S. and non-U.S. firms by industry relative size ratio of three largest corporations in each industry*[a]

	1957	1962	1967
Auto	11.6	6.2	6.4
Electrical machinery	4.2	2.5	2.7
Oil	1.3	1.9	1.9
Chemical	0.8	0.8	0.8
Food	2.5	2.1	2.1
Iron and steel	4.7	2.3	1.8
Nonferrous	1.8	1.5	1.3
Machinery and engineering	1.7	1.6	1.5
Rubber	3.3	2.2	2.2
Paper	n.a.	2.3	1.9
Textiles	n.a.	2.4	2.1
Aircraft	n.a.	3.4	4.1
Stone	n.a.	1.2	1.6

[a]Ratio of total sales of the three largest U.S. to total sales of the three largest non-U.S. firms.

relative size ratio (except in the largest size category) against U.S. corporations between 1957 and 1962, and an approximate stabilization thereafter. Table 6 indicates that this pattern holds for nearly all industries. There is thus a sense in which the U.S. corporations have been challenged rather than challenging.

To what extent was size an advantage in international competition during this period? To help answer this question a regression analysis was performed relating the data on growth of a corporation to its size, nationality, and industry. The size of a corporation S was measured in terms of its sales at the beginning of the period. The growth rate g was measured by the average annual percentage change in sales over the period.[8] Country and industry were indicated by a set of dummy variables C_i and I_j, where $C_i = 1$ for a firm from country i and 0 otherwise, and $I_j = 1$ for a firm from the jth industry and 0 otherwise.

For econometric reasons it was necessary to exclude the dummies of an arbitrary country (the United States) and an arbitrary industry (Miscellaneous). The basic estimating equations were then of the following form, where a_1 is coefficient of the country dummy variable for the United States and b_1 is the coefficient of the industry dummy variable for the Miscellaneous industry.[9]

$$g = \text{const} + \sum_{2}^{m} (a_i - a_1) C_i + \sum_{2}^{n} (b_j - b_1)I_j + eS + fS^2 + u$$

The sample for 1957 to 1962 and for 1957 to 1967 consisted of the 100 largest U.S. and the 100 largest non-U.S. corporations. The sample of the second period, 1962 to 1967, consisted of the 500 largest corporations, approximately 300 U.S. and 200 non-U.S. (A number of firms dropped off the *Fortune* list during the period, and so the actual number of firms which could be used was 188 for 1957 to 1962, 438 for 1962 to 1967, and 178 for 1957 to 1967). The main results are presented in Table 7. For simplicity, the constant term and the coefficients for industry dummies have been excluded, since they are not relevant to the hypothesis under test. Three regressions are presented for each period; first excluding the size variable altogether, second including it, and third using a logarithmic form. Regressions were also run separately for major industries, but the results are too long and involved to be presented here. For the moment we merely note that the main conclusions of Table 7 were broadly corroborated by the industry studies. We might also mention that the results were unaffected by additional tests involving changes in the sample, in the function fitted, and in the methods of estimation.

The first important feature to emerge from the investigation is the significant relationship between size and growth. The coefficients are negative for S and log S, and positive for S^2 and $(\log S)^2$. This indicates a U-shaped relationship in which size first has a negative effect and then a positive effect. The exact strength of the upward twist is not well established and differs substantially according to whether we use the parabolic equation, $f(s) = \text{const} + eS + fS^2$, or its log equivalent $f(S) = \text{const} + e \log S + f \log S^2$. In the former case, for example, the turning point occurs when a firm's sales reach $8 billion (according to the 1962 to 1967 equations); in log form, the turning point occurs at sales of $3.2 billion in this period. However, in 1962 there were only three corporations whose sales exceeded $8 billion (all from the United States) and nine corporations whose sales exceeded $3.2 billion (seven from the United States). In the earlier period, 1957 to 1962, the turning points are $5.4 billion for the parabolic form and $3.8 billion for the logarithmic form and the number of firms whose sales exceeded these figures were four (three from the United States) and seven (five from the United States), respectively. The upward twist therefore applies only to a handful of giants. For the rest of the sample the relationship between size and growth is clearly negative.

An examination of the residuals suggests that even this upward twist may be an illusion caused by the types of curve we have fitted. Indeed, for the period 1962 to 1967 the industry regressions show a negative relationship between size and growth rate over the whole range.

The second important conclusion of the regression analysis is that nationality has frequently been a significant variable in explaining the growth rates of firms. This is because many firms are national rather than multinational, and their fortunes depend very much upon the countries to which they are attached. Recalling that the coefficients measuring the country effects in Table 7 refer to the difference between the growth rate of companies based in a particular country and that of the United States, we note first that these

Table 7. Regressions results

Description	Germany–U.S.	France–U.S.	Benelux–U.S.	Italy–U.S.	U.K.–U.S.	Other EFTA–U.S.	Japan–U.S.	Canada–U.S.	Other–U.S.	S	S²	R²
1957 to 1962												
Excluding S												
Parameter estimate	7.1**	2.8	−4.5*	10.2**	−2.4**	4.7*	10.6**	−5.1**	4.3			0.314
t value	4.15	1.36	−1.73	2.82	−1.99	1.81	2.89	−2.18	0.96			
Including S												
Parameter estimate	5.8**	0.9	−2.8	8.6**	−3.2**	3.2	8.9**	−6.1**	2.9	−3.1067**	0.2923**	0.357
t value	3.42	0.45	−1.10	2.43	−2.65	1.22	2.47	−2.64	0.66	−3.27	2.75	
S in logs												
Parameter estimate	5.5**	−0.9	1.5	7.2**	−4.4**	1.0	7.2**	−6.7**	−0.2	−20.8217*	0.9880**	0.372
t value	3.25	−0.43	0.57	2.02	−3.41	0.36	1.96	−2.93	−0.05	−1.94	1.72	
1962 to 1967												
Excluding S												
Parameter estimate	−3.9**	−1.5	−1.2	−0.6	−0.8	0.2	6.9**	−0.0	1.4			0.206
t value	−3.22	−1.13	−0.61	−0.29	−0.94	0.13	6.26	−0.02	0.57			
Including S												
Parameter estimate	−3.6**	−1.9	−1.5	−0.8	−0.8	0.0	6.4**	−0.3	0.8	−1.8516**	0.1160	0.231
t value	−3.04	−1.38	−0.77	−0.36	−0.87	0.00	5.88	−0.19	0.32	−3.40	2.37	
S in logs												
Parameter estimate	−2.8**	−1.6	−1.3	0.0	−0.8	0.2	6.4**	−0.2	0.7	−11.5656**	0.5579*	0.254
t value	−2.34	−1.18	−0.65	0.01	−0.89	0.09	5.90	−0.13	0.30	−2.24	1.91	
1957 to 1967												
Excluding S												
Parameter estimate	2.6**	2.7**	3.4**	5.8**	−1.7**	2.4	11.3**	−0.4	4.5*			0.381
t value	2.44	2.12	2.01	2.74	−2.29	1.58	5.20	−0.27	1.72			
Including S												
Parameter estimate	1.9*	1.7	2.4	4.9**	−2.1**	1.5	10.3**	−0.9	3.8	−1.6455**	0.1409**	0.417
t value	1.76	1.28	1.43	2.35	−2.89	1.00	4.82	−0.59	1.46	−2.92	2.23	
S in logs												
Parameter estimate	1.6	0.5	1.7	4.0*	−2.9**	0.1	9.1**	−1.3	1.7	−12.8019**	0.6062**	0.439
t value	1.58	0.38	1.03	1.92	−3.72	0.07	4.22	−0.84	0.62	−1.97	1.74	

Note: t values are the coefficients divided by their standard errors. Two asterisks means significant at the 5% level with a two-tailed *t* test. One asterisk means significant at the 10% level with a two-tailed *t* test. *S* is measured in billions when regressions include *S*, and in hundreds of thousands when they coefficients are mainly positive from 1957 to 1962 and mainly negative from 1962 to 1967. This indicates a country effect or common factor for U.S. firms that was disadvantageous in the first period and advantageous in the second.

Surprisingly, when the regressions for 1962 to 1967 were run for a reduced sample of the 178 large continuing firms (i.e., those firms that were among the 100 largest U.S. or 100 largest non-U.S. firms in 1957 and were still on the *Fortune* list in 1967), the country coefficients were uniformly higher in nearly every case. This indicates that non-U.S. corporations held their own better in the middle and large range than they did in the smaller range. To put this another way, *small* U.S. corporations had some advantageous factor in common so that they performed better as a group than predicted by our equations relating size to growth.

As for other countries, in the first period it was disadvantageous to be a British or Canadian firm, relative to the United States, but this disadvantage was removed in the second period when the country effect came to closely approximate that of the United States. Germany and Italy showed the opposite pattern to the United States; a relatively strong positive country effect in the first period which disappears in the second (in the case of Germany it becomes strongly negative). Finally, the Japanese country effect, as expected, was strongly advantageous in both periods.

Before we apply these empirical findings to the second and third questions raised in the Introduction, we should perhaps stress their tentative nature. A number of empirical studies on the effect of size and growth have been conducted for samples drawn from within a country and these in general have concluded that there is little correlation between size and growth.[10] Since the problem of sorting out the effects of size, industry, and nationality is difficult and complex, our experiments far from exhaust the possible interrelationships that can be tested. However, it is clear that the data do not support the view that size has been an advantageous, much less a crucial, factor in growth during the first decade following the establishment of the common market.

Dialectics of the multinational corporation (1957 to 1967)

If the U.S. corporations did not grow faster than their European and Japanese rivals, where did the notion of the American challenge come from? We suggest it was due, in part at least, to myopia. Europeans felt threatened because they saw U.S. corporations gaining an increased share of the European market. They paid little attention to the fact that, in the world market taken as a whole, U.S. corporations were themselves being threatened by the rapid growth of the Common Market and the Japanese economy, and required a rapid expansion of foreign investment to maintain their relative standing. To understand the divergent views on who is being challenged, and who is challenging, it is useful to distinguish between Gp, the growth rate of the U.S. parent firm (including its subsidiaries), Gs, the growth rate of its subsidiaries, and Ge, the growth rate of non-U.S. firms. The stylized facts of the period were something like the following[11]:

$$Gs > Ge \geqslant Gp.$$

European firms compared Gs to Ge and felt they were being challenged. United States multinational corporations compared Ge to Gp and also felt a challenge. The fact that both parties could feel challenged stemmed from the difference in the horizons of national and multinational corporations. Multinational corporations see the world as their oyster, and judge their performance on a world-wide basis. They look to their global market position. National or regional firms keep their eyes close to the ground and concentrate on their share of particular submarkets. Thus the same phenomenon appears different according to the eyesight of the beholder. To the short-sighted European firm, whose markets are mainly European, U.S. investment seems to be an aggressive move to dominate Europe. To the long-sighted American firm, on the other hand, this investment appears to be a desperate attempt to defend its existing world share and keep up with the dynamic Europeans.

A more interesting interpretation of the ten years between 1957 and 1967 would recognize that a firm can be challenging and challenged at the same time, just as a military strategy can be both offensive and defensive. The rapid growth of the Common Market and Japan in the 1950s challenged the dominance of the U.S. giants, who responded with an aggressive policy of foreign investment. Their great strength, their past experience with continental and multinational markets, plus the open-door policy of European governments made this counterstrategy successful.

This invasion of Europe threatened the position of European firms which have now begun their countermeasures. The threats, of course, have not been felt evenly. The United Kingdom, for example, seems to have felt less challenged than other countries even though U.S. penetration of the United Kingdom is far higher than for the continent. This is because linkages are well established, and because many leading British firms are themselves multinational and think in terms of world markets. Japan also did not feel as threatened as other countries, but for different reasons. By virtually prohibiting foreign investment, the Japanese government reserved its rapidly growing market for its own firms and frustrated the attempts by U.S. corporations to redress the imbalance caused by the Japanese challenge. This has created considerable tension and may soon have to be modified since Japanese corporations encounter increased resistance to their penetration via exports.

What about the next round? It is a foregone conclusion that Europe will follow (is following) the policies advocated by Servan-Schreiber. The European merger movement is well under way and nearly all European governments are actively taking positive measures to strengthen their large corporations. Negative measures are out of favor, in part because they are unworkable in the context of the Common Market, where an American firm denied entry to one country can always locate in another and penetrate the forbidden market through exports. Unanimous agreement is therefore required but is not possible due to divergent interests and outlook. In any case, by now the die is cast, since all of the top U.S. corporations have staked their claim in the European economy.

Where will the positive measures lead? There is no reason to believe that newly enlarged European corporations will increase their rate of growth merely because of their increased size. On the contrary, the data of the past decade indicate that, if anything, most mergers will slow down the rate of growth.

With the exception of the very largest firms, for which there does not seem to be any well-established relationship between size and growth rate, most firms are located on the downward-sloping part of the curve, where the larger their size the slower their growth. These equations for 1957 to 1967 may well not apply to the future: But taking into account the numerous other studies on the relationship between size and growth cited above, we can predict with some confidence that an analysis in 1977 or 1987 of the growth rates of firms will at least not show any positive relationship between size and growth.

The European merger movement is, however, likely to result in a crucial *qualitative* change in the nature of European business. By increasing the average size of European firms it will make them less regional in outlook and more multinational, with the result that they, like American firms, will invest heavily overseas. Among the most important reasons for this change are:

1 Mergers and rationalizations will lead to corporate reorganization and the creation of new administrative structures more akin to those of the American corporation and better suited to multinational expansion. Or, to put the matter differently, as European firms increase in size and complexity their administrative "brain" will increase more than proportionately and their attention will focus not so much on national or European markets but on the world as a whole, including the U.S. market itself. In a sense, the vision of a firm depends on the height of its head office building.

2 Greater financial strength will enable European firms to invest more overseas. Investment in a foreign country often involves a more direct challenge to established firms than does exporting. Firms that were previously prepared to tolerate some competition in the form of exports may not be willing to tolerate competitive direct investment. To protect themselves against what they consider to be a policy of aggressive expansion, they may attempt

to drive the intruder out of the market before he gets too strong.
The outcome of this struggle is likely to depend upon the relative
financial strengths of the established firms and the firm attempting to increase its market share by investing, which in turn
depend upon their relative sizes.

The financial resources associated with size confer other
advantages on the big firm. It can buy its way into markets by
taking over local firms. It can afford to take risks. For a firm the
size of the American giants, with a capital of billions of dollars,
the purchase of an overseas plant costing say $20 million may be
a relatively minor affair. For a firm with a capital of millions of
dollars this plant would be a major undertaking to be contem-
plated only if it was fairly sure to succeed. Thus the smaller firm
must be cautious where the bigger firm can afford to experiment.

3   By consolidating the overseas sales of European firms, mergers
will make them better able to establish subsidiaries of an efficient
size. In any particular market a big firm is likely to have actual or
potential sales larger than those of a small firm, either because it
is already selling more in the form of exports or because it can
afford to finance a costly promotion and distribution program for
its products. Equally it can afford to establish a large and
efficient subsidiary which can produce the output necessary to
satisfy this larger market. From the point of view of both supply
and demand the big firm is therefore better able to produce on an
efficient scale.

As a hypothetical example, consider the ease of four European firms, each
with actual or potential sales of $20 million in the United States. At this level
it may be hopelessly inefficient to produce locally, and therefore they export
from their domestic plants. Suppose they now merge. Then the resulting firm
will have actual or potential sales worth $80 million – a significant share of
the American market – which may be high enough to justify setting up a local
subsidiary.

A brief examination of the relevant statistics[12] supports the view that size is
a major determinant of overseas investment. In 1957, out of 1,542 firms with
investments overseas, 15, each having foreign assets worth over $100 million,
accounted for 35% of total American manufacturing investments abroad.
Together with 64 others having investments worth over $25 million each, they
accounted for 69% of the total, leaving 1,463 firms to share the remaining
31%.[13] In the British case, the big investor is equally dominant. Some 46
firms, most of them large, accounted for 71% of manufacturing assets
overseas in 1962 and 3 firms owned virtually all petroleum assets overseas.[14]

Table 8. *Exports and local production (millions of dollars)*

	X	P	$X + P$	P/X	X	P (est)	$X + P$	P/X
Out of U.S.			1957			1966		
Europe	6,940	10,762	17,702	1.55	14,440	36,000	50,440	2.50
Into U.S.			1959			1966		
U.K., Netherlands, and Switzerland	2,320	4,657	6,977	2.01	3,740	7,400	11,140	1.97
Other Europe	4,580	559	5,139	0.12	8,050	1,271	9,321	0.16
of which:								
France	690	92	782	0.13	1,050	123	1,173	0.12
Germany	1,380	47	1,427	0.03	2,700	138	2,838	0.05

Definitions: X = exports (c.i.f.).
P = manufacturing and petroleum sales of local subsidiaries.
Methods: The rate of growth of sales up to 1966 is assumed to be the same as that of net assets in the appropriate industry (manufacturing, petroleum). A cross check with the sales of U.S. manufacturing subsidiaries for 1965 suggested that the original estimate of $39,600 million was too high by about 3,000 to 4,000 million. The estimate was therefore adjusted to the $36,000 million given in the table. For the United Kingdom, Netherlands, and Switzerland net assets by industry were not available for 1966. It was therefore assumed that sales grew at the same annual rate as net assets between 1959 and 1967. For France and Germany no breakdown of assets was available for 1966 and the growth rate assumed was that of net assets in all industries. This probably underestimates the growth of manufacturing and petroleum sales, but the error is not likely to be important.
Finally 50% was added to the f.o.b. figures for exports and imports given by the Department of Commerce to allow for insurance, freight, and other charges.
Sources: Survey of Current Business (Washington, D.C.: U.S. Department of Commerce), various issues. *Statistical Abstract of the United States* (Washington, D.C.: U.S. Government Printing Office), various issues. *U.S. Business Investments in Foreign Countries* (1960), and *Foreign Business Investment in the United States* (undated), U.S. Department of Commerce publications.

Among them they accounted for around 83% of all British investments in petroleum and manufacturing combined.

The role of investment in the expansion of American and European firms in each other's markets is well illustrated in Table 8, which shows the local production of foreign-owned subsidiaries in manufacturing and petroleum (P) and the exports (X) of various countries. Although some of the figures are rather rough estimates, the broad picture they reveal is accurate. Three European countries – the United Kingdom, the Netherlands, and Switzerland – account for about nine-tenths of the sales of all European subsidiaries in American manufacturing and petroleum. These sales are roughly twice as much as the total exports to the United States of these three countries combined. By contrast, other European countries rely mainly on exports to serve the American market, and of these the most striking is Germany, whose

Table 9. *Direct investment flows of industrial countries (millions of dollars)*

	Average 1957 to 1960			Average 1961 to 1964		
	Out-flows	In-flows	Net	Out-flows	In-flows	Net
United States	−2,830	330	−2,500	−3,210	310	−2,900
United Kingdom	− 510	310	− 200	− 670	480	− 190
Subtotal	−3,340	640	−2,700	−3,880	790	−3,090
Belgium	n.a.	n.a.	n.a.	n.a.	n.a.	n.a.
France	− 10	30	+ 20	− 100	280	+ 180
Germany	− 120	60	− 60	− 220	200	− 20
Italy	− 60	220	+ 160	− 170	350	+ 180
Netherlands	− 170	50	− 120	− 120	60	− 60
Subtotal	− 360	360	0	− 610	890	+ 280
Other EFTA countries	n.a.	20	n.a.	− 60	110	+ 50
Canada	− 60	550	+ 490	− 100	360	+ 260
Japan	− 50	20	− 30	− 90	80	− 10
Total industrial	−3,810	1,590	−2,220	−4,740	2,230	−2,510

Source: M. Diamond, IMF *Staff Papers* (March 1967).

firms exported 20 times as much in 1966 as they produced in the United States.

As a result of investment, firms of the first group have been able to maintain a clear lead in the American market over other European firms. Despite an impressive growth of exports to the United States, which doubled in nine years, German sales by 1966 were still only a quarter of those of the first group. Moreover, the absolute gap increased dramatically as this group's sales increased by over $4 billion as compared to 1.4 billion for Germany and 0.4 billion for France.

It is clear that if French or German firms wish to establish themselves extensively or even securely in the American market they will have to invest heavily, something they have not yet done.[15] Why have they not done so? After all, the American market is important to them, as their export performance shows. More to the point, they have been investing heavily in other countries, as Table 9 shows. During the years 1961 to 1964 German firms invested an average of $220 million a year abroad and French firms an average of $100 million, compared to which their investment in the United States looks trivial – an average of $5.5 million a year for the Germans and $9 million for the French.

Part, if not the whole, of the answer lies in the small size of French and German firms, particularly in those areas where European investment in the United States has been heavy. Using the sectoral distribution of investments in 1959 as a guide, we find that the bulk of them lie in areas where firms of the United Kingdom, the Netherlands, and Switzerland have a clear lead over other European firms and are of a size comparable to the American giants.[16] Unilever (Anglo-Dutch), Nestlé (Swiss), and British-American Tobacco (British) are many times larger than other European firms in their sectors of food and household products, and are about the same size or even larger than their American rivals. In petroleum Royal Dutch-Shell (Anglo-Dutch) and BP (British), which has recently begun a massive expansion into the United States, are several times larger than other European firms. In pharmaceuticals, a comparatively small-scale industry, Switzerland has the only four specialist companies on the *Fortune* list of non-American firms. In rubber and paper, British firms are the biggest in Europe and rival the Americans, and in electrical goods the Netherlands has the largest non-American firm. Of course, there are exceptions. Switzerland, for example, is mentioned by the U.S. Department of Commerce as having investments in the electrical industry, yet the largest Swiss firm is only fifth in Europe. But on the whole the correlation holds up fairly well. In industries where the three countries are not European leaders – iron and steel, machinery, automobiles – their firms are fairly small in comparison to American firms and they tend not to invest in the United States. Even the apparent exception of chemicals, where British ICI is the largest in Europe (excluding Unilever) and relies on exporting, reinforces our argument, for ICI is planning to expand rapidly in the United States from its comparatively small base·in artificial fibers.

As it stands, all this leaves the question of causality open, for it would be possible to argue that these firms are giants *because* they invest in the United States rather than the other way around, and that if European firms merge to become giants there is no reason to assume that they will follow the same path and also invest in the United States. If the European giants produced a third, a half, or more of their output in the United States, this argument would be plausible, but they do not. Over the last decade, for example, Unilever has never produced more than a sixth of its output in the American continent as a whole, both north and south. Even British-American Tobacco, perhaps the most dependent on its American investments, has only a third of its assets there. We can conclude, therefore, that as a rule the causality runs from giant size to investment in the United States at least as strongly as it does from investment to giant size. In cases such as ICI or BP, which are just beginning to invest seriously, the causality is clearly far stronger in the size-to-investment direction. This is not to deny that overseas investment does not or will not play a crucial part in the growth of large firms, particularly in the case of small countries such as Switzerland or the Netherlands. On the contrary, the most common path for European firms may well be domestic growth on the basis of home sales and exports up to the point where they are well enough established in foreign markets and financially strong enough to consider foreign investment. At first they begin by investing outside America in markets that are easier to enter. Eventually, when they have gained the experience, created the organizational structure, and, perhaps most important of all, gained the extra financial strength necessary, they invest in the United States.

Clearly, most European firms are still at the first or second stage. Either they have not invested abroad at all, or are investing outside of America. Mergers, by adding to their financial strength and consolidating their foreign sales, will enable these firms to accelerate the first and second stages or even to skip the intermediate stage so that they go straight from home production to investment in the United States. Rather than labor this point any longer, we shall assume that the European merger movement will result in both heavy overseas investment outside the United States, and in the slightly longer run in the United States itself.

How will U.S. corporations react to the challenge of outward investment by European firms? United States corporations have also been undergoing a large merger movement which may have maintained or increased their relative size. Since U.S. corporations are large and powerful there is no reason for them to accept a lower rate of growth. Moreover, precisely because they are the dominant firms, they must worry about losses in relative position and be prepared to adopt defensive measures when threatened. Although they might be willing to accept a loss of a few points in their market shares to a large number of medium and small rivals, they are not likely to regard even a small loss to a rival European giant with equanimity. Thus the merger movement makes it even more likely that they will do everything in their power to maintain the same rate of growth as non-U.S. firms: Since their resources and skills are very great they are likely on the average to be fairly successful in this effort. European firms will have the advantage at first of great government support, but if the world balance is threatened, the United States government can be counted on to come to the rescue of its corporations.

The American response is likely to assign an even greater role than in the past to increased foreign investment. For one thing, it is very costly for a dominant firm to resist incursions into its own market by serious rivals (since the loss caused by a 1% reduction in price is greater for the established firm than for the new entrant). Equally, European attempts to gain a foothold in the U.S. market are also likely to be successful, for it will be easier for the U.S. corporations to counterattack abroad, and to meet inward foreign investment with outward foreign investment. Indeed, U.S. corporations might even welcome an exchange of markets since it would create a better world-wide environment for multinationalism. Another factor is that the growth of the U.S. economy may slow down, if the new Republican administration adopts a deflationary monetary and fiscal policy over the next few years. To maintain their world position U.S. corporations would have to expand even more rapidly abroad in order to compensate for their slowly growing home base. A slowdown in the growth of the U.S. market would present less of a problem to non-U.S. firms because they start from a smaller base. Investment in the United States would likely continue, and combined with deflationary policies would improve the U.S. balance of payments and facilitate the outward migration of U.S. capital. Finally, added pressure to invest abroad comes from the fact that U.S. corporations will not be able to stand idly by and allow Europeans to capture important markets in the less-developed countries or in the communist countries.

We can therefore expect a period of intensified multinationalization (almost amounting to capital flight) over the coming decade as both U.S. corporations and non-U.S. corporations try to establish world-wide market positions and protect themselves from the challenges of each other.[17] The cross penetration implied by the simple oligopoly model we have just described has as its *logical* end a stable equilibrium where all of the dominant oligopolists have a similar world-wide distribution of sales. This logical end is not likely to be achieved in practice but the following equations are a useful device for illuminating current tendencies.

$$S_1 = a_{11} Y_1 + a_{12} Y_2,$$
$$S_2 = a_{21} Y_1 + a_{22} Y_2,$$

where S_1 equals the aggregate sales of the "dominant" U.S. corporations; S_2 equals the aggregate sales of the "dominant" non-U.S. corporations; Y_1, the size of the U.S. market; Y_2 the size of the non-U.S. market; and the a_{ij}'s represent the share of a firm from country i in the market of country j (obtained either through exports or local sales). The stylized fact of the present world structure of industry is that a_{21} (the European share in the U.S. market) is very low. Hence if Y_2 grows faster than Y_1, non-U.S. corporations will grow faster than U.S. corporations, unless Americans increase a_{12}. As we suggested above, this perhaps describes the period 1957 to 1967 in a rough sort of way. The increase in a_{12} and the slowing down in the rate of growth of Y_2 has threatened European firms and led them to take steps which increased a_{21}. This in turn we suggest will lead American firms to further increase a_{12}. As this dialectical process unfolds, the world distribution of sales of American and European firms will tend to approximate each other more closely. As a_{11}/a_{12} approaches a_{21}/a_{22}, relative size S_1/S_2 becomes less and less affected by differences in the rate of growth of Y_1 and Y_2. In other words, corporations of both centers will come to experience similar rates of growth regardless of whether Europe is growing faster than America or America is growing faster than Europe. But this solution to the American challenge on the level of oligopolistic competition will not remove conflicts at the political level. A breaking of the link between corporations and countries will create conflicts between the private and public interest and between one nation and another that are difficult to resolve. In the next section we turn to these more intractable and more important problems.

International capital and national interest

The concept of the American challenge as a diagnosis and prescription of Europe's current predicaments is in large part a myth resting on an exaggeration of the prowess of the large U.S. corporation and a myopic view of the dynamics of international competition. It is in fact one of the guises for a new form of protectionism and as such is an attempt to identify the national interest with the interest of certain dominant firms. The instruments of this neoprotectionism differ from those of the old. Instead of tariffs to preserve the domestic market for national firms, businessmen are asking for positive help to penetrate foreign markets. The theme, however, is the same: The growth of a certain sector of private business is elevated to a national goal and the economic problems of the entire country are viewed from a particularly restrictive vantage point.

Our analysis suggests that the main result of the strategy of "positive measures" to help large firms will be to change European business qualitatively towards multinationalism, rather than to raise the relative growth rates of European firms.

The increased multinationalism that follows increased size, by weakening the link between country performance and company performance, will help to equalize growth rates of firms of different nationality and make it easier for U.S. corporations to maintain their position.

If the goal were to develop a strong *national* business sector, it would probably be better to follow the Japanese example of fostering the growth of the internal market, restricting inward investment, and penetrating foreign markets through exports rather than investment (though this policy too has its limitations). The present strategy will strengthen a few very large corporations but divorce their interest from that of the national economy, and may well have a negative effect on international trade, since corporations concentrate on foreign investment rather than exports. For example, the data from the Reddaway report (Table 10) covering the 15 countries that receive most British direct foreign investment show that the big investors produce locally 20 times as much as they export. Furthermore, their exports to these markets have fallen by 7% whereas their local production has risen by 62%. In the same period, the exports of other British firms that did not have local foreign investments have risen by 42%. It seems inconceivable that the big investors, if not allowed to invest overseas, could not manage to raise their exports well above the £106.2 million that they presently export. More work is needed for other countries, but this example should serve as an illustration of

Table 10. *U.K. exports and local production (£ millions) in 15 countries*

	1956	1963	% change
1. U.K. exports (f.o.b.)	1,450.3	2,000.5	+38%
2. Exports of firms in Reddaway sample	114.2	106.2	− 7%
3. Local production of firms Reddaway sample	1,321.4	2,137.8	+62%
4. Total U.K. exports to 15 countries less those of firms in Reddaway sample (f.o.b.)	1,336.1	1,894.3	+42%

Notes and Sources: W. B. Reddaway, *Effects of U.K. Direct Investment Overseas: An Interim Report* (Cambridge: Cambridge University Press, 1967), Table VI 4.
Local production has been estimated by subtracting 150% of the value of exports (f.o.b.) of firms in the Reddaway sample from the total sales of these firms in the 15 countries. The extra 50% is to allow for the fact that sales are valued at selling price whereas exports are valued f.o.b.

the difference between policies to maintain a corporation's shares of the world market and policies to maintain a country's share.[18]

What will be the overall effect on economic performance and political independence of a world of multinational corporations, some from one side of the Atlantic, some from the other (and perhaps a few from the less-developed world)? We can here provide only the briefest summary of various approaches.

The United States antitrust tradition, as exemplified by Kaysen and Turner,[19] for example, would tend to view the current wave of national and international mergers and takeovers suspiciously, just as this tradition viewed with alarm the merger movement in the United States at the end of the 19th century. At that time the growth of the national corporation led to great concern in the agrarian and small business sectors about "the fate of small producers driven out of business or deprived of the opportunity to enter it, by 'all-powerful aggregates of capital,' " and about "the power of monopolists to hurt the public by raising prices, deteriorating product, and restricting production"; while on the political side, "concentration of resources in the hands of a few was viewed as a social and political catastrophe," a belief, as Kaysen and Turner point out, "rationalised in terms of certain Jeffersonian Symbols of wide political appeal and great persistence in American Life: business units are politically irresponsible and therefore large business units are dangerous." The antitrust tradition would argue for competition rather than size to obtain efficiency and innovations and would resolve doubts "in favour of reducing market power rather than maintaining it." These political forces, however, had little influence in the United States. As Mason points out in his preface to Kaysen and Turner, "the struggle against size was largely lost in the merger movement of 1897–1901."[20] Similarly the battle against size on the international plane is being lost in the current international merger movement, and international antitrust is not likely to challenge the resulting size structures in any serious way. Indeed, it is supporting them.

International trade economists have in general been less concerned about the dangers of high concentration and oligopoly, and have welcomed the free flow of capital as a device for integrating the world economy. They have stressed the advantages of scale and argued that the multinational corporation, because of its organizing ability, will be a powerful force in allocating capital efficiently, and spreading technology from advanced to less-advanced countries. They welcome an industrial structure where large firms span the entire world producing each component in the country where costs are lowest and making technical advances and product innovations quickly and evenly available throughout the world. Their suggested model is perhaps the United States economy, where major firms are spread over most of the country and take advantage of differences in relative supplies of labor, capital, or natural resources. On the international plane, the prototype is perhaps United States–Canadian integration, which, symbolically speaking, has proceeded on north–south lines, i.e., pairing of Canadian enterprises with their counterparts to the south, rather than on east–west lines, i.e., coordination within Canada of the various parts of its economy.

Socialist economics also stresses the advantages of scale in keeping with Marx's analysis of the increasingly social nature of production (including the increasingly social nature of management). However, it does not always agree with the international trade approach on the way in which capital should be concentrated and centralized. Whereas the trade approach argues for coordinating one industry across many countries, socialist economics points to the advantages of coordinating many industries within one country. It thus argues for combining oligopolies to form monopolies (because it views the choices offered by oligopolistic product-differentiation as usually meaningless and sometimes harmful); for combining industries to harmonize complementary and competing sectors, and of course for central planning to provide overall coordination of all enterprises. Most important, it stresses the need for political control of economic decision makers. This implies that the boundaries of an enterprise should be contained by the boundaries of the political unit, since enterprises that extend over several units can escape political regulation by any one unit (on this argument the conglomerate enterprises should perhaps be organized on regional rather than national levels in order to be more sensitive to local requirements).

Since the multinational corporate system is the prevailing one, we might spend some time discussing it in more detail and especially its relations to nation-states. George Ball has put the case for the withering away of the nation-state most succinctly: "The structure of the multinational corporation is a modern concept designed to meet the requirements of a modern age; the nation-state is a very old fashioned idea and badly adapted to serve the needs of our present complex world."[21] The idea behind this point of view, as expounded by Sidney Rolfe,[22] for example, is that the phenomenal progress in communications and transportation has created an interdependence of human activity that renders national boundaries obsolete. "The conflict of our era is between ethnocentric nationalism and geocentric technology." All countries, the United States included, must therefore realize that the multinational corporation is modern because it is the first of the major institutions to grasp the significant fact that "history is not of the essence here, evolution is," and "what the world faces is *le défi international* rather than *le défi Américain.*"

This argument contains a strong element of technological determinism, and in our view greatly oversimplifies and perhaps badly mistakes the trends of the modern world. Although it is quite true that modern world technology makes it possible to coordinate production and marketing on a global basis, it is also true that modern communications make centralized planning within one country possible. Moreover, the high productivity of the new technology allows countries greater scope for national independence, since it becomes far less urgent to concentrate on economizing scarce resources. Most important, improved communications make it easier for small regions and units to obtain the most advanced knowledge quickly and cheaply without formal institutional lines of communication. This provides increased scope for independence and reinforces polycentralism rather than centralism. It is not at all clear that hierarchical authoritarian corporate structures are well suited to this environment. In an age when it is possible for every nation or city to be almost instantaneously in communication with every other nation or city, the technological distinction between hinterland and center disappears, though it can still be maintained by political or economic institutions. In short, the options available under the new technology are much wider than those suggested by the proponents of the multinational corporation and it is unjustified to foreclose debate at this time.[23]

Whatever the force of technology, it is clear that the growth of multinational corporations, by itself, tends to weaken nation-states. Multinational corporations render ineffective many traditional policy instruments, the capacity to tax, to restrict credit, to plan investment, etc., because of their international flexibility. In addition, multinational corporations act as a vehicle for the intrusion of the policies of one country into another with the ultimate effect of lessening the power of both.[24] These tendencies have long been recognized in dependent developing countries, but it is now also evident that even the United States, as a *nation-state,* is losing some of its "independence" as it attempts to cope with the tangled web woven by its international business.[25]

The battle, however, is far from over. Nation-states are powerful and are not likely to die easily. Merely to ask which institution one expects to be around 100 years from now, France or General Motors, shows the nature of the problem. Moreover, the implication of Ball's point of view is that the United States must also wither away as a nation-state.[26] How exactly this is to occur is, to say the least, not clear. The growing feedback operations of U.S. corporation on the United States have already created considerable difficulty and can be expected to lead to increased attempts by the American state to control its corporations. Other countries will also try to control the eroding forces of multinational business. Even the government of Canada, which for unique reasons has been less resistant to giving up "independence" for foreign investment than other countries, has stopped short of full integration, and has, for example, used tariffs to interfere with corporate rationalization.

Nation-states and nationalism have in many ways been powerful supports of capitalism, for they have created the group solidarity that enabled the system to survive. In a private-enterprise system, some win and some lose, and a national government with the power to redistribute income and wealth is needed to convince losers to allow the game of competition to go on.[27] The manner of giving subsidies to the losers (e.g., price supports to farmers) has often been inefficient and has been subject to much criticism by economists; but this is not the same as saying the corporations can do without a strong nation-state to deal with the problems of the business cycle, social insecurity, unemployment, unbalanced regional growth, labor unrest, attacks on property and order, etc. If, for example, all countries lost their power of fiscal and monetary policy, as some observers believe Canada has, how would aggregate demand be stabilized? Or does multinationalism do away with Keynesian problems?

Hence the multinational corporations require multinational states. It is utopian to think that this will come about quickly enough to permit the full flowering of international business. It may be possible to stagger toward some level of cooperation at a higher plane on monetary and fiscal policy, tariff policy, and antitrust policy, but the degree of success will be limited. A most important obstacle to supranationality stems from the fact that many of the most important government policy instruments require patriotism to be effective. From the moral suasion exercised by governments on banks, to the voluntary guidelines established for capital flows, wages, and prices, to the demand for honesty in the payment of taxes, the government depends upon voluntary compliance by the majority of its citizens in order to operate effectively. Group loyalty of this kind does not exist at an international level. There does not yet seem to be any effective replacement for the nationalism that has in the past helped to dissolve class conflict and maintain social cohesion (witness how effectively patriotic sentiments have been used by Western governments to blunt the edge of social discontent during periods of economic hardship such as the years of postwar reconstruction).

In a regime of multinational corporations and weak nation-states, differences will become accentuated and will lead to international alliances and federations parallel to the multinational corporation.[28] And even if a strong world federal government could be established, many problems can only be solved at the national and local level. If nation-state governments are too greatly weakened, the model for the future may be the urban crisis, where strong national corporations confront weak city governments. In short, there is a conflict at a fundamental level between national planning by political units and international planning by corporations that will assume major proportions as direct investment grows.

In conclusion, we may return to the question raised in *The American Challenge* about the danger of Europe becoming a colony. Servan-Schreiber is perhaps correct that in the world of multinational corporations it is better to have some of your own than to have none at all. This does not, however, mean that European multinational corporations will enable Europeans to control their future. Instead, difficulties arising from the internationalization of wealth may well inhibit Europe's ability to cope with its internal problems and, in this regard, the problems faced by the United Kingdom in reconciling international finance and the national interest should serve as a warning (as should the current problems of the United States). The problem of colonialism is not really a European problem since European business, despite Servan-Schreiber's analysis, is strong, not weak. Colonialism is the problem of the less-developed countries, where both state enterprise and private capital are very weak and are in no way a match for the powerful business organizations of the advanced world. In the coming competition between European and U.S. corporations, the markets of the third world will be an important battleground, because the stakes will be not only the limited markets of Africa, Latin America, and Asia, but oligopoly equilibrium in the developed world itself. The lesson of Europe's past colonialism is that the harm it did to foreigners was not matched by benefit to itself (i.e., by a benefit to the country as a whole rather than to a particular group). Indeed, the nation was often called upon to sacrifice in order to maintain imperial connections benefiting only a few. Partly because of this, there is a tradition among some English economists of challenging the advantages of foreign investment (Keynes).[29] In following that tradition rather than the more prevalent one, which assumes international movements of capital to be guided by an invisible hand to improve human welfare, we are in no way suggesting policies to stop multinationalization, since we believe it to be a foregone conclusion. Our aim is to point out some likely consequences and contradictions of the laws of international industrial reorganization, as we see them. The propensity of multinational corporations to settle everywhere and establish connections everywhere is giving a new cosmopolitan nature to the economy and policies to deal with it will have to begin from that base.

9   United States investment abroad

The statistical evidence on foreign investment can hardly bear the weight of the policy proposals and value judgments all of us make, but it is mounting in quality and quantity and it is possible to isolate a few important features with reasonable confidence. This chapter presents a number of such empirical characteristics and draws out some of the value implications for present and future problems.[1]

The underlying framework of my essay can be summarized in the following equation describing the amount of United States direct investment in a country:

$$D = \sum a_i (1 - b_i) K_i$$

where D is total United States direct investment in a given country, a_i is the share of assets in industry i owned by American subsidiaries, b_i is the proportion of a subsidiary's assets financed locally, K_i is the capital stock of industry i. According to this equation, variations in United States direct investment from country to country can be attributed to variations in one of three factors. The first, *the industrial organization factor,* is represented by a_i, the American market share in each industry in the foreign country. This share is determined by oligopolistic competition and depends upon the strength of American firms, the strength of foreign competitors, and the accidents of oligopolistic rivalry. For most industries the a_is are zero, but in a few industries they are high on a world wide basis.

The second factor, the *international finance factor,* represented by $(1 - b_i)$, is the parent firm's financial share in its subsidiary's assets. This ratio depends mainly upon the state of the capital market in the host country and on political factors, though it is to some extent related to specific characteris-

This essay originally appeared in *Direct Foreign Investment in Asia and the Pacific,* P. Drysdale, ed. (Canberra: Australian National University Press, 1972), pp. 19–58. Copyright © 1972 by Australian National University Press. Reprinted by permission of Australian National University Press.

tics of the industry involved. Lastly, the volume of United States direct investment in a country depends upon the *composition of its industry*, a factor represented by the K_js, the vector of capital stocks in each industry. To a large extent, the amount of direct investment in a given country depends upon whether that country happens to have those industries with which direct investment tends to be associated or whether it has industries where the value of a_i tends to be low. This in turn is heavily dependent on the industrialization strategy of the government.

I want to try to use existing materials to study some of the characteristics of D, a_i, b_i and K_i through time as best I can and to relate them to other magnitudes. It should be noted, however, that by and large these quantities are not themselves the main objects of concern but are intermediaries in a more complex chain. At the deepest level, what concerns people is the degree of participation in the shaping and sharing of values. These include not only economic wealth, our primary focus of attention, but also power, well-being, enlightenment, skill, recitude, affection, and respect, to follow Harold Laswell's categories.[2] However, the connections between the empirical parameters of direct foreign investment and these values is not one upon which we can agree as easily as we can upon the "facts."

Another important feature to bear in mind is that, scientifically (econometrically) speaking, it is not proper to separate *economic* analysis from *political* analysis when interpreting data. The coefficients a_i, b_i, and K_i are not determined by economic forces alone. The effect of government in determining the size of specific industries, the amount a firm can borrow, and the share of the United States is obvious. Equally important, the size of a_i, b_i, and K_i affects government policy either through its effects on taxes or through its effect on interest groups pressuring the government. An increase in a_i, for example, may cause national firms either to pressure the government to curb American expansion or give American firms more of a stake and more say in determining policy. To ignore this relationship is to run the danger of interpreting a reduced form equation as a structural equation with consequent errors in prediction and policy.[3]

Historical perspective

Direct investment has a very long history (see Table 1). Most United States multinational firms began their international forays a long time ago, often before the Depression, sometimes before World War I. Some of the most important firms can trace the beginning of their foreign activities to before 1900. By 1914, the United States had $US2½ billion in direct investment. Thus, what seems to be a new phenomenon to a receiving country is often an old practice from the point of view of the firm.[4]

Corporations do not grow old and die. They are, as Harry Johnson has put

Table 1. *Expansion of United States multinational corporations through time*

	In all areas	Canada	Latin America	Europe	Southern dominions	Asia and other Africa
(a) Number of companies operating a foreign subsidiary						
1901	23	6	3	22	2	0
1913	47	27	9	37	8	4
1919	74	54	16	45	14	8
1929	123	92	36	95	34	23
1939	153	123	72	116	63	33
1945	158	128	93	120	69	33
1957	183	167	155	160	105	83
1967	186	174	182	185	154	158
(b) Number of companies operating a foreign manufacturing subsidiary						
1901	18	5	3	16	1	0
1913	39	24	6	26	3	1
1919	64	48	10	30	7	4
1929	110	79	24	76	20	15
1939	135	102	56	96	44	18
1945	138	107	73	96	50	17
1957	174	142	131	144	85	61
1967	185	161	171	183	135	134

Source: J. W. Vaupel and J. P. Curhan, *The Making of Multinational Enterprise* (Cambridge, Mass.: Harvard University Press, 1968), p. 69.

it, like California Redwoods, with perpetual life, and this is reflected in their international operations. There is little tendency for the activities of foreign enterprise to decline through time and their share of the market to fall. Instead their subsidiaries in each country, once established, tend to grow in step with that industry in that country except where interrupted by extraordinary events like war. When dealing with an international corporation, we are dealing with a long-run problem.[5]

Historical accident plays an important role in determining the market share of particular firms in a particular country. An old example contrasting the meat industry and the tobacco industry can help illustrate this important feature.[6] In the nineteenth century the United States exported meat to Great Britain and Europe. The advent of refrigerated shipping made it economical for Europe to switch its imports from the United States to Latin America. Both British and American firms established meat packing plants in Latin America. A bitter battle resulted but firms of both countries remained in the industry.

Contrast this with the tobacco case where the invasion of the British tobacco industry by American capital was met by amalgamations of British firms, a period of cut-throat competition, and a market sharing agreement which kept the American tobacco out of Britain, British capital out of

America, and established a joint venture to handle third markets. Later, as part of an antitrust decree, American Tobacco was forced to divest itself of its share of the British-American Tobacco Company. Similarly, in the chemical industry, a low level of direct investment in Europe by American firms and a high reliance on licensing reflects the particular form of oligopoly collusion reached in that industry characterized by large firms on both sides of the Atlantic. Also, the joint venture between Imperial Chemical and Du Pont in Canada was broken up by an antitrust decree.

Wars have also been an important factor determining market shares. In the United States, in contrast to the general pattern, firms formerly owned by foreigners have in some industries given way to local firms. But many of these were special cases resulting from the war, when German subsidiaries were seized, and some British firms sold to meet exchange requirements of the United Kingdom. Some of the British firms later bought back their interests.

Thus we can observe a wide variety of historical patterns. In one industry firms may divide the world into spheres of interest, with, say, American firms restricting themselves to Latin America, European firms to Asia and Africa, and all competing with Canada. In another industry, firms may co-operate more closely and establish joint ventures to operate in regions outside their home countries. In still other industries, the firms may compete instead of collude and each establish branch plants in most foreign countries. It is not possible to specify *a priori* which of the many permutations and combinations will be chosen; the indeterminacy of oligopoly theory reflects itself in the indeterminacy of direct investment and there is great difficulty in predicting the a_is with any degree of accuracy.

But the system underlying direct investment tends to be characterized by positive feedback and a structure, once established, tends to reproduce itself. This underlines the importance of initial positions in determining future profits and explains in part the emphasis placed by businessmen on market position rather than profitability in determining their investment strategy (this can also be used as an argument for government restrictions, that is, the infant *firm* argument for protection).

It would be quite wrong, though, to project the past pattern into the future. We seem now to be witnessing a major upheaval. Market patterns, sometimes set early in the century, remained stable until the fifties, but now radical shifts are occurring in the structure of the international economy, and many industries are characterized by intense oligopolistic competition between firms of different nations. During the next few years, we may expect shifts and fluctuations in the pattern of market shares; but if the past is any criterion, we may hazard the guess that a new pattern will emerge which will remain stable for another long period. The European situation seems to have begun already to work towards stabilization in terms of market shares; but in Eastern Europe, Asia, Africa and Latin America, the battle is probably just about to begin.

Table 2. Scale of United States business in foreign countries ($US billion except where noted)

	All foreign subsidiaries				Subsidiaries in Latin America				Comparable data for United States 1962–3			
					All industries		Manufacturing		All corporations	Largest 50 firms	Next 50 firms	Largest 200 firms
	1950	1957	1966	1970	1957	1966	1957	1966				
U.S. investment	11.8	25.3	54.8	70–75	6.6	11.4	1.2	3.3				
Total assets	22.2	42.5							291.0	136.2		165.3
Sales		38.1		120–150	7.2	12.9	2.3	6.5	420.3	25%	9%	42%
Value added		16.0		40–50	4.0	6.7	.7	2.1	191.9	25%	8%	41%
Employment (millions)		3.2		5–6	.8	1.2	.319	.475	17.0	19%	6%	31%
Wages and salaries		6.7	5.7	12.0					99.7	24%	8%	39%
Earnings	2.0	3.6			1.3	2.5	.354	1.147	19.3	11.1		13.0

Source: Cols. 1–3: *Census of 1950, Census of 1957,* and *Survey of Current Business,* October 1969. Value added for foreign subsidiaries obtained by subtracting materials, supplies, and services purchased from total costs. Cols. 5–8: *Census of 1957* and preliminary results of *Census of 1966* as reported by the Council for Latin America (1970). Cols. 9–12: U.S. Congress *Economic Concentration, Hearings* before the Subcommittee on Antitrust and Monopoly, May–June 1965 (U.S. Government Printing Office, Washington, 1965), Part I, p. 5 and p. 1894, Part II, pp. 113–14. Total assets and earnings refer to 1962 rather than 1963. Total earnings (profit after tax) were available on a quarterly basis and were multiplied by four. They refer to earnings of manufacturing corporations only. The figure for Sales ($US420.3 billion) refers to value of shipments.

Table 3. *Measures of penetration by multinational corporations for Canada, Australia, and New Zealand (per cent)*

	Canada				
	All industries		Large firms		
	1945	1954	1961	Australia	New Zealand
Fixed assets					
Land and buildings				6.9	25
Plant and					
machinery				10.2	35
Value of output	20	30	49	7.0	26
Value added	20	29	47	—	26
Employment	16	21	44	5.1	20
Salaries and wages	—	—	42	—	—
Profits	18	25	—	—	—
Establishments	1.3	2.0	37	—	5
Replacement to					
Land and buildings				14.8	
Plant and machinery				13.1	

Source: Canada: Dominion Bureau of Statistics, *Canada's International Investment Position 1926–1954;* Gideon Rosenbluth, "Foreign Control and Industrial Concentration," *Report for the Task Force on the Structure of Canadian Industry* (Ottawa: Queen's Printer, 1969). Large firms refers to manufacturing establishments belonging to entrepreneurs with capital investment of more than $25 million in Canada. Australia: Donald T. Brash, *American Investment in Australian Industry.* Data refer to United States firms responding to his questionnaire. New Zealand: R. S. Deane, *Foreign Investment in New Zealand Manufacturing.* Data for all foreign firms.

The rapid growth of United States business abroad

Adequate data on the degree to which United States corporations have penetrated foreign markets are not available but the aggregate investment of American corporations in all foreign countries is very large. At present it totals $US70-75 billion and in recent years it has grown on the order of $US5-7 billion annually (see Table 2). These numbers, it should be noted, represent only the capital invested by the American parent in its foreign subsidiary and not the total assets under its control. The total assets of American corporations operating abroad are much larger than the capital invested and probably equal $US110 billion at book value. American corporations, on the average, are able to borrow 40 per cent of their subsidiaries' capital requirements locally in the country of operation.

The foreign penetration of United States industry differs considerably from country to country. In Canada and some underdeveloped countries, foreign investment represents a very large amount of the capital stock. In the rest of the world the American share is considerably lower. In Europe it is still

Table 4. *Expenditures by United States companies on plant and equipment in the United States and abroad ($US billion)*

Year	In United States	Abroad	Ratio of foreign to domestic
1957	18.2	4.8	26
1958	13.8	4.1	30
1959	14.1	3.7	26
1960	16.4	3.8	23
1961	15.6	4.1	26
1962	16.5	4.6	28
1963	17.5	5.1	29
1964	20.7	6.1	29
1965	24.9	7.4	30
1966	29.8	8.6	30
1967	30.2	9.2	37
1968	30.0	9.4	31
1969	33.6	11.4	34
By industry for 1966			
Food	1.440	0.205	
Paper and pulp	1.460	0.271	
Chemicals	2.960	1.159	
Rubber	0.430	0.188	
Printing	1.802	0.463	
Machines	2.990	0.765	
Electrical machines	1.120	0.265	
Transport equipment	2.990	1.119	
Mining and petroleum	5.910	3.553	

Source: *Survey of Current Business,* September 1965, September 1966, January 1970, March 1970.

small, relatively speaking, but as it is associated with dynamic industries, it is growing rapidly and of considerable importance. In Japan, it is less than one per cent.

The question is how big is big? To what should we compare foreign investment in order to evaluate its importance; to national income, aggregate capital stock and employment, or to the value of these variables in the manufacturing sector alone, or in selected industries within manufacturing?

In general the subsidiaries of multinational corporations are larger than average, more capital intensive, and pay higher wages than those of the host country. Their share of capital and profits therefore usually exceeds their share of output which in turn exceeds their share in employment (see Table 3 for some examples). On the other hand, the subsidiaries of United States multinational corporations have less capital per man than their parents and pay lower wages; the foreign share in employment of multinational corporations thus exceeds their foreign share of output or profits.

There is room for a vast number of indicators depending upon the purposes, theory, and biases of the observer. However, since direct foreign investment is growing more rapidly than most other economic series, whatever ratio is chosen, the critical point where a quantitative change becomes a qualitative change is likely to be reached fairly shortly, if present trends continue. The examples that follow are indicative.

First, the $US6 billion of value added by all United States foreign business in 1957 was only about 13 per cent of the total United States national income generated in mining and manufacturing that year (about $US12 billion); but whereas foreign activity probably tripled between 1957 and the present, activity in the United States only doubled (see Table 4). Plant and equipment expenditure by United States business abroad was about one-quarter of domestic expenditure in 1957 and rose to about one-third by 1969. These ratios are much higher in certain industries.

Secondly, Table 5, which compares United States firms abroad with *Fortune*'s 500 largest United States industrial corporations and 100 (or 200) largest non-American corporations, shows that American industry abroad is by itself equal to the industrial sector of a sizeable country and that it is expanding rapidly relative to its parent firms. To large American firms, foreign operations are of considerable importance and growing rapidly.

Thirdly, whereas United States production abroad grew at about 10 per cent per year over the last twenty years, United States exports grew at only 5.4 per cent, indicating a dramatic shift in United States corporate strategy for meeting the challenge of the world market.

Fourthly, and finally, we should note the growing importance of manufacturing, and, in particular, its rapid rate of growth in Latin America, perhaps a portent for the future of other developing countries (see Table 6).

What happens if these trends are projected into the future? Judd Polk, for example, taking into account all United States investment abroad and all foreign investment in the United States and elsewhere, estimates that the internationalized production associated with that investment is about one-quarter of the total world product.[7] To obtain this rate, he assumes that two dollars' worth of international products is associated with a dollar's worth of direct investment, and less for other kinds of investment. According to Table 5 this is not unreasonable for sales but it is too high for value added. On the assumption that the internationalized sector grows at 8 percent and the non-internationalized sector at 4 per cent, international production will account for 50 per cent of the total world production by the year 2005 and 80 per cent by the year 2040.[8]

In sum, the growth of the United States investments has been very rapid (10 per cent per year from 1950 to 1970). At this rate it doubles every seven years. When projected over the next thirty or fifty years the repercussions of this rate of growth are very large. What are the prospects that will be sustained? Economic conditions, that is, the size of market and state of

Table 5. *Total sales, assets, income, and employees of the industrial corporations on the* Fortune *list*

	500 largest United States firms[a]				100 or 200 largest non–United States firms[a]				Foreign subsidiaries of United States firms[a]					
	Sales	Assets	Income	Employees	Sales	Assets	Income	Employees	Sales	Assets	Book value of U.S. investment	Income	Employees	Value added
1957	188.3	148.8	11.6	9,078	55.2	42.6	2.5	4,800	38.1	42.5	25.4	3.6	3,200	16
1958	176.8	154.4	9.6	8,523	51.6	47.2	2.2	5,000			27.4	3.0		
1959	197.4	168.5	12.0	9,052	55.2	53.1	2.5	5,200			29.8	3.2		
1960	204.7	176.2	11.6	9,179	62.7	60.1	2.9	5,700			31.8	3.6		
1961	209.2	186.8	11.6	9,266	67.8	67.0	2.8	6,000			34.7	3.8		
1962	229.0	197.0	13.4	9,652	98.4	102.9	3.8	8,893			37.3	4.2		
1963	245.1	208.7	14.8	9,966	108.3	114.2	4.1	9,249			40.7	4.6		
1964	266.5	224.7	17.3	10,464	121.2	131.3	4.6	9,804			44.5	5.0		
1965	298.1	251.7	20.1	11,279	130.8	143.4	5.1	9,853			49.5	5.5		
1966	332.6	282.1	22.1	12,307	143.1	159.1	5.2	9,962			54.8	5.7		
1967	358.9	216.9	21.4	13,079	155.1	171.3	5.5	10,113			59.5	6.0		
1968											64.8	7.0		

[a]Value of sales, assets, and income in $US billion; numbers of employees in thousands.
Sources: Fortune Magazine, Census of 1957, and Survey of Current Business Statistics.

Table 6. *Growth of United States foreign investment*

Year	Value of direct investment at year's end ($US billion)	Earnings ($US 000)	Manufcturing investment	Latin America ($US billion) Total	Latin America ($US billion) Manufacturing
1950	11.8	1,766	3.8	3.6	.781
1951	13.0	2,236			
1952	14.7	2,327			
1953	16.3	2,258			
1954	17.6	2,398			
1955	19.4	2,878			
1956	22.5	3,298			
1957	25.4	3,561	8.0	8.6	1.3
1958	27.4	3,014			
1959	29.8	3,241			
1960	31.8	3,566	11.0	8.4	1.5
1961	34.7	3,815	12.0	9.2	1.7
1962	37.3	4,325	13.2	9.5	1.9
1963	40.7	4,587	14.9	9.9	2.2
1964	44.5	5,077	16.9	10.3	2.5
1965	49.5	5,460	19.3	10.9	2.9
1966	54.8	5,702	22.1	11.5	3.3
1967	59.5	6,034	24.2	12.0	3.6
1968	64.8	7,010	26.4	13.0	4.0

Sources: Survey of Current Business (various issues), *Census of 1950*, and *Census of 1957*.

competition are favourable. The world market for products associated with multinational corporations (consumer durables, other items for the mass middle class market, plus key producer's durables) is expanding rapidly. Important competitors in other countries are ready to take advantage of these markets if United States firms do not. Pressure to continue to invest abroad is thus high.

Political forces are a different matter. They tend to exert a resisting pressure likely to turn the exponential expansion of the last twenty years into an S-shaped Lorenz curve. The question is when the turning points will come and how.

The problem as John Powers of the Chas. Pfizer Corporation has put it is that "practice is ahead of theory and policy."[9] Multinational corporations in their everyday business practice are connecting consumers and producers on a world-wide basis and creating a new world structure. This will require correspondingly radical changes in the legal, political, and ideological framework if it is to be sustained. Therefore, the multinational corporations will have to mobilize political power to bring about these changes, or they will not be able to continue growing as in the past. Can they do so?

As a headline to George Ball's now famous argument that corporations are modern while nation-states are old-fashioned institutions rooted in archaic concepts, *Business Week*[10] wrote: "For a worldwide enterprise, national boundaries are drawn in fading ink." The task of the multinational corporations is to convince nation-states including the United States to accept a greater degree of interdependence; to surrender a wide variety of traditional policy instruments – tariffs, balance of payments controls, and probably monetary and fiscal policy; to sacrifice certain sectors of their economy to the interests of the multinational sector; and to accept the cost of protecting and maintaining a system of international private property.

The positive attitude of most nation-states towards multinational corporations during the last twenty years may not be a good indicator of future practice. Multinational corporations, because of their favorable position (large size, wide horizons, and proximity to new technology) and the favorable environment (the initial large gold reserves of the United States, the formation of the Common Market, the small size of foreign investment), were in the vanguard of the revolution in world economic structure. The next round is likely to be characterized by increased emphasis on politics rather than economics and a much less free hand for business. The conflict is not so much between nationalism and internationalism, as the supporters of the multinational corporations like to put it; or between corporations and nation-states, as others prefer; but between groups of people within corporations and nation-states struggling over who decides what and who gets what – that is, between large corporations over their share of the world market, between big business which is internationally mobile and small business and labor which are not, between the middle classes of different countries over managerial positions, between high-wage labor in one country and low-wage labor in another, and between excluded groups in each country and their elites in that country.

Continued expansion of foreign investment will intensify some of these conflicts. In the case of the United States, for example, it has made the economy more open and difficult to manage and cleavages have already appeared between the interests of international investors and the rest of the domestic economy over taxation, balance of payments policy, extraterritoriality, and foreign aid. Multinational corporations want lower taxation on foreign income and freedom from anti-trust and other regulations. They want the United States to adjust its balance of payments through deflation or import control rather than foreign investment, and they want lower tariffs on some goods to permit an expansion of certain cheap-labor imports to the United States, and they want foreign aid to complement their foreign investment. Given the present economic and political tensions in the United States, it is far from certain that multinational corporations will be able to form the alliance necessary to overcome resistances to their expansion.

If multinationalization provided quick rewards perhaps it could be done. But United States foreign investment is often defensive rather than offensive: That is, to protect an existing position rather than to capture a rich new market. Moreover, the gradual erosion of traditional monetary, fiscal, and other policy instruments before new supranational ones are built, may create a gap in government effectiveness which could lead to a loss of national income and perhaps even a serious economic crisis. Finally the cost of protecting international private property from expropriation is rising and will continue to rise, since, as I argue below, a system of multinational corporations holds little promise for promoting widespread participation and its benefits are largely restricted to a minority of population, in the world as a whole and within the United States itself.

The above analysis is speculative and controversial. The important point is to raise, *as a scientific issue,* the question of whether foreign investment will continue to expand – something which involves political analysis as well as economic analysis. Much work needs to be done in this direction. Our work is only half done when we analyze the effect of foreign investment on income and its distribution without looking at the political strength and reactions of the various groups affected. The practice of multinational corporations with regard to countries can perhaps serve as a model. Dupont is one company that is making a stab in the direction of formally measuring environmental uncertainty, basically as a tool for capital budgeting decisions. The project is still in the research stage, but essentially the idea is to try to derive estimates of the potential of a foreign market, which is, of course, affected by economic conditions. The state of the economy in turn, is partly a function of the fiscal and monetary policies the foreign government adopts. Policy decisions depend on the real economic forces, and on the attitudes of various interest groups in the country, and on the degree to which the government listens to these groups.

In the fiscal and monetary part of their broad economic model, the Dupont researchers have identified fifteen to twenty interest groups per country, from small land-owners to private bankers. Each interest group has a "latent influence" which depends on its size and educational level and the group's power to make its feelings felt. This influence, subjectively measured, is multiplied by an estimate of "group cohesiveness": that is, how likely the group is to mobilize its full resources on any particular issue. The product is a measure of "potential influence". This in turn must be multiplied by a factor representing the government's receptivity to each influence group.[11]

The growth of non-American multinational corporations

Much less is known about non-American direct foreign investment than about American. According to OECD-DAC data (Table 7) it is about 60 per cent

Table 7. *Book value of direct foreign investment by major countries, 1966 ($US billion)*

Investing country	All foreign investment	Foreign investment in underdeveloped countries
United States	54.6	16.8
United Kingdom	16.0	6.2
France	4.0	2.1
Germany	2.5	0.9
Sweden	0.8	0.161
Canada	3.2	0.534
Japan	1.0	0.605
Total[a]	89.6	30.0

[a]Includes countries not listed separately.
Source: Based on OECD-DAC data and Sidney E. Rolfe, *The International Corporation* (New York: International Chamber of Commerce, 1969).

the size of United States direct investment, whereas total manufacturing production outside the United States, excluding socialist countries, is about equal to that of the United States and total exports of manufacturing by the United States are only about one-quarter of world exports of manufactures, although some investment and exports of other countries arise from the operations of American multinational corporations.[12]

The rate of growth of non-American direct investment is difficult to ascertain with precision. Investment by foreign firms in the United States grew slowly during the fifties and early sixties but, in recent years, has been averaging almost 10 per cent (from $US9.0 billion in 1966 to $US9.9 billion in 1967, and $US10.8 billion in 1968). There are reasons to expect an increased emphasis on foreign investment by European and Japanese firms in the future. Their strategy of expanding through exports rather than investment becomes increasingly difficult as they saturate markets. Their capability to invest will increase as they grow in size[13] and develop more modern systems of business administration. Lastly, the loss by the United States of its gold reserves will work to remove the asymmetries in government policy which in past years discouraged outward investment by non-American firms.

In addition to Europe and Japan, one must speculate what Russia will do. Her exports are increasing. How long will it be before she finds it desirable or necessary to set up local assembly and distribution facilities in order to service her markets?

Increased direct foreign investment by non-American enterprises is both competitive and complementary to the expansion of United States investment. As European and Japanese firms exploit their particular advantages, the hegemonic position of American corporations will be reduced. These advantages include: Greater flexibility in dealing with Russia and China;

certain special relations with former colonies; special experience in utilizing cheap labor in the case of Japan; greater flexibility with regard to joint ventures, management contracts, and the like; and less of an association with United States domestic political problems. These firms could provide a formidable challenge to United States firms, just as they did in the sixties through growth in production and exports. Leading non-American firms grew faster than American firms from 1957 to 1962 and at about the same rate from 1962 to 1967. Japanese firms grew much faster throughout the period.[14]

The complementary side to the growth of non-American firms can be illustrated by a simple model (used in collaboration with Robert Rowthorn):

$$S_1 = a_{11}Y_1 + a_{12}Y_2 + a_{13}Y_3$$
$$S_2 = a_{21}Y_1 + a_{22}Y_2 + a_{23}Y_3$$

where S_i is the total size of large firms in country i, Y_i is total production in country i, and a_{ij} refers to the market share of firms from country i in country j. The subscript 1 refers to the United States, 2 refers to Europe and Japan, and 3 refers to other countries.

At present the non-American share of the United States market (a_{21}) is very small. It is possible for the overall growth of American and non-American firms to be roughly equal (thus maintaining present oligopoly balance) and for both kinds of firms to expand faster abroad than at home if European firms become more multinational by increasing a_{21} and a_{23} while American firms increase a_{11} and a_{13}.

This would tend to equalize (a_{11}, a_{12}, and a_{13}) on the one hand, and (a_{21}, a_{22}, and a_{23}) on the other. The world would come more and more to resemble the United States market where each of the large firms is spread into every market and roughly speaking has the same share in each submarket as it does in the total.

The stability properties from such investment come from two sources. In the first place, the relative growth rates of firms of different countries come less and less to depend on differences in the growth of individual markets, that is, the ratio S_1/S_2 becomes independent of Y_1, Y_2, and Y_3. This permits oligopoly equilibrium with constant market shares in the large, independent of differential rates of growth in different countries.

In the second place, increased multinationalization on the part of European and Japanese firms would give them an increased stake in a world of free capital movements. This enhances the political leverage of American multi-national corporations and helps them to mobilize governments around the world for the task of reforming the world economy in the direction they desire. The close association between national firms and their national economy would be broken as well as their dependence on particular national

Table 8. *United States direct foreign investment by size of investment*

Value of direct investment by size classes	Number of firms		Percentage of total	
	All industries	Manufacturing	Industries	Manufacturing
$US100 million and over	45	15	57	35
$US50–100 million	51	24	14	18
$US25–50 million	67	40	9	17
$US10–25 million	126	64	8	11
$US5–10 million	166	89	5	7
Total	455	232	93	88

Source: Census of 1957, Table 55, p. 144.

governments. In the extreme, all multinational firms would tend to pressure all governments in similar directions.

Such a state, however, is still very much in the future. Inter-penetration of European and United States firms is well advanced but Japanese enterprises (and Russian) are outside this system and still closely tied to national governments. Similarly, the nascent capitalists of underdeveloped countries are closely tied to their governments. The critical point has not been reached, though the rapid development of the international communications system which will give multinational corporations the power to reach 500 to 700 million consumers at one blow, may soon give them the decisive edge.

Association with a few large firms

Though many firms have some international operations, the number of important investors is relatively small. Fifty American firms, each with foreign investment of over $US100 million (in 1957) accounted for nearly 60 per cent of all United States direct investment abroad. The next fifty largest investors accounted for another 10 per cent. Ninety per cent of all United States direct investment is accounted for by 300 firms (see Table 8). To this must be added a dozen or so large European and Canadian concerns that qualify as multinational corporations.

Given the major expansion of foreign investment since 1957, the number of large foreign investors must have increased and the distribution may have become less skewed. We shall know better when the results of the 1966 census are published. However, it is unlikely that this expansion has changed the fact that the largest part of direct foreign investment is accounted for by a relatively small number of firms in an even smaller number of industries.[15]

The large size of the multinational corporation is a major feature of all discussions. They are described as "giants" or "mastodons." They are large

Table 9. *Distribution of major foreign investors in manufacturing by market structure compared to all United States industry*

Market structure: concentration ratios for 4 largest companies	Major foreign investors		All U.S. industry	
	No. of firms	Percentage total no. of firms	No. of industries	Percentage total value of shipments
75 to 100%	32	44	40	8
50 to 74%	11	15	101	17
25 to 49%	28	39	157	35
less than 25%	1	1	136	40
Total	72	99	434	100

Source: The Distribution of American Industries by Concentration ratio is taken from U.S. Senate *Concentration in American Industry*, Report of the Subcommittee on Antitrust and Monopoly pursuant to S. Re 57 (85th Congress), Table 17, p. 23. The data on major investors were obtained from Annual Reports. It was possible from this source to trace about 92 of the major foreign investors in manufacturing (Food, Paper, Chemicals, Metals, Machinery, Automotive and Electrical, and Other). A more complete analysis would now be possible using the data collected by the Harvard Business School and in the report of Bruck and Lees. Though there is some uncertainty surrounding certain of these firms, probably at worst no more than five are wrongly included. These firms were classified into industries which were then grouped according to concentration level. Twenty of these firms were in industries for which it was difficult to assign concentration ratios: general food products, general chemicals, metals, electrical equipment, paper products. For some of these industries concentration ratios are probably low; however, the foreign investments may well be in specialized segments more concentrated than the average. See Table 10 for a more detailed listing.

relative to their markets and large relative to the governments with which they deal. The parent firms occupy a dominant position in the United States economy and feature prominently in the list of the 200 largest firms that account for over half of the value in industry in the American economy. The subsidiaries are often amongst the largest firms in the countries in which they operate.

Direct investment tends to be associated with oligopolistic industries. The major investors are dominant producers in industries where a few firms account for a large part of industry output.

Table 9 classifies the major United States direct investors in manufacturing industries by the level of concentration of their industries and presents evidence for the United States. Approximately 40 per cent of these firms are in industries where the concentration ratio is greater than 75 per cent (a detailed list of the industries in each category is found in Table 10). For the United States as a whole the corresponding figure is much lower; only 8 per cent of the total value of shipments occur in industries where the concentration is higher than 75 per cent. Note that firms have been classified according to their major product, while their direct investments are often restricted to

Table 10. *Distribution of major manufacturing foreign investors by market structure (detailed listing)*

Less than 25% concentration	25–49% concentration	50–74% concentration	70–100% concentration	Unclassified
Construction and mining machinery 1	Meat products 4	Biscuits and crackers 1	Cereal breakfast foods 2	Chemicals 5
	Dairy products 2	Corn wet milling 1	Chewing gum 2	Metals 1
	Canned fruits and vegetables 3	Abrasives 1	Flavoring syrups for soft drinks 3	Food 2
	Flour and meal 1	Asbestos 1	Hard surface floor coverings 1	Paper products 9
	Cement 1	Photographic equipment 1	Tires and inner tubes 5	Electrical machinery 3
	Refractories 1	Cleaning and polishing soaps and glycerine 2	Flat glass 1	
	Surgical appliances 1	Plumbing fixtures 2	Tobacco 1	
	Mattresses and bed springs 1	Elevators and escalators 1	Aluminum 1	
	Medicinal chemical and pharmaceutical preparations 6	Vacuum cleaners 1	Tin cans and other tinware 2	
	Paints and varnishes 1		Razors and razor blades 1	
	Tractors and farm machinery 5		Computing machines and typewriters 4	
	Oil field machinery and tools 1		Sewing machines 1	
	Printing trade equipment and machinery 1		Shoe machinery 1	
			Motor vehicles 6	
			Locomotives and parts 1	
Total 1	28	11	32	20

Source: See Table 9.

Table 11. *Distribution of American-owned enterprises in United Kingdom by market structure*

	Number of enterprises	Number of employees
Group A – U.S. firm the dominant producer	12	32,000
Group B – U.S. firm one or more of a small number of strong producers	136	200,000
Group C – U.S. firm one of a number of producers of modest size	57	14,000
Total	205	246,000

Source: Dunning, *American Investment in British Manufacturing Industry*, pp. 156–7. Dunning believes the 205 firms in his sample account for between 90 and 95 per cent of the total labor force of the United States financial and manufacturing units in the United Kingdom. This presentation underestimates the monopolistic characteristics of the industries; the Group C category contains proprietary medicines, beauty and toilet preparations, and foundation garments, which are industries where brand names are very important.

one or two specialties where the firm has particular advantages and where concentration is much higher; a better industry definition would, I suggest, show an even stronger association.

Still the best and most detailed study of the association of foreign investment with concentration is that of John Dunning, undertaken in 1957. Dunning's classification is reproduced as Table 11. *Nearly every branch plant is an industry where it is the dominant producer or one of a small number of producers.* As Dunning concluded, "three-quarters of the employment in the United States affiliated firms is concentrated in industries where the five largest competitors supply 80 per cent or more of the total output." Dunning's rough measure of the importance of the American subsidiaries in their industries, though not as systematic as one would wish, is nonetheless clear: American subsidiaries have a very high share in these highly concentrated industries.[16]

Evidence from other countries, though available only in less convenient form, confirms the finding that direct investment is associated with oligopolistic industries.[17]

A number of important implications follow from these characteristics. First, the large size of multinational corporations implies an interaction between them and the government quite different from the traditional view, which pictures a large state acting on a plane above business. Large corporations, because of their cohesiveness, their access to information and modern technology, their world-wide network of communication, and their long time perspectives, often act alongside the state or above it. In theory, the corporation is a person operating under the sovereignty of the state. In practice, the actual power of many national governments, relative to multinational corporations, is more like that of city governments than sovereign states.

Second, a dichotomy of interest often exists between those firms which have large investments and those which do not. Arguments framed in terms of protecting the national interest are often the rationalization of national capital attempting to protect itself from the competition of international capital. Similarly, much of the talk about "one world" and "le defi international" should be viewed as an ideological banner for the few, but important, firms with international strategies.

This cleavage shows up in many ways. One of them is the debate over balance of payments adjustment. Those firms which cannot invest abroad want help in exporting to meet the challenge of international competition. Those firms which can invest argue about the virtue of locating production where it is "efficient" and adjusting the local economy accordingly.

This cleavage, it should be noted, does not increase but diminishes with the growth of foreign investment. Small businesses can be divided into three types: those in direct conflict with multinational corporations, those in symbiotic relation as suppliers or distributors, and those which are unaffected. The first group is often destroyed by competition. It is soon out of the picture, unless it acts quickly, as far as political or economic power is concerned. The interest of the second group basically lies in promoting multinational corporations, despite conflict over how rewards are to be shared. The third group of capital also tends to become increasingly favorable to multinational corporations as the advantages it derives from an open international economy become clear, that is, the opportunity to trade and the ability to protect its wealth. In a closed system of economy, national capital is constantly in fear of expropriation and capital controls. When the national economy becomes integrated into an open international system, Swiss Bank accounts become less necessary, as small capital is sheltered by the umbrella of a multinational corporate system emphasizing the rights of international private property.

Association with special industries

Multinational corporations tend to be concentrated in a few industries with special characteristics.[18] Table 12 shows the industrial distribution of direct investment by American firms and the direct investment in the United States by foreign firms. The great bulk of the investment is in "heavy" industry rather than light, that is, in industries characterized by large firms, high capital intensity, advanced technology, and differentiated products. Gruber, Mehta, and Vernon found little association with capital intensity. However, they restricted their definition to fixed capital (as measured by depreciation and net fixed assets) and not variable capital. Often the strength of the

Table 12. *Industrial distribution of foreign investments*[a]

	1950		1962		1959	
	Foreign investment of United States companies	Ratio of foreign investment to total assets	Foreign sales of United States companies	Percentage distribution of sales of all corporations in the United States	Foreign business in the United States investment	Sales
20 Food	483	4.0	3,410	15.5	931	2,299
20 Paper and allied	378	8.4	1,180	2.0		
28 Chemicals	513	5.3	4,400	7.9	465	891
drugs	—	—		1.2		
other	—	—		6.7		
29 Petroleum	3,390	19.4	n.a.	8.9	1,184	n.a.
30 Rubber	182	8.9	1,332	2.5		
33 Primary metals						
34 Fabricated metals	385	2.1	2,053	12.5	125	276
35 Machinery,						
except electric	420	4.4	3,359	7.6	275	432
36 Electrical machinery	386	8.2	3,571	8.6	83	289
37 Transportation						
equipment	—	—	6,680	13.5		
aircraft	—	—		3.7		
motor vehicles						
and parts	485	6.1				
Other				9.5		
All other manufactures	599	2.4	2,938		592	944

[a]Industry definitions not exactly comparable.
Sources: Cols. 1–2, *Census of 1950* and FTC-SEC *Quarterly Industrial Financial Reports,* First Quarter 1950.
Cols. 3–4, *Survey of Current Business* and FTC-SEC *Quarterly Industrial Financial Reports* as reproduced in Gruber, Mehta, and Vernon, "The R & D Factor," p. 24.
Cols. 5–6, *Census of 1959.*

modern firm stems from its ability to advance wages to skilled personnel for long-term developments. Because these are treated as current costs, profits and investment are underestimated. A more detailed analysis within two digit categories would show foreign investment to be concentrated in speciality industries; and that, within firms, foreign investment usually does not cover the full product range but is concentrated in lines where the firm is particularly strong (see Table 10).

A full explanation of the factors which determine whether an industry has foreign investment or not is still lacking but the existing studies point to three features: Firstly, there must be some kind of barrier to entry in the industry

Table 13. *Examples of cross-investment*

Industry in which United States has major investments	Foreign-controlled firm operating in United States
1. Concentrated milk	Nestle
2. Soft drinks	Orange Crush
3. Biscuits	Westons
4. Paper	Bowater
5. Pharmaceuticals	BASF, Bayer, Hoechst, Ciba
6. Soap	Lever Brothers
7. Petroleum	Shell
8. Tires and tubes	Dunlop
9. Aluminum	Pechiny
10. Farm machinery	Massey-Harris-Ferguson
11. Business machines	Olivetti, Moore, Philips
12. Sewing machines	Necchi
13. Automotive parts	Bosch
14. Fountain pens	Bic, Waterman

Source: A fuller list of American subsidiaries in the United States, unfortunately without any index of the scale of operations, is found in Appendix A of S. Rolfe and W. Damm, *The Multinational Corporation in the World Economy* (New York: Praeger, 1970), pp. 131–67.

(technological, economies of scale, or differentiated products) so that local firms cannot compete with profits below a level which compensates the multinational corporation for the extra costs of operating in a foreign country and integrating geographically dispersed operations; secondly, it must be advantageous to produce locally rather than export from a single production center (this depends upon tariffs, the size of the market, and the threat of local competition); and, thirdly, the firm must find it more profitable to exploit the foreign advantage through direct investment rather than licensing. Hence a technological lead is not a sufficient explanation of foreign investment. One must also explain why the technology is not sold like other commodities. The answer usually lies in the marketing characteristics of the advantage, that is, the difficulty of extracting full quasi-rent where markets are imperfect.

Non-American multinational corporations tend to be in the same kind of industries as American corporations. Perhaps the most intriguing characteristic of direct investment is the number of cases of foreign companies which have branch plants in the United States in the *very same* industries that American firms have branch plants abroad. Table 13 lists fourteen important industries in which American firms have large foreign investments, and where one of the major firms operating in the United States is a branch plant of a foreign firm. This cross-investment shows that American direct investment cannot be explained simply in terms of better access to capital, better entrepreneurship, better technology, or higher profits abroad, since the flow takes place in two directions. Analysis of oligopolistic bargaining strategy is, however, helpful; it is not unusual for leading oligopolists to establish inroads into their competitor's home territory to strengthen their position; cross-investment may be a reflection of this tactic on the international level.

The industries associated with multinational corporations tend to grow more rapidly than aggregate national income. This suggests a steady increase of direct investment in Western Europe and the growing importance of the Eastern European market. It also implies that the developing countries offer a more important market than might at first seem the case. Development programs over the decades have created in many countries a large urban proletariat, a considerable increase in the stock of education, a nascent industrial capitalist class, the beginnings of a physical infrastructure suitable for manufacturing, and an expanded modernized government sector. These elements are likely to grow rapidly in the next decades, given the level of past and existing government programs. Though many problems remain, rapid industrialization is indicated. Since the strategy of most countries is to stress the expansion of the small privileged "modern" sector rather than the development of the lower two-thirds of the population, demand will shift more and more in the direction of consumer durables and brand name products (processed food, drugs and medicines, cosmetics, etc.) – that is, towards the mass middle-class market.

These markets are important to the American multinational corporations since the marginal costs of serving them are low (the costs of product development and marketing knowledge is a fixed cost). Not to fill them would open spaces for rival multinational firms or lead to the emergence of serious local competition which could eventually threaten the home market in developed countries. The motives for direct investment are thus both offensive and defensive – the seeking out of new sources of profit, and protection from future attack.

In making a foreign investment the strategy of the firm is to maximize the return on its advantage while consolidating its ability for self-sustained growth. This involves getting control of marketing facilities through advertising, or dealer networks, and continuous heavy expenditure on product development to maintain high barriers to entry. Smaller firms can often do better than the large firms at one point of the product cycle. The large corporation gains its strength by planning and co-ordinating over the whole product cycle, and absorbing successful small firms when they reach a certain stage in their growth. Given the revolution in communications and the rapid growth of industry abroad, the product cycle comes more and more to include the stage of foreign marketing and production as well. Hence, the importance to large American firms of free capital movements and free entry to new markets if they are to maintain their world share.

From the point of view of the United States, the ability of its firms to innovate continuously and to spread their advantages widely has considerable importance. In 1908, Alfred Marshall analyzed the problem of the then dominant economic power as follows:

England will not be able to hold her own against other nations by the mere sedulous practice of familiar processes. These are being reduced to such mechanical routine by her own, and still more by American ingenuity that an Englishman's labour in them will not continue long to count for very much more than that of an equally energetic man of a more backward race. Of course, the Englishman has access to relatively larger and cheaper stores of capital than anyone else, but his advantage in this respect has diminished, is diminishing, and must continue to diminish; and it is not to be reckoned on as a very important element in the future. England's place among the nations in the future must depend on the extent to which she retains industrial leadership. She cannot be *the* leader, but she may be *a* leader.

The economic significance of industrial leadership generally is most clearly illustrated just now by the leadership which France, or rather Paris, has in many commodities which are on the border-line between art and luxury. New Parisian goods are sold at high prices in London and Berlin for a short time, and then good imitations of them are made in large quantities and sold at relatively low prices. But by that time Paris, which had earned high wages and profits by making them to sell at scarcity prices, is already at work on other things which will soon be limited in a like way. Sixty years ago England had this leadership in most branches of industry. The finished commodities, and still more, the implements of production, to which her manufacturers were giving their chief attention in any one year, were those which would be occupying the attention of the more progressive of Western nations two or three years later, and of the rest from five to twenty years later. It was inevitable that she should cede much of that leadership to the great land which attracts alert minds of all nations to sharpen their inventive and resourceful faculties by impact on one another. It was inevitable that she should yield a little of it to that land of great industrial traditions which yoked science in the service of man with unrivalled energy. It was not inevitable that she should lose so much of it as she has done.[19]

The United States is now in a similar position to Great Britain. Its great strength in innovation and organization cannot be denied. But a striking feature of recent decades is the narrowing of lead-times and the shortening of the product cycle. Direct foreign investment provides one way of meeting this challenge.

Note that this new international division of labor implies a continued dependence on the part of underdeveloped countries as they specialize in the later stages of the product cycle. Direct investment thus has a dual aspect: It brings capital, technology, and managerial skill, but it centralizes the means for producing capital, technology, and organizing ability. The relationship between the developed and underdeveloped countries may become like the relationship between major and minor cities, the one continuously innovating and dispersing activity to surrounding areas, the other having continuously to adjust to changes in the center. The gap could then remain permanent as the relationship between leader and lagger is reproduced through the vehicle of corporate control.

Table 14. *United States and foreign patterns of financing direct investments*

	Direct investment by United States in foreign countries (1957) (per cent)			Direct investment by foreigners in the United States (1959) (per cent)		
	Equity capital	Debtor capital	All capital	Equity capital	Debtor capital	All capital
United States share	86	25	61	14	81	50
Non-United States share	14	75	39	86	19	50
	100	100	100	100	100	100

Sources: Census of 1957 and *Foreign Business Investments in the United States.*

Capital

The structure of international ownership and control varies considerably as firms choose between many devices for international operations: licensing agreements, management contracts, minority interest, joint ventures, or wholly-owned branch plants. Within any one system, the degree of control can vary from complete centralization to a great degree of local autonomy.

For the United States there seems to be a strong preference for the wholly-owned subsidiary, although this may be changing. At the time of the last United States census of foreign investments, ownership of foreign branch plants or subsidiaries was 95 per cent or more in 75 per cent of the cases of American investments.[20] A similar pattern is found for foreign investment in the United States: 76 per cent of the foreign investment in the United States was owned 95 per cent or more and 20 per cent was owned between 50 and 95 per cent.

The basic pattern of financing direct investment is illustrated in Tables 14 and 15. Multinational corporations make a sharp distinction between equity and non-equity capital. The parent company's share of equity capital in foreign subsidiaries averages 85 per cent while the share of non-equity capital is only 25 per cent. On average, firms finance only about 8 per cent of total assets through equity securities, in contrast to about 31 per cent in the form of creditor capital.

This pattern of finance is as true for corporations investing in the United States as it is for American corporations investing abroad, suggesting that it is a feature of the multinational corporation in general and not the particular countries in question.

The high share of equity securities can to some extent be explained by the imperatives of global profit maximization. The multinational corporation is a substitute for the market as a method of co-ordinating decisions in different

Table 15. *Financing of United States foreign subsidiaries*

Area	Percentage of liabilities held by U.S. parent	Percentage of net worth held by U.S. parent	Percentage of total assets held by U.S. parent
All areas	25	86	61
Canada	37	79	62
Latin America	25	93	69
Western Hemisphere	17	87	65
Europe	11	84	46
Africa	24	81	52
Asia	13	94	62
Oceania	29	84	53

Source: Census of 1957, p. 108.

countries. It centralizes control in order to take advantage of the effects of decisions in one country on profits in another. Local shareholders interested only in local profits would ignore externalities and frustrate their goal.

We may state the argument more precisely as follows. Direct investment occurs because the profits of an enterprise in one country, II_1, are dependent on the profits of an enterprise in another country, II_2, that is,

$$II_1 = F(II_2). \tag{1}$$

To maximize global profits ($II_1 + II_2$) the following must hold:

$$\frac{\partial II_1}{\partial II_2} = -1. \tag{2}$$

But if the parent firm owns only λ (less than 100) per cent of the enterprise in country *2*, it will maximize ($II_1 + \lambda II_2$), by setting

$$\frac{\partial II_1}{\partial II_2} = -\lambda \tag{3}$$

which only partially exploits global interdependence. For example, concentration of production in a low-cost partially-owned subsidiary, rather than a high-cost fully-owned one might increase total profits, but the firm shares the gains in profits in one country with local shareholders, while it stands the loss in the other alone. A corollary of this is that a local investor might be reluctant to participate in a venture with an international firm which has the power to siphon off profits to one of its wholly-owned subsidiaries located elsewhere.

A similar problem arises in the case of vertical integration, for example, the selling of a patent. The real marginal cost of using the patent is zero. To maximize global profits, the branch plants should produce where its marginal revenue product also equals zero. But how will profits be allocated between enterprises? If there are local shareholders in the foreign country, the profits accruing to the branch plant must be separated from the profits of the parent firm. To do so, some price must be used to value the patent. But if a price is charged, managers, attempting to maximize profits of the branch plant, will economize on the use of the patent accordingly. Production will be restricted and total profits lowered.

The usefulness of complete ownership as a device for appropriating externalities and maximizing joint profits constrains the financial flexibility of multinational corporations. No matter how cheap capital is in a given country, there is a disadvantage to selling equity securities because of the distortions introduced by local partners. However, this applies only if one assumes firms try to maximize profits legally belonging to shareholders in the home country. An alternative assumption is that firms view all dividends, including those paid to shareholders in the home country, as a cost of borrowing and attempt to maximize retained earnings. Letting d_1 and d_2 dividends paid in country 1 and 2 respectively, the firm maximizes $(II_1 + II_2 - d_1 - d_2)$ instead of $(II_1 - \lambda II_2)$ as above. Provided dividends in each country do not depend on profits earned in that country, that is, provided they depend only on total profits and the conditions prevailing in the capital market in each country, equity securities introduce no distortion in the production decision of the type described above.[21] In the future, it may be increasingly possible for firms to do this in practice by issuing European or Latin American equity securities, for example, and declaring dividends and profits in such a way as to minimize borrowing.

Once the equity constraint is fulfilled, the firm is free to choose between capital markets according to relative interest rates. However, their behavior appears paradoxical at first sight. We find American subsidiaries in Europe borrowing 80 per cent of their non-equity needs in Europe, while at the same time European subsidiaries in America also borrow 80 per cent of their needs in America. It appears therefore that to Americans capital is cheaper in Europe, while to Europeans it is cheaper in America. Moreover, American firms seem to find capital cheaper abroad in nearly all instances of direct investment, for in every country they borrow something locally and almost never finance completely from the American sources (Table 15). Yet America is usually thought of as a source of cheap capital. One would expect that large American firms, with easy access to the American capital market and branch plants scattered throughout the world, would be anxious to act as a financial intermediary investing as much as possible in subsidiaries abroad and lending to unaffiliated foreign enterprises as well.

One reason for not doing this may be that firms have nationality and tend to calculate profits in terms of the currency in which they pay dividends.

When comparing the costs of borrowing at home to the cost of borrowing abroad, the firm must add a risk premium to the home interest rate and in the usual case this will outweigh the difference in interest rates. If r equals the capital costs of borrowing in America, r' the capital cost of borrowing abroad, and t the risk premium, the firm bases its decision to borrow on whether

$$r + t \gtrless r'$$

because international arbitrage will ensure that the interest rates in two countries do not differ by more than the cost of professional arbitrage. Letting a equal this cost, then $(r + a)$ will be equal to or greater than r' and $(r + t)$ will be greater than $(r + a)$. The primary occupations of firms with direct foreign investments are mining, manufacturing, or distribution, and not finance: In the difficult act of arbitrage they are likely to be at a comparative disadvantage relative to the banks and other financial institutions which specialize in these activities. Some large international firms, at a given point of time, may have better facilities for transferring capital between two countries than financial firms, but by and large the division of labor can be expected to apply here as elsewhere.[22]

The same principles will of course apply to firms investing in the United States. They too should borrow locally and avoid taking a position. Thus, to a multinational firm, the question of where capital is cheapest is not simply a question of prevailing interest rates in various countries, but also its own vantage point. There is a sort of relativistic effect, as firms facing the same world structure of interest rates add different risk premiums.

Thus, multinational corporations do not necessarily move from where it is abundant to where it is scarce since, within an industry, capital will flow from the parent to the subsidiary. At the turn of the century, for example, Europe had cheap capital, and America was technologically dynamic; portfolio investment flowed from Europe to America but direct investment flowed from America to Europe. Interest rates affect the size of the flow but they may have a perverse effect. Cheap capital in a country may attract equity capital because of the greater leverage it permits.

If capital markets were perfect, the direction and the amount of direct investment would be of no importance. In the above example, for instance, the outflow of direct investment from the United States would raise interest rates in New York and cause a compensating inflow of capital from Europe until interest rates were again equalized. The method of financing the branch plant would determine the gross flows of capital but not the net flows and would have no effect on overall distribution.

The financing practice of firms may be changing. In addition, as foreign investment grows, creating a world climate favorable to multinational corporations, more and more companies including smaller ones may expand

Table 16. *Employment and wages in United States business abroad, 1957*

	Wages and salaries ($US billion)	Employees (000s)	Average compensation per employee (dollars per year)			
			All industries	Manufacturing	Mining and smelting	Petroleum
All areas	6.9	3,200	2,100	2,100	1,800	3,200
Canada	2.6	670	3,900	4,000	3,600	6,000
Latin America	1.4	950	1,400	1,100	1,500	5,000
Europe	2.0	1,080	1,800	1,600	—[a]	2,100
Africa	0.1	100	1,200	1,400	550	2,200
Asia	0.4	240	1,500	1,000	—[a]	2,200
International	0.2	20	2,100	2,100	—[a]	2,200

[a]Number of firms not large enough to be representative.
Source: Census of 1957.

international operations. Many of these will use management contracts of licenses to avoid the difficulties of establishing a wholly owned subsidiary. In addition, larger companies may also show greater ingenuity in devising new forms of international associations which maximize rent on their particular advantage but allow more local participation in other areas. This has the advantage of creating local political allies and also has cost advantages. The small local firms typically pay lower wages and can gain certain concessions from government, thus lowering their cost and prices. The large firms can specialize more and more on software, that is, their organizing and marketing ability, and shift the burden of owning the hardware, that is, fixed capital, and managing labor to outsiders. Large Japanese firms to some extent follow this practice.

Labor

The employment associated with direct investment will not be known until the results of the 1966 census are published. In 1957, when direct investment was only about one-third of its 1970 level, the number of people employed in foreign countries by United States business firms was 3.2 million (1957 census). Employment must have grown more slowly than capital since then, but a figure of 5 or 6 million does not seem unreasonable. For Latin America excluding Cuba the preliminary results of the 1966 census indicate that employment rose 50 per cent from 1957 to 1966 while direct investment doubled (Table 1).

The area distribution of foreign employment, wages, and compensation per employee in various countries is shown in Table 16. In general wages are

Table 17. *Employment structure of United States business abroad*

	United States business abroad 1957		United States business in Latin America (excluding Cuba) 1966	
	Total	Sent from U.S.	Total	Sent from U.S.
Managers, technical and	178,000	14,000	1,600	1,200
professional			31,000	800
Other salaried wage earners	1,251,000	5,000	136,000	—
			292,000	—
Total	1,942,000	19,000	475,000	2,000
Estimated grand total	3,200,000			

Source: Census of 1957, p. 22, and report of the Council for Latin America (1970).

lower abroad than at home but are higher than average for the host country, in part because the subsidiaries are larger and more capital intensive than other firms and in part because of political vulnerability. Wages are particularly high for the few employed in highly capital intensive petroleum production.

The number of Americans sent abroad to work in the subsidiaries in American multinational corporations is small – about 1 per cent concentrated in higher posts (see Table 17). At first sight this would seem to indicate a high degree of local participation. In fact it does not since levels of decision-making are not specified. A company can offset pressure to hire nationals for top management posts by downgrading the functions of the office and centralizing control.

To indicate the kinds of data we require on the structure of employment, we refer to the management literature on corporate administrative structures and span of control.[23] In the version presented by Simon, for example, it is assumed that each executive can supervise n employees and that the ratio of wages at any level of the hierarchy to the one below is b. Since this model is used only for illustrative purposes, the many complications involved will not be discussed. This leads to an employment pyramid as depicted in Table 18.

Location theory suggests that while employment at lower levels will be spread throughout the world rather widely, executives at higher levels will tend to be concentrated in a few locations in the home country.

The main argument can be summarized briefly as follows. Increased division of labor within the corporation which accompanies the growth of the corporation increases productivity and the variety of tasks the organization can accomplish. If all employees do the same thing, the range of their combined activity is limited; if each employee is assigned to one of n tasks,

Table 18. *International corporate structure*

Levels of corporate hierarchy	Number of persons	Salary per person	Share of employees located in the U.S.	Nationality and class
Executive level 1	1	b^6w	100%	Mostly American and
Executive level 2	n	b^5w	very high	upper middle class
Executive level 3	n^2	b^4w		
Executive level 4	n^3	b^3w	(declining)	(increasingly heterogeneous)
Executive level 5	n^4	b^2w		
Executive level 6	n^5	bw		
Operatives	n^6	w	50% (?)	Many races and nationalities

Source: See text.

then *m* employees can jointly accomplish *mn* different activities. This would result in chaos if it was not co-ordinated. Hence increased differentiation and subdivision require elaborate organs of integration at higher levels.

For this complex hierarchical system to work, the organization must develop efficient vertical communications so that their information flows up and orders flow down easily. It must also have strong lateral communications at the higher levels so that decisions will be co-ordinated and integrated. But for lower levels it is usually necessary to restrict lateral communications to eliminate noise and to prevent the lower echelons from organizing themselves in opposition to the higher ones.

The general pattern therefore is that the higher one goes in the hierarchy, the greater the need for lateral communication. At the highest levels, continuous face to face contact and a large measure of common understanding are necessary. Hence the need for a common background and a common meeting place.

This applies to communications between business enterprises as well as within business enterprise. Corporations differ greatly in the geographical distribution of their operatives, depending upon the industry – specific pull of men, markets, and raw materials; but they tend to locate co-ordinating offices in the same major cities in order to benefit from common communications networks, specialized personnel, and other infrastructure. The higher levels, where strategy is made, tend to be even more concentrated geographically. It is almost true that nearly every major corporation in the United States must have its general office in New York or else maintain a large proportion of its higher personnel there if it is to operate effectively in the capital market, be in touch with the media, and have access to the pool of specialized knowledge and service concentrated there.

In sum, the growth of firms involves a double movement; expansion or spread at the bottom, concentration at the top. Local firms differ from national firms in the location of top executives as well as in the scope of operations. The local firm is directed locally; national firms are controlled from the strategic metropolis. Similarly, national firms differ from multinational firms not only in the geographical scope of their operations but also in where their strategy is made. Multinational corporations are connected to the world's major financial capitals and linked to each other by a variety of special networks. National firms do not move in these circles.

This means that the international distribution of high level employment will depend crucially upon the degree to which economic activity is organized multinationally or nationally. A world dominated by multinational corporations would tend to concentrate higher level decision-makers in a few centers in the advanced world. Other places would conduct only intermediate or lower level activity and would have a correspondingly truncated employment structure.[24] In addition, nationality at higher levels would tend to be more homogeneous (that is, upper- and middle-class European) than at the bottom where people of all races and nationalities are represented. This is still true in the United States where conditions of upward mobility are most favorable.

Stratification along these lines would have important political consequences. Unfortunately the data are poor and we are very much in the dark about this aspect of multinational corporations. Surveys showing the following type of data for employees of multinational corporations are badly needed if we are to begin evaluating the impact of a world of free capital movement:

— salary structure, which would indicate status within the organization better than job title;

— level of decision-making, which could be defined in terms of the amount of money the person was authorized to spend, the time span of discretion, authority for promoting subordinates, etc.;

— nationality, which would include educational and class background;

— geographic location, including per cent of time spent in various countries and amount of travel.

The meager data currently at hand hardly confront the issue.

10   The United States multinational corporations and Japanese competition in the Pacific

1927   The world's centers of gravity are always in process of change. Old centers lose their relative importance as new factors enter to disturb the equilibrium. . . The world is gradually becoming a closed area. The pioneer conditions which gave economic unity to the British Empire are rapidly passing. New centers of dominance are arising and producing new combinations of regional interdependence which are often quite at variance with the existing political structure.
R. D. McKenzie, "The Concept of Dominance and World Organization," *American Journal of Sociology,* July 1927, p. 42

1943   Whereat "Winston" had jumped up and said "How so? How so? Don't you remember that at the beginning of the war Britain owned twice the size merchant marine that the United States did?" The President retorted, "Well how about the fact that at the end of the war the U.S. will own twice as large a merchant marine as Britain has then."
Stimson Diary, November 5, 1943, quoted in Lloyd C. Gardner, *Economic Aspects of New Deal Diplomacy,* p. 275

1969   Time is pressing on Japan to decide in what tones to speak in the councils of the world.
Fortune, August 1, 1969, p. 101

I. Transition in the world economy

Everywhere about us there are signs of change in the international economy. Three aspects are particularly important for this essay.

1. *Industrialization of the underdeveloped countries.* The old international economy developed underdeveloped countries as primary producing export economies. During the 1930s, 1940s, and 1950s mass national movements, reacting to this position, combined with weakness at the center, led to a

Hymer intended this analysis of Japanese economic development to be a case study applying the concepts and methodology he discusses in his paper, "The Multinational Corporation and the International Division of Labor," published as Chapter 6 of this book. This essay originally appeared, in *Chuokoron-sha,* Spring 1972. Copyright © 1972 by *Chuokoron-sha.* Reprinted by permission of *Chuokoron-sha.*

radical switch in government policies. One by one, governments of under-developed countries changed over from a strategy of cheap labor and export biased infrastructure to one of *education, urbanization,* and *protection.* During the last few decades, a succession of development programs have created a large proletariat concentrated in urban areas, a significant increase in levels of education and training, and a great expansion of government infrastructure and support services needed for industry. These elements are likely to grow rapidly in the next decades, given the level of past and existing government expenditure programs. The question is not so much whether industry will grow rapidly but who will organize it – *national* capital, *state* capital, or *foreign* capital. What direction will it take and who will benefit from it?

2. *A changing pattern of regional interdependence.* The old colonial partitioning directed the trade of each underdeveloped country toward its particular metropolis. This is giving way to *multilateralism* as developed countries penetrate each other's spheres of interest, and underdeveloped countries, as part of their assertion of national independence, open their doors to new trading partners (including other underdeveloped countries).

This development is associated with changes in the world's centers of gravity. After the Second World War the old centers in Europe lost ground to the United States. Now the United States is losing its hegemonic position with the recovery of Europe and Japan. In the next years Russia certainly and China probably will play an increasing role in the international economy. The center is no longer a point or a triangle but a pentagon.

3. *The emergence of the multinational corporation.* A new element on the scene is the multinational corporation. Metropolitan expansion is now going beyond the traders' frontier, the settlers' frontier, the planters' frontier (to use Hancock's terminology)[1] to the corporate frontier, as large business enterprises establish worldwide networks of manufacturing and marketing connections. "American imperialism," wrote *Fortune* magazine in May 1942, "can afford to complete the work the British started; instead of salesmen and planters, its representatives can be brains and bulldozers, technicians and machine tools. American imperialism does not need extraterritoriality; it can get along better in Asia if the tuans and the sahibs stay home."[2] This strategy is now a general one as businessmen from all major countries scurry over the globe buying, selling, building, investing, consulting, contracting, licensing, and in general forming partnerships and alliances to control raw materials and markets.

What will come of all this? Most people hope it will result in a polycentral world that will give all countries and regions more breathing space to develop along their own lines. But this need not be the case. In a sense there is a race going on between a mass awakening, the revolution of rising expectations, on the one hand, and the threatened elites on the other. Those at the bottom of the pyramid of power hope to use the new industrial base and the decline in imperialism to appropriate a greater share of values to themselves. Those at the top are trying to use their privileged positions of power and information to form new alliances and structures to maintain their control and power.

The multinational corporation is an interesting focus for studying this problem because it is in the vanguard of the current revolution in world structure. Closest to the new technology, possessing great funds of capital and knowledge, it is the first major institution to establish global perspectives and identity. Only the U.S. military can match it in modernity and breadth of operations and horizons. In the first round it is likely to have many successes. Indeed, it has already staked out major positions around the globe, and probably brought about an irreversible new cosmopolitanism in the international economy, a qualitative change comparable to the establishment of the world market in the late nineteenth century.

But in the second round we are likely to see many other groups react to the realities of the new environment. On the ideological plane the battle will probably center on internationalism versus nationalism, technology versus quality of life. But these are in a sense false issues, for the struggle is between different groups in different countries – international business, small national business, labor, professionals, the large mass of excluded groups, etc. – over what kind of international associations are to be fostered and what use is to be made of the common heritage of science.

The purpose of this essay is not to predict the outcome of this tension, but to identify some of its features. The original intention implied in the title, to confine the analysis to the Pacific and to Japanese competition, is too narrow. The Pacific is a crucial area, but the phenomenon is global and the multinational corporation is not just an aspect of the American empire, but something beyond it!

The essay contains *speculations* on four major questions:

1 How does Japanese business fit into the multinational corporate system established in the North Atlantic in recent years?

2 What international division of labor and combinations of regional interdependence are implied by the multinational corporate system? In short, who will do what? Who will get what? And where?

3 What conflicts between multinational capital and national interests might arise in the countries of the center?

4 How might the various development strategies of underdeveloped countries fit into the system being planned in the center?

II. The multinational corporation

A. The Atlantic

The multinational corporation is in the first instance an American phenomenon. Its precursor is the U.S. *national corporation* created at the end of the nineteenth century when American capitalism developed a multicity continent-wide marketing and manufacturing strategy. The chief characteristic of the national corporation was its elaborate administrative structure to coordinate and control mass production and mass marketing in geographically dispersed branch plants and sales outlets. Business administration became a highly specialized field of activity and U.S. capitalism gained a lead in management and marketing techniques over Europe, where the older type of family firm continued to prevail.

Though many U.S. corporations began to move to foreign countries almost as soon as they completed their continent-wide integration, the term *multinational* came to prominence only after 1960. Many definitions of the term have been offered. The one used in this essay is based upon the horizons, or cognitive map, of the firm. National firms think in terms of the national market; multinational firms see the whole world as their market and plan manufacturing and marketing on a global scale. Few firms actually fit this ideal, and the term should be interpreted as a direction of change rather than as a description of the actual state of affairs.

The shift in business horizons is closely connected to the aeronautical and electronic revolution that made global planning possible. However, its proximate cause was the rapid growth of the European economy and of European firms. The formation of the Common Market combined with a slow rate of growth in the U.S. economy in the 1950s challenged the dominant position of many American corporations. Had they not been allowed to invest in Europe, they would have been unable to maintain their world market share and they would have lost a valuable base for future growth. However the liberal attitude of European governments and the gold reserves of the United States made foreign investment possible and in a short time most major U.S. corporations established or expanded a base within the Common Market. Even so, U.S. firms were not outstanding performers during this period–*pace* Servan-Schreiber.[3] The leading U.S. firms grew slower on average than non-American firms from 1957 to 1962 and only just kept pace from 1962 to 1967.

The reaction of European business was to join the multinational corporate system rather than to challenge it. Several leading European firms were already multinational, though their overseas expansion had been somewhat frustrated by balance of payments restrictions. Other firms became better equipped for multinational operations as a result of mergers, nationalization, and growth and began to extend their international operations in other European countries, in underdeveloped countries, and in the United States. The multinational corporate system is no longer an American system, but is, at the very least, a North Atlantic system both in the sense that Europeans have joined the ranks and in the sense that American firms have become less tied to the United States. Many leading U.S. firms now have 30 percent, 40 percent, and sometimes even more of their operations abroad, and feel somewhat constrained by their ties to the United States. (George Ball, for example, has been the leader of a group calling for international incorporation to free the multinational corporation from its U.S. identity and from U.S. laws.) These tendencies, plus the integration of capital markets as Europeans purchase equity securities in American firms and vice versa, are leading to a new system characterized by a common outlook rather than nationalistic rivalry on the part of big business in the North Atlantic area. The oil industry provides a model. It is hard to see much difference in behavior, outlook, and interest of the oil giants, even though some are Americans, some are owned by European governments, and one is jointly owned by two countries. This does not mean that oil companies do not need the support of nation-states, but rather that to a large extent they have transcended nationality and try to use all governments. Instead of dividing the world into spheres of interest, as was the case in the old imperialism, they now interpenetrate each others' markets, recognize their interdependence, and overtly or tacitly collude to achieve common goals on a global basis.

B. The Pacific

What role will Japan play in this system? Until recently, Japan has been an outsider because it would not allow foreign capital in and because of its vigorous competitive challenge to dominant North Atlantic corporations. Recently, there are signs of change and our discussion below focuses on the possibility of a turning point in Japan's role.

Our basic underlying hypothesis is as follows. Japan's economy and Japanese firms are growing much faster than anyone else's. As they increase their share of the world market, they will meet increasing resistance from other corporations and governments. The bigger they get, the more difficult they will find it to continue as before. Several resolutions of this contradiction between size and rate of growth are possible. We cannot pretend in this essay to be attempting to predict the future. We wish only to map out one scenario that might be of interest to underdeveloped countries wishing to use the space created by Japanese-American-European competition to strengthen their own position.

The following table, taken from a recent article by Koichi Hamada, indicates current trends:[4]

Investing country	Share of world direct investment in 1968	1968 ratio of direct investment:		Annual rate of growth of foreign investment 1966–8
		to export	to GNP	
U.S.	61%	183	7	9%
U.K.	17%	109	17	8%
France	4%	37	4	8%
Germany	4%	12	3	25%
Canada	3%	34	6	3%
Japan	2%	10	1	40%

Japan has only a small share of the world's foreign investment and the lowest ratio of accumulated direct investment to exports of the major industrial nations. But the fact that its foreign investment is growing the most rapidly may indicate the beginning of a take-off period. (Germany, which has the next to the lowest ratio, also has the next to the highest rate of growth.) Given the expected large surplus in the balance of payments, the new liberalization policy toward outward foreign investment, the reorganization, rationalization, and concentration of industrial structure that is occurring, and an increased capacity to invest abroad through learning by doing, Hamada feels that it is not unreasonable to expect Japanese direct foreign investment to rise to 10 or 20 billion dollars (American) by 1975 from its 1968 level of 2 billion.[5] Because the Japanese gross national product is expected to rise from 200 to 400 billion from now to 1975, its ratio of accumulated direct investment to gross national product would still be only 2.5 to 5 percent, a low figure for an industrialized nation.

A qualitative analysis of Japan's economy supports the view that Japan will play an increasing role in actively organizing the international division of labor through direct investment, contracts, licenses, etc., in the "new age of economic internationalization." The need to assure supplies of raw materials has already led Japanese firms to construct an extensive network of exploration and production around the Pacific rim – Siberia (timber, copper, oil, etc.), Alaska–Yukon–British Columbia–Alberta–Washington–Oregon–Idaho–Montana (coal, oil, copper, lumber, fish, food processing), Australia (coal, copper, oil, timber, salt), Indonesia (oil, nickel, lumber, copper, fishing, pearl cultivation, rice, maize), Malasia (oil, tin, timber, sugar), Philippines (copper, iron, forestry, fishing), Burma (oil), Thailand (tin, tungsten, agriculture), and South Korea (oil, copper, zinc).

This system is sure to expand in the coming years. Many of these ventures do not take the form of the wholly owned subsidiary or branch plant used by American multinational corporations. Instead, they frequently involve production sharing, guaranteed demand contracts, technical assistance, and portfolio capital. (Indeed, some countries, Russia in particular, are trying to get the Japanese to put up *more* capital!) The quantity of direct foreign investment is thus not a good measure of the degree of Japanese involvement in international production relative to North American companies.

Involvement in overseas manufacturing is also likely to grow. The leading Japanese firms are already multinational as far as their sales frontier is concerned. In order to maintain their position and continue to grow they will have to make increasing use of direct investment, local assembly, and local manufacturing. A cycle beginning with exports and ending with local production has long been noted for American and European firms. Pressure on Japan to progress through it rapidly will mount through time as their sales penetration increases. The larger the market share, the greater the negative pressures from local governments and foreign competition, and the greater the positive incentives from economies of scale and increasing capacity to produce locally. Moves in this direction are already evident in numerous industries in numerous countries and it is clear that Japan cannot continue to penetrate foreign markets at the past rate without changing form.

In addition, rapid capital accumulation in Japan raises wages and cuts into its cost advantage in many industries. Many Japanese firms, including small ones, have been establishing production facilities abroad, especially in Taiwan and South Korea, for export to Japan and in anticipation of special preferences being granted by developed countries to manufacturing exports from underdeveloped countries.

These trends foreshadow new forms of association with Western multinational corporations, including a new attitude toward investment in Japan. Policies that were possible when Japan had a small share of the market and relied solely on exports will no longer be tenable when Japan is a major producer in an oligopolistic industry and an important capital exporter. Multinational firms from other countries cannot afford to stand idly by and allow their market shares to continue to shrink. They have already begun countermoves and will continue to do so in the future. Many American firms are establishing branch plants in Asia in electronics and other industries to take advantage of cheap labor and to meet Japanese competition. They are also increasing their pressure to gain entry into Japan. The multinational corporations are large and powerful and have enormous financial and political resources to draw upon in a serious oligopolistic fight, and the greater the Japanese share of the market, the more vulnerable are Japanese firms to oligopolistic price cutting and other forms of warfare. Moreover, the United States remains Japan's largest trading partner. This market serves as a hostage to encourage Japan to play the game. Pressure can also be put on third countries.

In addition, as Japanese business moves into more modern advanced sectors – atomic energy, pollution, ocean, housing, etc. – for which they need the most advanced technology, their bargaining position weakens and they have to accept direct investment and partnership rather than rely on licensing and copying. Japanese policy can be expected to move more and more from undercutting to interlocking. As the president of the Japan Iron and Steel Federation put it, "Now is the time for us to drop the mean idea of trying to beat foreign competitors and face the reality of Japanese interdependence with them."[6]

In the agreement of a Japanese firm to establish a chain of Howard Johnson franchise restaurants in Japan, the appointment of a Japanese executive as a director of AMF, the Joint Venture between Burlington Industries and Mitsubishi Rayon to manufacture carpets in Japan, an agreement between Nippon Steel Corporation and a West German firm to establish a joint steel pipe manufacturing venture in Canada, the proposed scheme that "Japan and West Germany should jointly finance development of new raw material projects overseas with the output of Asian projects going to Japan and African projects to Germany,"[7] we can see possible patterns of future cooperation. (Including the type of integration implied by General Electric's request to two Japanese firms for help in producing certain electrical components on its behalf owing to a protracted strike.)

The automobile industry may serve as a model for future industrial organization. Japan is fast becoming a "major" rather than a "minor" oligopolist. Japanese firms are already assembling in underdeveloped countries and at least one, Nissan Motor Company, envisages auto production set-ups in Western Europe as well. American firms have at last broken some of the barriers to entry into the Japanese market[8] and are pursuing a number of other counterstrategies as well.

One of General Motors' plans is "to advance into neighboring countries such as Taiwan and the Philippines, in an 'encirclement' strategy against Japan's automobile industry."[9] Ford is using its Australian subsidiary to develop plans to build an inexpensive car in the poor countries of Asia, Africa, and the Pacific. The operation will be supervised from Melbourne, but will manufacture parts in different nations and ship them between countries for assembly.[10] In addition, both GM and Ford are thinking of purchasing steel from Japan,[11] and Chrysler plans to import Japanese cars to compete in the rapidly growing subcompact market in the U.S.[12]

In sum, the logic of oligopolistic rivalry suggests that, more often than not, each move of Japan to compete in the international markets draws it further into the multinational corporate system. True, the Japanese system differs in many ways from the U.S. multinational corporate system (just as the European system has special features). But these differences, far from signaling the end of this system, probably indicate a more refined and advanced form. Japanese firms, for example, are much more flexible in their attitudes toward Russia, China, North Korea, and North Vietnam (see the report in *The Japan Economic Journal*[13] of a visit of a Japanese trade mission to explore economic possibilities for Japan in the *postwar* rehabilitation of North Vietnam), and state enterprises in nonsocialist countries. But American firms are also trying to free themselves from Cold War rigidity and to extricate themselves from U.S. extraterritoriality. They too want to enter China (some are trying to use Japan as a base) and other socialist countries, and to form an interface with the state sector in other countries. The decline in U.S. hegemony does not imply the decline of multinational capitalism, which now goes well beyond the U.S. nation-state.

Similarly, Japan's flexibility in designing new forms of association and using joint ventures, subcontracting, etc., rather than wholly owned subsidiaries, also indicates a trend U.S. and European firms are following and will follow. If Japan continues on the path suggested by the above analysis, it will be helping to develop the multinational corporate system rather than overthrow it.

In conclusion, Japan's position may be changing from *interloper* to *imperial power*. Japan's recent growth has taken place under the umbrella of the United States. As its involvement grows, it will be forced to share increasingly in designing and maintaining the world economic system. It is becoming a major financial center as its banks and securities firms spread abroad, as it builds an international "aid" program to support its position, as it attracts foreign money – the ratio of foreign ownership to the total value of all stocks in the top fifty-five Japanese corporations was over 10 percent[14] – as the yen becomes internationalized and is increasingly used abroad as a means of exchange, and as Tokyo moves in the direction of becoming the major money market of the East. Japan's interest will become more and more that of the *mature creditor* rather than the *young challenger*. It will develop a vested interest in maintaining international private property and free international capital. This would have important implications for underdeveloped countries planning to use Japanese firms as a bargaining lever in dealing with American firms. Just as these countries find that the major creditor countries compete vigorously in offering suppliers credit but form a united front when collecting the debt, they may also discover that the business competition to establish branch plants, joint ventures, technical assistance agreements, purchasing contracts, etc., though improving their bargaining position in the short run, draws them into a system of continued dependency as the big countries collude more and more.

III. The multinational corporate system

To the multinational corporation, "national boundaries are written in fading ink."[15] The expansion of the multinational corporation involves a double movement. On the one hand, it spreads capital and technology. On the other hand, it centralizes control by establishing a vertically integrated network in which different areas specialize in different levels of activity.

This double movement – decentralization and centralization, differentiation and integration – in the development of a corporation resembles the development of a human being. As a child grows it learns to move the various parts of its body separately. This differentiation increases the variety of activities it can perform. At the same time, integration occurs at a higher level as the brain grows in complexity in order to consciously control the various relatively independent subparts.[16]

In a similar way, as a corporation develops from workshop to factory to multiplant, multifunction corporation to multiproduct corporation to multinational corporation the space over which it operates becomes increasingly differentiated. It comes to consist of more and more subparts that can move relatively independently of each other. This increases the corporation's flexibility and potential. But the greater the variety of possible outcomes, the more complex must be its brain to choose among the many alternatives and to give overall direction. Hence the importance of the administrative structure of the corporation and its evolution through time.

The twofold nature of corporate expansion needs stressing because it is so often misunderstood in analysis of international business. Decentralization within a corporation is often not the opposite of centralization, but the complement; for decentralization at one level is often accompanied by centralization at a higher level. As corporations have developed through time, their capacity for higher-level, more abstract planning covering longer time horizons and broader geographical space has increased greatly. This enables and even may require greater autonomy at lower levels. The granting of independence to lower levels does not imply a surrender of strategic control but an increase in tactical flexibility combined with an increase in planning capacity.

For example, when production is the crucial element, ownership of plant and equipment may be essential for control. But where product design becomes the dominant element, investment in development and marketing is more important. The large corporations might then prefer to allow small businesses to own the plant and equipment (along with the associated risks) while it concentrates on intangibles (just as capitalists prefer the government to own the large capital stock in highly capital-intensive sectors such as transportation and communication, so long as this infrastructure does not share in surplus by receiving profit). A corporation that concentrates on softwear, allowing small businesses to participate in owning and operating the hardware through partnerships and licensing franchises, is not surrendering control, but is extending it more widely.

Similarly, when there are only a few sources for a raw material, it may be necessary for a large user to integrate backward to control that raw material.

But if there are many sources of supply the corporation might welcome local participation in order to save its capital for other stages. In the oil industry, for example, it seems that the multinational corporations are gradually retreating from previous levels of ownership of crude oil production; they appear to be concentrating more and more on the marketing function. They use their large computers and their vast knowledge of demand and supply for each of the many varieties of oil and alternative transportation facilities to profit by buying cheap and selling dear. Again, it is not clear that their control is declining even though their share of ownership might be. Similarly, a metal company may welcome a scheme of progressive nationalization in one country, because it is already developing new replacements in another country.

In summary, modern business has come more and more to think in terms of product cycles lasting perhaps from two to fifteen years. At any one time they have projects in the initial stage, products in the middle stage, and products in the final stage. Their strength comes from being able to deal with all three at once and to *couple* the various stages of research, production, and marketing by integrating information. At any moment of time they may bring capital and technology to a country. But at the same time they are retaining control over the production of capital and technology. In this way the dependency relationship is often reproduced from period to period and a country may find itself relatively as far behind at the end of a project as it was at the beginning.

The relevant classification scheme for understanding division of labor may no longer be industry versus agriculture, but level of function within the corporation. The main divide in the corporation is between capital and labor, between management and operations, between the head and the hand. As Marshall aptly put it, this method of dividing labor within a firm so that "the planning and arrangement of business, its management and its risks, are borne by one set of people, while the manual work required for it is done by other labor" stands out "for good and evil as the chief fact in the form of modern civilization, the 'kernel' of the modern economic problem."[17]

The modern multinational corporation has an elaborate vertical structure with many levels of intellectual work. The higher up the ladder, the higher are wages and status, the more abstract the level of planning, the longer the time horizons, the greater the scope for discretion and judgment. At bottom one supervises a few people, remains rooted in one spot, and deals with narrow specialties. At the top, the budget runs in 10s or 100s of millions, the time horizon covers decades, and vision covers the world. (For a detailed discussion of location theory as it applies to multinational corporations and an analysis of the emerging hierarchy of cities, see Chapters 2 and 6.)

The multinational corporate system does not seem to offer the world national independence or equality. Instead, it would keep many countries as branch-plant countries, not only with reference to their economic functions but throughout the whole gamut of social, political, and cultural roles. The subsidiaries of multinational corporations in the country of operations and their top executives play an influential role in the political, social, and cultural life of the host country. Yet these people, whatever their titles, occupy at best a medium position in the corporate structure and are restricted in authority and horizons to a lower level of decision making. The governments with whom they deal tend to take on the same middle management outlook, since this is the only range of information and ideas to which they are exposed. In this sense, one can hardly expect such a country to bring forth the creative imagination needed to apply science and technology to the problems of degrading poverty.

IV. Cleavages in the center

Where are the cracks in this satellite system?

Analysis of the dynamics of oligopolistic rivalry suggests that competition between business firms of different countries provides only a temporary respite for dependent countries. During the next ten years, the challenge of European and Japanese firms to American corporations will increase the maneuverability of the Third World. But increasingly, as firms interpenetrate each other's markets and develop global outlooks, competition will turn to collusion as dominant firms of the center present a united front. The choices available to the lesser cities will be narrow and restricted, like the choice between a Chevrolet and a Ford, or worse still, between a Chevrolet and a Pontiac.

Political integration of the ruling cities of the inner circle is a different matter. The capital cities have the advantage that they are few in number and comparatively well connected. They can act in unison much more easily than can the provincial capitals or small towns of the imperial system. When a revolt occurs, they can combine forces and information to act swiftly and powerfully. Thus, even though they are encircled overall, in each battle, they encircle their enemy.

But there are many divisions between the major powers. There is little Moscow fears more than an alliance between Peking and Tokyo. There is little the United States fears more than an alliance between Tokyo and Moscow. And so on. "When thieves fall out . . . ."

The multinational corporation itself increases divisiveness in a number of ways. As a viaduct for transmitting pressure from one country to another, it intensifies interaction. At the same time it erodes the power of nation-states by extending itself beyond the reach of traditional policy instruments. Thus the ability of a nation-state to stabilize its economy through monetary and fiscal policy decreases as multinational corporations spin their webs of interdependency. It is possible, for example, that national policy instruments will be reduced in effectiveness more quickly than international policy instruments can be built, and that another world depression will threaten to occur because the multinational corporations have destroyed the corporate business interface of the national welfare state.[18]

More important, the multinational corporate system creates contradictions between the interests of big business, which is internationally mobile, and small business and labor, which are not, as well as between the middle classes of different countries over managerial position, between high-wage labor in one country and low-wage labor in another; between elites who share in some of the benefits of the system and excluded groups that do not.

The importance of these conflicts depends upon the scale of foreign investment. In the United States, for example, the rapid growth of foreign investment over the last twenty years has already revealed many cleavages between the interests of international investors and the rest of the domestic economy over taxation, balance of payments, extraterritoriality, and foreign aid. Multinational corporations have pressed for relief from taxation on foreign income and from regulation by antitrust and other laws. They would like the United States to adjust to balance of payments problems by deflating the economy or controlling imports rather than controlling foreign invest- ment. At the same time, they would like freedom to produce where costs are lowest and unhampered by tariffs and trade. On these issues they conflict with other taxpayers who wish equal taxation for foreign income, with firms who cannot meet the challenge of foreign competition through investment but must rely on exports or on the domestic market, and with certain classes of labor threatened by foreign competition. Moreover, the costs of administering the empire are rising more rapidly than any benefits it brings to the United States, and these costs are borne by the nation as a whole while the benefits are reaped by a small group. The current troubles in the United States are in no little way associated with the cost of imperialism and are weakening its ability to maintain the system. This accounts in part for the decline in its hegemony and the opportunities this has provided certain countries in Latin America to take important steps to strengthen their position.

The system can survive despite the weakening of the United States if it can mobilize fresh political power in Europe and Japan. London is rising as a center for Europe, just as Tokyo is strengthening in the Pacific. They may provide new strategies and tactics to replace those of Washington and New York. The multinational corporations are well established in London, and if they can form alliances in Japan, regroupings are possible to build a new superstructure for international development using multilateral institutions like the UN, the World Bank, etc.

But as these other countries become enmeshed in supporting this new system, they too will develop the strains of empire. London in particular and

Europe in general have only recently extricated themselves from the old empire entanglements; though they seem ready to jump in again, it is unlikely they will have much staying power. The Golden Age of Europe's empire was only forty-four years, from 1870 to 1914. Their initial position is now much weaker and history moves much more quickly. Perhaps they will have only one-third as long to restructure the world economy. In fourteen years, it will be 1984.

Tensions in Japan may become particularly acute. Japan's economy has been based on a particularly tight-knit interface between government and business, between big business and small business, between capital and labor. This fabric will be torn apart by continued international expansion and multinationalization of production. The large multinational Japanese firm, though strategically controlled from Tokyo, will have its thoughts elsewhere. Like American capital, it will have a large number of foreign employees, numerous partnerships and alliances with foreign small businesses and large business, many interfaces with a variety of foreign governments, and a large vested interest in foreign countries. Japanese society needs restructuring, but not in this way.

Nobutane Kiuchi, in an article titled "Japan at the Threshold of a New Era," notes the serious choice faced by his country as to which growth path to choose. His starting point is "a peculiar coincidence of particular importance."

The United States has been capably assuming the leadership of the Free World during the postwar decade – but this leadership has become uncertain recently. Coincidentally, the U.S.S.R. has begun to lose its grip on the leadership within the Communist bloc.[19]

He offers two possibilities for consideration. The first is outward expansion.

Now, suppose the people realize that they have more power at their disposal than they thought and their aspirations remain as before. The outcome will be a still greater pursuit of material wealth, the components of which must be faster growth, larger exports, etc. It is quite probable that the future Japan would pay more attention to its own defense and would do more in the field of aid to the developing countries. This is some consolation, but to those with a discerning eye, to whom the present state of "despoiled land" is already unbearable, there should remain no doubt that this accelerated rush for more material wealth means not only a ravaged land, but a ruined people.[20]

As opposed to this path of international business, aid, armaments, air pollution, defiled rivers, overcongested roads, noisy cities, damaged natural beauty, injustice, and civil strife – in a word the United States in the sixties – Kiuchi clearly prefers his second one, which he labels an "inward-looking" Japan, which concentrates its surplus energy in the domestic field and in which "what the new Japan seeks will reflect as closely as possible what the heart of Japan demands."[21]

V. Underdeveloped countries

An underdeveloped country does not face free markets in which it can sell goods, buy technology, and borrow capital. The basic repository of technological knowledge, capital, and access to markets lies in an interlocking system of large private companies outside their control. To get what it wants it must bargain and negotiate with these business enterprises as well as the national governments and international institutions that back them up. What strategies can it pursue and what resources can it draw upon?

On the international front, its problem is to change the flow of information. The control structure found within the corporation and reproduced on a broader scale in the multinational corporate system is based on three features:

1   strong vertical links so that information can pass up and orders can pass down;

2   strong lateral communications at the top so that information can be pooled and actions harmonized;

3   weak lateral links at the bottom, so that the bottom elements in the pyramid cannot communicate with each other and mobilize their strengths.

To change the basic dependency relations underdeveloped countries must welcome and take advantage of divisions on the top; introduce interference in vertical links so that the center does not have an accurate picture; and cement links at the bottom so that forces are combined. Ideally we would change the pattern from an axial pattern to a polycentric system where there would be many centers, each communicating *with* every other. The system would resemble an electronic grid rather than a hierarchy, and the distinction between margin and center would disappear. Modern technology makes such a grid more possible than ever, for it is now relatively cheap to send messages efficiently and quickly from any point to any other. However, to take advantage of modern technology, the underdeveloped countries must fight against the attempt to impose legal and political asymmetries on the essential symmetrical technology. Ironically, the forces it must oppose claim to represent technological imperatives while they in fact try to monopolize them. Multinational corporations, like pine trees, spread their cones on the ground so that nothing else will grow.

Conflicts between America, Europe, and Japan present one source of opportunity to the underdeveloped countries, but we have argued that this contradiction may have a short half-life and the current breathing space may not last very long. Contradictions between socialist countries and nonsocialist countries provide another possibility, though discussion of its opportunities and dangers would require a full essay in itself. The possibilities of cooperation between underdeveloped countries also require a separate extensive treatment; here we might merely point out the lesson of Europe, that a common market can easily fortify rather than strengthen multinational corporations from outside the common market and from within. Similarly, we must note that international institutions often cement the partnership between the capitals rather than promote the "global partnership" they proclaim.

What about internal resources? One possibility, in fact pursued by many countries, is to try to build up a national capitalist class to defend the national interest. My own view is that this is not a promising path. The national bourgeois of most underdeveloped countries are very weak and in no way a match for international capital. Moreover, the tastes of the middle class are for goods innovated in the high-income countries, that is, for the brand names and quality products in which multinationl corporations specialize. Every attempt to squeeze the population at large to build up the middle class increases the need for the particular technologies and specialties of multinational corporations. Only a strategy of producing basic goods for the mass of the population can release an underdeveloped country from its dependency on foreign know-how and capital equipment; for, in that area, the multinational corporation has few advantages.

Finally, a native capitalist class would have a vested interest in supporting private property. Their capital stock is always subject to expropriation by the excluded class. Only under a regime of free transfer of capital can they obtain real security for their wealth. Thus in the last analysis their interest lies with the international system. Consider, for example, the case of a successful entrepreneur who has accumulated a large quantity of capital under the protection of tariffs and other subsidies. Suppose a multinational corporation attempts to take over his enterprise in exchange for its own shares freely traded on the international financial markets. At one blow, the national capitalist exchanges a fixed investment continuously threatened by nationalization into a highly liquid and secure asset. How many capitalists can resist this opportunity? (The multinational corporation has less to fear from nationalization because it is backed up by international law and its national government, which may even guarantee it against expropriation.) If the national bourgeois could promise rapid growth and widespread benefit, they might be free of such fears. But even their staunchest supporters admit they need protection and subsidy for a long time, and for the next twenty or thirty years can offer little in return. Although national business has an important role, it cannot, it seems to me, play a dominant role because of its vulnerability.

The multinational corporations are aware that national capitalists and the middle class are their staunchest supporters. Daniel Parker, chairman of the board of the Parker Company, states:

The multinational corporation has assets, tangible and intangible, and they will not come into a market if doing so involves a dilution of their equity. For instance, the arrow clip on this Parker Pen – it enhances not one whit the writing capability per se of this pen, but we have found that it produces confidence in the mind of the buyer, even to the extent that people in less-developed parts of the world who are illiterate seek to buy the cap only, without the writing part, to use the arrow clip as a symbol. In this manner, an important part of Parker's assets is not just being able to make superior writing instruments, but the share of mind that we have in the markets of the world. We will not come in and share ownership with local nationals on the basis of balance sheet costs. Multinationalism, be it European or Japanese or American, involves similar principles – the values that go beyond the *pro forma* balance sheets of a proposed local national company. Such sharing is unlikely and illogical. But each such endeavor can be benefitted from and needs industrial infrastructure. The nationality of the source of supply is an unimportant matter. This is where the external economies' opportunity really is, where the local national opportunity really lies.[22]

The counterstrategy for the underdeveloped country is national planning. To put the matter most starkly, the multinational corporation is a private organization that organizes one industry across many countries. Its polar opposite is a public institution that organizes many industries across one country, or better still across one region. To put this another way, there are two issues involved. First, the question of centralization of capital, that is, how many enterprises should be coordinated by one decision-making center. Second, there is the issue of the internationalization of capital, that is, to what extent should coordination and control spread across countries or regions? The argument for building institutions with a full complement of skills and resources but that are confined to one region is that it allows scope for the economies of planning while subordinating economic decisions to political and social requirements. It seems to me that only such an organization could be efficient in mobilizing the strengths of the population as a whole in the interest of the population as a whole. Problems of ensuring democracy within a region would remain, but they would seem to be more tractable than the ones associated with world stratification by multinational corporations.

In short, in order to build a system that will reflect as closely as possible what the heart of the people demands, we need a world economy where information can move freely between nations but capital, that is, power, cannot.

11   International politics and international economics: a radical approach

To be radical, or to be a scientist, is the same thing; it is a question of trying to go to the root of the matter. For Marx, this meant trying to uncover the "economic laws of motion of modern society," that is, first of all, seeing society as an organism in motion constantly changing and developing as it moves from its beginning to its end, and second of all, searching in the economy, i.e., in changing conditions of production and exchange, for the underlying basis of this motion.

In this essay, I wish to follow Marx's approach by viewing the present conjuncture of international politics and economics in terms of the long-term growth and spread of capitalist social relations of production to a world level. More concretely, I want to try to relate the current crises in national and international politics to the world market created during the last twenty-five years by the American Empire, firstly by examining Keynes's 1933 warnings of the difficulties and dangers for the development of modern society posed by the world market, and secondly, by using Marx's analysis of the general law of capitalist accumulation, and, in particular, his theory of the reserve army to go deeper into the roots of our present difficulties.

The basic text for this analysis is a provocative statement Marx wrote to Engels in October 1858:

We cannot deny that bourgeois society has experienced its Sixteenth Century a second time – a Sixteenth Century which will, I hope, sound the death-knell of bourgeois society just as the first one thrust it into existence. The specific task of bourgeois society is the establishment of a world market, at least in outline, and of production based upon this world market. As the world is round, this seems to have been completed by the colonization of California and Australia and the opening up of China and Japan. The difficult question for us is this: on the Continent the revolution is imminent and will immediately assume a socialist character. Is it not bound to be

This essay originally appeared in *Stress and Contradiction in Modern Capitalism*, L. Lindberg, R. Alford, C. Crouch, and C. Offe, eds. (Lexington, Mass.: Lexington Books, 1975), pp. 355–72. Reprinted by permission of the Estate of Stephen Hymer.

crushed in this little corner, considering that in a far greater territory the movement of bourgeois society is still in the ascendent?[1]

The beginnings of industrial capitalism

Capitalism began as a world market system in the Mercantilist age of the sixteenth and seventeenth centuries when the discovery of America and the rounding of the Cape led to an explosion of maritime commerce and the creation of the first international economy. The epoch-making significance of this great burst of international trade, however, did not lie in the world market itself, but in the transformation of the home market that it unwittingly brought about.

It has been said of Columbus, who died thinking he had discovered a new route to India, that he was a man who, when he set out, did not know where he was going, that when he got there did not know where he was, and that when he returned did not know where he had been. The same irony characterized the Mercantilist system as a whole. The merchants, adventurers, financiers, and sovereigns of this age set out on an international quest for gold, spices, and new lands, but the really important discoveries were made at home. Specifically, the expansion of foreign trade and the growth of merchants and finance capital resulted, along with other factors, in the disintegration of the traditional nonmarket domestic economy and the setting free of labor from its precapitalist forms of production. This newly-created wage-labor force, when harnessed by industrial capital first into manufacturing and then into modern industry, unleashed an explosion in productivity that provided society with an entirely new material basis for its existence and ushered in the modern world.

Once the force of this great discovery of the value of labor power had been demonstrated by the English industrial revolution, other nations were compelled either to adopt this new mode of production or to be subdued by those countries which did. The mercantilist era had been characterized by active state intervention and acute national rivalry. At first, the new world economy of the nineteenth century took on an internationalistic or a nationalistic guise as it seemed that this age of industrial capital would be dominated by market principles and a government that governed best by governing least.

This was certainly the trend in Britain where the newly-triumphant capitalist class set about (1) to systematically dismantle the state apparatus used by Feudalism and Mercantilism to control production and trade, and (2) to enlarge the extent of the market internally and externally. To some extent this tendency was followed by other nations, but actually a double movement was involved. On the one hand, they too had to dismantle the system of pre-capitalist controls, but at the same time, they had to unify the nation and strengthen the state in order to industrialize.

The first focus of the new industrial state was primitive accumulation, i.e., a conscious political effort to establish the conditions of modern capitalist production by setting free a wage-labor force to work and fostering a national industrial class to organize it. Those countries which did not effect such a transformation of the domestic economy soon fell prey to one imperial power or another and became underdeveloped.

Once industrial capitalism got going, a second task emerged; namely, that of keeping it going by mediating the contradictions it inevitably produced. These contradictions stemmed from two basic interconnected conditions: (1) the anarchic relations between capitalists which produced great waste and resulted in periodic crises, (2) the concentration of people into factories and cities and their growing politicization. With the accumulation of capital, these contradictions intensified and a large and elaborate superstructure was formed to contain them.

Thus we find during the late nineteenth and early twentieth centuries that the growth and spread of industrial capitalism was accompanied by a strengthening and not a declining nation state and an intensification of national rivalry rather than its withering away. Internally, the visible hand of the state operated continuously alongside the invisible hand of the market. Internationally, one by one, countries erected national barriers against trade and in the late nineteenth century a scramble began to divide the underdeveloped countries into exclusive spheres of interest and into a new colonial system. The end result of Laissez-Faire, Pax Britannica, and Free Trade was the "welfare state," the First World War, and the complete breakdown of the international economy during the Depression.

The world market versus national welfare

It is at this point that our story begins. We find in 1930 a world economy in which:

1) The industrial revolution has more or less spread to Western Europe, America, Russia, and Japan, but is far from complete in the sense that to varying degrees large pockets of non-industrial, non-capitalist sectors remain in each country. Although certain beginnings towards industrial capitalism have been made in isolated spots in Latin America, Asia, and Africa, the vast majority of the world's population lives outside these enclaves.

2) There is a strong disenchantment with capitalism and internationalism and a belief that the nation-state and not the invisible hand will play the dominant role in economic development. (Even the Fascists call themselves National Socialists.) On the other hand, thinking still remains one-dimensionally capitalist as far as production is concerned since no alternative has emerged to the alienated work process of the capitalist factory. Marx had felt that the working class would organize itself in revolt against the dominance of capital and create a new system of production, but in the 1930's

an international revolutionary working class to lead us beyond capitalism still had not emerged.

It is in this context that we turn to Keynes's analysis of the conflict between a world market and national welfare as presented in his 1933 article on "National Self-Sufficiency." In this article Keynes argues that a restoration of the world market would unnecessarily prolong capitalism with its inherent evils and interfere with our progress towards the good society.

Describing himself as a man "who in the last resort prefers anything on earth to what the financial reports are wont to call 'the best opinion of Wall Street'," he argues that world peace, prosperity, and freedom could best be achieved by emphasizing non-capitalist national self-sufficiency rather than international market capitalism.[2] In stronger language than almost any other economist would dare use, he came to the following conclusion:

I sympathize, therefore, with those who would minimize, rather than with those who would maximize, economic entanglement among nations. Ideas, knowledge, science, hospitality, travel – these are the things which should of their nature be international. But let goods be homespun whenever it is reasonably and conveniently possible, and above all, let finance be primarily national.[3]

He supports his case with three basic arguments. First, he notes that contrary to the belief of the nineteenth century free traders, the world market created in the Golden Age of Pax Britannica did not ensure peace but ended in war and a depression. In his words:

To begin with the question of peace. We are pacifist today with so much strength of conviction that, if the economic internationalist could win this point, he would soon recapture our support. But it does not now seem obvious that a great concentration of national effort on the capture of foreign trade, that the penetration of a country's economic structure by the resources and the influence of foreign capitalists, and that a close dependence of our own economic life on the fluctuating economic policies of foreign countries are safeguards and assurances of international peace. It is easier, in the light of experience and foresight, to argue quite the contrary. The protection of a country's existing foreign interests, the capture of new markets, the progress of economic imperialism – these are a scarcely avoidable part of a scheme of things which aims at the maximum of international specialization and at the maximum geographical diffusion of capital wherever its seat of ownership.[4]

Second, he deals with the question of economic efficiency. He argues that the spread of modern technology makes it easier to produce locally the basic needs of a community and makes the argument for international specialization and export-oriented growth less compelling.

Third, and I think this is the most important part of his case, he argues that the free trader's economic internationalism assumes the whole world was, or would be, organized on the basis of private competitive capitalism. In contrast, Keynes felt that we had to go beyond capitalism if the fruits of the industrial revolution were to be realized in a humane and rational way. But a world market would prevent experimentation in socio-economic organization and thus inhibit the free and full development of our potential.

Expressing a view that is not very popular today except among socialists, Keynes argues:

> The decadent international but individualistic capitalism, in the hands of which we found ourselves after the war, is not a success. It is not intelligent, it is not beautiful, it is not just, it is not virtuous – and it doesn't deliver the goods. In short, we dislike it, and we are beginning to despise it. . . .
>
> We each have our own fancy. Not believing that we are saved already, we each should like to have a try at working out our own salvation. We do not wish, therefore, to be at the mercy of world forces working out, or trying to work out, some uniform equilibrium according to the ideal principles, if they can be called such, of *laissez-faire* capitalism. . . . We wish – for the time at least and so long as the present transitional, experimental phase endures – to be our own masters, and to be as free as we can make ourselves from the interferences of the outside world.[5]

The internationalization of capital

Keynes's view, as expressed in this article, had little effect on the policies which governed the post–Second World War reconstruction and development plans for the world economy. Instead, the best opinion of Wall Street and the City prevailed.

"Let there be no mistake about it," wrote *The Economist* in 1942 in an article on "The American Challenge," "the policy put forward by the American Administration is revolutionary. It is a genuinely new conception of world order."[6] In this way *The Economist,* reflecting the policy discussions taking place in London during the war, welcomed the plan to create a postwar world economy based on international capitalism under American hegemony.

The goal of this plan was " 'a new frontier, a frontier of limitless expanse, the frontier of human welfare,' " and " 'the instrument will be industrial capitalism, operating, broadly speaking, under conditions of private enterprise'."[7] Or, as *The Economist* put it, "the idealism of an international New Deal will have to be implemented by the unrivalled technical achievements of American business. The New Frontier will then become a reality."[8] Or as *Fortune* expressed it with regard to underdeveloped countries, "American imperialism can afford to complete the work the British started; instead of salesmen and planters, its representatives can be brains and bulldozers, technicians and machine tools."[9]

As we now know, this plan was highly successful. The world experienced a twenty-five year long secular boom in which employment, capital, and technology grew rapidly and even the Socialist countries began to be drawn away from autarky into the whirlpool of the international market.

Ironically, Keynes's theory of State policy, which he himself believed to be a tool for bringing about the end of capitalism, was used to preserve it. In the *General Theory*, Keynes argued that by restoring full employment through government intervention, we could in a reasonable time destroy capital's monopoly and free ourselves from its grip. He judged that "it might be comparatively easy to make capital goods so abundant that the marginal efficiency of capital is zero," and that this peaceful evolution might "be the most sensible way of gradually getting rid of many of the objectionable features of capitalism."[10] In his view technological change could rather quickly (one or two generations) reduce the rate of profit and thus bring about "the euthanasia of the rentier, and, consequently, the euthanasia of the cumulative oppressive power of the capitalists to exploit the scarcity-value of capital."[11] And at the same time we could save money on management through "a scheme of direct taxation which allows the intelligence and determination and executive skill of the financier, the entrepreneur *et hoc genus omne* (who are certainly so fond of their craft that their labour could be obtained much cheaper than at present), to be harnessed to the service of the community on reasonable terms of reward."[12]

Keynes was as far off the mark here as he was in his call for national self-sufficiency. One generation has already passed. The rate of profit has not fallen; instead, the state has been harnessed to shore it up and ensure the continued growth of private wealth nationally and internationally. Neither have managers' salaries been reduced. Rather the techno-structure has gained in status and income as it has become an even more crucial element in supporting the expansion of capital and preventing its euthanasia.

Thus, contrary to Marx and Keynes, the world market and the welfare state have not sounded the death-knell of capitalism. At least not yet. Instead capitalism revived from the interwar crisis and flourished in the quarter century following the war.

Now, however, there are signs of strain in the system and a wave of reexamination and reconsideration of its basic framework is taking place in the light of emerging contradictions and crises, national and international. The tightening of the web of interdependence, to use a now popular phrase, seems to be becoming increasingly uncomfortable as we progress into the 1970's. There is a certain unease in many quarters (dramatized by the oil crisis) that we may be too much at the "mercy of world forces" and too little "our own masters." And there are signs of an outbreak of the national rivalry that Keynes thought was scarcely avoidable if we placed too much emphasis on the world market.

I have argued elsewhere[13] that due to the internationalization of capital, competition between national capitalists is becoming less and less a source of rivalry between nations. Using the instrument of direct investment, large corporations are able to penetrate foreign markets and detach their interests from their home markets. At the same time, capitalists from all nations, including underdeveloped countries, are able to diversify their portfolios internationally through the international capital market. Given these tendencies, an international capitalist class is emerging whose interests lie in the world economy as a whole and a system of international private property which allows free movement of capital between countries. The process is contradictory and may break down, but for the present there is a strong tendency for the most powerful segments of the capitalist class increasingly to see their future in the further growth of the world market rather than its curtailment.

In the next section of this essay, I would like to turn to the other side of the coin and examine the interests of labor in the world market. The main theme is that labor will tend to become more nationalistic and possibly more socialistic as the continued growth of the world market undermines its traditional strategy.

Labor and the world market stage of capitalism

"Accumulation of capital is, therefore, increase of the proletariat."[14] This is the key concept in Marx's analysis of the general law of motion of capitalist society. Capitalist competition leads, at one level, to the concentration and centralization of capital in large corporations tied together by a capital market and unified at the political level by the state. At another level, it draws an ever-increasing portion of the population into the wage laboring class, concentrates them into large factories and urban centers and develops in them a group cohesiveness which makes them a political force in opposition to capital. In this way, capitalism, which is based on the competitive wage labor system, creates within itself forms of social organization which are antithetical to competition and the market system and which, in Marx's view, serve as the embryo of a new society beyond capitalism.

The trend towards class consciousness is, however, a long-drawn-out process that proceeds dialectically out of the competition between workers. On the one hand, the continuous expansion of capital and extension of the market unifies wage workers into larger and larger groupings as they strive to eliminate competition between themselves; on the other hand, it also introduces new elements of competition which divide workers into antagonistic groups and inhibit their realizing the latent potential of their unity.

Marx identified two major forces in the development of capitalism (in addition to the ideological superstructure of the corporation and the state) which continually create competition between workers and allow capitalism to reproduce itself on an expanded scale and to survive even its worst crises. First, technological change substitutes machinery for labor: By throwing, or threatening to throw, the worker out of the factory and into the market, it breaks up the cohesiveness of labor organization and reduces workers to individuals or small groups competing with each other instead of cooperating. Secondly, capitalism continuously breaks down pre-capitalist areas – what Marx calls the latent surplus population – thus forming a fresh supply of non-class conscious workers to compete in the labor market.

These two dynamic forces create a stratified labor force which keeps the pretensions of the working class in check. Above the proletariat stands a vast officer class of managers, technicians, and bureaucrats to organize it and to overcome its resistance by keeping it divided. Below it is a pool of unemployed, underemployed, and badly-paid strata continuously fed by technological change and the opening up of new hinterlands, which undercut its position and inhibit its development towards class consciousness. This reserve army drives the labor aristocracy to keep on working and keeps it loyal to the capitalist system from fear of falling from its superior position. By the nature of things, these different strata often come from different regions within a country, different racial or ethnic groups, and different age and sex classes. Thus, the competitive cleavages between workers often reflect lines of race, creed, color, age, sex, and national origin, which make working class consciousness more difficult.

The significance of the world market stage of capitalism into which we have now entered is that this competitive process, which both brings labor together and separates it, has now taken on an international dimension. The growth of world trade brings labor of different countries into closer contact and competition; the internationalization of production via the multinational corporate system was a reaction on the part of capital to this fact. American firms, for example, found that the recovery of Europe and the development of labor surplus economies in the Third World made it possible to produce certain things more cheaply abroad than in the United States; and competitive pressure from emerging non-American capitalists forced them to invest abroad or enter into licensing and management contracts in order to preserve their position and maintain their growth. More generally, the emergence of a unified world commodity market, which in effect is the emergence of a unified world labor market, switched the domain of competition and its accompanying tendencies towards concentration and centralization from the national to the international plane. But this quest for profit, which led capital to shed its national character and escape the narrow confines of the nation-state, has also intensified competitive pressure on labor and undermined its traditional organization and strategy. This, I suggest, is bound to bring about a new stage of development of labor organization, and it is here we must search for the root of the matter if we wish to understand our present predicament and the development track we are on.

In short, we must view present developments in terms of the long-term spread of commodity production, based on wage labor, from the local towns of the Middle Ages and the small enclaves of the transition period, to the national market and now the world market. The process of concentration and centralization of capital occurring within this framework led both to the steady growth and development of modern enterprise from the workshop to the factory to the national corporation to the multidivisional corporation and now to the multinational corporation, and to the parallel spread of the financial system from the local to the national and now to the international plane. At the same time, this growth has led to the continuous spread of labor organization in response to the opening up of new sources of competition and the emergence of new contradictions. This took place partly through the spread of the trade union movement to a broader and broader basis, and partly through the joint action of workers of different industries in the struggle over the working day, health, education, social security, unemployment, etc., at the political level. Workers' organization has so far taken place almost entirely within national boundaries through a struggle to obtain civil rights and national laws to protect labor from some of the vicissitudes of the competitive labor process. Now internationalization of capital, combined with certain domestic contradictions of the welfare state, has brought the established structure of labor organization to a critical juncture, and it is to this problem that we must now turn.

The political role of labor

From a Marxist perspective, the main theoretical shortcoming of Keynes's analysis is that he paid no attention to the conditions of production and the political role of labor. He viewed the market system, based on greed and selfishness, with considerable disdain and wanted to go beyond the profit motive towards a society managed by a society-oriented elite, operating in a loose framework that combined state planning and large quasi-public operations. He did not believe that either the capitalists or the "boorish proletariat" could or would lead us to this higher form of organization, but felt that the process of capital accumulation and technological progress would achieve this end naturally despite the wrong-headed interferences by capital and labor. Thus, neither in his political nor his economic writings, did he pay attention to class struggle as a moving force in capitalist development.

Ironically, this limited perspective was also in one sense his genius, for in fact during the post-war period, the issue of class struggle was highly subdued and labor did not form a serious challenge to capitalism as a system, but instead cooperated within its framework. This was one of the reasons capitalism grew so rapidly and one of the reasons Keynes's theory of monetary and fiscal policy could work.

In the *General Theory*, Keynes shifted the focus of discussion away from the labor market to the capital market. Classical economists saw unemployment and stagnation as the result of too high a level of wages. (In Marxian terms, too low a rate of surplus value.) Keynes instead postulated an elastic supply of labor at the going wage and sought the breakdown of the system in the contradictions between savers and investors, i.e., the rentier class and the entrepreneurial/managerial class. Keynes's preferred way out of this dilemma seemed to be through an expansion of the state and public consumption at the expense of the rentier class, but the alternative preferred by the capitalist was an expansion of the state to promote the growth of private wealth through the stimulation of private investment and private consumption. It was this path that finally predominated.

This strategy was possible because of specific conditions emerging from the Great Depression and the War which restored the workings of the labor market. In Marxist theory, the functioning of the wage labor market, upon which capitalist expansion depends, is maintained in the first instance through the institutions of the reserve army.

The industrial reserve army, during the periods of stagnation and average prosperity, weights down the active labour army; during the periods of over-production and paroxysm, it holds its pretensions in check. Relative surplus-population is therefore the pivot upon which the law of demand and supply of labour works. It confines the field of this law within the limits absolutely convenient to the activity of exploitation and to the domination of capital.[15]

In this sense, the long period of large scale unemployment of the Thirties served as a disciplinary action on labor to make it ready, willing, and anxious to work again in the postwar period. But action at the political level was needed as well.

As soon, therefore, as the labourers learn the secret, how it comes to pass that in the same measure as they work more, as they produce more wealth for others, and as the productive power of their labour increases, so in the same measure even their function as a means of the self-expansion of capital becomes more and more precarious for them; as soon as they discover that the degree of intensity of the competition among themselves depends wholly on the pressure of the relative surplus-population; as soon as, by trade unions, etc., they try to organize a regular cooperation between the employed and unemployed in order to destroy or to weaken the ruinous effects of this natural law of capitalistic production on their class, so soon capital and its sycophant, political economy, cry out at the infringement of the "eternal" and so to say "sacred" law of supply and demand. Every combination of employed and unemployed disturbs the "harmonious" actions of this law. But on the other hand, as soon as (in the colonies, e.g.) adverse circumstances prevent the creation of an industrial reserve army and, with it, the absolute dependence of the working class upon the capitalist class, capital, along with its commonplace Sancho Panza, rebels against the "sacred" law of supply and demand and tries to check its inconvenient action by forcible means and State interference.[16]

The New Deal, the World War, and the Cold War made it possible in the United States to purge the labor movement of its radical elements and create a system of collective bargaining within the framework of the welfare state. This system left the basic capitalist institutions of private wealth and wage labor largely untouched and channeled labor protest into narrowly-defined trade unionism, which concentrated on selling labor at a more advantageous price without challenging the prerogatives of management and capital, either inside the plant or out of it. Trade unions confined their horizons to the interests of their own membership and instead of unifying all of labor in a class perspective, maintained cleavages within the best-paid aristocracy of the working class and between it and the reserve army. The law of supply and demand was thus altered by the growth of unions, but still kept working within conveniently confined limits. The history of the European movement was different in content but similar in effect, that is, the elimination of radical perspectives and the creation of a framework in which labor was willing to submit to the dictates of capital in order to obtain economic growth and capitalism's "New Frontier."

A major factor in making the system work was the existence of a latent surplus-population in the underdeveloped countries and backward sectors of advanced countries which could be broken down to form a constantly flowing surplus population to work at the bottom of the ladder. In the United States the replacement of southern sharecropping agriculture by modern capitalist methods created a flow of black labor to the northern cities, just as the "development" of Puerto Rico led to large-scale immigration into the eastern United States. Similarly, in Europe modernization of agriculture and the importation of labor from foreign countries played a major role in creating the labor supply needed for capitalist expansion. In addition, the advanced countries benefited from cheap prices for raw materials made possible by the creation of a labor surplus economy in the underdeveloped countries.

Thus, during this twenty-five year period, labor was able to enjoy prosperity and growth as it concentrated on working harder for steadily increasing standards of living and refrained from challenging the system politically. By and large the major source of rebellion and protest did not come from the established proletariat during the Fifties and Sixties, but from the new strata being incorporated into the wage labor force from their previous position in the latent surplus population. These groups were highly critical of the conditions of capitalist production, as they found themselves caught between the breakdown of the old system and the unfulfilled expectations of the new one. They were acutely aware of the coercive nature of the capitalist work relationship, since, unlike the traditional working class, they were "disadvantaged," i.e., they had not yet internalized the capitalist values of alienated work. And they were also extremely bitter at the inequality of their position and the discriminations they suffered.

These factors, which gave such great force to their reaction, also limited the scope of their challenge to capitalism. Because they were outside production and at odds with the privileged strata, they were relatively powerless to actually transform the capitalist system. Their programs often tended to be backward-looking, harking after a return to older forms of community production, and/or anarchistically radical, seeking to burn, destroy, and sabotage the system which oppressed them, rather than to seize it for their own. They were caught in a dilemma. On the one hand, they were antagonistic to capitalism, but on the other hand, they also wanted to get into it and share its benefits and privileges. The result of this dualism was a tendency for their group to split as some entered the labor force and became part of the system, while others fell down into the stagnant part of the reserve army with extremely irregular employment, well below average conditions of life, and into the lowest sediments which dwell in the sphere of pauperism, thus forming an incredible pool of wasted human beings in the slums, ghettos, and rural hinterlands of the capitalist economy.

Thus the uneven development of capitalism, accumulating wealth at one pole and misery at the other, was from the political point of view a stabilizing force because it divided the potential opposition to capitalism into conflicting groups. The question is, then, for how long can this go on? In the next section, I examine the pressures on the labor aristocracy which I believe are bringing this phase of capitalist expansion to an end and leading us to a period when class conflict between capital and labor will be a major force in the economy and polity, nationally and internationally.

The seeds of a new class conflict

The success of the "American Challenge" and the "New Frontier," we have argued, rested on a particular set of initial conditions arising out of the great depression and the World War. These wore down the resistance of labor, destroyed its radical wing, and made organized labor into a willing partici- pant in a strategy based on strong state action to promote growth and international expansionism. But the very success of the plan has tended to undermine these initial conditions and to lead us to a stage marked by crisis and reorientation of basic strategies.

In the first place, memories of the Thirties and Forties have faded in this period of affluence, while the "New Frontier" has turned out to be less rewarding than it promised. The growth of national income satisfied some of the pent-up needs of previous decades and created new needs which the market system cannot fulfill. The consumer durable revolution provided most families with a car, a television set, and a refrigerator, but also resulted in overcrowding, pollution, and an energy crisis. The middle class standard of living, towards which the working class aspired, is predicated in large part on only a few people having it. When everybody has a car, the result is not freedom to escape from overcrowded cities into the countryside, but a crowded countryside. Similarly, when everybody has access to higher education, its elite qualities and privileges are destroyed and a college degree no longer means a ticket to the top of the hierarchy, but an upgraded job at the lower level. Thus, many of the promises of capitalistic consumption tend to be illusory, while alienation and exploitation in the work process remain an ever-present reality. Therefore, job dissatisfaction and a decreased motivation to work has increased steadily over the last twenty-five years, and resulted in the productivity crisis causing so much discussion and concern in business circles.

In the second place, the latent surplus population has been steadily drying up, thus exhausting national pools of cheap labor and lessening the competitive pressure on the work force. Moreover, as more and more people from the nonwage sector are drawn into the wage labor force, the locus of their struggle against discrimination, alienation, and exploitation shifts from outside to inside, thus infusing the labor movement with new dimensions of protest and militancy. At the same time, the demands for welfare and other support programs by those who are nonincorporated into the wage labor force eat up the surplus and limit the scope for expanding wages.

These two trends have seriously threatened the collective bargaining strategy which dominated the trade union movement over the last twenty-five years. Trade unions can obtain higher wages within capitalist expansion only to the extent that they are matched by increased productivity or passed on to lower strata of the labor force. However, the tightening of the labor market that accompanies capitalist expansion increases the pretensions of the working class, both with regard to wages and relief from work, at the same time that it diminishes the possibility of placing the burden on disadvantaged sectors. Hence, wage demands result in inflation and a crisis in labor organization. (A recent article in *Business Week,* for example, focused on three crises in the union movement: dissatisfaction on the part of consumers concerning the inflationary consequences of wage demands, dissatisfaction on the part of businessmen over the ability of the unions to deliver the intensity of work contracted for, and dissatisfaction on the part of the rank and file over the responsiveness of union leadership to their needs.[17])

These tendencies in the labor market, which are occurring throughout the advanced capitalist world as capital expansions occur (usually called a shift in the Phillips Curve by non-Marxist economists), have led to the widespread adoption of wage and price controls, thus signalling the de facto end, or at least the beginning of the end, of the era of collective bargaining. Trade unions can no longer confine their horizons to the struggle between their membership and its employers, but must bargain politically at the national level over the share of wages in national income. In Marxian terms, the material conditions of trade union consciousness are coming to an end in advanced capitalism since the trade unions can no longer confine themselves to wages, but must deal directly with the problem of the aggregate rate of surplus value which is a class phenomenon. At this point of development, they soon find out that there is very little that can be done about the rate of surplus value within a capitalist framework, since increases in the share of wages cut down on investment and result in unemployment and a slackening of growth. A socialist alternative, under which the working class seizes control of the investment process, could open new possibilities of organizing production and promoting the growth and development of the potential of social labor. Failing this radical break, the working class is a hostage to the capitalist class on whom they depend for capital accumulation and to whom they must provide incentives in the form of profit and accumulation of capital, that is, more work.

Thus, labor organizations must shift their horizons from the industrial to the national level, that is, they must shift from economic to political action. At the same time, the growth of the world market and the internationalization of capital implies they must also shift their horizons to the world level. Once again, they discover how limited their options are if they do not challenge the capitalist system. If, for example, they adopt a protectionist policy, they can lessen the competition from imports, but they cannot insure a high rate of national investment if capitalists can escape their national demands by investing abroad. If they try to control capital flight, they then discover that the size and complexity of multinational corporations and the international financial market provide capitalists with numerous escape valves and that unless they take over the whole system, they can only achieve partial control.

Another strategy is international trade unionism, which can alleviate competition in certain industries but is still partly limited on two accounts. First, organizing workers in developed countries for higher wages at the cost of reduced employment, though it obtains the support of some groups, increases the gap between the small local labor aristocracy and the vast reserve army and creates politically volatile conditions which have to be brutally suppressed. Second, international trade unionism can only struggle over industry wage and working conditions. But a great part of labor's historical gains have occurred at the political level and are embodied in national social infrastructure in the fields of health, education, welfare, social security, etc. Equalization of this infrastructure to remove competition involves far more political unification than a simple trade unionist strategy can provide.

Therefore, on both counts – the internal reserve army and the external reserve army – labor is in an objective crisis where its old institutions and policies no longer work, and, what amounts to the same thing, so is capitalism. This is what I believe to be the radical view of international economics and international politics at this juncture in history.

The next twenty-five years

Work in the Marxist framework is a political relationship. In the market, where workers sell their labor in exchange for wages, it seems to be only an economic phenomenon, but this is an illusion. What the workers sell is not labor but labor power, that is, their life activity. How this labor power will be used, its duration and intensity, is not settled by competition but by struggle and force. Hence there arises within the business enterprise a political superstructure whose function is in part to coordinate work and in part to overcome the resistance of workers arising out of the antagonistic social relations of production. Similarly, the struggle over work leads to the capitalist state whose function in the last instance is to insure the reproduction of the basic structural elements of the work relationship – capital and labor. The rise and spread of the market system is thus closely connected to a political struggle to create and maintain the wage labor force, divided by competition, upon which capitalism rests.

Politics – the getting, keeping, and using of power – is mainly a question of uniting your allies and dividing your enemies. Marx's analysis of the general laws of capitalist accumulation is an attempt to uncover the tendencies towards concentration and class consciousness that develop in the two main contending parties as capitalism progresses.

The peculiar feature of capitalism is that it obtained power and in some sense maintains it with an inherently limited degree of class consciousness. Capitalism is a system based on the mutual indifference of its participants, operating in a structure of competition and the pursuit of selfish interests. In economists' terms, it is a highly decentralized system based on private profit maximization and united through the invisible hand of the market, that is, the law of value. The great strength of this system, which differentiates it from all previous modes of production, is that the competition between capitalists and between capital and labor forces a continuous revolution in technology and an epoch-making expansion of material production. But this competitive market nexus is also its chief limit, for it prevents the development of a total view of society commensurate with the increasingly interdependent social division of labor that it is creating. The capitalist state attempts to provide some sort of total view, but is sharply limited by the divisions in capitalist society between capital and labor and between capitalists themselves. As capitalism progresses, this contradiction intensifies. The problems of "externalities," to use economists' language, and "socialization" and "legitimization" become more important as more and more problems arise which cannot be managed by the invisible hand of the market. The world market, created since World War II, has brought things to a critical point. Capital has expanded to global dimensions, but still maintains a consciousness based on narrow private calculation. The structure of the American Empire, which kept some sort of order on this process in the past, is dissolving and a Hobbesian-like struggle of all against all seems to be emerging at the world level. As the anarchy of competition asserts itself, we find ourselves facing numerous crises, with even greater ones looming in the background.

Labor, in contrast to capital, though it too is divided by competition, steadily struggles to eliminate this competition at higher and higher levels until it reaches a world historic perspective far more total than capital and replaces capitalism by socialism. This unification, however, is a long-drawn-out process, requiring a high development of material forces, i.e., a long expansion of capitalist production.

Competition separates individuals from one another, not only the bourgeois but still more the workers, in spite of the fact that it brings them together. Hence it is a long time before these individuals can unite, apart from the fact that for the purpose of this union – if it is not to be merely local – the necessary means, the great industrial cities and cheap and quick communications have first to be produced by big industry. Hence every organized power standing over against these isolated individuals who live in relationships daily reproducing this isolation, can only be overcome after long struggles. To demand the opposite would be tantamount to demanding that competition should not exist in this definite epoch of history, or that the individuals should banish from their minds relationships over which in their isolation they have no control.[18]

In this paper we have tried to suggest that the world market, by expanding the edge of competition, has created a critical juncture in the labor movement which will force a change in its strategy and structure. During the last twenty-five years, capital has been able to expand and internationalize, first by strengthening and then by eroding the powers of the nation-state. During the next twenty-five years we can expect a counter-response by labor and other groups to erode the power of capital. This response will take a political form, i.e., a struggle over state power around the central issue of capitalism and its continuance. Since states are territorial, the locus of the struggle will be largely national, or at least regional, even though the context is international. In the United States, it will probably tend to the formation of some sort of labor party. In Europe, it will probably lead to unification and a closer union between Social Democratic and Communist parties. In the underdeveloped countries, it will lead to an increased role of labor in politics as the new proletariat emerges. And so on.

In this paper we cannot even begin to examine the complexity of the struggle and the numerous paths it can take between the following two extremes:

1 A privileged part of the new working class in the advanced countries joins with capital in a new imperialistic alliance to get higher benefits in return for suppressing blacks, Third World people, foreign workers, women, the aged, etc. I personally think that this extreme is unlikely due to the large numbers and

strength of the disadvantaged groups and the enormous brutality it would take to contain them.

2   At the other extreme, we can imagine a socialist consciousness which unites the disparate elements of labor to effect the transition from capitalism to socialism. Since socialism implies that communities obtain control over their own work and consumption, it would probably have to be based on national or regional self-sufficiency, as Keynes suggested; though with a great deal of international cooperation to permit the free flow of ideas, hospitality, etc.

Much research needs to be done on both labor and non-labor political groups before we can sort out the possible sets of intermediate alliances that might emerge, and analyze their implications for the balance between capitalism and socialism, internationalism and nationalism. This paper merely attempts to point to the crucial role of the capital–labor struggle that we can expect in the future. We might end by noting that whatever the outcome – international fascism, socialism, or mixed free enterprise – a great deal of conflict and struggle domestically and internationally is in store for us, especially in the Third World, as the powerful forces unleashed by advanced capitalism come to a head. Our main problem as social scientists and human beings is not only to analyze what is happening, but also to decide which side we want to be on. That is why I spent so much time on Keynes, who asked the right questions, even though he was sharply limited in his answers – because he tried to think history without Marx.

On becoming a radical economist

A brief biography of
Stephen Herbert Hymer (1934-1974)

We have to invent new wisdom for a new age. And in the meantime we must, if we are to do any good, appear unorthodox, troublesome, dangerous, and disobedient to them who begat us.
— From Stephen Hymer's notes for an autobiographical essay, 1973

Stephen Hymer was a complex person. To those he befriended, he was one of the most original and challenging thinkers they had known. Many believed he was the best Canadian-born economist of his generation. Both his wide-ranging academic interests and his increasing involvement in political issues enriched and enlivened many of the projects on which he worked. People always felt his presence. He both commanded attention and devoted himself intensely to friends and family, colleagues, and comrades.

And Steve changed continually. His eclecticism was apparent early, during his graduate student years at M.I.T., when he began to apply the neoclassical paradigm in an unorthodox way to unravel the forces behind U.S. foreign investment. From that period in the late fifties until his death, his analysis became increasingly radical. Eventually he became a professed Marxist and committed his intellectual work to the expansion of Marxist theory and to the worldwide struggle for a new social order.

Those of us who knew him have sought to understand how Steve's work and life progressed. In preparing this biography, we talked and corresponded with many people who worked with Steve. We hope that it will help convey something about the development of Steve's work and his relationship with the world around him.

The changes in Steve's thinking emerged continually but fitfully. His own nature drove him forward: He read insatiably and wanted to probe to the "bottom of things"; he hungered to understand the roots of economic and social change; and he struggled to contribute to people's understanding of the forces that controlled their lives. But he was not changing in a vacuum. The political and economic developments around him influenced Steve's develop-

273

ment forcefully. He himself traced much of his later appreciation of capitalism's contradictions to his early life in Canada; that he was born Canadian no doubt influenced his conceptions of imperialism, dependency, and economic development. Steve's work and life also reflected the developments of the 1960s; his growing awareness, disillusionment, and political activism parallel the movements that emerged during those years. And Steve always worked with others in study groups, collectives, and discussion groups both inside and outside academia; people from these experiences probably influenced him at least as much as his more formal training and academic work.

We feel that Stephen Hymer must be remembered partly as a pioneer. He was the first person to investigate the overseas expansion of U.S. multinational corporations and to elucidate the economic forces behind their foreign investment. With the exception of Charles Kindleberger, few in the United States gave this early work the recognition it undoubtedly deserved, and Steve sometimes appeared to feel the personal disappointment that a pioneer must often sense.

Yet he eventually gained an international reputation and became involved with events on an international scale. His ability to synthesize masses of empirical data became one of his formidable strengths. He developed an integrated and almost prescient capacity to identify important and emergent tendencies in capitalist development. In later years, growing numbers sought Steve's opinions because he was beginning to develop and apply Marxist insights with a stunning blend of clarity and originality.

Stephen was born in Montreal, Canada, on November 15, 1934, to Leo and Bernice Hymer. His father was a Jewish immigrant from Eastern Europe who ran a small clothing store where his mother worked as a bookkeeper. These early Depression years in a lower-middle-class environment clearly influenced his subsequent intellectual and political development. His view of the world was colored by a strong sense of individualism and by his community's envy and awe of the rich and powerful. In his autobiographical notes, Steve wrote of his feelings as a young man:

We were aliens in a land where large corporations and government were monopolized by the English and French. Politics were outside our control but had an immediate impact on our lives. We were outsiders who moved from country to country in response to political events, whose lives were dominated by economic activity. We lived in the interstices of society always trying to take advantage of shifts in power, tastes, and social relations in order to survive and at times to prosper. We always felt the outsider trying to understand what was happening inside and we always understood the importance of money as social power.[1]

It was not surprising that both he and his younger brother Bennett went on to study economics. Steve spent his undergraduate years at McGill. Early in his studies, he began to ask questions about the influence of economic forces on the great events of his time – the Depression, the Second World War, the Cold War. And he and his fellow Canadians at McGill were beginning to develop their budding nationalism – they saw Canada as something more than a colony but something less than a nation. In his notes Steve tells the story of a small bird who lives off the food it picks from between the teeth of a crocodile. The bird, out of necessity, becomes an expert on crocodiles. So, "in Canada, our eyes were always turned outward to the great metropolitan centers that dominated us."[2]

Although this nationalism was important to Steve, he chose to pursue his economic studies at M.I.T. – located in the metropolis and known as the center for the economics profession. After graduating from McGill with first-class honors in politics and economics, Steve moved to Cambridge with his wife, Gilda Guttman. He and Gilda had two sons, David, born in 1962, and Jonathan, born in 1965.

During the late 1950s, Steve was affected by the exuberance of the Cambridge, Massachusetts economists who were shaping the "grand neoclassical synthesis" and preparing for their influence in the Kennedy administration. But he was disturbed by the inadequacy of their framework. He doubted the coherence of traditional theory and was troubled by those M.I.T. economists who reasoned only in pure theory and yet adopted the policies of the Democratic Party. He was more impressed with the unorthodox than the mainstream. He felt special respect, for instance, both for M. A. Adelman, who claimed neoclassical theory was unable to answer questions about economic concentration, and for Milton Friedman, whose economics was closely integrated with his politics. Paul Samuelson also intrigued Steve; although he was a major proponent of the new neoclassical synthesis, Samuelson periodically resumed his study of Marx.

Increasingly skeptical, Steve and some other students, including Ronald Findlay and B. P. Pashigian, formed a study group to criticize conventional theory and examine questions excluded from the M.I.T. curriculum. For instance, Steve had become interested in the history of class struggle from his work in labor economics, and he wondered whether or not it was necessary to study Marx and particularly the labor theory of value in order to understand the basis of class struggle.

But the issues on which his years in Canada had focused his attention remained paramount. His earlier awareness of domination by "large corporations and government" pointed him toward the field of industrial organization. And, with other Canadians who became economists like Harry Johnson and Jacob Viner, his preoccupation with trade relationships led him to international economics. It was Charles Kindleberger – for whom Steve had developed a great admiration and affection – who suggested that Steve could integrate these two fields by studying the multinational corporation and its effects upon world development. Kindleberger supervised Steve's thesis on

"The International Operations of National Firms, a Study of Direct Foreign Investment."[3]

The framework Steve applied in his thesis illustrates how he was beginning to challenge neoclassical theory. For instance, Steve attempted to account for the foreign operation of national firms – or the role of direct foreign investment. However, he recognized that traditional theory could not answer a number of questions raised by its own postulates about capital movements. Searching for an alternative explanation, he distinguished direct from port-folio investment and traced the different movements of each. Steve noted that, counter to the orthodox theory that capital moves in response to interest rates, the large, oligopolistic firm invests capital in order to obtain and retain advantages over its competitors. Firms located in countries with high interest rates had international operations in countries where the interest rate was low; thus direct investment moved in a direction opposite to the one implied by traditional theory. He developed in his thesis an explanation for direct investment within the framework of oligopoly theory and, in so doing, criticized the limitations of traditional theory.

Although Kindleberger was enthusiastic about Steve's results, others were not. The M.I.T. Economics Department refused to sponsor publication of the thesis. It was not until 1976 – sixteen years after the thesis was completed – that Kindleberger was finally able to arrange for its posthumous publication.

Following his graduation from M.I.T., Steve planned to continue his study of the effects of foreign direct investment on a "host" country. He chose to spend a year in Ghana. There he met a group of intellectually stimulating and politically aware people who had been drawn to Ghana by the promise of a new political and economic order under Nkrumah. Their impressive presence helped his investigations into the Ghanaian economy and he began to appreciate the deep-rooted nature of the problems created by the British colonial legacy. He could not yet decide whether the economic chaos and "underdevelopment" were the results of bureaucratic incompetence or the symptoms of more fundamental forces. In the first article he wrote on Ghana, co-authored with R. H. Green, he traced the relationship between govern-ment practice and economic development, documenting the colonial govern-ment's virtual disruption of the cocoa industry.[4]

Although he came back to the United States and taught at M.I.T. and Yale for two years, Steve remained fascinated by his experiences in Ghana and the issues they raised for his work. He returned again in 1963. In order to pursue his original questions about British colonialism, he sifted through voluminous statistics. (He later published a collation of these data in one of the more extensive statistical portraits of a newly independent nation.[5]) As a result of his research, one idea that struck him was that the British may have discouraged the development of capitalism in Ghana because they feared that the proletariat in the colonies would aggravate problems with the British working class at home. In this work, Steve was beginning to unleash his earlier curiosity about the class struggle. A germ of his later approach had been planted.

His new, largely tentative soundings reflected not only the political and economic situation in Ghana, but also the ideas of the people with whom he worked there. Steve was active in an informal group called the Marxist Forum, which included Paul Semonin and Geoffrey Kay. The group focused on Marxian theory and development. Steve was particularly impressed with Roger Genoud, a Swiss linguist and one of the first dedicated Marxists Steve had met. Genoud played an especially important role in the group because he challenged the others to abandon their neoclassical thinking.

Genoud's challenge pricked Steve, but he wasn't ready to join the Marxian ranks. His work on Ghana made him aware of the limitations of neoclassical theory and suggested the value of a Marxian analysis. But he was not yet convinced of the validity of the Marxian approach. Reflecting on this experience in his notes, Steve later tried to explain why he was unable to adopt Marxism in those years:

Both in my study on Ghana and my study of direct foreign investment the disproportion between the questions I was asking and the tools I had to deal with them grew daily. But I was a reformist and tried to incorporate what I was learning about society and politics into the analytic framework of economics. I held on too fast to what I learned in school. I think in retrospect that this was because I was too much interested in advancing my career. A *petit bourgeois* outlook dies hard.[6]

Steve returned to New Haven in 1964, rejoined the Yale faculty, and resumed his work at the Economic Growth Center. He remained interested in Third World economies and met other colleagues with similar reactions to their work in developing countries. Stephen Resnick's experiences in the Philippines had been so similar to Steve's in Ghana that they collaborated on several articles about development – one of which, "International Trade and Uneven Development," appears as Chapter 5 of this book – and planned to write a book together.

Steve also began to study the works of Marx. During his years at Yale from 1964 to 1969, he began to pursue an alternative framework. He and Steve Resnick read *Capital* together and "discovered" in Marx's writings numerous parallels to their own observations on development. But Steve was to go through many personal, political, and intellectual changes before he was able fully to embrace Marx's analysis and adapt it to his work.

One significant experience that helped him sharpen his analysis was his work on the Canadian government Task Force on the Structure of Canadian Industry.[7] Steve was appointed to this task force in 1967 because Canadian officials had been impressed with the findings of his thesis, which were summarized in an article, "Direct Foreign Investment and the National Economic Interest" (Chapter 7), published in *Nationalism in Canada*.[8] The

278 On becoming a radical economist

thesis provided the principal framework for the task force study. Steve and Mel Watkins, who had been a graduate student with him at M.I.T., analyzed the role of the multinational corporation in host nations and predicted that the global, long-term strategies of multinationals would eventually conflict with the more limited investment perspectives of the nation-state. In a paper prepared for the task force entitled "National Policies Towards Multinational Corporations," Steve argued that the conflict between the multinationals and the nation-state would become most acute over issues of innovation, invention, and corporate political power. If nations could prevent multinational corporations from monopolizing industries by establishing agencies that would screen foreign investment and modernize domestic corporations, they might be able to maintain their independence.[9] The final report essentially called for antitrust priorities. It argued so persuasively for government regulation of multinationals that the report had a great impact on the thinking of Canadian economists. Its recommendations were considered too radical to form the basis for government policy, however, and the report was tabled for some time.

Steve was quite pleased with the task force report when it was completed and he considered doing similar studies for other nations. He continued to work on the problem of the multinationals and the nation-state, presenting a more critical analysis of multinationals in a Yale Economic Growth Center paper, "Transatlantic Reactions to Foreign Investment."[10] In this paper, he argued that multinational corporations could in fact have a *negative* influence upon "host" countries, especially upon their economic *and* social, political, and cultural development. Pursuing the implications of his argument, he suggested that the internationalization of capital would have to be counteracted by the international organization of trade unions and political parties. He was already beginning to move beyond the regulatory position of the task force report.

At the time that Steve was abandoning his nationalist antitrust approach and adopting a more critical view of capitalism, his personal life was also undergoing major changes. He was greatly affected by the social and political movements of the late 1960s. "Things started to come to a head for me in 1967," he wrote in his notes:

I was 34 at the time and discovered one day that I would retire in the year two thousand. I wondered what lay ahead of me in these next thirty years. I had already lived hard, been marked by the rise and fall of Hitler, the rise and fall of the American Empire from Korea to Vietnam. It was at this point that I began to study Marx seriously and to re-think my professional and personal life. It was the days of the American movement, when we were gripped by a certain spirit and dared to question all the institutions of our society – the state, the school, the family, and to examine all its ideas of liberty, love and life.[11]

The student-worker uprisings of May 1968 strengthened Steve's resolve to become more involved in radical analysis. In order to expand his contacts with radicals, Steve spent the fall of 1968 with Robert Rowthorn at Cambridge University in England, where they worked on a joint study of the growth of the U.S. and European multinational corporations in Europe (later published as *International Big Business 1957–1967*[12]). While in England, Hymer joined an informal discussion group that included Rowthorn, Robin Murray, Geoffrey Kay, Sean Gervasi, and several others. This group had a significant influence on Steve's development because its members abandoned conventional theory and attempted to work explicitly within a Marxian framework. The vibrant political atmosphere of 1968 permitted them to combine Marxian analysis with activist, anticapitalist politics. Steve returned to the United States fully committed to the study of Marx.

Steve attempted to apply Marx's method to his study of the organization of the modern corporation. He had been interested in the work of Marshall McLuhan. Mel Watkins introduced him to McLuhan in the late 1960s. Although Steve disagreed with McLuhan's anti-Marxism, he was intrigued by his approach to social control and its parallels to his own developing critique of the multinational corporation. Steve combined McLuhan's ideas with Alfred Chandler's concept that firms were reorganized in order to establish control over their own operations and labor forces. He focused more and more carefully on the organizational mechanisms of the multinational corporation, tracing their implications for internal control and for corporate location across space. One of his important and original essays, "The Multinational Corporation and the Law of Uneven Development" (Chapter 2 of this book), grew out of this train of analysis.

While he was developing his ideas on hierarchy and the role of the corporation in the Third World, Steve was influenced by two important trips during 1969. Steve received a research fellowship at the University of the West Indies in Trinidad. He met Lloyd Best and Kari Levitt, who were researching the development of plantation economies, during his visit there. He also talked with Norman Girvan, whose investigations into the raw materials industries interested him greatly. Through their work and his visit Steve was observing once again how imperialism disrupted and destroyed people's cultures and livelihoods. Now, several years after his Ghanaian visits, he connected his experience in the West Indies with his stay in Africa. He had less hope than ever that government regulation of multinationals could somehow mitigate the excesses of imperialism.

Following his stay in the West Indies, Steve spent the summer at the Institute for International Studies of the University of Chile. During this trip, he finally and irrevocably changed his perception of international capital. At the Yale Economic Growth Center, the research program developed experts on specific nations. Steve was beginning to realize that such expertise could only serve the interests of capitalists who wished to further their political and economic influence in the Third World. His visit to Chile convinced him that it was necessary to counter this expertise, to educate economists who would provide information to people in the Third World about the strategies of capitalists in the developed nations. This was especially true as more and more radicals were beginning to take power and would need to know how to deal with international capital. Steve highlighted these new concerns in a paper presented a few years later at a conference in Chile, "The United States Multinational Corporations and Japanese Competition in the Pacific" (Chapter 10 of this book).

While at Yale during 1968 and 1969, Steve continued to analyze the dimensions of control in the multinational corporation. Much of this work was done in collaboration with Paul Semonin and a collective of researchers that included Leah Margulies, Judith Miller, Joan Gambos, and Florika Remetier. These women influenced Steve's thinking about hierarchy, social control, and the role of family organization. They, together with Steve's wife, Gilda, were in a women's group in New Haven that raised issues about the hierarchical organization of people's daily lives. They also were concerned about patriarchy and the family and about the ways parents could share responsibilities for child care and housework. At the same time, Steve participated in the Morning Sun Daycare and School and joined in a number of debates about how to attain a nonhierarchical and non-male-chauvinist education for the children in that collective. Steve struggled intensively over these issues, and those personal struggles both changed his attitude and influenced the content and process of his academic work.

Steve was also influenced and radicalized by the mass movements of those years. The Vietnam War showed him that American technological sophistication could not subdue liberation movements; he and others would no longer need to cavil before the power of American business. He was also affected by student movements; he often tried to organize his classes to encourage collective work among the students. And he confronted hierarchy and status distinctions in his own life. He was aware that he was considered to be an authority on multinational corporations, yet he actively sought funds to enable younger people to attend conferences. He included less-knowledgeable people in his working groups. He joined the Union for Radical Political Economics, which was becoming an important vehicle for shared work among radical economists, and he participated in a study group on Marxian economics with Peter Bell, Vahid Nowshirvani, Stephen Resnick, Heidi Hartmann, the late Peggy Howard, and others.

In the spring of 1970, Steve taught his first course on Marx. Nonuniversity, "movement" people were invited as well as Yale students. Steve tried to encourage everyone in the class to participate in order to overcome hierarchical distinctions between student and teacher and among students. Although this approach did not entirely succeed, Steve became convinced of its importance for teaching. Not only was it an appropriate method to encourage collective relations between people, but it also reinforced his ideas about the way Marx's analysis should be used to understand contemporary issues. He wished to teach Marx politically. For him this meant that he and his co-workers would strive to understand the importance of class struggle both locally and globally. He wanted to suggest that both cooperation and confrontation would have to permeate our daily lives as well as our international political struggles if capitalism were to be overthrown.

Steve was also aware that several students and activists wanted to engage in a serious study of the works of Marx. Many recognized the need – often as a result of their political involvement – to deepen their analysis of contemporary society in order to carry on their political work in a more sophisticated way. Experience was showing the need for theory. Deeper theoretical understanding would help sharpen practice. But the academy was still a hostile place for Marxists. Steve hoped that he could in some way help develop an atmosphere in the university more favorable to the study of Marx. He recognized the need to express both a personal and public commitment to Marxism. In 1969, at a conference of the Union for Radical Political Economics at M.I.T., he and his colleague Stephen Resnick publicly announced that they were Marxists. This was a cathartic moment for Steve. He was pleased to have made a public commitment, but he also believed that his open support jeopardized his position with the university. When he was denied promotion and tenure at Yale, he believed it was because of his radicalism. He was bitter and disillusioned with "academic freedom." It seemed that the struggle for Marxian studies would simply have to intensify.

He was offered a position both at the University of Toronto and at the New School for Social Research in New York City. He decided to remain in the United States, and, in the fall of 1970, joined the faculty of the New School as a professor of economics. Steve was the first tenured faculty member with responsibility for shaping a student-designed program in political economy. He was now free to teach courses on Marx and to develop his criticisms of economic theory. He continued to work on multinational corporations, incorporating much of what he had learned politically and intellectually into his analysis; he now saw the multinationals as a particular form of capitalist development and no longer viewed them as institutions that could be explained by the theories of oligopoly and the dynamic growth of firms.

He taught introductory courses in Marxian theory that emphasized the basic social and economic relationships of capitalism; many of the insights developed in this work were embodied in his paper "Robinson Crusoe and the Secret of Primitive Accumulation" (Chapter 4 of this book). He taught a course on the international economy that illustrated the different phases of mercantilism discussed in the paper he co-authored with Stephen Resnick, "International Trade and Uneven Development" (Chapter 5), but that also explored the characteristics of different modes of production, the transition from feudalism to capitalism, theories of imperialism, and the internationalization of capital. The course on the international economy formed the basis for a course in socioeconomic formations, applying and developing the tools of historical materialism.[13]

Steve also continued to work with groups in New Haven. His former researchers founded a consulting and research group that hoped to provide Third World countries with information on multinational corporations. The group examined how multinationals used women as a source of labor and affected most all aspects of their lives. Their research resulted in the publication of *A Bibliography on the Multinational Corporation*.[14] Steve continued his work with the Morning Sun Daycare and School, which his sons attended, and participated in meetings of the New Haven Union for Radical Political Economics. However, Steve and Gilda separated, and in the summer of 1973 they were divorced; Steve relocated in New York City.

By this time Steve had developed extensive international contacts in France, Italy, Latin America, and Africa. He spent several months in 1973 working with researchers at the Max-Planck-Institut at Starnberg, West Germany, on the internationalization of capital and labor.[15] He testified before the United Nations study group on multinational corporations.[16] In Canada, Steve's approach to economics influenced both academics and nonacademics. He visited Canada frequently to attend conferences, give seminars, and appear on the CBC. Indeed, he was often unaware of how important his influence was on the work of his fellow economists. Several people contacted him to arrange for translations of his collected essays, which have been published in Spanish, Italian, and Japanese.

At the end of his life, Steve's intellectual work was considerably enriched by his personal and political experiences. He had been struggling to combine analysis and practice, to integrate the personal and political as parts of his understanding and his being. The women's movement had helped focus his attention on hierarchy and authority. National liberation movements at home and abroad convinced him that these struggles would play a critical role in reshaping the world order. He hoped that his application of Marxian insights could aid these transformations. Toward that end, he was starting to work on a book that would pull together his work on capital accumulation, labor, and the international class struggle. The notes for this work were almost completed before his death.

Through all of this work, he was still developing his radical ideas about pedagogy. He was probably not appreciative of the strides he had made. He was one of the most exciting and inspiring teachers we had known. Many sat spellbound in his classes, following his brilliant insights and connections, until they were drawn, almost in spite of themselves, into lively discussions as Steve challenged and encouraged them to sharpen their ideas. During his early years at the New School, Steve doubted the importance of teaching – he was concerned that it reproduced certain authoritarian tendencies that he was trying to counter. Gradually, he came to see that teaching was an important political act. He believed that by encouraging the study and the application of Marxian ideas, he could make a substantial contribution to the broader movement. That commitment fueled his final efforts at developing a political economy program where students and activists could come together to study and to share ideas and experiences. He placed a high priority on joining with others to build this program at the New School. He lived to see the enrollment increase considerably and new faculty hired to teach political economy. The program was not seriously disrupted nor diminished as a result of his death, even though he was a principal founder; he had helped develop and encourage a group that could carry on what he helped to begin, and his spirit seemed to spark continuing effort.

His death was a great personal loss to many. At the time of his tragic accident, Steve had become one of the world's best-known Marxian scholars. He was making major contributions through fresh applications of Marxian analysis to new areas of research. He had integrated the dialectical method into his work and was, at the end of his life, finally integrating personal, political, and intellectual experiences in a way that permitted him to break out of the constraints of the traditional disciplines and his own personal habits of thought and action. One of the most tragic aspects of his death was that it happened just as he was finally beginning to put together a new personal and intellectual synthesis.

The late 1960s had been somewhat painful for him; he had been forced and was forcing himself to reexamine many of the traditional premises that had framed his personal life. In his last year or so, he was beginning to feel a sense both of personal accomplishment through continued struggle and of great excitement at the new directions and relationships that now seemed possible.

Many of his friends emphasized the extraordinary intellectual excitement Steve generated among his colleagues. His insights – brilliant, ordinary, and sometimes banal – stimulated many people to take substantial risks necessary for growth and development beyond the ordinary, beyond political timidity. Although he encouraged people to write, he believed more strongly in the importance of the oral tradition – the importance of sharing ideas and helping nurture them. We hope this book can convey some of the appreciation, love, and respect we had for him. So much of his later work remains in the form of notes, unwritten manuscripts, and in the "souls" of those he worked with and inspired. Perhaps the great contribution he would have made to a radical analysis of society remains unfinished, but he has shown the way for some, and brought so many of us to the point where we can begin.

For Stephen Hymer – a propos 1966

A memorial poem by Ama Ata Aidoo, Cape Coast, Ghana

Steve,
When we try
To be fair
       and
Objective
       like they
Keep
Whining at us to be:
Such painful
Such grudging
Admissions
Break –

On
Who came good-intentioned.

And
We silently cry for
All wonder-face clouded
By the dust of
Bitter history,
As we sit beside
This
Latter-day Babylon,
Our minds
Aching for the respite of
Ancient glorious gone, and
Future miracles unperformed.

Yet
Who could have done more with
Time flying on complex skates
Abreast
Fanged doomcasters and

Their agents who lick

Bloody lips
Savoring –
     in advance –
The Fall
For which they had
Schemed?

Some brotherhood of man.

While
Siblings, friends, and
Comrades
Endlessly fought, disputed, bitched
On such
Great questions as

Where
Our well-wishers chose to grow
Their
Rice!!

So that if we still grieve
For you and Roger* and
Us – the so-called Living –
It's only because
Death visits us in more ways
Than One,
Stephen.

But enough.
We have been back to the old
Campsite.
Not
All the grains you scattered
Died.

Some have
Sprouted too –
Fighting their slow way
Through sharp thorns
Long droughts
Brutal Fingering and
Such
     and such and
Such . . .

*Roger Genoud – a mutual friend, ex-member of the Swiss Communist Party, and
first Director of the Ghana Institute of Languages, who died in June 1973.

Publications and research papers of Stephen Herbert Hymer

1960

The International Operations of National Firms: A Study of Direct Foreign Investment (Cambridge, Mass.: M.I.T. Press, 1976). Hymer's doctoral dissertation, Massachusetts Institute of Technology, June 1960.

1962

"Turnover of Firms as a Measure of Market Behavior," *Review of Economics and Statistics,* Vol. XLIV, No. 1, February 1962, pp. 82–7, with B. P. Pashigian.
"Firm Size and Rate of Growth," *Journal of Political Economy,* Vol. LXX, No. 6, December 1962, pp. 556–69, with B. P. Pashigian.

1964

"Reply: Firm Size and Rate of Growth," *Journal of Political Economy,* Vol. LXXII, No. 1, February 1964, pp. 83–4, with B. P. Pashigian.

1965

"Investment in the Ghana Cocoa Industry: Some Problems of Structure and Policy," *Economic Bulletin,* Vol. IX, No. 1, 1965, pp. 16–23, with Reginald H. Green.

1966

"The Introduction of Cocoa in the Gold Coast: A Study in the Relations between African Farmers and Colonial Agricultural Experts," Yale University Economic Growth Center Discussion Paper No. 1, February 18, 1966, with Reginald H. Green. Published as "Cocoa in the Gold Coast: A Study in the Relationship between African Farmers and Agricultural Experts," *Journal of Economic History,* Vol. XXVI, No. 3, September 1966, pp. 299–319, with Reginald H. Green.
"Antitrust and American Direct Investment Abroad," *International Aspects of Antitrust,* Hearings before the Subcommittee on Antitrust and Monopoly of the Committee on the Judiciary, U.S. Senate, 89th Congress: 2d Session, April 20, 1966, pp. 19–32.

"Comments on the Transfer of Technical Knowledge by International Corporations to Developing Economies," *Papers and Proceedings of the American Economic Association,* May 1966, pp. 275–7.

"Cocoa in the Gold Coast: A Study in the Relationship Between African Farmers and Agricultural Experts," *Journal of Economic History,* Vol. XXVI, No. 3, September 1966, pp. 299–319, with Reginald H. Green.

"Direct Foreign Investment and the National Economic Interest," in Peter Russell, ed., *Nationalism in Canada* (Toronto: McGraw-Hill Ryerson, 1966), pp. 191–202.

"The Decision to Own a Foreign Enterprise," Yale University Economic Growth Center Discussion Paper No. 13, Nov. 16, 1966.

1967

"The Responsiveness of Agrarian Economies and the Importance of Z Goods," Yale University Economic Growth Center Discussion Paper No. 25, April 29, 1967; revised as Discussion Paper No. 39a, October 1, 1967, with Stephen Resnick.

"A Note on the Constancy of the Real Wage," Yale University Economic Growth Center Discussion Paper No. 39, October 17, 1967, with Stephen Resnick.

1968

"Transatlantic Reactions to Foreign Investment," Yale University Economic Growth Center Discussion Paper No. 53, April 18, 1968.

"The Radical Centre – Carter Reconsidered," *Canadian Forum,* June 1968, with Melville H. Watkins.

Review of *The Teaching of Development Economics,* Kurt Martin and John Knapp, eds. (Chicago: Aldine, 1967), *Journal of Finance,* Fall 1968, pp. 719–21.

"Offering Options to the 'Third World,' " in University League for Social Reform, Toronto, *An Independent Foreign Policy for Canada?,* Stephen Clarkson, ed. (Toronto: McClelland and Steward, 1968), pp. 226–43, with Brian Van Arkadie.

"The Impact of the Multinational Firm," in Colloque sur la politique industrielle de l'europe integrée et l'apport des capitaux extérieurs, Paris, 1966, M. Byé, ed., *La Politique industrielle de l'europe integrée et l'apport des capitaux extérieurs* (Travaux et recherches de la Faculté de droit et des sciences economiques de Paris, Série Europe, No. 7) (Paris: Presses Universitaires de France, 1968). Also published as Yale University Economic Growth Center Discussion Paper No. 6, May 17, 1966.

"The Multinational Corporation: An Analysis of Some Motives for International Business Integration," *Revue Economique,* Vol. XIX, No. 6, November 1968, pp. 949–73.

"National Policies Towards Multinational Corporations," a background report prepared for the study: Canada, Task Force on the Structure of Canadian Industry, *Foreign Ownership and the Structure of Canadian Industry* (Ottawa: Queen's Printer, 1968). This report is in mimeographed form.

1969

"Interactions Between the Government and the Private Sector: An Analysis of Government Expenditure Policy and the Reflection Ratio," in Ian Stewart, ed., *Economic Development and Structural Change* (Edinburgh: Edinburgh University Press, 1969), pp. 155–80, with Stephen Resnick. Published in French as "Les Interactions entre le Gouvernement et le Secteur Prive," *L'Actualite Economique,* No. 3, October–December 1968.

"A Note on the Capacity to Transform and the Welfare Costs of Foreign Trade Fluctuations," *Economic Journal,* December 1969, pp. 833–46, with R. Albert Berry.

"A Model of an Agrarian Economy with Nonagricultural Activities," *American Economic Review,* September 1969, pp. 493–506, with Stephen Resnick.

"The Crisis and Drama of the Global Partnership," *International Journal,* Winter 1969–70, pp. 184–91, with Stephen Resnick.

"Capital and Wealth in the Development Process," Yale University Economic Growth Center Discussion Paper No. 63, 1969, with Stephen Resnick.

1970

"External Aid in the Region: Effects and Influences," International Conference on Hemispheric Relations in the Caribbean, University of the West Indies, Mona, Jamaica, Jan. 5–8, 1970.

"Multinational Corporations and International Oligopoly: The Non-American Challenge," in C. P. Kindleberger, ed., *The International Corporation* (Cambridge, Mass.: M.I.T. Press, 1970), pp. 57–91, with Robert Rowthorn.

"Economic Forms in Pre-Colonial Ghana," *Journal of Economic History,* Vol. XXX, No. 1, March 1970, pp. 33–50.

"Notes on Dependency and Interdependency in the World Economy," April 1970, with Osvaldo Sunkel.

"The Efficiency (Contradictions) of Multinational Corporations," *American Economic Review,* Vol. LX, No. 2, May 1970, pp. 441–8.

"Capital and Capitalists," foreword to Polly Hill, *Studies in Rural Capitalism in West Africa* (Cambridge: Cambridge University Press, 1970).

Statement in *The Multinational Corporation and International Investment,* Hearings before the Subcommittee on Foreign Economic Policy of the Joint Economic Committee, 91st Congress, 2d Session, July 30, 1970.

International Big Business 1957–67 (Cambridge: Cambridge University Press, 1970), by Robert Rowthorn in collaboration with Stephen Hymer.

"International Trade and Uneven Development," in J. N. Bhagwati, R. W. Jones, R. A. Mundell, and Jaroslav Vanek, eds., *Trade, Balance of Payments and Growth* (Amsterdam: North-Holland Publishing Co., 1970), pp. 473–94, with Stephen Resnick.

1971

"The Multinational Corporation and the Law of Uneven Development," in J. W. Bhagwati, ed., *Economics and World Order* (New York: World Law Fund, 1971), pp. 113–40. Published in German as "Multinationale Konzerne und das Gesetz der ungleichen Entwicklung," in Dieter Senghass, ed., *Imperialismus und Structurelle Gewalt: Analysen über abhängige Reproduction* (Frankfurt: Suhrkamp Verlag, 1972).

"International Production," Discussion Meeting Report, Council on Foreign Relations, New York, March 23, 1971.

"Comment on R. J. Barnet, 'Can the United States Promote Foreign Development,' " Overseas Development Council Paper 6, July 1971.

"Robinson Crusoe and the Secret of Primitive Accumulation," *Monthly Review,* September 1971, pp. 11–36.

"Partners in Development: The Multinational Corporation and its Allies," *Newstatements,* Vol. I, No. 1, 1971. Published in French as "La Croissance de la Grande Firme Multinationale," Colloques Internationaux du Centre National de la Recherche Scientifique, Centre National de la Recherche Scientifique, Rennes, September 28–30, 1972.

"Comments on Public and Private Enterprise in Africa," in G. Ranis, ed., *Government and Economic Development* (New Haven, Conn.: Yale University Press, 1971), pp. 123–5.

"The Political Economy of the Gold Coast and Ghana," in G. Ranis, ed., *Government and Economic Development* (New Haven, Conn.: Yale University Press, 1971), pp. 129–78.

1972

"Is the Multinational Corporation Doomed?," *Innovation,* No. 28, February 1972, pp. 3–16.

"The Internationalization of Capital," *Journal of Economic Issues,* Vol. 6, No. 1, March 1972, pp. 91–111.

"The Multinational Corporation: Your Home is Our Home," *Canadian Dimension,* March/April 1972, pp. 29–38.

"On Tinkering with Takeovers and Leaving Capitalism to Flourish," *Canadian Dimension,* June 1972, pp. 7, 47.

"Statistical Abstract," in G. B. Kay, ed., *The Political Economy of Colonialism in Ghana* (Cambridge: Cambridge University Press, 1972), pp. 305–419, with G. B. Kay.

"The United States Multinational Corporation and Japanese Competition in the Pacific," *Chuokoron-sha,* Spring 1972.

"Some Empirical Facts about U.S. Investment Abroad," in P. Drysdale, ed., *Direct Foreign Investment in Asia and the Pacific* (Canberra: Australian National University Press, 1972), pp. 19–58.

"The Political Economy of the New Left," *Quarterly Journal of Economics,* November 1972, pp. 644–57, with Frank Roosevelt.

1973

"Comment on Louis T. Wells, Jr.," in Eliezer B. Ayal, ed., *Micro Aspects of Development* (New York: Praeger, 1973), pp. 177–180.

"Notes on the United Nations Report on International Corporations in World Development," *Testimony Before the Group of Eminent Persons to Study the Impact of Multinational Corporations on Development and on International Relations* (Geneva: United Nations, November 6, 1973), UN Document No. E.74.II.A.9.

1975

"International Politics and International Economics: A Radical Approach," in Leon N. Lindberg, R. Alford, C. Crouch, C. Offe, ed., *Stress and Contradiction in*

Modern Capitalism (Lexington, Mass.: Lexington Books, 1975), pp. 355–72. Published posthumously.

1977

A Bibliography on the Multinational Corporation, by Leah Margulies, Judith Miller, Paul Semonin, Florika Remetier (San Francisco: Earthwork, April 1977), with Stephen Hymer.

Unpublished manuscripts and research

"The Impact of the International Economy on the Gold Coast 1900–1950," 1962, work in progress.

"Direct Foreign Investment and International Oligopoly," June 30, 1965.

"International Firms and International Capital Markets," November 15, 1965.

"Historical Economic Documents and Statistics of Ghana," April 27, 1966, draft of a book, with G. B. Kay and Reginald H. Green.

"The Multinational Corporation and the Nation-State," outline and reference bibliography, January 1968.

"The Multinational Corporation: An Analysis of Some of the Motives for International Business Integration," 1968.

"The Political Economy of Capital in the Gold Coast and Ghana," 1969, draft manuscript for a country study of Ghana.

"Multinational Corporation Bibliography (Draft)," report to the Canadian Science Council, July 1970, with Paul Semonin.

"The Multinational Corporation and the International Division of Labor," 1970.

"Corporate Structure and Urban Dualism: A Research Proposal," Stephen Hymer, Thomas Vietorisz, William W. Goldsmith, Bennett Harrison, Robert B. Cohen, Matthew Edel, and Thomas Reiner, background paper, Session on Social Stratification, Econometrics Society, New Orleans Meeting, December 1971, mimeograph.

"Political Economy of International Oil," 1972.

"Labor Unions and Economic Transformation in Advanced Industrial Countries," a proposal, 1973, with David M. Gordon, mimeograph.

Translations

Empresas Multinacionales: La Internacionalizacion Del Capital (Buenos Aires: Ediciones Periferia, 1972). Editions of *Essays on the Multinational Corporation* are also published in Italian and Japanese.

Notes

General introduction

1 Stephen Hymer, *The International Operations of National Firms: A Study in Direct Foreign Investment* (Cambridge, Mass.: M.I.T. Press, 1976). Hymer's doctoral dissertation, Massachusetts Institute of Technology, June 1960.

2 C. Fred Bergsten, Thomas Horst, and Theodore H. Moran, *American Multinationals and American Interests* (Washington, D.C.: Brookings Institution, 1977), Chapter 8, p. 6.

3 Bertil Ohlin, *Interregional and International Trade* (Cambridge, Mass.: Harvard University Press, 1933).

4 Charles P. Kindleberger, *International Economics*, 5th edition (Homewood, Ill.: Richard D. Irwin, 1973), p. 227.

5 R. Z. Aliber, "The Theory of Direct Foreign Investment," in C. P. Kindleberger, ed., *The International Corporation* (Cambridge, Mass.: M.I.T. Press, 1970), pp. 17–34.

6 David Forsyth, *United States Investment in Scotland* (New York: Praeger, 1972), p. 211.

7 Kindleberger, *International Economics, op cit.*, p. 210.

8 Hymer, *International Operations of National Firms, op. cit.*, p. 25.

9 *Ibid.*, p. 91.

10 *Ibid.*, p. 94.

11 Charles Cooper, "The Transfer of Industrial Technology to the Underdeveloped Countries," *Bulletin*, Institute of Development Studies, University of Sussex, England, Vol. 3, No. 1, October 1970, p. 3.

12 For a more complete discussion concerning the types and effects of technology transfers on development, see: Cooper, "Transfer of Industrial Technology," *op. cit.*, pp. 3–7; Constantine V. Vaitsos, "Bargaining and the Distribution of Returns in the Purchase of Technology by Developing Countries," *Bulletin*, Institute of Development Studies, University of Sussex, England, Vol. 3, No. 1, October 1970, pp. 16–23; G. K. Helleiner, "Transnational Enterprise, Manufactured Exports and Employment in Less Developed Countries," *Economic and Political Weekly*, Vol. XI, Nos. 5, 6, and 7, February 1976, pp. 247–62; "Special Issue on Conflict and Bargaining," Sanjaya Lall, ed., *World Development*, Vol. 4, No. 3, March 1976 (see especially the article by Raphael Kaplinsky, "Accumulation and the Transfer of Technology: Issues of Conflict and Mechanisms for the Exercise of Control," pp. 197–224).

13 C. P. Kindleberger, *American Business Abroad* (New Haven, Conn.: Yale University Press, 1969). This part of the introduction draws much of its review of the work of Kindleberger and Dunning from the survey article by the late György Ádám, *The World Corporation Problematics: Apologetics and Critique* (Budapest: Hungarian Scientific Council for World Economy, 1971).

14 Kindleberger, *American Business Abroad, op. cit.*, p. 35, as cited in Ádám, *World Corporation, op. cit.*, p. 15.

15 Kindleberger, *American Business Abroad, op. cit.*, pp. 179–82.

16 This critique is made by Ádám, *World Corporation, op. cit.*, p. 15, and also has been made by Professor Melville Watkins, in the *Proceedings* of the Conference on the Politics on International Business, sponsored by *Daedalus*, Journal of the American Academy of Arts and Sciences, December 6–7, 1968, mimeograph.

17 Richard E. Caves, *International Trade, International Investment, and Imperfect Markets* (Princeton, N.J.: International Finance Section, Department of Economics, Princeton University, 1974), p. 26.

18 Adolf Berle and Gardiner C. Means, *The Modern Corporation and Private Property* (New York: Macmillan, 1932).

19 Edith Penrose, *The Large International Firm in Developing Countries: The International Petroleum Industry* (London: George Allen and Unwin, 1968), p. 272.

20 *Ibid.*, p. 273.

21 *Ibid.*, p. 268.

22 See Penrose's written and oral statement and replies to questions in "The United Nations Report on International Corporations in World Development," *Testimony before the Group of Eminent Persons to Study the Impact of Multinational Corporations on Development and on International Relations* (Geneva: United Nations, November 6, 1973), UN Document No. E.74.II.A.9, pp. 336–48.

23 John Dunning, *The Role of American Investment in the U.K. Economy*, Broadsheet No. 507, Political and Economic Planning, February 1969, as cited in Ádám, *World Corporation, op. cit.*, pp. 25–6.

24 John Dunning, "Further Thoughts on Foreign Investment," *Moorgate and Wall Street*, Autumn 1966, p. 26, as cited in Ádám, *World Corporation, op. cit.*, p. 28.

25 *Ibid.*, p. 32, as cited in Ádám *World Corporation, op. cit.*, p. 29.

26 *Ibid.*

27 R. Vernon, *Sovereignty at Bay* (New York: Basic Books, 1971), p. 109.

28 R. Vernon, "Storm Over the Multinationals: Problems and Prospects," *Foreign Affairs*, January 1977, pp. 243–62, and R. Vernon, "An Interpretation," in R. Vernon, ed., *The Oil Crisis* (New York: W. W. Norton, 1976), pp. 1–14.

29 Vernon, "An Interpretation," in Vernon, ed., *Oil Crisis, op. cit.*, pp. 12–14.

30 Y. Tsurumi, "Japan," in Vernon, ed., *Oil Crisis, op. cit.*, pp. 113–28.

31 Vernon, *Sovereignty at Bay*, pp. 134–45.

32 Vernon, "An Interpretation," in Vernon, ed., *Oil Crisis, op. cit.*, p. 8.

33 Vernon, "Storm Over the Multinationals," *op. cit.*, p. 251.

34 *Ibid.*, pp. 252, 260.

35 Vernon, "The Distribution of Power," in Vernon, ed., *Oil Crisis, op. cit.*, pp. 245–57.

36 G. W. Ball, *Diplomacy for a Crowded World: An American Foreign Policy* (Boston: Little, Brown, and Company, 1976), pp. 278–9.

37 *Ibid.*, p. 280.

38 *Ibid.*, p. 291.

39   *Ibid.*, p. 293.
40   *Ibid.*, p. 294.
41   *Ibid.*
42   R. Vernon, "Introduction," in D. Kujawa, ed., *International Labor and the Multinational Enterprise* (New York: Praeger, 1975), p. ix.
43   *Ibid.*, pp. viii, ix.
44   *Ibid.*, p. ix.
45   *Ibid.*, p. x.
46   *Ibid.*
47   *Ibid.*, p. xi.
48   *Ibid.*
49   D. Kujawa, "Transnational Industrial Relations: A Collective Bargaining Prospect," in Kujawa, ed., *International Labor and the Multinational Enterprise, op. cit.,* p. 97.
50   *Ibid.*, p. 97.
51   *Ibid.*, pp. 97–119.
52   *Ibid.*, p. 126.
53   *Ibid.*, p. 127.
54   D. Kujawa, ed., *American Labor and the Multinational Corporation* (New York: Praeger, 1973), p. 4.
55   J. Polk, "American Labor and the United States Multinational Enterprise in an Emerging World Economy," in Kujawa, ed., *American Labor and the Multinational Corporation, op. cit.*, pp. 270–85.
56   *Ibid.*, p. 279.
57   *Ibid.*, pp. 279–80.
58   *Ibid.*, 280–1.
59   *Ibid.*, p. 281.
60   *Ibid.*
61   C. Levinson, *Capital, Inflation and the Multinationals* (New York: Macmillan, 1971), p. 217.
62   *Ibid.*, p. 205.
63   *Ibid.*, pp. 205–6.
64   *Ibid.*, p. 221.
65   R. Cox, "Labor and the Multinationals," *Foreign Affairs*, Vol. 54, No. 2, January 1976, pp. 344–65.
66   *Ibid.*, pp. 351–2.
67   *Ibid.*, pp. 353–5.
68   *Ibid.*, p. 356.
69   *Ibid.*, p. 359.
70   *Ibid.*, p. 365.
71   P. P. Streeten and S. Lall, *Summary of Methods and Findings of Private Foreign Manufacturing Investment in Six Developing Countries* (Geneva, UNCTAD, May 1973) (in 3 parts), part i, *Methodology Used in Studies on Private Foreign Investment in Selected Developing Countries*, TD/B/C 3(VI)/Misc. 6, p. 1.
72   P. P. Streeten and S. Lall, *Summary, op. cit.*, part iii, *Main Findings of a Study of Private Foreign Investment in Selected Developing Countries*, TD/B/C 3/111, p. 21.
73   *Ibid.*
74   *Ibid.*, p. 62.
75   *Ibid.*, pp. 25–6.
76   *Ibid.*, pp. 27–9.

77   R. Barnet and R. Müller, *Global Reach: The Power of the Multinational Corporations* (New York: Simon and Schuster, 1974), p. 133.
78   *Ibid.*, p. 134.
79   *Ibid.*, p. 135.
80   *Ibid.*
81   *Ibid.*, p. 214.
82   *Ibid.*, p. 216.
83   *Ibid.*, p. 363.
84   *Ibid.*, p. 364.
85   *Ibid.*, p. 367.
86   *Ibid.*, p. 369.
87   *Ibid.*, p. 370.
88   *Ibid.*, p. 373.
89   *Ibid.*, p. 366.
90   *Ibid.*, p. 367.
91   *Ibid.*, p. 368.
92   V. I. Lenin, "Imperialism, the Highest Stage of Capitalism," *Selected Works in 3 Volumes* (Moscow: Progress Publishers, 1967), Vol. 1.
93   *Ibid.*, p. 745.
94   *Ibid.*, pp. 745–6.
95   *Ibid.*, p. 683.
96   *Ibid.*
97   *Ibid.*, p. 774.
98   *Ibid.*
99   P. A. Baran and Paul M. Sweezy, "Notes on the Theory of Imperialism," *Monthly Review*, March 1966, pp. 15–31.
100 H. Magdoff, "Notes on the Multinational Corporation," in Paul M. Sweezy and Harry Magdoff, *The Dynamics of American Capitalism* (New York: Monthly Review Press, 1972), pp. 88–112.
101 *Ibid.*, p. 102.
102 *Ibid.*, p. 95.
103 Baran and Sweezy, "Notes on the Theory of Imperialism," *op. cit.*, pp. 15–31.
104 S. Amin, "Towards a New Structural Crisis of the Capitalist System?," in Carl Widstrand, ed., *Multinational Firms in Africa* (Dakar and Uppsala: African Institute for Economic Development and Planning and Scandinavian Institute of African Studies, 1975), pp. 3–25.
105 *Ibid.*, p. 3.
106 *Ibid.*, p. 7.
107 S. Amin, *Accumulation on a World Scale, Vol. 1* (New York: Monthly Review Press, 1974), p. 25.
108 *Ibid.*, pp. 91–136.
109 Stephen Hymer, New Haven Marxist History Conference, New Haven, Conn., February 25, 1973.
110 Stephen Hymer, "The Multinational Corporation and the Law of Uneven Development," Chapter 2 of this volume.
111 Christian Palloix, "The Self-Expansion of Capital on a World Scale," *Review of Radical Political Economics*, Vol. 9, No. 2, Summer 1977, pp. 1–28; and "The Internationalization of Capital and the Circuit of Social Capital," in Hugo Radice, ed., *International Firms and Modern Imperialism* (Harmondsworth, England: Penguin Books, Ltd., 1975), pp 63–88.
112 Amin, *Accumulation on a World Scale, op. cit.*, p. 35.

113   *Ibid.*, p. 96.
114   *Ibid.*, pp. 122–3.
115   Stephen Hymer, "The United States Multinational Corporations and Japanese Competition in the Pacific," Chapter 10 of this volume.
116   *Ibid.*, pp. 253-4.
117   R. Hilferding, *Das Finanzkapital* (Vienna: 1910), and V. I. Lenin, "Imperialism," *op. cit.*
118   Nikolai Bukharin, *Imperialism and World Economy* (New York: Monthly Review Press, 1973; originally published in 1929), p. 106.
119   S. Hymer, "The Internationalization of Capital," Chapter 3 of this volume, p. 75.
120   *Ibid.*
121   Karl Marx, *Capital,* 3 vols. (New York: International Publishers, 1967), Vol. III, p. 198.
122   S. Hymer, "International Politics and International Economics: A Radical Approach," Chapter 11 of this volume, pp. 271–2.
123   G. Ádám, "Multinational Corporations and Worldwide Sourcing," in Radice, ed., *International Firms and Modern Imperialism, op. cit.*, pp. 89–103; and Palloix, "Internationalization of Capital," *op. cit.,* pp. 63–88.
124   Stephen Hymer, from notes on K. Marx, *Capital,* unpublished ms., 1972, no pagination, New York City.
125   Ádám, "Multinational Corporations and Worldwide Sourcing," *op. cit.*, p. 90.
126   Baran and Sweezy, "Notes on a Theory of Imperialism," *op. cit.*, pp. 15–31.
127   Magdoff, *Dynamics of American Capitalism, op. cit.*, pp. 88–112.
128   *Ibid.*, p. 111.
129   Bill Warren, "How International is Capital?," in Radice, ed., *International Firms and Modern Imperialism, op. cit.*, pp. 135–41.
130   *Ibid.*, p. 138.
131   *Ibid.*, pp. 139–40.
132   R. Murray, "The Internationalization of Capital and the Nation-State," in Radice, ed., *International Firms and Modern Imperialism, op. cit.*, pp. 110–15.
133   *Ibid.*, pp. 117–19.
134   Stephen Hymer, "The Efficiency (Contradictions) of Multinational Corporations," Chapter 1 of this volume.
135   Stephen Hymer and Robert Rowthorn, "Multinational Corporations and International Oligopoly: The Non-American Challenge," Chapter 8 of this volume.
136   Hymer, "Internationalization of Capital," *op. cit.*, pp. 19–20.

Part I. The nature and contradictions of the multinational corporation: introduction

1   Kari Levitt, "Economic Dependence and Political Disintegration: The Case of Canada," *New World Quarterly,* Jamaica, 1968.
2   Kari Levitt, *Silent Surrender: The Multinational Corporation in Canada* (Toronto: Macmillan of Canada, 1970).
3   Lloyd Best and Kari Levitt, "Externally Propelled Growth and Industrialization in the Caribbean," McGill University, Montreal, 1968, mimeographed.
4   Stephen Hymer and R. H. Green, "Investment in the Ghana Cocoa Industry: Some Problems of Structure and Policy," *Economic Bulletin,* Vol. IX, No. 1, 1965, pp. 16–23. Stephen Hymer and R. H. Green, "Cocoa in the Gold Coast: A

Study in the Relationship between African Farmers and Agricultural Experts," *Journal of Economic History,* Vol. XXVI, No. 3, September 1966, pp. 299–319. Stephen Hymer and Stephen Resnick, "A Model of an Agrarian Economy with Nonagricultural Activities," *American Economic Review,* September 1969, pp. 493–506. Stephen Hymer, "Economic Forms in Pre-Colonial Ghana," *Journal of Economic History,* Vol. XXX, No. 1, March 1970, pp. 33–50.

5   Lloyd Best, "Outline of a Model of Pure Plantation Economy," *Social and Economic Studies,* Vol. XVII, No. 3, May 1968, pp. 283–326. G. L. Beckford, "The Economics of Agricultural Resource Use and Development in Plantation Economies," *Social and Economic Studies,* Vol. XVIII, No. 4, December 1969, pp. 321–47. G. L. Beckford, "The Dynamics of Growth and the Nature of Metropolitan Plantation Enterprise," *Social and Economic Studies,* Vol. XIX, No. 4, December 1970, pp. 435–65. Norman Girvan, *The Caribbean Bauxite Industry* (Kingston, Jamaica: Institute for Social and Economic Research, University of the West Indies, 1967). Norman Girvan, "Multinational Corporations and Dependent Underdevelopment in Mineral Export Economies," *Social and Economic Studies,* Vol. XIX, No. 4, December 1970, pp. 490–526.

6   Stephen Hymer, "External Aid in the Region: Effects and Influences in 1970," International Conference on Hemispheric Relations in the Caribbean, University of the West Indies, Mona, Jamaica, January 5–8, 1970.

7   O. Sunkel, "Politica Nacional de Desarrollo y Dependencia Externa," *Estudios Internacionales,* Vol. I, No. 1, April 1967, pp. 43–75. O. Sunkel, "Capitalism o Transnacionale y Desintegracion Nacional en la America Latina," *Estudios Internacionales,* Vol. IV, No. 16, January 1971, pp. 3–61.

8   D. H. Robertson, quoted in R. H. Coase, "The Nature of the Firm," *Economica* (N.S.), Vol. IV, 1937, pp. 386–405.

9   Alfred D. Chandler, Jr. *Strategy and Structure: Chapters in the History of the American Industrial Enterprise* (Cambridge, Mass.: M.I.T. Press, 1962). Alfred D. Chandler, Jr. and Fritz Redlich, "Recent Developments in American Business Administration and their Conceptualization," *Business History Review,* Spring 1961, pp. 103–28.

10 Joseph A. Schumpeter, *The Theory of Economic Development* (Cambridge, Mass.: Harvard University Press, 1949).

11 George Ball, *The Global Companies: The Political Economy of World Business* (Englewood Cliffs, N.J.: Prentice-Hall, 1975).

1. The efficiency (contradictions) of multinational corporations

1   D. H. Robertson, quoted in R. H. Coase, "The Nature of the Firm," *Economica* (N.S.) Vol. IV, 1937, pp. 386–405. Reprinted in G. S. Stigler and K. E. Boulding, *Readings in Price Theory* (Homewood, Ill.: Richard D. Irwin, 1937).

2   Alfred D. Chandler, Jr., *Strategy and Structure: Chapters in the History of the American Industrial Enterprise* (New York: Doubleday & Co., 1961).

3   Alfred D. Chandler, Jr., and Fritz Redlich, "Recent Developments in American Business Administration and their Conceptualization," *Business History Review,* Spring 1961, pp. 103–28.

4   Stephen Hymer and Stephen Resnick, "International Trade and Uneven Development," in J. N. Bhagwati, R. W. Jones, R. A. Mundell, and J. Vanek, eds., *Trade, Balance of Payments and Growth* (Amsterdam: North-Holland, 1970), pp. 473–94 (reprinted as Chapter 5 of this volume).

5   See also Stephen Hymer, "Direct Foreign Investment and the National

Economic Interest," in Peter Russell, ed., *Nationalism in Canada* (Toronto: McGraw-Hill Ryerson, 1966), pp. 191–202 (reprinted as Chapter 7 of this volume); "The Impact of the Multinational Firm," in Colloque sur la politique industrielle de l'Europe integrée et l'apport des capitaux extérieurs, Paris, 1966. M. Bye, ed., *La Politique industrielle de l'europe integrée et l'apport des capitaux extérieurs* (Travaux et recherches de la Faculté de droit et des sciences economiques de Paris, Série Europe, No. 7) (Paris: Presses Universitaires de France, 1968).

6 Sean Gervasi, "Publicité et Croissance Economique," *Economie et Humanisme,* November–December 1964; Harry Johnson, "The Political Economy of Opulence," *The Canadian Quandary* (Toronto: McGraw-Hill Ryerson, 1962).

7 Alfred Marshall, *Principles of Economics, 9th ed.* (New York: Macmillan, 1961), p. 745.

8 This point is developed more fully in Stephen Hymer, "The Multinational Corporation and the Law of Uneven Development," in J. Bhagwati, ed., *Economics and World Order* (New York: World Law Fund, 1971) (reprinted as Chapter 2 of this volume).

9 For a stimulating analysis of the relationship of multinational corporations to economic development, see: G. Arrighi, "International Corporations, Labour Aristocracies, and Economic Development in Tropical Africa," in Robert I. Rhodes, ed., *Imperialism and Underdevelopment* (New York: Monthly Review Press, 1970), pp. 202–67; N. Girvan, "Regional Integration vs. Vertical Integration in the Utilization of Caribbean Bauxite," Lewis and Matthew, eds., *Caribbean Integration* (San Juan: Institute of Caribbean Studies, University of Puerto Rico, 1967).

10 Stephen Hymer and Stephen Resnick, "Interactions Between the Government and the Private Sector: An Analysis of Government Expenditure Policy and the Reflection Ratio," in Ian Stewart, ed., *Economic Development and Structural Change* (Edinburgh: Edinburgh University Press, 1969), pp. 155–80; published in French as "Les Interactions entre le Gouvernement et le Secteur Prive," *L'Actualite Economique,* October–December 1968.

11 For an attempt to predict the trend toward multinationalism and the problems it causes, see Stephen Hymer and Robert Rowthorn, "Multinational Corporations and International Oligopoly: The Non-American Challenge," in C. P. Kindleberger, ed., *The International Corporation* (Cambridge, Mass.: M.I.T. Press, 1970), pp. 57–91 (reprinted as Chapter 8 of this volume).

2. The multinational corporation and the law of uneven development

1 See Karl Marx, *Capital,* 3 vols. (New York: International Publishers, 1967), Vol. I, Chapter XXV, "The General Law of Capitalist Accumulation," Chapter XIII, "Co-operation," and Chapter XIV, part 4, "Division of Labour in Manufacture and Division of Labour in Society"; and *Capital,* Vol. III, Chapter XXIII, "Interest and Profit of Enterprise."

2 Phrase used by A. M. Salomon in *International Aspects of Antitrust,* Part I, Hearings before the Sub-Committee on Antitrust and Monopoly of the Senate Committee on the Judiciary, April 1966, p. 49.

3 These trends are discussed in S. Hymer and R. Rowthorn, "Multinational Corporations and International Oligopoly: the Non-American Challenge," in C. P. Kindleberger, ed., *The International Corporation* (Cambridge, Mass.: M.I.T. Press, 1970) (reprinted as Chapter 8 of this volume).

4 Substituting the word *multinational corporation* for *bourgeois* in the following quote from *The Communist Manifesto* provides a more dynamic picture of the multinational corporation than any of its present-day supporters have dared to put forth.

"The need of a constantly expanding market for its products chases the multinational corporation over the whole surface of the globe. It must nestle everywhere, settle everywhere, establish connections everywhere. The bourgeoisie has through its exploitation of the world-market given a cosmopolitan character to production and consumption in every country. To the great chagrin of Reactionists, it has drawn from under the feet of industry the national ground on which it stood. All old-established national industries have been destroyed or are daily being destroyed. They are dislodged by new industries, whose introduction becomes a life and death question for all civilized nations, by industries that no longer work up indigenous raw material, but raw material drawn from the remotest zones; industries whose products are consumed, not only at home, but in every quarter of the globe. In place of the old wants, satisfied by the production of the country, we find new wants, requiring for their satisfaction the products of distant lands and climes. In place of the old local and national seclusion and self-sufficiency, we have intercourse in every direction, universal interdependence of nations. And as in material, so also in intellectual production. The intellectual creations of individual nations become common property. National one-sidedness and narrow-mindedness become more and more impossible, and from the numerous national and local literatures there arises a world literature."

"The multinational corporation, by the rapid improvement of all instruments of production, by the immensely facilitated means of communication, draws all, even the most barbarian, nations into civilization. The cheap prices of its commodities are the heavy artillery with which it batters down all Chinese walls, with which it forces the barbarians' intensely obstinate hatred of foreigners to capitulate. It compels all nations, on pain of extinction, to adopt the bourgeois mode of production, it compels them to introduce what it calls civilization into their midst, i.e., to become bourgeois themselves. In a word, it creates a world after its own image."

"The multinational corporation has subjected the country to the rule of the towns. It has created enormous cities, has greatly increased the urban population as compared with the rural, and has thus rescued a considerable part of the population from the idiocy of rural life. Just as it has made the country dependent on the towns, so it has made barbarian and semi-barbarian countries dependent on the civilized ones, nations of peasants on nations of bourgeois, the East on the West."

"The multinational corporation keeps more and more doing away with the scattered state of the population, of the means of production, and of property. It has agglomerated population, centralized means of production, and has concentrated property in a few hands. The necessary consequence of this was political centralization. Independent, or but loosely connected provinces, with separate interests, laws, systems of taxation, and governments, became lumped together in one nation, with one government, one code of laws, one national class-interest, one frontier, and one customs tariff."

5 John Powers, *The Multinational Corporation* (New York: Pfizer Public Relations Department, 1967).

6 See R. H. Coase for an analysis of the boundary between the firm and the market: "Outside the firm, price movements direct production which is coordinated through a series of exchange transactions on the market. Within the firm

these market transactions are eliminated and in place of the complicated market structure with exchange transactions, is substituted the entrepreneur co-ordinator who directs production." R. H. Coase, "The Nature of the Firm," reprinted in G. J. Stigler and K. E. Boulding, *Readings in Price Theory* (Homewood, Ill.: Richard D. Irwin, 1952).

7   "Even in the very backward countries we find highly specialized trades: but we do not find the work within each trade so divided up that the planning and arrangement of the business, its management and its risks, are borne by one set of people, while the manual work required for it is done by hired labour. This form of division of labour is at once characteristic of the modern world generally and of the English race in particular. It may be swept away by the further growth of that free enterprise which has called it into existence. But for the present it expands out for good and for evil as the chief fact in the form of modern civilization, the 'kernel' of the modern economic problem." Alfred Marshall, *Principles of Economics*, 9th edition (New York: Macmillan, 1961), p. 745. Note that Marshall preferred to call businessmen undertakers rather than capitalists (p. 745).

8   "Division of labour within the workshop implies the undisputed authority of the capitalist over men that are but parts of a mechanism that belongs to him. . . . The same bourgeois mind which praises division of labour in the workshop, life-long annexation of the labourer to a partial operation, and his complete subjection to capital, as being an organisation of labour that increases its productiveness – that same bourgeois mind denounces with equal vigour every conscious attempt to socially control and regulate the process of production, as an inroad upon such sacred things as the rights of property, freedom and unrestricted play for the bent of the individual capitalist. It is very characteristic that the enthusiastic apologists of the factory system have nothing more damning to urge against a general organization of the labour of society, than that it would turn all society into one immense factory." Karl Marx, *Capital, op. cit.*, Vol. I, p. 356.

9   The following analysis by E. S. Mason of current attempts to justify hierarchy and inequality by emphasizing the skill and knowledge of managers and the technostructure is interesting and of great significance in this connection:

"As everyone now recognizes, classical economics provided not only a system of analysis, or analytical 'model,' intended to be useful to the explanation of economic behaviour but also a defense – and a carefully reasoned defense – of the proposition that the economic behaviour promoted and constrained by the institutions of a free-enterprise system is, in the main, in the public interest."

"It cannot be too strongly emphasized that the growth of the nineteenth-century capitalism depended largely on the general acceptance of a reasoned justification of the system on moral as well as on political and economic grounds."

"It seems doubtful whether, to date, the managerial literature has provided an equally satisfying apologetic for big business."

"The attack on the capitalist apologetic of the nineteenth century has been successful, but a satisfactory contemporary apologetic is still to be created. I suspect that, when and if an effective new ideology is devised, economics will be found to have little to contribute. Economists are still so mesmerized with the fact of choice and so little with its explanations, and the concept of the market is still so central to their thought, that they would appear to be professionally debarred from their important task. I suspect that to the formulation of an up-to-date twentieth-century apologetic the psychologists, and possibly, the political scien-

tists will be the main contributors. It is high time they were called to their job."
(Edward S. Mason, "The Apologetics of Managerialism," *Journal of Business of the University of Chicago,* January 1958, Vol. XXXI, No. 1, pp. 1–11.)

10 This analysis of the modern corporation is almost entirely based on the work of Alfred D. Chandler, *Strategy and Structure* (New York: Doubleday & Co., 1961), and Chester Barnard, *The Functions of the Executive* (Cambridge, Mass.: Harvard University Press, 1938).

11 Alfred D. Chandler and Fritz Redlich, "Recent Developments in American Business Administration and their Conceptualization," *Business History Review,* Spring 1961, pp. 103–28.

12 Neoclassical models suggest that this choice was due to the exogenously determined nature of technological change. A Marxist economic model would argue that it was due in part to the increased tensions in the labor market accompanying the accumulation of capital and the growth of large firms. This is discussed further in Stephen Hymer and Stephen Resnick, "International Trade and Uneven Development," in J. N. Bhagwati, R. W. Jones, R. A. Mundell, and J. Vanek, eds., *Trade, Balance of Payments and Growth* (Amsterdam: North-Holland Publishing Co., 1970) (reprinted as Chapter 5 of this volume).

13 The reasons for foreign investment discussed here are examined in more detail in Stephen Hymer, "The Multinational Corporation: An Analysis of Some Motives for International Business Integration," *Revue Economique,* Vol. XIX, No. 6, November 1968, pp. 949–73, and in Hymer and Rowthorn, "Multinational Corporations," *op. cit.*

14 At present U.S. corporations have about 60 billion dollars (American billion) invested in foreign branch plants and subsidiaries. The total assets of these foreign operations are much larger than the capital invested and probably equal 100 billion dollars at book value. (American corporations, on the average, were able to borrow 40 percent of their subsidiaries' capital requirements locally in the country of operation.) The total assets of 500 large U.S. firms are about 300–350 billion dollars, while the total assets of the 200 largest non-U.S. firms are slightly less than 200 billion dollars. See U.S. Department of Commerce, *Survey of Current Business,* September 1969, and *Fortune* list of the 500 largest U.S. corporations and 200 largest non-American.

15 At present unequal growth of different parts of the world economy upsets the oligopolistic equilibrium because the leading firms have different geographical distributions of production and sales. Thus, if Europe grows faster than the United States, European firms tend to grow faster than American firms, unless American firms engage in heavy foreign investment. Similarly, if the United States grows faster than Europe, U.S. firms will grow faster than European firms because Europeans have a lesser stake in the American market. When firms are distributed evenly in all markets, they share equally in the good and bad fortunes of the various submarkets, and oligopolistic equilibrium is not upset by the unequal growth of different countries.

16 Chandler and Redlich, *op. cit.*

17 Chandler and Redlich, *op. cit.,* p. 120.

18 See H. A. Simon, "The Compensation of Executives," *Sociometry,* March 1957.

19 Sean Gervasi, "Publicité et Croissance Economique," *Economie et Humanisme* (November/December, 1964).

20 Lloyd A. Fallers, "A Note on the Trickle Effect," in Perry Bliss, ed., *Marketing and the Behavioral Sciences* (Boston: Allyn and Bacon, 1963), pp. 208–16.

21 See Raymond Vernon, "International Investment and International Trade in the Product Cycle," *Quarterly Journal of Economics,* LXXX, May 1966.

22   An interesting illustration of the asymmetry in horizons and perspectives of the
       big company and the small country is found in these quotations from *Fortune*.
       Which countries of the world are making a comparable analysis of the Multina-
       tional Corporation?
       "A Ford economist regularly scans the international financial statistics to
       determine which countries have the highest rates of inflation; these are obviously
       prime candidates for devaluation. He then examines patterns of trade. If a
       country is running more of an inflation than its chief trading partners and
       competitors and its reserves are limited, it is more than a candidate; it is a
       shoo-in. His most difficult problem is to determine exactly when the devaluation
       will take place. Economics determines whether and how much, but politicians
       control the timing. So the analyst maintains a complete library of information on
       leading national officials. He tries to get "into the skin of the man" who is going
       to make the decision. The economist's forecasts have been correct in sixty-nine of
       the last seventy-five crisis situations."
       "Du Pont is one company that is making a stab in the direction of formally
       measuring environmental uncertainty, basically as a tool for capital budgeting
       decisions. The project is still in the research stage, but essentially the idea is to try
       to derive estimates of the potential of a foreign market, which is, of course,
       affected by economic conditions. The state of the economy in turn is partly a
       function of the fiscal and monetary policies the foreign government adopts. Policy
       decisions depend on real economic forces, on the attitudes of various interest
       groups in the country, and on the degree to which the government listens to these
       groups."
       "In the fiscal and monetary part of their broad economic model, the DuPont
       researchers have identified fifteen to twenty interest groups per country, from
       small land-owners to private bankers. Each interest group has a "latent
       influence," which depends on its size and educational level and the group's power
       to make its feelings felt. This influence, subjectively measured, is multiplied by
       an estimate of "group cohesiveness"; i.e., how likely the group is to mobilize its
       full resources on any particular issue. The product is a measure of "potential
       influence." This in turn must be multiplied by a factor representing the govern-
       ment's receptivity to each influence group." (Sanford Rose, "The Rewarding
       Strategies of Multinationalism," *Fortune,* September 15, 1968, p. 105.)

23   A. A. Berle, Jr., has put the problem most succinctly: "The Industrial Revolution,
       as it spread over twentieth-century life, required collective organization of men
       and things. . . . As the twentieth century moves into the afternoon, two systems –
       and (thus far) two only – have emerged as vehicles of modern industrial
       economics. One is the socialist commissariat; its highest organization at present is
       in the Soviet Union; the other is the modern corporation, most highly developed in
       the United States." (Foreword to *The Corporation in Modern Society,* E. S.
       Mason, ed. New York: Atheneum, 1967, p. ix.)

24   S. Kuznets, *Modern Economic Growth* (New Haven, Conn.: Yale University
       Press, 1966), pp. 423–4.

25   See K. Polanyi, *The Great Transformation* (New York: Farrar and Rinehart,
       Inc., 1944), on the consequences after 1870 of the repeal of the Corn Laws in
       England.

26   See Kari Levitt, *Silent Surrender: The Multinational Corporation in Canada*
       (Toronto: Macmillan Company of Canada, 1970), and Norman Girvan and
       Owen Jefferson, "Corporate vs. Caribbean Integration," *New World Quarterly,*
       Vol. IV, No. 2.

27 See Adam Smith, *The Wealth of Nations* (New York: Modern Library, 1937), pp. vii, 1.
28 See Theodor Mommsen, *The History of Rome* (New York: Meridian Books, 1958), p. 587.

3. The internationalization of capital

1   Franz Oppenheimer, *The State* (New York: B. W. Huebsh, 1922; Arno, 1972), p. 110.
2   Robert Heilbroner, "Paradox of Progress," in Andrew S. Skinner, ed., *Essays on Adam Smith* (Oxford: Clarendon Press, 1975).
3   Karl Marx, *Capital,* 3 vols. (New York: International Publishers, 1967), Vol. III, p. 266.
4   Karl Marx, *Capital, op. cit.,* Vol. I, p. 329.
5   Karl Marx, *Capital, op. cit.,* Vol. II, p. 34.
6   Many of the ideas presented here are further developed in S. Hymer and R. Rowthorn, "Multinational Corporations and International Oligopoly: The Non-American Challenge," in C. P. Kindleberger, *The International Corporation* (Cambridge, Mass.: M.I.T. Press, 1970) (reprinted as Chapter 8 of this volume); S. Hymer, "The Efficiency (Contradictions) of the Multinational Corporation," *American Economic Review,* May 1970 (Chapter 1 of this volume); S. Hymer, "The Multinational Corporation and the Law of Uneven Development," in J. Bhagwati, ed., *Economics and World Order* (New York: Macmillan, 1972) (Chapter 2 of this volume); and S. Hymer, "Robinson Crusoe and the Secret of Primitive Accumulation," *Monthly Review,* September 1971 (Chapter 4 of this volume).
7   Karl Marx, *Capital, op. cit.,* Vol. III, p. 198.
8   *Ibid.,* p. 385.
9   Karl Marx, *Capital, op. cit.,* Vol. I, p. 332.
10 Karl Marx, *Grundrisse,* Martin Nicolaus, ed. (Harmondsworth, England: Penguin Books, 1973), p. 92.
11 Karl Marx, *Economic and Philosophical Manuscripts of 1844* (New York: International Publishers, 1964), p. 148.
12 *Ibid.,* p. 155.
13 Phrase used by Anthony M. Salomon in *International Aspects of Antitrust,* Part I, Hearings before the Sub-Committee on Antitrust and Monopoly of the Senate Committee on the Judiciary, April 1966, p. 49.
14 Crane Brinton, *The Anatomy of Revolution* (Englewood Cliffs, N.J.: Prentice-Hall, 1952).
15 J. M. Keynes, "National Self-Sufficiency," *Yale Review,* Vol. 22, Summer 1933, p. 761.

4. Robinson Crusoe and the secret of primitive accumulation

1   Karl Marx, *Capital,* 3 vols. (New York: International Publishers, 1967), Vol. I, p. 751.
    "This primitive accumulation plays in Political Economy about the same part as original sin in theology. Adam bit the apple, and thereupon sin fell on the human race. Its origin is supposed to be explained when it is told as an anecdote of the past. In times long gone by there were two sorts of people: one, the diligent, intelligent, and above all, frugal elite; the other, lazy rascals, spending their

substance, and more, in riotous living. The legend of theological original sin tells us certainly how man came to be condemned to eat his bread in the sweat of his brow; but the history of economic original sin reveals to us that there are people to whom this is by no means essential. Never mind! Thus it came to pass that the former sort accumulated wealth, and the latter sort had at last nothing to sell except their skins. And from this original sin dates the poverty of the great majority that, despite its labor, has up to now nothing to sell but itself, and the wealth of the few that increases constantly although they have long ceased to work. Such insipid childishness is everyday preached to us in the defense of property. . . . In actual history it is notorious that conquest, enslavement, robbery, murder, briefly force, play the great part. In the tender annals of Political Economy, the idyllic reigns from time immemorial. . . . As a matter of fact, the methods of primitive accumulation are anything but idyllic." *Ibid.*, p. 713.

2   For studies of Defoe dealing with economic aspects see: E. M. Novak, *Economics and Fiction of Daniel Defoe* (Berkeley: University of California Press, 1962); H. M. Robertson, *Aspects of the Rise of Economic Individualism* (Cambridge: Cambridge University Press, 1933); Ian Watt, *The Rise of the Novel* (Berkeley: University of California Press, 1957); Dorothy Van Ghent, *The English Novel* (New York: Harper & Row, 1961), chapter on Moll Flanders; Brian Fitzgerald, *Daniel Defoe* (London: Secker and Warburg, 1954); Pierre Macherey, *Pour une Theorie de la Production Litteraire* (Paris: François Maspero, 1966); John Richetti, *Popular Fiction Between Defoe and Richardson* (New York: Oxford University Press, 1969). All quotations and excerpts in the text of this article are from Daniel Defoe, *Robinson Crusoe* (New York: New American Library, 1961).

3   J. M. Keynes, "Economic Possibilities for our Grandchildren," in *Essays in Persuasion* (New York: W. W. Norton, 1963), p. 370.

4   See Karl Polanyi, "Aristotle Discovers the Economy," in Karl Polanyi, et al., *Trade and Market in the Early Empires* (New York: Free Press, 1957), pp. 64–94; and A. French, *The Growth of the Athenian Economy* (London: Routledge and Kegan Paul, 1964).

5   J. M. Keynes, "National Self-Sufficiency," *Yale Review,* Vol. 22, Summer 1933, pp. 755–69.

6   R. D. Laing, *The Politics of Experience* (New York: Pantheon, 1967), p. 36.

7   Aristotle, *The Politics* (New York: Oxford University Press, 1946), Book I, Chapter V, 1254 b 9.

8   *Ibid.*, Book I, Chapter V, 1254 b 7.

5. International trade and uneven development

1   By trade theory we mean the classic law of comparative advantage: "Under a system of perfectly free commerce, each country naturally devotes its capital and labour to such employments as are most beneficial to each. This pursuit of individual advantage is admirably connected with the universal good of the whole. By stimulating industry, by rewarding ingenuity, and by using most efficaciously the peculiar powers bestowed by nature, it distributes labour most effectively and most economically: while, by increasing the general mass of productions, it diffuses general benefit, and binds together, by one common tie of interest and intercourse, the universal society of nations throughout the civilized world. It is this principle which determines that wine shall be made in France and Portugal, that corn shall be grown in America and Poland, and that hardware

and other goods shall be manufactured in England." [David Ricardo, *Principles of Political Economy and Taxation* (London: J. M. Dent & Sons, 1948), p. 81.] Since Ricardo's time, numerous qualifications have been added to his statement, and now the orthodox model recognizes exceptions to the "gains from trade argument." The qualifications are not the ones we shall be concerned with in this essay.

2   It is unlikely that h and n are independent, but it is convenient to postpone discussion of this until after the model is presented.

3   S. Hymer and S. Resnick, "A Model of an Agrarian Economy with Nonagricultural Activities," *American Economic Review,* September 1969, pp. 493–506.

4   See S. Hymer, "Economic Forms in Pre-Colonial Ghana," *Journal of Economic History,* Vol. XXX, No. 1, March 1970, pp. 33–50, for a discussion of the African case.

5   K. A. Wittfogel, *Oriental Despotism* (New Haven, Conn.: Yale University Press, 1957).

6   Three men working one-third of the time can nearly always duplicate the work patterns of one man working full time. The opposite is not true. For example, one full-time agriculturalist cannot be in more than one place at one time. If ϵ_1 is the set of activities achievable under part-time work in the African mode, and ϵ_2 is the set possible for full-time specialists in the Asian mode, then $\epsilon_1 \subset \epsilon_2$ but $\epsilon_2 \not\subset \epsilon_1$. The African societies could spread themselves over the land and take advantage of nature, while Asian societies had to concentrate around the river where it was possible to grow water-crops which allow for more equal spacing of work over time.

7   The Asian case is, however, complex even if, on balance, there was a net improvement of welfare. An interesting example is provided by India. The Indian ruling class began to decline prior to the coming of the West and Indian society might have been in a state of transition that would have led to the growth of indigenous merchant-capitalism. Although there is some historical evidence supporting this view, colonialism in fact ended the possibility of such a path and created an underdeveloped country.

8   For an historical account of the decline of traditional life and the effects on the distribution of income brought about by the export economy, see S. Resnick, "Decline of Rural Industry under Export Expansion: A Comparison among Burma, Philippines and Thailand, 1870–1938," *Journal of Economic History,* March 1970, Vol. XXX, No. 1, pp. 51–73.

9   C. P. Kindleberger, "Group Behavior and International Trade," *Journal of Political Economy,* Vol. LIX, No. 1, February 1951, pp. 30–46.

10 *Ibid.,* pp. 32–3.

11 See Kindleberger's discussion of Italy, *op. cit.,* p. 34.

12 We are gratful to Lloyd Best of the University of the West Indies for this distinction. See Lloyd Best and Kari Levitt, *Externally Propelled Growth and Industrialization in the Caribbean* (Mona, Jamaica: University of the West Indies, 1969), mimeograph.

13 These issues are discussed more fully in S. Hymer and R. Rowthorn, "Multinational Corporations and International Oligopoly: The Non-American Challenge," in C. P. Kindleberger, ed., *The International Corporation* (Cambridge, Mass.: M.I.T. Press, 1970) (reprinted as Chapter 8 of this volume), and S. Hymer, "The Multinational Corporation and the Law of Uneven Development," in J. Bhagwati, ed., *Economics and World Order* (New York: World Law Fund, 1971) (Chapter 2 of this volume).

6. The multinational corporation and the international division of labor

1   Richard Austin Smith, "European Nationalism Threatens U.S. Investment," *Fortune,* August 1965, p. 126.
2   George W. Ball, "The Promise of the Multinational Corporation," *Fortune,* June 1967, p. 80.
3   "Management Outlook," *Business Week,* February 17, 1968, p. 112.
4   The ideas of this section on pyramids of power rely heavily on Harold D. Lasswell's analysis of the transition from national to international identity patterns and the implications this has for a realignment of political forces in the world. See Harold D. Lasswell's *Future Systems of Identity in the World Economy* (mimeo), prepared for the Tokyo Conference of the World Order Models Project, 1970, for a discussion of the changing identity patterns and the various combinations of forces making either for an alliance between elites or more popularly based groups.
5   Concerning the pyramids of power and the possibility of them flattening, see Harold D. Lasswell and Abraham Kaplan, *Power and Society* (New Haven, Conn.: Yale University Press, 1950). See also R. M. McIver, *The Modern State* (London: Oxford University Press, Clarendon Press, 1926). We do not necessarily share McIver's view on the question of the extent to which power has become diffused in free-enterprise democracy, but we found this a helpful framework for viewing the pyramid of power.
6   Harold D. Lasswell's discussions on "The Unspeakable Revolution" are to be found in Chapters 1, 2, and 3 of *World Revolutionary Elites* (Cambridge, Mass.: M.I.T. Press, 1966), which contains a summary of the major world revolutions of our time as well as a discussion of the possibilities and dangers for the future. See also his "Must Science Serve Political Power," *American Psychologist,* Vol. 25, No. 2, February 1970, pp. 117–23, for the problem that is the central theme of our essay, namely the question whether the monopoly of knowledge by elites can be broken. Our study of the multinational corporation is essentially a study of the way corporate capital uses information to shape our values and way of life. Like Lasswell, we study power in the same spirit as Machiavelli: "I come now to the last branch of my charge: that I teach princes villainy, and how to enslave. If any man will read over my book . . . with impartiality and ordinary charity, he will easily perceive that it is not my intention to recommend that government or those men there described to the world, much less to teach men how to trample upon good men, and all that is sacred and venerable upon earth, laws, religion, honesty, and what not. If I have been a little too punctual in describing these monsters in all their lineaments and colours, I hope mankind will know them, the better to avoid them, my treatise being both a *satire* against them, and a true character of them . . . ." Niccolo Machiavelli, from a Letter to a Friend, cited by James Burnham, *The Managerial Revolution* (Bloomington: Indiana University Press, 1941), frontispiece.
7   Kurt Lewin, *Field Theory in Social Science* (London: Social Science Paperbacks, 1952), p. 105.
8   Herbert A. Simon, *Administrative Behavior* (New York: Free Press, 1945), p. 2.
9   G. H. Clee and Alfred di Scipio, "Creating a World Enterprise," *Harvard Business Review,* September–October 1960, p. 67.
10 Alfred D. Chandler and Fritz Redlich, "Recent Developments in American Business Administration and Their Conceptualization," *Business History Review,* Spring 1961, p. 89.

11 Chester I. Barnard, *The Functions of the Executive* (Cambridge, Mass.: Harvard University Press, 1938), pp. 104–6.
12 Herbert A. Simon, "The Compensation of Executives," *Sociometry,* March 1957, pp. 32–5.
13 Alfred Marshall, *Principles of Economics,* 9th ed. (New York: Macmillan, 1961), pp. 1–2.
14 Karl Marx, *Capital,* 3 vols. (New York: International Publishers, 1967), Vol. I, p. 356.
15 J. K. Galbraith, *The New Industrial State* (New York: Houghton Mifflin, 1967).
16 H. Igor Ansoff and John M. Stewart, "Strategies for a Technology-Based Business," *Harvard Business Review,* November–December 1967, pp. 71–83.
17 E. Raymond Corey, "The Rise of Marketing in Product Planning," in the *First International Seminar on Marketing Management,* published as a Special Supplement to *Business Horizons,* School of Business, Indiana University, February 1961, p. 79.
18 Robert Keith, "The Marketing Revolution," *Journal of Marketing,* January 1960, p. 37.
19 George W. Ball, "Promise of the Multinational," *op. cit.,* p. 80.
20 Max Ways, "The Deeper Shame of Our Cities," *Fortune,* January 1968, p. 208.
21 Chester I. Barnard, *Functions of the Executive, op. cit.,* p. 91.
22 Karl W. Deutsch, *The Nerves of Government* (New York: Free Press of Glencoe, 1963).
23 R. M. Haig, "Toward an Understanding of the Metropolis," *Quarterly Journal of Economics,* February 1926, p. 427.
24 *Ibid.,* p. 427.
25 Sune Carlson, *Executive Behavior* (Stockholm: Strombergs, 1951), p. 96; also Herbert A. Simon, *Administrative Behavior, op. cit.,* p. 158, for the quote within the Carlson quote.
26 R. M. Haig, "Metropolis," *op. cit.,* p. 415.
27 R. D. McKenzie, "The Concept of Dominance and World Organization," *American Journal of Sociology,* Vol. 33, July 1927, p. 32.
28 Karl Marx, *Pre-Capitalist Economic Formations,* E. J. Hobsbawm, ed. (New York: International Publishers, 1964), p. 124.
29 R. D. McKenzie, "Concept of Dominance," *op. cit.,* p. 33.
30 Henri Pirenne, *Medieval Cities* (Princeton, N.J.: Princeton University Press, 1969).
31 Walter Cristaller, *Central Places in Southern Germany* (Englewood-Cliffs, N.J.: Prentice-Hall, 1966).
32 R. D. McKenzie, "Concept of Dominance," *op. cit.,* p. 37.
33 Mark Jefferson, "The Law of the Primate City," *Geographical Review,* April 1939.
34 R. D. McKenzie, *The Metropolitan Community* (New York: McGraw-Hill, 1933), pp. 162–5.
35 First National City Bank (now Citibank), "Plan for New York City – A Review," *Monthly Economic Letter,* January 1970, p. 7.
36 Lloyd A. Fallers, "A Note on the Trickle Effect," *Marketing and the Behavioral Sciences,* Perry Bliss, ed. (Boston: Allyn and Bacon, 1963).
37 "One World," *Forbes,* November 15, 1968, p. 90.
38 *Ibid.,* p. 93.
39 R. D. McKenzie, "Concept of Dominance," *op. cit.,* p. 34.
40 Sidney Rolfe, "Updating Adam Smith," *Interplay,* Vol. 2, November 1968.

7. Direct foreign investment and the national economic interest

1 See, for example, Irving Brecher and S. S. Reisman, Royal Commission on Canada's Economic Prospects, *Canada–United States Economic Relations,* Ottawa, 1957; Harry G. Johnson, *The Canadian Quandary,* Toronto, 1963; A. E. Safarian, "Foreign Ownership and Control of Canadian Industry," in Abraham Rotstein, ed., *The Prospect of Change,* University League for Social Reform, Toronto, 1965.

2 For the official meaning of "direct investment" and "control," see Dominion Bureau of Statistics, *Canada's International Investment Position 1926–1954,* Ottawa, 1956, p. 24. For a discussion of the complexities that inhere in these concepts, see Safarian, as cited, pp. 224–5.

3 For a fuller discussion of the theoretical structure and empirical evidence on which this paper is based, see my *The International Operations of National Firms: a Study in Direct Foreign Investment* (Cambridge, Mass.: M.I.T. Press, 1976), doctoral dissertation, Massachusetts Institute of Technology, June 1960.

4 Safarian, as cited, pp. 226–8.

5 This list of factors draws on the responses of American parent firms to a campaign by the Montreal Stock Exchange to increase access of Canadian investors to the equity of Canadian subsidiaries. See Appendix XII of the submission of the Montreal Stock Exchange to the Royal Commission on Banking and Finance. The response was described as "completely negative" by the Hon. Eric W. Kierans in an address to the Toronto Society of Financial Analysts, February 1, 1966.

6 See above, papers by John Dales and H. Ian MacDonald. My paper has ignored the much-discussed phenomenon of the tariff factor, that is, of foreign firms attracted into Canada by the Canadian tariff. This has been done in the interest of focusing on neglected issues, and does not imply that the role of the tariff in foreign ownership is unimportant.

8. Multinational corporations and international oligopoly: the non-American challenge

1 The research for this paper was in part financed by a grant from the Council on Foreign Relations in the case of Stephen Hymer and by the Faculty of Economics of Cambridge University in the case of Robert Rowthorn. Preliminary versions of this paper were presented at seminars at the University of Toronto, Cambridge, M.I.T., and the Instituto de Estudios Internacionales of the University of Chile, where much helpful criticism was obtained. (Geoffery Whittington also made a number of helpful comments on a preliminary version.) The authors would also like to thank Miss P. Cunningham, Miss J. McKenzie, Miss R. Henderson, and Miss H. Lackner for their help in preparing the statistical material of this essay. Finally, they would like to thank Miss J. A. Barnes and Mrs. M. N. Simmonds, who typed the manuscript.

2 The Editor, "The Multinational Corporation: the Splendors and Miseries of Bigness," *Interplay,* November 1968, p. 15. This source provides as good a definition of the multinational corporation as any – "an organization which, while remaining in private hands, transcends national boundaries and national regulation."

3 J.-J. Servan-Schreiber, *The American Challenge* (New York: Atheneum, 1968). Servan-Schreiber is chosen because he is the most articulate propagator of a certain view. The literature on the subject is too extensive to be quoted here, but at the very least we must mention C. Layton, *Trans-Atlantic Investments*

(Boulogne-sur-Seine: Atlantic Institute, 1966); Colloque sur la politique indus-trielle de l'europe integrée et l'apport des capitaux extérieurs, Paris, 1966, M. Bye, ed., *La Politique industrielle de l'europe integrée et l'apport des capitaux extérieurs* (Travaux et recherches de la Faculté de droit et des sciences economi-ques de Paris, Série Europe, No. 7 (Paris: Presses Universitaires de France, 1968); C. P. Kindleberger, "European Integration and the International Corpo-ration," *Columbia Journal of World Business,* Vol. I, No. 1, Winter 1966, pp. 65–73; G. Y. Bertin, *L'Investissement des firmes etrangères en France* (Paris: Presses Universitaires de France. 1963); S. H. Robock, "The American Chal-lenge – an Inside Story," *The Hermes Exchange,* Vol. 1, No. 2, October 1968, pp. 9–12; B. Balassa, "American Direct Investments in the Common Market," *Banca Nazionale del Lavoro Quarterly Review,* No. 67, June 1966, pp. 121–46; E. Mandel, "International Capitalism and Supra Nationality," in *The Socialist Register 1967,* R. Milliband and J. Saville, eds. (London: Merlin Press, 1967); G. Ádám, "Standing up to the American Challenge," *New Hungarian Quarterly,* Vol. IX, No. 3, Autumn 1968, pp. 57–139.

4   J. K. Galbraith, *The New Industrial State* (Boston: Houghton Mifflin Company, 1967).

5   The data are taken from *Fortune* magazine's annual listing of the 500 largest industrial corporations in the United States and the 200 largest industrial corporations outside the United States (100 in 1957). The data are subject to numerous deficiencies but are the only ones available, since government statistics typically use the industry rather than the corporation as the unit of analysis. *Fortune* ranks firms by sales rather than assets or employees and we have accordingly used sales for most of the tests in this paper. To the extent that *Fortune* correctly reflects business thinking on the "best" measure of size, sales may well be the appropriate index for analyzing oligopoly strategy.

6   We have counted Unilever as a chemical firm rather than a food firm. If Unilever is excluded from chemicals, the relative size-ratio shifts in favor of the U.S. firms in this industry.

7   See A. D. Chandler, Jr., *Strategy and Structure* (New York: Doubleday & Co., 1961), for an analysis of the development of the United States' structure of business organization in response to the challenge of the continental market and the rapidly changing composition of output.

8   Certain adjustments were made to deal with inaccuracies in the *Fortune* data and mergers. The adjusted data yielded better results than the crude data and only equations for adjusted data have been reported. The differences, however, were small.

9   Suppose we had instead estimated

$$g = \text{const} + \sum_{i=1}^{m} a_i C_i + \sum_{j=1}^{n} b_j I_j + eS + fS^2 + u. \tag{1}$$

Since every firm belongs to exactly one country, $\Sigma_1^m C_i = 1$. Similarly since every firm belongs to exactly one industry $\Sigma_1^n I_i = I$. The set of variables $(C_1 \ldots C_m)$ and $(I_1 \ldots I_n)$ are thus linearly dependent. To get around this problem we chose an arbitrary country (country 1) and note

$$a_i c_i = (a_i - a_1) c_i + a_1 c_i \tag{2}$$

$$\sum_i^m a_i c_i = \sum_2^m (a_i - a_1) C_i + a_1 C_i \tag{3}$$

$$= \sum_{2}^{m} (a_i - a_1) C_i + a_i, \tag{4}$$

since $\Sigma C_i = 1$. Similarly, letting industry 1 be an arbitrary industry,

$$\sum_{2}^{n} b_i I_i = \sum_{2}^{n} (b_i - b_2) I_i + b_2. \tag{5}$$

Substituting Equations 4 and 5 into 1 gives us the equation in the text which can be estimated, since the vectors $(C_2 \ldots C_m)$ and $(I_2 \ldots I_n)$ will normally be linearly independent.

10 See, for example, H. A. Simon and C. P. Bonini, "The Size Distribution of Business Firms," *American Economic Review,* Vol. XLIII, No. 4, September 1958, pp. 607–17; P. E. Hart and S. J. Prais, "The Analysis of Business Concentration," *Journal of the Royal Statistical Society,* Part 2, 1956, pp. 150–81; S. Hymer and P. Pashigian, "Firm Size and Rate of Growth," *Journal of Political Economy,* Vol. LXX, December 1962, pp. 556–69; E. Mansfield, "Entry, Gibrat's Law, Innovation, and the Growth of Firms," *American Economic Review,* Vol. LII, No. 5, December 1962, pp. 1023–51; A. Singh and G. Whittington, in collaboration with H. T. Burley, *Growth, Profitability and Valuation* (Cambridge: Cambridge University Press, 1968). These studies, as well as a number of others, have for the most part found that above a certain minimum size, large firms do not perform better (or worse) than small firms when judged by costs, profits, or propensity to grow. This evidence on the existence or nonexistence of economies of scale is, however, far from conclusive for an important theoretical reason. Small firms are often complementary to large firms, acting as suppliers to the large firms or filling the gaps left by large firms. The two sets are in ecological equilibrium, as bees are to apple orchards or as any parasite is to its host. International size comparisons, though subject to their own special difficulties, get around this problem, in part, since the smaller firms outside the United States are not in ecological equilibrium with the larger firms but in competition.

11 It is well known that U.S. subsidiaries in Europe have, on average, been growing faster than their European rivals. Between 1950 and 1965, for example, the value of U.S. direct investment in Western Europe rose from $1,720 million to $13,894 million. Few European firms, even the heavy overseas investors, could have matched this growth rate of 14.9% a year sustained for 15 years. Assuming that these figures are a reasonable guide to the relative sales performance we can conclude that $G_s > G_e$ is a fair stylization of the facts. Our regressions and tables show that, on average $G_e \geqslant G_p$. Indeed, for the period 1957 to 1967, as a whole, the inequality is strict.

12 More evidence will be provided when G. Bertin (Université de Rennes) completes his econometric investigation of the relationship between size and foreign investment.

13 U.S. Department of Commerce, Office of Business Economics, *U.S. Business Investments in Foreign Countries* (Washington, D.C.: U.S. Government Printing Office, 1960).

14 W. B. Reddaway, *Effects of U.K. Direct Investment Overseas* (Cambridge: Cambridge University Press, 1967).

15 At present there is a great asymmetry between commodity flows and capital

flows. Europe's exports of manufactures to the United States are about equal to its imports from the United States, but direct investment by European corporations in the United States is much smaller than United States direct investment in Europe. The theory of the product cycle (from innovation to exports to foreign investment) seems to apply more closely to the experience of U.S. corporations than to the experience of non-U.S. corporations, where the sequence often runs from innovation to exports to loss of market, as the European firm's advantage is eroded by competition.

16 U.S. Department of Commerce, *U.S. Business, op. cit.*

17 Cross-investment is a long-standing feature of direct foreign investment. In many industries where U.S. corporations have substantial direct investment in foreign countries, one of the leading firms in the United States is a foreign firm, e.g., oil, soft drinks, paper, soaps, and detergents, farm machinery, business machinery, tires and tubes, sewing machines, concentrated milk, biscuits, chemicals.

18 Note that local production abroad by U.S. corporations is growing much faster than exports. See also C. A. Van den Beld and D. Van der Werf. "A Note on International Competitiveness," Berlin, 1965, published as "Nota Sulla Competitivita Internazionale," in *Economia Internazionale,* Vol. XIX, 1966, pp. 325–37; Table 6, p. 14, shows that Germany has done far better than either the United Kingdom or the United States *even when price has been allowed for.* Similarly H. B. Junz and R. R. Rhomberg, "Prices and Export Performance of Industrial Countries, 1953–63," IMF *Staff Papers,* July 1965, show that Germany and Japan did better relative to the United Kingdom and the United States than prices would explain. In each of the above two studies the bad performance of the United Kingdom and the United States *could* be explained by the fact that their firms have tended to expand by investing rather than exporting.

19 C. Kaysen and D. F. Turner, *Antitrust Policy* (Cambridge, Mass.: Harvard University Press, 1959). The quotations are from pp. 19 and 17, respectively.

20 E. S. Mason, preface to Ref. 19, p. xi.

21 G. W. Ball, "The Promise of the Multinational Corporation," *Fortune,* Vol. 75, No. 6, June 1, 1967, p. 80.

22 S. Rolfe, "Updating Adam Smith," *Interplay,* Vol. 2, November 1968, pp. 15–19.

23 For an important discussion of technology and nationalism in the tradition of Harold Innis, Karl Polanyi, and Marshall McLuhan, see A. Rotstein, "The 20th Century in Prospect: Nationalism in a Technological Society," and M. Watkins, "Technology and Nationalism," in *Nationalism in Canada,* P. Russell, ed. (Toronto: McGraw-Hill Ryerson, 1966).

24 For a discussion of the limitations on a nation-state brought about by multinational corporations, see M. Watkins *et al., Foreign Ownership and the Structure of Canadian Industry,* Report of the Task Force on the Structure of Canadian Industry (Ottawa: Queen's Printer, 1968). See also K. Levitt, "Canada: Economic Dependence and Political Disintegration," *New World,* Vol. IV, No. 2, 1968, pp. 57–139. An incisive treatment designed for less-developed countries but perhaps soon to be of some relevance for developed countries is found in R. Demonts and F. Perroux, "Large Firms, Small Nations," *Présence Africaine,* Vol. 10, No. 38, 1961, pp. 3–19.

25 Some interesting aspects of the problem are explored in L. Model, "The Politics of Private Foreign Investment," *Foreign Affairs,* Vol. 45, June 1967, pp. 639–51.

26 The arguments put forward by Ball and the large corporations for an interna-

tional system of incorporation are, of course, as much as attempt by firms to escape from U.S. regulation as anything else.

27 Cf. C. P. Kindleberger, *International Economics,* 3rd edition (Homewood, Ill.: Richard D. Irwin, 1963), p. 627.

28 E. Mandel, "International Capitalism," *op. cit.,* and "Where is America Going?," *New Left Review,* No. 54, March/April 1969, pp. 14, 15.

29 J. M. Keynes, "Foreign Investment and National Advantage," *The Nation and the Athenaem,* Vol. XXXV, No. 19, August 1924, pp. 584–6.

9. United States investment abroad

1 The hypothesis in this paper is based on my doctoral dissertation, *The International Operations of National Firms,* submitted to the Massachusetts Institute of Technology in May 1960 [published posthumously as *The International Operations of National Firms* (Cambridge, Mass.: M.I.T. Press, 1976)]. An attempt is made to bring empirical evidence contained in the thesis up to date using the material in the *U.S. Business Investments in Foreign Countries: Census of 1957* (Washington: U.S. Government Printing Office, 1960) (hereafter *Census of 1957*) and the *Foreign Business Investments in the United States, Census of 1959* (Washington: U.S. Government Printing Office, 1962) (hereafter *Census of 1959*), as well as the many important empirical and critical studies published since 1960. Unfortunately the *Census of 1966* had still not been released at the time of writing (except for some preliminary results on Latin America contained in the report by the Council for Latin America).

  The empirical material used here is illustrative rather than exhaustive. We are now reaching the point where full scaled econometric analysis will be possible for many hypotheses previously evaluated only in qualitative terms. The accompanying data indicate some relations which can be tested. In some cases, where data are not available but soon could be, an attempt is made to suggest lines of approach.

2 Harold P. Lasswell and Abraham Kaplan, *Power and Society* (New Haven, Conn.: Yale University Press, 1950).

3 This point is developed more fully in Stephen Hymer and Stephen Resnick, "International Trade and Uneven Development," in J. Bhagwati *et al.* (eds.), *Trade, Balance of Payments and Growth: Papers in International Economics in Honour of Charles P. Kindleberger* (Amsterdam: North-Holland Publishing Co., 1970) (reprinted as Chapter 5 of this volume). See also H. G. Johnson, "A Theoretical Model of Economic Nationalism in New and Developing States," *Political Science Quarterly,* Vol. 80, June 1965, and Albert Breton, "The Economics of Nationalism," *Journal of Political Economy,* Vol. 72, No. 4, August 1964, for articles which integrate political and economic equations in the analysis of foreign investment.

4 Other evidence on the venerability of foreign investment is as follows: The *Census of 1957* showed that 65 per cent of total investment is concentrated in plants which were established before 1946 (p. 99). Since few plants were established during either the depression or the war, most of these plants must have started before 1930. This is confirmed in the *Direct Private Foreign Investments of the United States: Census of 1950* (Washington: U.S. Government Printing Office, 1953) which found that almost 60 per cent of 1950 investment was in plants established before 1930 (p. 50). In the United Kingdom, fully one-half of the

employment in United States controlled enterprises in 1953 was in firms established before 1914: John H. Dunning, *American Investment in British Manufacturing Industry* (London: George Allen and Unwin, 1958), p. 95. In Australia, Brash found over half of the 1962 employment in his sample of American firms began operations before 1929, mainly between 1920 and 1929: Donald T. Brash, *American Investment in Australian Industry* (Canberra: Australian National University Press, 1966). Two-thirds began before 1939. In New Zealand, Deane found 34 per cent of its 1965 employment of respondent companies from all countries to be in firms established before 1930, 50 per cent before 1939: R. S. Deane, *Foreign Investment in New Zealand Manufacturing* (Wellington: Sweet and Maxwell, 1970). These statistics refer to the date on which the branch plant began operations. The relevant concept is the date the *parent firm* first went abroad. If data were available on this basis, they would indicate a much smaller percentage of investment being accounted for by new entrants. See also the case histories reported in Cleona Lewis, *America's Stake in International Investments* (Washington, D.C.: Brookings Institution, 1938); H. Marshall, F. A. Southard, and K. Taylor, *Canadian-American Industry* (New Haven, Conn.: Yale University Press, 1936); D. M. Phelps, *Migration of Industry to South America* (New York: McGraw-Hill, 1936); and F. A. Southard, *American Industry in Europe* (Boston: Houghton Mifflin Co., 1931). In this last work, Southard was able to trace the origins of many firms back to the late nineteenth century. Direct investment by foreigners in the United States appears also to be in old, well-established subsidiaries. Of the $US6 billion of direct investment in the United States in 1959, almost 80 per cent was established before 1941 (*Census of 1959*).

5   In Canada, for example, the share of foreign firms has shown no tendency to fall and is increasing: Dominion Bureau of Statistics, *Canada's International Investment Position, 1926–1954* (Ottawa: Queen's Printer, 1958), and *Foreign Ownership and the Structure of Canadian Industry* (Ottawa: Queen's Printer, 1968). For England, only a very slight decline, helped by the war, was found by Dunning in his investigation of the trend in the American share of British industry (Dunning, *op. cit.*, p. 184); of the 115 firms questioned, only 15 claimed their share decreased; 63 firms reported an increase and 37 no change.

6   L. Corey, *Meat and Man* (New York: Viking Press, 1950), pp. 202–6. On tobacco see Dunning, *American Investment, op. cit.*, pp. 30–1.

7   Rates of growth estimated by Judd Polk, Irene W. Meisler, and Laurence A. Viet, *United States Production Abroad and the Balance of Payments* (New York: National Industrial Conference Board, 1966).

8   Judd Polk, "Internationalization: A Production Explosion and a Political Challenge," *Business Abroad,* Vol. 95, No. 2, February 1970.

9   John Powers, *The Multinational Company* (New York: Pfizer Public Relations Department, 1967).

10 "Management Outlook," *Business Week,* February 17, 1968, p. 112.

11 Stanford Rose, "The Rewarding Strategies of Multinationalism," *Fortune,* 15, September 1968, p. 105.

12 A. Maizels, *Industrial Growth and World Trade* (Cambridge: Cambridge University Press, 1963), pp. 23, 85, 430, 431.

13 Gilles Bertin of the University of Rennes is conducting an econometric study of the propensity to invest abroad. His preliminary findings seem to indicate a sharp positive (discontinuous) relation to size and a general upward shift in the curve for European firms in recent years.

14 See S. Hymer and R. Rowthorn, "Multinational Corporations and International Oligopoly: The Non-American Challenge," in C. P. Kindleberger, *The International Corporation* (Cambridge, Mass.: M.I.T. Press, 1970) (reprinted as Chapter 8 of this volume) for evidence on the growth of American and non-American firms and for the basis of the next paragraph.

15 The data reported for Sweden in Sidney E. Rolfe, *The International Corporation* (New York: International Chamber of Commerce, 1969), p. 175, show that twenty-one companies account for 80 per cent of total sales of foreign subsidiaries; the largest of these, SKF, accounts for one-quarter, and the five largest account for almost 50 per cent.

16 Dunning, *American Investment, op. cit.*, pp. 60–78.

17 Maureen Brunt (Statement on Australia in *International Antitrust*, United States: Hearings before the Subcommittee on Antitrust and Monopoly, April and June 1966) in her testimony before the Senate, for example, noted: "It is striking to observe that characteristically these industries which are dominated by foreign firms are all highly concentrated industries" (p. 263) and "almost invariably the foreign firm in Australia operates in a highly oligopolistic market setting." She recorded that in 1964, 41 of the 100 largest mining and manufacturing companies were foreign subsidiaries or affiliates (p. 263). Brash's survey of American firms also provides evidence of this for Australia. A similar pattern was found by Deane, *Foreign Investment, op. cit.*, in New Zealand.

Official publications in Canada show that half of the United States investment is in industries where the American share is 50 per cent or more (Dominion Bureau of Statistics, *Canada's International Investment Position, 1926–1954*, pp. 4292–3). This underestimates the extent of high concentration.

In Europe, too, we know from Southard's study, *American Industry, op. cit.*, that industries in which American investment is prominent were characterized by a high degree of concentration.

18 See W. Gruber, P. Mehta, and R. Vernon, "The R & D Factor in International Trade and International Investment of United States Industries," *Journal of Political Economy*, Vol. 75, February 1967; R. E. Caves, "International Corporations: The Industrial Economics of Foreign Investment," *Economica*, Vol. 48, No. 149, February 1971; Raymond Vernon, "International Investment and International Trade in the Product Cycle," *Quarterly Journal of Economics*, Vol. 80, May 1966; and Raymond Vernon, "Future of the Multinational Enterprise," in Charles Kindleberger, *The International Corporation* (Cambridge, Mass.: M.I.T. Press, 1970).

19 Quoted by S. H. Frankel in "Industrialisation of Agricultural Countries and the Possibilities of a New International Division of Labour," *Economic Journal*, June–September 1943. Frankel deals with the challenge of new countries, especially Japan. His article contains other citations in the same vein, for example, by Loveday who in 1931, said: "The future lies with the countries whose whole economic organisation is most mobile, with those which have the imagination to foresee future needs."

20 Three-quarters of the employment of Brash's sample of United States subsidiaries in Australia was in firms 100 per cent owned (p. 64). Deane found 63 per cent of the foreign subsidiaries in New Zealand completely owned (p. 24).

21 I am grateful to Edith Penrose for this point.

22 Borrowing costs change this model but little. As they are a rising function of the quantity borrowed, the supply curve of capital is tilted upwards. This has two effects, the substitution effect encouraging firms to finance a greater proportion

from home, and the scale effect discouraging investment in the country where capital is expensive because of low overall profitabilities.

23 On the levels of authority within the corporations see: Herbert A. Simon, "The Compensation of Executives," *Sociometry,* March 1957; Norman H. Martin, "The Levels of Management and Their Mental Demands," in *Industrial Man, Businessmen and Business Organizations* (New York: Harper Bros, 1959); William M. Evan, "Indices of the Hierarchical Structure of Industrial Organizations," *Management Science,* April 1963; M. F. Hall, "Communication Within Organizations," *Journal of Management Studies,* February 1965; J. H. Horne and Tom Lupton, "The Work Activities of Middle Managers: An Exploratory Study," *Journal of Management Studies,* Vol. 2, No. 1, February 1965; John Dearden, "Timespan in Management Control," *Financial Executive,* August 1968; Robert E. Thompson, "Span of Control Conceptions and Misconceptions," in *Emerging Concepts in Management* (London: Macmillan Co., 1969); Thomas L. Whisler, "Measuring Centralization of Control in Business Organizations," in W. W. Cooper *et al.,* eds., *New Perspectives in Organizational Research* (New York: John Wiley & Sons, 1964); and Hans B. Thorelli, "Salary Span of Control – A Study in Executive Pay," *Journal of Management Studies,* October 1965. This last work is a study of executive pay in Sears Roebuck's Latin American branches. Thorelli found that a large part of the variation could be explained by the executive's level in the overall corporate hierarchy and the total wage bill of all employees under him.

24 See R. M. Haig, "Toward an Understanding of the Metropolis," *Quarterly Journal of Economics,* February 1926, and R. D. McKenzie, "The Concept of Dominance and World Organization," *American Journal of Sociology,* Vol. 33, July 1927, for an analysis of the hierarchy of cities.

10. The United States multinational corporations and Japanese competition in the Pacific

1 W. K. Hancock, *Survey of British Commonwealth Affairs,* Vol. 2, *Problems of Economic Policy, 1918–1939* (New York: Oxford University Press, 1942).
2 "An American Proposal," *Fortune,* May 1942, p. 63.
3 J.-J. Servan-Schreiber, *The American Challenge* (New York: Atheneum, 1968).
4 Koichi Hamada, "Japanese Investment Abroad," in P. Drysdale, ed., *Direct Foreign Investment in Asia and the Pacific* (Canberra: Australian National University Press, 1972), p. 190.
5 *Ibid.,* p. 193.
6 *Montreal Star,* January 24, 1970.
7 Gregory Clark, "Triangles and Pentagons," *Far Eastern Economic Review,* January 22, 1970, p. 7.
8 John G. Roberts, "To Arms Dear Friends," *Far Eastern Economic Review,* July 31, 1969, points to certain possible deeper implications of the automobile agreements: "Significantly, the business managers who have been pressing for easier entry of foreign investment into the motor industry have now almost unanimously begun to call for expansion of the defense programme. This indicates that the forthcoming arms boom will not be entirely spontaneous. Indeed, a military and industrial complex is undoubtedly at work in Japan. Some observers believe that the Chrysler–Mitsubishi tie-up has "internationalized" it. The partnership of the two firms makes sense especially as both are thoroughly experienced in the armaments business."

9   *Japan Economic Journal,* December 2, 1969, p. 1.
10   "International Outlook," *Business Week,* August 22, 1970, p. 54.
11   *Wall Street Journal,* June 1, 1970, p. 1.
12   *Wall Street Journal,* May 15, 1970, p. 1.
13   *Japan Economic Journal,* March 10, 1970, p. 12.
14   John G. Roberts, "Because Japan's Economy is Strong and Steady," advertisement, *Wall Street Journal,* July 1, 1970, p. 13.
15   "Management Outlook," *Business Week,* February 17, 1968, p. 112.
16   Kurt Lewin, *Field Theory in Social Science* (London: Social Science Paperbacks, 1952).
17   Alfred Marshall, *Principles of Economics,* 9th edition (New York: Macmillan Company, 1961), p. 745.
18   This may not be undesirable for underdeveloped countries. As Andre Gunder Frank points out in his analysis of underdevelopment, it is, ironically, in periods of crisis in the center that underdeveloped countries often make the most important strides toward escaping from their underdevelopment.
19   Nobutane Kiuchi, "Japan at the Threshold of a New Era," *The President Directory 1969* (Tokyo: President's Magazine, 1969), pp. 3–4.
20   *Ibid.,* p. 5.
21   *Ibid.*
22   Daniel Parker, Chairman of the Board of Parker Pen Company, in a speech at Georgia State College, Atlanta, Georgia, November 12, 1968, on the "International Dimensions of Business."

11. International politics and international economics: a radical approach

1   "Marx to Engels in Manchester, London, October 8, 1858," in Karl Marx and Friedrich Engels, *Selected Correspondence* (Moscow: Progress Publishers, 1975), pp. 103–4.
2   John Maynard Keynes, "National Self-Sufficiency," *Yale Review,* Vol. 22, Summer 1933, p. 766.
3   *Ibid.,* p. 758.
4   *Ibid.,* p. 757.
5   *Ibid.,* pp. 760–2.
6   "The American Challenge," *Economist,* July 18, 1942, p. 67.
7   Sumner Wells, quoted in "The New Frontier," *Economist,* June 13, 1942, p. 824.
8   "The New Frontier," *op. cit.,* p. 825.
9   "An American Proposal," *Fortune,* May 1942, p. 63.
10   John Maynard Keynes, *The General Theory of Employment, Interest and Money* (London: Macmillan & Co., 1964), p. 221.
11   *Ibid.,* p. 376.
12   *Ibid.,* pp. 276–377.
13   Stephen Hymer, "The Internationalization of Capital," *Journal of Economic Issues,* Vol. 6, No. 1, March 1972, pp. 91–111 (reprinted as Chapter 3 of this volume).
14   Karl Marx, *Capital,* 3 vols. (New York: International Publishers, 1967), Vol. I, p. 614.
15   *Ibid.,* p. 639.
16   *Ibid.,* p. 640.
17   "Trouble Plagues the House of Labor," *Business Week,* October 28, 1972, pp. 66–76.

18   Karl Marx and Friedrich Engels, *Selected Works* (Moscow: Progress Publishers, 1973), Vol. 1, p. 63.

On becoming a radical economist

1   This is from Hymer's notes for an autobiographical essay, which was to be an introduction to a book of essays on political economy, 1973.
2   *Ibid.*
3   Stephen H. Hymer, *The International Operations of National Firms: A Study of Direct Foreign Investment* (Cambridge, Mass.: M.I.T. Press, 1976).
4   Stephen H. Hymer and Reginald Green, "Investment in the Ghana Cocoa Industry: Some Problems of Structure and Policy," *Economic Bulletin,* Vol. IX, No. 1, 1965, pp. 16–23.
5   "Statistical Abstract," in G. B. Kay, ed., *The Political Economy of Colonialism in Ghana* (Cambridge: Cambridge University Press, 1972), pp. 305–419, in collaboration with G. B. Kay.
6   Stephen Hymer, autobiographical notes, *op. cit.*
7   Canada, Task Force on the Structure of Canadian Industry, *Foreign Ownership and the Structure of Canadian Industry* (Ottawa: Queen's Printer, 1968).
8   Stephen Hymer, "Direct Foreign Investment and the National Economic Interest," in Peter Russell, ed., *Nationalism in Canada* (Toronto: McGraw-Hill Ryerson , 1966), pp. 191–202 (reprinted as Chapter 7 of this volume).
9   Stephen Hymer, "National Policies Towards Multinational Corporations," background report prepared for the study: Canada, Task Force on the Structure of Canadian Industry, *Foreign Ownership and the Structure of Canadian Industry* (Ottawa: Queen's Printer, 1968).
10   Stephen Hymer, "Transatlantic Reactions to Foreign Investment," Yale University Economic Growth Center Discussion Paper No. 53, April 18, 1968.
11   Stephen Hymer, autobiographical notes, *op. cit.*
12   Robert Rowthorn, *International Big Business 1957–1967* (Cambridge: Cambridge University Press, 1970), in collaboration with Stephen Hymer.
13   Stephen Hymer, "Course Outline for the International Economy," *Reading Lists in Radical Political Economics,* Vol. 2, Union for Radical Political Economics, Ann Arbor, Michigan, December 1971, pp. 95–112, annotated by Robert B. Cohen.
14   Leah Margulies, Judith Miller, Paul Semonin, and Florika Remetier, *A Bibliography on the Multinational Corporation* (San Francisco: Earthwork, April, 1977), in collaboration with Stephen Hymer. The researchers also produced an as yet unpublished reader called *Managing Social Change,* which describes four dimensions of multinational corporations in business literature articles.
15   Folker Fröbel, Jürgen Heinrichs, Otto Kreye of the project group, "Development and Underdevelopment," at the Max-Planck-Institut zur Erforschung der Lebensbedingungen der wissenschaftlich-technischen Welt, Starnberg, Federal Republic of Germany. The paper is entitled, "The Internationalization of Capital and Labor," August 10, 1973.
16   Stephen H. Hymer, "Notes on the United Nations Report on International Corporations in World Development," *Testimony Before the Group of Eminent Persons to Study the Impact of Multinational Corporations on Development and on International Relations* (Geneva: United Nations, November 6, 1973), United Nations Document No. E.74.II.A.9.

Index